MILTON

SUNIL KUMAR SARKER

ATLANTIC PUBLISHERS AND DISTRIBUTORS

Published by
ATLANTIC PUBLISHERS AND DISTRIBUTORS
B-2, Vishal Enclave, New Delhi-110 027
Phones 5413460, 5429987

Sales Office
4346/4C, Ansari Road, Darya Ganj,
New Delhi-110 002
Phones 3273880, 3285873, 3280451
Fax 91-11-3285873
e-mail gupta.atlantc@axcess.net.in

ISBN 81-7156-794-0

Typeset at
APD Computer Graphics, Delhi

Printed in India at
Mehra Offset Press, Delhi

DEDICATED TO

MY LOVING 'ELDER SISTER', MRS. AKHTARUNNISA,
AND
MY AFFECTIONATE 'NIECE', MRS. TAJKIRAT,
(BOTH OF BANGLADESH),

I DEDICATE THIS BOOK.

PREFACE

This is not a book meant for those thousands of people who know Milton much, much more than I do, but for those hundreds of thousands of students who have, perhaps, only heard the name of the poet, but have found not very many books with which to strike an acquaintance with him. Therefore, my sole objective, while writing this thin book, is to bring into relief the different salient facets of the poet, in plain and simple terms, so that, once equipped with these things, the initiates may go to the savants for a better understanding of him: in short, the book may be treated as an introduction to Milton and his works. And, as such an introduction should be a compendious treatment of the whole gamut, I have tried to net in, as much as possible within the little space of this book, specimens of the works of the poet, and their critical evaluations, as it may be evident in the 'Contents' of this book.

My wife, Smt. Manju Sarker, has typed out a portion of the manuscript of this book, and so I am grateful to her. My two sons, Suman and Sutanu, always kept me buoyant while I was preparing the manuscript, with extreme dearth of helpful books, and so they deserve my thanks. Dr. K.R. Gupta, Managing Director of the M/s Atlantic Publishers and Distributors, New Delhi has always been kind to me: he is ready to publish whatever I write. Many, many, and again many thanks to him.

SUNIL KUMAR SARKER

CONTENTS

1

MILTON : THE AGE, THE LITERARY ENVIRONMENT, THE MAN AND HIS WORKS

1
(THE AGE)

As India can boast of Valmiki's epic *Ramayana* and Vyasa's epic *Mahabharata*, as Greece can be proud of Homer's epic *Iliad*, or as Rome may exalt herself for Virgil's epic *Aeneid*, so England can boast of Milton's epic *Paradise Lost*. *Paradise Lost* is not only the most famous epic of England but also of the English language. This is certainly a great achievement of Milton who, in general evaluation, is second only to Shakespeare, in poetic height. Both of them contributed greatly to English literature: Shakespeare gave it suppleness and efficacy, and Milton grandeur. Shakespeare has shown us how best English can serve as a medium of dramatic height, and Milton has shown us how best English can serve as a medium of epical poetry. In 1616, when Shakespeare died, he, as if, handed down the charge of English literature to the eight-year-old boy, Milton, and bade him to see that it did not fall to commonalty. Milton amply proved worthy of that charge. He was a multifaceted personalty: besides being primarily a poet of high calibre, he was a pamphleteer, an active advocate of puritan persuasion, a government functionary, a largely passive politician, and a fighter for liberalism and freedom and democracy. His being all these and many things more was largely due to the turbulent time in which he breathed, his sublime poetic quality being his only innate possession.

Milton was born in the reign of King James (1603-1625) who was James VI of Scotland and James I of England. His reign saw a turbulent England — turbulent because of political and religious reasons. With the ascension of James I, the Tudor dynasty came to an end, and the Stuart dynasty came into existence. James I lacked in gubernatorial skill and let him be manoeuvred by some of his unworthy and self-seeking courtiers, so much so that the people used to call him the 'wisest fool in Christendom'. The foolery of James I invited extra troubles in the country. For one thing, James waywardly believed in the out-moded concept of Divine Right of Kings, which the people rose up to crush. Secondly, and this we should particularly notice, James ardently continued the religious policy of the late queen Elizabeth — the policy of Protestant ascendency — and showed particular favour to episcopacy or the government by the bishops who belonged to the Church of England, as against both the Catholics and the Puritans. At first James showed some tolerance to the Catholics, but in course of time he became hard towards them, and for this reason the Catholics also revolted against him. In 1605, the Catholics planned to blow up both the King and the already weakened Parliament, at one mighty stroke. This plan is known as the Gun-powder Plot. The plot was busted beforehand, and one of the conspirators, Guy Fawkes, was arrested and executed. But this in no way unnerved the Catholics, but rather aggravated their ire. Thirdly, James also made enemies of the Puritans. Soon after his ascension, the Puritans submitted a petition before James in which they begged relaxation of some religious ceremonies which they abhorred. This petition is known as the Millenary Petition, and James rejected it outright. Though James minded to get the Vulgate translated into English for the first time, this brow-beating attitude of the King alienated the Puritans from him. Our poet, John Milton, was of this Puritan persuasion, and so, later on, he was deeply aggrieved at the treatment of the King meted out to the Puritans. Fourthly, the people could not take the whimsical execution of the multifaceted genius, Sir Walter Releigh, by the orders of James I, easy.

But the two great jactating events of the reign of James I, as also of the early Stuart period, were the Parliamentary Revolution and the Puritan Revolution. The supercilious James, as he believed in the Divine Right theory of kingship, did not give ear to the protestations of the House of Commons against this illusory concept of the king. Further, the king levied taxes without the concurrence of the House of Commons, and ardently tried to restrict the freedom of speech of the Commons and also of the people as a whole. Again, as we have said, the king was showing undue favour to the Protestants as against both the Catholics and the Puritans. And lastly, the king even hob-nobbed with the process of electing representatives of the people to the House of Commons. All these and other causes gave rise to the two great revolutions — the Parliamentary Revolution and the Puritan Revolution. However, at long last, James I was forced to yield to the third and the fourth Parliaments, the first and the second Parliaments being too weak for the supercilious and whimsical king.

James I, though he was inimical to the people, had some saving graces. It was he who first established English colonies beyond the seas, such as in Virginia (1607), Bermudas and Maryland; and it was he who, as told earlier, got the Vulgate (the Latin Bible) translated into English, for the first time. Again, it was also he who granted commission to the East India Company that fetched for England a fabulous amount of wealth from India. But, James' successor Charles I (1625-1649) could not show any such commendable achievements; rather, on the contrary, he superseded his predecessor in all his vices: hauteur, obstinacy and foolery. He believed, like his father James I, in the Divine Right theory of kingship and, consequently, again like his father, Charles I involved himself in controversy with the Parliament and with the Puritans. Charles I faced three Parliaments, in the third of which the Commons, led by John Eliot, submitted before him the famous Petition of Right, and condemned the arbitrary rule perpetrated by him. But, undaunted, Charles set aside all the parliamentary practices, and continued to rule autocephalically. He declared that, whosoever would try to reform the existing religious doctrine and rituals adopted by the state, would be severely punished. This irked, particularly, the Puritans; but the Commons, the Puritans and the public in general reacted unitedly and severally. But, yet not unnerved, Charles continued to disregard the wounded sentiment of the people, imposed his own religious discipline on the people, imposed on them excruciating burden of taxation, levied more money from them by all evil means to strengthen his hand, and whimsically sent to gaol the recalcitrant Commons. To teach the Puritans a lesson, Charles I made Laud, the Archbishop of Canterbury, and through his agency demanded of the people greater conformity with the ceremonial rituals of Christianity, which the Puritans rejected as Popish practices. He tried to suppress all religious dissensions from the Prostant doctrine and practices, and for this purpose created two courts: the Court of Star Chamber and the Court of High Commission. The former dealt with breaches of the king's ordinances, while the latter was meant for seeing that the people abided by Laud's religious promulgations made out from time to time. The tyranny of Charles I reached its apogee when he indiscriminately determined to impose upon the people a new religious order, in both England and Scotland.

The Scots were the first to rise against the religious tyranny of Charles. They would not part with their traditional Presbytarianism, and so they made a National Covenant to fight Charles' religious tyranny. Charles responded through his army, and consequently, the First and the Second Bishops' Wars were fought between the king's army and the people of Scotland. Ultimately, Charles had to yield, and he reluctantly called the Short and the Long Parliaments, successively. The Long Parliament abolished all the excesses of the king and circumvented the powers of the crown. The House of Commons framed the Grand Remonstrance under the leadership of Pym, and enlisted therein the tyrannical adventures of the king. The king retaliated by trying to punish five front-ranking Commons, and infringing their parliamentary immunity. As a result Civil War broke out in 1642. It was in this Civil War that Oliver Cromwell had his steep rise in power, and it was this Civil War that in course of time and events made him the head of the state. Cromwell organised the Eastern Countries and raised from there the new army called Ironsides, to fight against the king. Scotland joined Cromwell's army along with other auxiliary anti-royalist forces. Ultimately, Charles surrendered to the Scots in 1649, and the Scots handed the royal captive to the forces of Cromwell, only to be executed in the same year at the hands of the Rump (the association of a number of Commons), under the charges of tyranny, duplicity and treason. With the execution of Charles I, the monarchy was abolished, and England was declared a Commonwealth. Our poet, Milton, fought with his pen on the side of his hero, Cromwell, to help him bring in the Commonwealth, as Dryden (1631-1700) later on used his pen to denounce this revolution and to support the Restoration of Kingship, that occurred in 1660.

According to G.M. Trevelyan, "The Cromwellian revolution was not social and economic in its causes and motives; it was the result of political and religious thought and aspiration among men who had no desire to recast society or redistribute wealth" (Trevelyan, 248). Unlike modern men, the people of the early Stuart period were instinctively religious. They wanted peace and were interested in plain living, horticulture and forestry and gossip : and tumultuous life and revolutions they abhorred. Regarding the life in the country during the reign of Charles I, G.M. Trevelyan writes that the country house was not a centre "only of estate management but of domestic industry, in which the members of the family, as well as their army of servants and dependants of both sexes, have essential parts to play" (Trevelyan, 264). Such an idyllic life we may find in *Paradise Lost.*

Milton's literary life extended from the second quarter of the seventeenth century to 1671, in which year he published both *Paradise Regained* and *Samson Agonistes,* and, therefore, he lived upto, and died in, the Restoration period that began with the ascendancy of Charles II (ruled 1660-1685), son of Charles I. Further, though *Paradise Lost*, Milton's masterpiece, was conceived and perhaps was began in the period of the Commonwealth, it was completed in the Restoration period. For this reason, we should acquaint ourselves, at least, a little bit, with the general events of the early part of the reign of Charles II. Charles II was hilariously received by the traditionally loyal and royalist people, because they could not bear with the aggressively high-handed and imperialist rule of Cromwell. Nevertheless, the new king also had to face difficulties, particularly with the Puritans. For one thing, the people, after eleven years of asceticism during the Commonwealth, revived their general profligacy in the relatively freer environment in the reign of Charles II, and this profligacy the Puritans could not tolerate. Secondly, the king himself had not the desirable amount of probity, and this too hurt the sentiment of the Puritans. Thirdly, the Catholic king Charles II shrewdly tried to uphold Catholicism over against both Protestantism and Puritanism. Fourthly, the Cavalier Parliament (so called because it showed Cavalier-like loyalty to the king), under the aegis of the Crown, showed sympathy to Anglican Catholicism, and hated the Puritans. Fifthly, the Cavalier Parliament passed four Acts which compelled everyone to conform to Catholicism: the Corporation Act, the Act of Uniformity, the Conventicle Act and the Five Miles Act. The Corporation Act demanded everyone within a municipal corporation to abide by the rules of the Church of England; the Act of Uniformity provided that every bishop must receive episcopal ordination; the Conventicle Act debarred any congregation of more than five persons for religious activities which are not allowed by the Anglican Church and the Five Miles Act forbade clergymen expelled by the Anglican Church to teach in any school outside the radius of five miles of a corporation town. All these measures went particularly against the Puritans, and as a result, the relation between the Puritans and the king became overtly inimical; and to teach the Puritans and the Dissenters a lesson, the king managed to get the oppressive Clarendon Code Bill passed by the Parliament. G.M. Trevelyan writes that "Throughout the reign of Charles II, religious non-conformists suffered severely through intermittent persecution, under the laws of the 'Clarendon Code' " (Trevelyan, 268). And, curious enough, this age of religious bigotry was a time when experimental science spread itself fast throughout England, and it was also this age in which the 'English genius and civilization' shone brighter than earlier. G.M. Trevelyan writes about this age : "The age which produced Newton's *Principia*, Milton's *Paradise Lost*, Dryden's *Absalom and Achitophel*, Purnell's music, and Wren's churches, and all the varied interests and curiosities of the daily life recorded by Evelyn and Pepys, such an age was one of the greatest for English genius and civilization" (Trevelyan, 277).

The age in which Milton's creative faculty matured and blossomed is called the Puritan Age (1620-1660). Earlier, the Renaissance gave England an aesthetic boost in the 15th and the 16th centuries, and now the Puritan movement of the 17th century gave her a moral boost. The Puritans distinguished themselves by laying emphasis on moral purity and on freedom in religious observances. This was their only distinguishing quality or characteristic. So Puritanism did not connote any definite religious sect or any religious philosophy. Actually, the Puritans were the English Calvinists or the followers of John Calvin (1509-1564), the French Protestant theologian, who in his *Institutes* laid much emphasis on faith and moral probity. The Puritans wanted to give a fillip to the on-going Reformation movement of the 16th and the 17th centuries in England. The Reformation movement was touched off by Martin Luther in Germany in 1517. Calvinism, Protestantism and Puritanism are the three denominations of more or less the same religious philosophy. However, the Puritans demanded abolition of Church hierarchy, simplification of rituals, reduction of Church interferences in secular matters, and allowance of more liberty to the people. At first only those persons who were obsequious about certain religious rites of the Church were called Puritans, but gradually Puritanism turned into a National movement that brought within its fold all shades of Christianism and all sorts of Christians: Calvinists, Covenanters, Separatists, etc.

Soon the movement for reforming the Church gathered momentum, in the wake of which a Commonwealth was established in England — a lone instance of Commonwealth in that country. H.G. Wells, in his *A Short History of the World*, writes about those who involved themselves in the reforming movement: "They refused the disciplines of a state church. In England these dissentients were the Non-conformists who played a very large part in the politics of that country in the seventeenth and eighteenth centuries. In England they carried their objections to a princely head of the church as far as to decapitate King Charles (1649), and for eleven prosperous years England was a republic under Non-conformist rule" (Wells, 214). The Commonwealth was established largely owing to the energy of the Puritans. The Great Rebellion, or the Civil War, broke out in 1642, when the Puritans were very much active, and ended in the jugulation of Charles I and in the establishment of the Republic or the Commonwealth. The Civil War was led by Oliver Cromwell who himself was of puritan persuasion. After the Commonwealth was established, Milton became the Latin Secretary to the new government, and continued to produce propagandistic pamphlets in support of the Commonwealth, denouncing the reign of the late king, Charles I. Milton wrote such philippics as *De Doctrina Christiana, The Tenure of Kings and Magistrates, Areopagitica, A Treatise on Civil Power in Ecclessiastical Causes, Considerations touching the likeliest means to remove hierlings out of the Church, The Ready and Easy Way to Establish a Free Commonwealth,* etc. Milton was highly influenced by the ideas of the Renaissance while in the Cambridge University, and by the notions of the Reformation when, after completing his studies, he was preparing for public life, and engaging himself in the religio-political controversy and turmoil in the country. So, he is rightly called the child of both Renaissance and Reformation.

The Puritan Age in which Milton lived was an age of utter confusion in all spheres of life: religious, political and literary. In all these fields, the Puritans held their preferred views which were opposed by the inimical forces of the royalists. In the religious and political spheres what the Puritans of England wanted was recorded in the Covenant of 1643 which they signed with the anti-royalists of Scotland: "To bring the churches of God in the three kingdoms [of England, Wales and Scotland] to uniformity in all religion and government, to preserve the rights of the Parliament and the liberties of the kingdom; ... that we and our posterity may as brethren live in faith and love, and the Lord may delight to live in the midst of us' " (Long, 188). In the sphere of literature, the age could neither sustain the old medieval ideology of chivalry, romantic love, absolute religious and moral standards of the Spenserian type, nor could it substitute these with other appropriate ideals compatible with the changed socio-religio-political scenario. There was also no measuring rod for literary values, and this non-existence of literary ideals created a state of gloom in the sphere of literature. And in this state of affairs, literature took a new turn.

2
(THE LITERARY ENVIRONMENT)

With the advent of a complex religio-political environment, the Elizabethan literary sense was no more prevalent, and in its stead the Puritans, who dominated the go of the day, brought in a new literary value-system. The Elizabethan literature was undisturbed and uninfluenced by the religio-political trend of the period, and so it had uniformity and cohesion. On the contrary, in the Puritan Age, the people were divided into two identifiable and bickering camps. In the Puritan Age, *i.e.* in the Stuart period, which was roughly coeval with the Puritan Age, therefore, literature was also divided into two distinct camps: the puritan literature and the non-puritan literature. The Elizabethan literature was inspiring and romantically tinged, but the Puritan literature was overcast with the gloomy spirit of the age. The Puritan Age lacked in the medieval chivalry and the romantic imagination, and in the musicality of Edmund Spenser, and also in the dramatic genius of Shakespeare. However, the poets of the Puritan Age can roughly be divided into two broad categories: the royalist Cavalier poets, and the metaphysical poets. The poets of both the categories are sometimes collectively called Caroline poets, because they all belonged to the period of king Charles II (Latin 'Carolus' for English 'Charles'). The poems of the Cavalier poets are based particularly on the theme of love, and are light in treatment, though witty and elegant. Some of the Cavalier poets are: Lovelace, Harrick, Carew and Sir John Suckling. On the other hand, the Cavalier dramatists produced some uninspiring and decadent plays written in artificial style. Suckling, James Shirley and Thomas Killigrew were the foremost Cavalier dramatists.

The term 'metaphysical poet', as it is generally understood, was coined by Dr. Johnson. But J.A. Cuddon says that the term was first used by William Drummond of Hawthornden "in a letter written to Arthur Johnston c. 1630" (Cuddon, 392). Donne, Carew, George Herbert, Crashaw, Henry Vaughn, Andrew Marvell, Cleveland, Cowley, and such others were the foremost metaphysical poets. The poems of the metaphysical poets are distinguished by their satire, philosophical bent, crispness and terseness of phraseology, amorous tinge, dissonance in melody, far-fetched similes and metaphors, *i.e.* conceits, etc. In addition, the poems have a predominance of wit, colloquialism, flexibility of rhythm and metre, dramatic quality, directness, delicacy, and deeper passion and feeling. The following two stanzas from Marvell's Poem

'The Definition of Love' may show some of the salient qualities of the metaphysical poetry:

> My Love is of a birth as rare
> As 'tis for object strange and high:
> It was begotten by despair
> Upon impossibility.
>
> Magnanimous Despair alone
> Could show me so divine a thing,
> Where feeble hope could ne'er have flown
> But vainly flapt its Tinsel Wing.

In his early life, Milton was a Spenserian, but he soon abandoned Spenserianism in favour of the style of the metaphysical poets who dominated the stage of poetry of that period. Some of the metaphysical poets contemporary with Milton were Samuel Daniel (1562-1619), Giles Fletcher, the Younger (1585-1623), Henry Vaughan (1622-1695), Andrew Marvell (1621-1678), John Donne (1573-1631) and George Herbert (1593-1633). Milton grew up in the literary climate which was being largely dominated by the poetry of these poets. Samuel Daniel was one of the first batch of metaphysical poets. He is now remembered principally for his *Delia* which is a collection of sonnets on the theme of love. Daniel rejected the prevailing medieval tendency in poetry, and tended to be realistic and modernistic. He was profusely praised by such great poets as Wordsworth, Southey, Lamb and Coleridge. Giles Fletcher, the Younger, Published his *Christs Victorie and triumph in Heaven and Earth, over and after Death* in 1610. It is rich in rhetoric, imagery, didacticism and eroticism, and was written in the Spenserian style. Milton was much influenced by this book of Fletcher, especially in his *Paradise Regained.* Abraham Cowley (1618-1667) was also a poet to reckon with. In his own time, he was considered to be the greatest poet of England. He was a versatile poet writing Pinderic odes; poems on love; anacreontics or a collection of sixty-odd poems on love, wine and song, in imitation of Anacreon (6th c. B.C.) — a rare variety of English poem practised by few poets like Thomas Campion (1567-1620) —; and elegies. His love poems are contained mostly in his *The Mistress*. Cowley should be accredited much for his eipcesque poem *Davideis* which "is the first attempt at a genuine, neo-classical, biblical epic in English" (Daiches, 1971, 123). Cowley, therefore, should be credited for conceiving of the idea of an English epic even before Milton who was perhaps influenced by Cowley's *Davideis*, in his *Paradise Lost*. But, *Davideis* "was not suited to Cowley's genius, and the *Davideis* lacks the grandeur and power necessary to such a poem, but it does show a superb mastery of heroic couplet from which Dryden learnt and developed his skill" (Daiches, 1971, 123). Henry Vaughan and Andrew Marvell were also metaphysical poets, and contemporaries of Milton; Marvell, in addition, was a close friend of Milton. Vaughan's poems are suffused with religious and spiritual undertones. Marvell, like Milton, was a pamphleteer, besides being a poet of considerable worth, but unlike his friend, Marvell kept company with the Royalists and not with the Puritans, during the Civil War.

John Donne and George Herbert are the two other metaphysical poets of eminence, of the age of Milton. According to Ben Jonson, Donne was "the first poet of the world in some things". In his early life, Donne participated in the pamphleteering industries of his day. Two of his famous pamphlets are: *Pseudo-Martyr* and *Ignatius his Conclave*. Donne was a deeply religious poet, though he craved secular career advancement as well as religious serenity. In 1614, he entered the Parliament which was dissolved by the king within only two months. His ecclesiastical sonnets are a proof of his deep religious convictions and sentiments. So much religious was also George Herbert whose *The Temple* consists of one hundred and fifty poems of devotion to the church.

Among the Cavalier poets contemporary with Milton, Thomas Carew (1598?-1639?), Sir John Suckling (1609-1642) and Sir Richard Lovelace (1618-1658) were front-ranking. Carew's poems betray wit, sensuality, courtly style, grace and cynical charm, but lack in profundity of thought and emotion. Suckiing was both a dramatist (he wrote three plays) and a poet. His poems could attract public attention for their "lucidity, conceited wit, polite language, and down-to-earth sentiment" (Daiches, 1971, 506). However, in such a literary environment, our poet John Milton was born and grew up to become a great poet.

3
(THE MAN AND THE POET)

The Puritan age of Milton lacked in nothing essential to literature but only in high religious and moral ideals and lofty spirituality, that Milton soon injected into it; and all these he did not borrow from elsewhere but these were his inalienable qualities and possessions that were inspired to get expressed by his immediate environment and filliped by some events in his life. Milton contributed to his age the sense of republicanism, the sense of liberty, and the spirit of Puritanism. He was born between six and seven in the morning of ninth December 1608 at Spread-Eagle in Bread Street in London, three years after the hatching of the famous Gun Powder Plot to overthrow both King Charles I and the Parliament, and thus to put an end to the evil episcopacy and the autocracy of the king. Eight years after Milton was born, Shakespeare died, leaving the charge of English literature to his worthiest successor John Milton. Milton's grand-father was one John Milton (Sr.) and his father was also one John Milton (Jr.) Milton's grand-father was the 'Keeper of the Forest of Shotover', and he was a 'zealous papist'. Milton's father John Milton (Jr.), while studying at Oxford, first turned a renegade and then became a Puritan. Milton's grand-father could not tolerate this obvious effrontery of his son (Milton's father) and so disinherited him. After this, Milton's father became a scrivener (a sort of notary public, or a scribe or a copyist, or one who 'lays out money at interest for others'), and in course of time amassed enough money. He then married Caston (Milton's mother) and got two sons — our poet John and his brother Christopher — and a daughter, Ann, by her. Christopher, in his later life, was knighted and became a Judge. Our poet's father was a scholarly person, a musician, a lover of art and literature, and a businessman. Milton's father composed some delightful and deeply sentimental hymns which were sung long after his death. Regarding politics, he sympathised with radicalism and Puritanism. Milton's mother was a lady of cultivated taste with deep religious conviction and sentiment. The Milton family had a tradition of music. Milton's father was a noted music composer. Milton, perhaps, got his knack for music and his taste for musicality in poetry from his father. And, likewise, he perhaps learned to value charity from his mother who herself was full of charity.

In his early years, Milton received a very good education under the supervision of his loving father who wanted that Milton should become learned in literature. In his later years, Milton claimed that his father " 'destined [him] from a child to the pursuits of literature' " (Daiches, 1971, 364). In *Defensio Secunda* (1654), Milton writes about his early education : " 'My father destined me from a child to the pursuits of literature; and my appetite for knowledge was so voracious, that, from twelve years of age, I hardly ever left my studies, or went to bed before midnight. This, primarily, led to my loss of sight. My eyes were naturally weak, and I was subject to frequent headaches; which, however, could not chill the ardour of my curiosity, or retard the progress of my improvement. My father had me daily instructed in the grammar school, and by other masters at home. He then, after I had acquired a proficiency in various languages, and had made a considerable progress in philosophy, sent me to the University of Cambridge' " (Tillyard, 1956, 200). However, Milton's father first sent the poet to St. Paul's school, and there the poet was much influenced by the Christian humanist teachings — a sort of humanism propounded by the two great humanists: Colet and Erasmus. Alexander Gill, the headmaster of St. Paul's used frequently to quote from English poets, and this, perhaps, early imbibed the latent poetic genius of Milton. At St. Paul's, Milton was thoroughly trained in Latin and Greek, and at home he was taught Hebrew by a private tutor, Thomas Young, who was a divine from Scotland. From the very beginning of his school career, Milton was being attracted to art, literature and music, and he was developing a sense of devotion to duty, and all these commendable qualities he preserved in himself till his death. Finishing his studies at St. Paul's, Milton went to Christ's College, Cambridge, in 1625 — the year in which Charles I ascended the throne, and angry protestation against his autocratic rule began brewing. The public resentment reached the academic circle, and Milton was influenced thereby. In those days the study materials of colleges and universities largely included theological, escatological and stereological teachings. Milton protested against this conservative curriculum and pleaded for introduction of such secular subjects as physics, astronomy, geography, history and 'manners of men'. Curious enough, in those days, cudgelling was in vogue even in colleges, and we know that at least once Milton had to undergo treatment with a cudgel. He was once even rusticated, but was allowed to return to the college, later on.

Milton went to the university with the aim of entering the church, but soon changed his mind. At Cambridge, he began his literary career by writing both in Latin and English. At that time he preferred Latin to English as his medium, because he was more proficient in Latin than in English. In Latin he wrote elegies in Ovidian style, and in English he paraphrased in verse some of the Psalms, partly in the style of Joshua Sylvester's *Divine Weeks and Works*. But within two years he changed his mind and decided to write principally in English, and since then became an English poet, his model poet being Edmund Spenser (?1552-1599). Nevertheless, next year he wrote a group of sonnets in Italian, expressing his love for an Italian singer, Emilia.

Milton graduated from Cambridge in 1629, in which year he wrote a famous poem entitled 'On the Morning of Christ's Nativity'. It is a brilliant poem in baroque style. Three years after his taking B.A. degree,

Milton also took M.A. degree, both from Cambridge. At Cambridge he was a very serious student, having no taste for fun and keeping shy — characteristics that earned for him, from his friends, the nickname 'Lady'. The nickname was also due to the fact that — he was inordinately beautiful to look at. Milton could not stand the imputation of such a queer appellation, and so hit back the mean fellows who called him 'Lady' in a pungent passages: " 'Some people have lately nicknamed me the Lady. But why do I seem to them too little of a man? I suppose because I have never had the strength to drink off a bottle like a prize-fighter; or because my hand was never grown horney with holding a ploughshare; or because I was not a farm hand at seven, and never took a midday nap in the sun — last perhaps because I never showed my virility in the way these brothellers do. But I wish they could leave playing the ass as readily as I the woman.' " (Tillyard, 1956, 29). Before leaving Cambridge, Milton wrote two other famous poems: 'L'Allegro' and 'Il Penseroso'.

Milton now retired to his father's estate at Horton, Buckinghamshire, and remained there from 1632 to 1638. This period is known as Milton's Horton period. Milton's parents wanted him entered into the career of the church, and now they thought that as his education was over, he must obey. But by this time, Milton was confirmed not to enter the career of the church. He had at least four reasons for spurning away the monastic career. Firstly, he regarded church life as a life of servitude. Secondly, he could not tolerate the autocracy of the Anglican church and the bickerings among the different sects of the same religion. Thirdly, he thought himself to be a Puritan, a Separatist, an Independent, and a Congregationalist. And fourthly, his interest in poetry and music, and the influence of Pythagoreanism and Platonism on him made him averse to the career of the church. The life that Milton sought after was that of a Pilgrim Father. However, at Horton he poured himself into piles of books, an avid reader as he was. Though in *Paradise Regained*, he wrote 'many books,/Wise men have said, are wearisome', Milton never took leisure from books. But, he was never 'Deep-versed in books and shallow in himself' (*Paradise Regained*). He had a great regard for knowledge, and yet, curiously enough, he wrote, in *Paradise Regained* (Book IV), deridingly about all knowledge other than the knowledge of God. In *Paradise Regained*, when Satan tries to allure Christ with vast knowledge of the creation, Christ tells him: " 'he who receives/Light from above, from the Fountain of Light,/ No other doctrine needs, though granted true". However, at their residence at Horton,

Milton began to study voraciously everything that came to hand — mathematics, science, theology, music, Greek, Latin, Hebrew, Spanish, French, Italian and English literatures. The house at Horton was the new residence of the Milton family. By the time Milton graduated, his father retired from his business in London and took residence at Horton, seventeen miles from London. Milton's interest in music may be said to be hereditary, his father being a music composer, as we said earlier. Milton derived from his father his life-long passion for music, and this passion of his is reflected in the balance, melody and rhythm of his poetry. His taste for music is particularly evident in such poems of his as 'At a Solemn Musick' and 'Arcades'. Milton was also interested in the mystic philosophy of Pythagoras and Plato, and in the theory of harmony and music of the spheres.

Milton consummated his university learning and private study with a world tour. In 1637, his mother died, and in the next year he set sail for Greece, his tour being funded by his father. On way to Greece, he visited France and Switzerland. Even in his young age Milton's poetic fame and his fame as a man of learning travelled far and wide in Europe, and as a result, wherever he went on his world tour, he was given warm welcome. In Paris, he struck a friendship with the famous Dutch scholar Grotius, and in Italy, he met the noted astronomer Galilio who then had been serving his prison term for discovering that creation is not confined within this planet only. It was perhaps while he had been touring Italy that Milton first conceived of the idea of writing an epic in English which, he thought, the English People would 'not willingly let die'. While he was on board his ship towards Italy, he heard the news of the breach of trust between the king and the Parliament, and of the resultant breaking out of the Civil War in England, and so, apprehending a holocaust at home, he cut short his stay in Italy, and hurried towards England.

On his coming back to England, Milton's dear dream of becoming a poet of great worth and particularly of writing an English epic was shattered into pieces, because he was immediately involved in the political turmoil of the country. As we have seen, he was a staunch Puritan, and so he could not bear with the ill behaviour meted out to the Puritans. He was also a fierce anti-royalists : he could not compromise with the idea that "equal over equals monarch reign — " (*Paradise Lost*, Book V, line 831). Milton, therefore, willingly sacrificed his dream of becoming a great poet to the cause of the country, and came down heavily upon the royalist forces, to save the freedom of the people. He began to turn out sequences of anti-royalist pamphlets in invective prose. For nearly twenty years, since his coming back from Italy, the poet of an assuredly bright future engaged himself in turning out denouncing articles or pamphlets, setting aside songs and sonnets. He wrote such Pamphlets as *Epitaphium Damonis* (1639). *On Reformation in England* (1641), *Of Practical Episcopacy* (1641), *Animadversions upon the Remonstrant's Defence* (1641), *Reason of Church Government* (1641), *Apology for Smectymnuus* (1642) and *Areopagitica* (1644). Milton's opportunity of, and inspiration for, writing more piquant, invective and philippic pamphlets than all these came in after the killing of the king, Charles I, in 1639. In support of those who worked for the liberty of the people and compelled the king to pay the heavy penalty of his head for his autocephalic and biased episcopacy, Milton wrote the pamphlet *Tenure of Kings and Magistrates*. In it he justified his theory that even Kings, like the common people, are subject to the eternal laws, and that the people had the inalienable right to protect their liberty. In producing a spat of pamphlets, Milton was much inspired by his tutor, Thomas Young, who was also a Puritan and who himself published some anti-royal and anti-episcopal pamphlets. In fact, it was in support of Young that Milton first published pamphlets, anonymously. How much Milton valued liberty can be guessed from his sonnet 'To Mr. Cyriack Skinner Upon His Blindness' where says :

> What supports me dost thou ask?
> The conscience, friend, to have lost them overplied
> In Liberty's defence, my noble task.

Milton's pamphleteering period began just after his returning to England from Italy, as we have said, but just before that he shed a few tears for his close Italian friend and classmate Diodati who was drowned in a boat-capsise. He wrote the elegy 'Lycidas' in remembrance of Diodati.

On the establishment of the Commonwealth or the Republics in 1649, after the cessation of the Civil War and the jugulation of Charles I, Milton was appointed Secretary for Foreign Tongues of the nascent Cromwellian government. He soon rose very high in public estimation. People used to think that in the whole of the Commonwealth there were only two men — Oliver Cromwell, the man of action, and John Milton, the man of thought. In 1657, Cromwell was urged to become the king of England, but he declined the offer. So great was the estimation about Cromwell, and Milton had no less popularity and received no less praise as the greatest poet of the time. But, unfortunately, Milton's vision from now on was getting blurred, and ultimately by 1652 he became completely blind. His blindness, at least partially, was due to his overmuch study. His blindness was the cause of his continuous and silent suffering. Besides, he had some other personal tragedies. In 1643, he very impetuously married Mary Powell, a young 'shallow and pleasure-loving girl' who was the daughter of a staunch Royalist, and a Justice of the Peace in Oxfordshire. Powell was no scholar like Milton, and unlike Milton she was an extravert. She was brought up in a family where company and merriment were galore. The difference between the personal equations of the husband and the wife did not allow the two to come closer to each other in deep love. They could not adjust with each other, and so incessant bickerings continued to widen the gulf between them. The reasons were more than one. For one thing, as told before, they were temperamentally quite different from each other. Secondly, the jolly Powell could find nothing attractive in the pensive intellectual that Milton had been. And thirdly, the Royalist mentality of Powell always jarred against the sincere Puritanism of Milton. As a result, within a short space of only one month or so after their marriage, Powell retired to her father's house, leaving Milton in the lurch. This sad incident caused Milton to write the famous tracts or pamphlets justifying the necessity of divorce: *Doctrine and Discipline of Divorce* and *Tetrachordon*. However, before long, good sense prevailed over Powell and she returned to the fold of Milton, expressing deep repentance for deserting him, and Milton accepted her without showing any resentment. This certainly proves the magnanimity of Milton. Milton has, perhaps, depicted the weeping and returning Powell in *Samson Agonistes* (3rd Episode or Act, lines 726-731), where Dalila may be the replica of Powell, and where the Chorus sings Dalila's dithering approach towards Samson thus :

> Yet on she moves; now stands and eyes thee fixed,
> About t' have spoke; but now, with head declined,
> Like a fair flower surcharged with dew, she weeps,
> And words addressed seem into tears dissolved,
> Wetting the borders of her silken veils
> But now again she makes address to speak.

It is said that after Powell suddenly deserted him, immediately after their marriage, Milton used, for some time, to frequent the house of one Lady Margaret Leigh "whom he has mentioned in one of his sonnets" (Johnson, 76).

Mary Powell died in 1653, and a few years afterwards Milton married Catherine Woodcock who died in childbed in 1658, after only fifteen months of their marriage. Milton then married Elizabeth Minshull in 1663, when he was 54. Minshull survived him by about half a century. She bore Milton no children, but the other two wives did. Milton had perhaps more affection for his second wife than for the other two, though Minshull was a very kind, sympathetic and affectionate wife. Milton's relation with his wives was never ideal, and this might be one of the causes of his strained relation with his daughters. And this may be the reason of Milton's having no favourable opinion about womenfolk in general. His attitude towards women is well expressed in *Paradise Lost* (Book X, lines 888-895), where Adam, being a prey to the gullibility and wiles of Eve, is being driven out of Paradise, and is mourning, therefore thus :

Oh, why did God,
Creator wise, that peopled highest Heaven
With spirits masculine, create at last
This novelty on Earth, this fair defect
Of Nature, and not fill the world at once
With men as Angels, without feminine;
Or find some other way to generate Mankind?

Most of Milton's invectives against the womenfolk are expressed through Adam who calls the feminine kind 'mischief', 'female snares', 'frailty' and 'infirmer sex'. Nevertheless, as we indicated earlier, Milton had inordinate love for his second wife Catherine Woodcock for whom he wrote the sonnet 'Methought I saw my late espoused saint'.

After he became purblind, around 1652, Milton was shorn of his office of Secretary of Foreign Tongues, but was allowed an assistant for his poetical works. He then moved to a place called Petty France in Westminster. Even when he was engaged in the business of the state and even when he became blind, Milton continued to engage himself in study (with assistance) and writing. Long ago in 1645, *i.e.* two years after his marriage with Powell, Milton published his first volume of poems, which contained almost all his poems written upto then. Even in his blindness he continued to write such pamphlets as *A Treatise of Civil Power in Ecclesiastical Causes* (1659), *The Readie and Easie Way to Establish a Free Commonwealth* (1660). Then after a gap of nearly thirteen years, he wrote another pamphlet, *Of True Religion*, in which he pleaded for freedom of interpreting the Scriptures. During this long period of time, he interspersed his pamphlets with sonnets. He also tried his hand in historical writings. In the middle of the 1640s, he worked on his *History of Britain*.

Milton's life took a sharp turn after the Restoration. In 1658 Oliver Cromwell died, and his son, Richard Cromwell, became the Protector of the Commonwealth. Richard was a weak and incapable ruler, and soon resigned his post. At this critical juncture, the royalist army came forward and restored the Rump Parliament which included a group of about one hundred members of the Long Parliament of the time of Charles I, who were royalists and Presbyterians, and who formed the dominant group in the Rump Parliament. It was this group of the members of the Parliament which helped the army restore the Rump Parliament. But soon a quarrel broke out between the army and the Rump, leading the country to a deeper crisis, and consequently the prospect of the reign of the Stuart dynasty for the second time became brighter. And before long, General Monk, who had once been Cromwell's general, restored the Long Parliament. But this Parliament was soon dissolved by itself and a new Parliament — the Convention Parliament — was called, and this Convention Parliament made Charles II, son of the decapitated Charles I, the king in 1660. Charles was coronated on May 8 of the same year.

After the Restoration, Milton feared persecution at the hands of the royalists, and he was right, because immediately after the Restoration he was arrested though he was soon released (*Encyclopaedia Britanica*, Vol. VI, entry: Milton). Some believe that Milton had even harder days after the fall of the Commonwealth: "After the Restoration copies of his works were publicly burned. In danger of execution, he was initially a fugutive, then a prisoner, though after payment of a massive fine he was finally released into a life of relative retirement — owing partly, it is said, to the intercession of Marvell [the poet Andrew Marvell (1621-1678) who once had been Milton's assistant when Milton had been the Secretary for Foreign Tongues, under Cromwell] (who spoke for him in Parliament) and D'Avenant" (Wordsworth Reference, 624). But even after his release, Milton could not think himself fully free from the vengeance of the royalists, and so he went underground, and remained there for several months. And there being no source of income, he was reduced to a virtual pauper. Further, after the Restoration, all his published books were set on fire for his being a defender of the late Commonwealth. The poet now felt extremely dejected, his hope of fighting for liberty and rationalism being gone for ever, and his public stature being reduced to the minimum. Now his only friend was his misery — misery for his fortune and for his blindness. It is said that just after the Restoration, Milton was destined for the scaffold, but how he could evade it we do not know. Hardin Craig writes about this: "How Milton escaped the scaffold is still a mystery. Biographers have attributed his escape to the intercession of Marvell and Davenant or to the safe Royalist position of his nephews. One would prefer to think that he was simply forgotten" (Craig, 247). This may be true, because after the Restoration, the officials were certainly busy otherwise. Further, the king, Charles II, was not by nature very much vindictive, and after the Restoration, Milton's pamphlets were not so much read by the public. However, during this time, Milton's only relief was his third wife Minshull who helped him much in his distressful state. Once he thought the Commonwealth a 'paradise on earth'. Now this 'paradise' was gone, and further, he being purblind, the 'paradise' of the sensible world was also no more there for him. Therefore, he now planned to create a paradise in verse — the paradise of *Paradise Lost.*

Milton began dictating *Paradise Lost* to his unwilling daughters, perhaps in the year 1658 and finished it after long seven years, in 1665. At Charles II's ascendency, he became frustrated, but John Dryden the royalist, became elated. Dryden expressed his elation in his *Astraea Redux* which begins with the line "Now with a general Peace the World was blest"; and Miltton continued to pour out the pain from his abraded heart in his *Paradise Lost.* Milton wrote at least a part of this epic, as Matthew Arnold informs us, at St. Margaret's, Westminster. He also wrote (by dictating) the whole of *Paradise Regained* and *Samson Agonistes*, here. A great plague took its toll in London in 1665, and a great fire reduced about two thirds or 13,000 houses of London to ashes, in 1666. During this disastrous time, Milton wrote *Paradise Regained* and *Samson Agonistes*, and also gave finishing touches to *Paradise Lost*, and all these in his utter loneliness. During the writing of *Paradise Lost*, Milton had to face several obstructions, such as his blindness, his poverty, the frequent refusals of his daughters to take dictations for the epic from him and to read source books to him, etc. After *Paradise Lost* was completed, Milton gave a copy of it to his friend Thomas Ellwood who delighted in this epic and requested the poet to write another poem on the theme of 'paradise regained'. Milton took the suggestion of his friend and began *Paradise Regained* in 1666 (the year of the great fire in London) and completed it in 1671. As *Paradise Lost* reflects Milton's rebellious spirit, expressed through the character of Satan, so *Paradise Regained* reflects his frustration with the 'showy public gestures' after the Restoration. His sentiment of resignation is particularly apparent in the last line of the second epic :

"Home to his mother's house private returned." This same mood of frustration and resignation appears once again in his only play, *Samson Agonistes*, that he finished also in 1671, especially in the last line of it : "And calm of mind, all passion spent." After the completion of *Samson Agonistes*, the old, blind and crestfallen poet said good-bye to his creative power, as Shakespeare did after his *The Tempest*, and began to live a lonely, sinecure and barely vegetative life, and, not long after, on 8 November 1674 peacefully passed away in London. Dr. Johnson writes that Milton died "about the tenth of November 1674, at his house in Bunhill-fields; and was buried next his father in the chancel of St. Giles at Cripplegate. His funeral was very splendidly and numerously attended" (Johnson, 105).

For some years before his death, Milton had been suffering excruciating pain of his gout. Dr. Johnson reports that in the intervals of the recurrent shattering pains, "he used to swing in a chair, and sometimes played upon an organ" (Johnson, 95). We know very little about Milton in his last few years. Hardin Craig, however, writes of his last years and about his habits during this period: "There is relatively little account of Milton's life during his last fourteen years, but much evidence of high performance. He had a good wife, many admirers — Marvell, Ellwood, and Dryden among them. We have records of his neat personal appearance, his cheerful good humour, his early rising, his love of music, and his habit of smoking his pipe before his door" (Craig, 261). Even "in later life he always looked much younger than his years, and his beautiful grey eyes never betrayed their sad secret" (Compton-Rickett, 177). There is no doubt about the personal beauty of Milton. Matthew Arnold, in his poem 'Cromwell', has written about the personal charms of Milton:

Lo ! Milton there
Stood like a statue; and his face was fair —
Fair beyond human beauty; and his eye,
That knew not earth, soar'd upwards to the sky !

Dr. Johnson also says that Milton was 'eminently beautiful'. Dr. Johnson further writes about Milton's personal appearance, habits, etc.: "His hair which was of a light brown, parted at the foretop, and hung down upon his shoulders, according to the picture which he has given of Adam. He was, however, not of the heroick stature, but rather below the middle size, according to Mr. Richardson, who mentions him as having narrowly escaped from being *short and thick.* He was vigorous, and active, and delighted in the exercise of the sword, in which he is related to have been eminently skilful. His weapon was, I believe, not the rapier, but the backsword, of which he recommends the use in his book on Education" (Johnson, 105). Johnson further goes on: "his domestic habits, so far as they are known, were those of a severe student. He drank little strong drink of any kind, and fed without excess in quantity, and in his earlier years without delicacy of choice. In his youth he studied late at night; but afterwards changed his hours, and rested in bed from nine to four in the summer, and five in the winter. The course of his day was best known after he was blind. When he first rose, he heard a chapter in the Hebrew Bible, and then studied till twelve; then took some exercise for an hour; then dined; then played on the organ, and sung, or heard another sing; then studied to six; then entertained his visitors till eight; then supped, and after a pipe of tobacco and a glass of water, went to bed" (Johnson, 106). Hardin Craig, as we have seen before, says that Milton was a cheerful person, and Dr. Johnson writes that Milton, perhaps joyfully, entertained guests and visitors, but C.V. Wedgwood differs from both of them. Wedgwood writes about Milton: "In private and public life he cuts a slightly ridiculous figure, a fact which enhances the solitary tragedy and grandeur of his achievement. That he was humourless and vain cannot be denied; his failings as a husband, a tutor, and a father have been fairly dwelt on and exaggerated" (Wedgwood, 108).

Milton had only three issues, and those only by his first wife — Anne, Mary and Deborah, all daughters. Barring Minshull, he was not in good terms with the other two wives. Milton was perhaps suffering from misogyny, and, may be, would like to say like the philosopher Nietzsche "When you go to a woman, take your whip with you." To him, the word 'woman', it is said, was the conjugation of two sounds: 'wo', meaning 'woe', and 'man'. Milton was, at first, a Calvinist, but later on subscribed to Arminianism. Dr. Johnson writes about his religious belief and observances that he had a profound faith in Christianity and in the holy Scriptures, and held a "confirmed belief of the immediate and occasional agency of Providence, yet grew old without any visible worship. In distribution of his hours, there was no hour of prayer, either solitary, or with his household; omitting public prayers, he omitted all" (Johnson, 108).

As a man of deep and wide learning, Milton was of a very serious sort. He could say with Lord Bacon 'Every province of knowledge is my province' — he was interested in almost everything of almost all branches of knowledge. Though he had a profound faith in God, he was never a dogmatist. He worshipped liberty and rationality, like Gods: all throughout his life he wrote for the cause of liberty and rationality. He was very steadfast; never did he budge even an inch from his conviction. But, all the same, he had enough magnanimity: we find him, for instance, accepting Mary Powell, who once left him temerariously in the lurch, with a magnanimous heart and without any impugnment. Milton had great courage and patience to bear great tragedies: he did never whimper after becoming blind. However, we sometimes hear of at least two deficiencies in his character: he was cruel to his daughters, and he was sexually deficient. Of the accusation relating to his relation with his daughters, we can say that we do not know much about the facts and the reasons and the circumstances behind his being cruel to his daughters, if he ever actually had been so. We are, of course, not trying to exonerate him, but we must take into account his deplorable condition — his blindness, his poverty, his other frustrations, particularly those due to the failure of the wished-for Commonwealth, etc. before we want to pronounce any final verdict on his character. And we should remind those who see sexual deficiency in him that a man with sexual debility would not marry as many as three times, in quick succession. His amorous awareness is well expressed in *Paradise Lost* (Book IV, lines 492-502) where Adam and Eve are in an amorous tangles :

> So spoke our general mother, and, with eyes
> Of conjugal attraction unreproved,
> And meek surrender, half-embracing leaned
> On our first father; half her swelling breast
> Naked met his, under the flowing gold
> Of her loose tresses hid. He in delight
> Both of her beauty and submissive charms,
> Smiled with superior love, as Jupiter
> On Juno smiled when he impregns the clouds
> That shed May flowers, and pressed her matron lip
> With kisses pure.

Other instances of Milton's amorous awareness are also present in the same epic, but let us cite only one more from the same. In Book VIII, lines 54-57, of *Paradise Lost*, Milton writes of Adam and Eve:

> He, she knew would intermix
> Grateful digressions, and solve high dispute
> With conjugal caresses: from his lip
> Not words alone pleased her.

Maybe, Milton underestimated the fair sex, but, if one likes to defend the poet, one may say that even the Christian Scriptures have not done justice to them; and further, Milton held the consummate love between man and woman to be divine.

Critics are not unanimous regarding the quality of Milton's personality: some are sympathetic to him, considering his misfortunes, and appraise his moral consternity, but others are arrogant and depreciative, Johnson for instance. Hardin Craig has a sympathetic attitude towards Milton's personality when he writes about the poet: "There was about him a sort of lofty and unmalicious arrogance that demanded expression. He was John Milton, and, as the world affected him, it revealed its general nature and principles. He stood forth to himself as a typically human personality endowed with unquestionable moral seriousness, intellectual integrity, and unswerving purposes. One might be disposed to cavil at this when one feels the rough edges of Milton's sternness if it were not true that Milton was, so far as justice can determine, exactly the upright and gifted creature that he thought himself" (Craig, 234). It is true that Dr. Johnson, for reasons known to him, detested Milton, the man as much as the poet Hardin Craig guesses some of the reasons: "In considering Dr. Johnson's attitude towards Milton one should remember not only the obvious fact that Milton's politics were obnoxious to Johnson, but also that, at the time Johnson wrote, the works of Milton were relatively fashionable. His [Milton's] imitators were creating a sort of romantic poetry to which Johnson objected" (Craig, 236 f.n.).

But whatever Milton might have been as a man, whatever flaws might have been there in his character, we should not forget that he was primarily a poet, and hence our evaluation of his personality will not be just unless we take him to be so. Milton was a poet even from his boyhood, and since then he reacted to everything with a poet's sentiment. David Daiches writes about Milton's life-long calling of a poet: " 'Anno Domini 1619, he was ten years old; and was then a poet.' So wrote John Aubrey in his 'brief life' of Milton, and though he may have exaggerated somewhat the information is essentially true, for Milton was dedicated to literature from early childhood more consciously and more deliberately than any other English poet" (Daiches, 1968, 7). Milton thought the calling of a poet to be a lofty one, as Wordsworth also thought two centuries later, and, moreover, he thought himself to be a 'consecrated spirit'. None can deny the depth and width of his knowledge, or the power of his imagination, or the profundity of his philosophy. C.V. Wedgwood writes about Milton's wisdom and poetic faculty : "Milton's acquired qualities were an understanding of several foreign and classical tongues, which enriched his experience in handling metres; a colossal learning which widened his vocabulary and his command of allusion and metaphor; and at the end, a resigned philosophy of existence" (Wedgwood, 110). Milton's personality was perhaps a blend of several contrary traits: he was generous but resolute; religiously meek but politically defiant; democratic but supercilious; and as a nationalist violently this-worldly, but as a God-fearing Christian abstractedly other-worldly. Behind his suave and serene personality, there lived a defiant and violent man who could say "When I die, let the earth be rolled in flames" (*Apology for Smectymnuus*, 1641).

4
(WORKS)

Milton's works may broadly be divided into three categories that belonged to the three different periods of his life: the early period of minor poems, the middle period of prose pamphlets, and the late period of two major poems and a drama : *Paradise Lost, Paradise Regained* and *Samson Agonistes*. In his writings, Milton was influenced principally by Spenser and Donne, and to an extent by Ben Jonson. He gave his successors much more than he received from his predecessors. One may identify three great stages in the history of English literature upto Milton, each stage showing one particularly striking quality: the period of Chaucer, when literature got from him a 'robust force'; the period of Spenser and Shakespeare, when literature received from them 'sweetness and variety'; and the third period, which came into being after a stage of fallow and imitative literature, when literature received from Milton what may be called 'greatness' (Milton's grand style).

No work of Milton, if there be any, while he was in the school, has come down to us. His first published work is *Elegy on Death of Fair Infant* which he wrote in the winter of 1625-1626, when he was only 17 or 18. It was followed by a Latin elegy, *Eligia Prima*, which Milton wrote in 1626 on the death of his class-mate and friend, the Italian boy Diodati, who was drowned in an accident. The same year Milton produced five other works: *Eligia Tertia* (written on the death of the Bishop of Winchester), *In Obitum Praesulis Eliensis, In Obitum Procancellarii Medici*, and *In Quintum Novembris* (written on the Gunpowder Plot). After this an unproductive year, 1627, elapsed, and in 1627 he wrote *Eligia Septima* (Milton's first, and perhaps only, love poem), 'Letter to Gill' (in verse), *Naturam non pati Senium*, and *Sixth*

Proclusion. In 1629, Milton wrote *De Idea Platonica; Eligia Quinta, in Adventum*; 'Nativity Ode'; and *Eligia Sexta*. Till 1629, *i.e.* the year in which he took his B.A., Milton had obvious preference for Latin as the medium of his poetry.

In 1630, when he was 21, Milton largely came back to his mother tongue English, and produced 'The Passion', 'Song on May Morning', some Italian sonnets and canzoni, and also some English sonnets, such as 'O Nightingle' and 'On Shakespeare'. Next, he wrote 'Epitaphs on Hobson', 'Epitaph on the Marchioness of Winchester' and 'Seventh Proclusion'. In 1632, *i.e.* the year in which he took his M.A. degree, Milton wrote the sonnet 'How soon hath Time'. The year 1633, again, was perhaps unproductive, like the year 1627. But we are not sure about this, for we do not know the exact dates of composition of such short works as 'Arcades', 'On Time', 'Upon Circumcison', and 'At a Solemn Music'; and of such long poems such as 'L'Allegro' and 'Il Penseroso'. We know this much that all these were written between the years 1632 and 1634. The beautiful masque *Comus* was also written in 1634. The year 1636 too was relatively unproductive, if we agree with E.M.W. Tillyard in supposing that the poem '*Ad Patrem*' was written in 1637, in which year Milton wrote the famous poem 'Lycidas'. In 1638, as we have said, Milton went to Italy. There he wrote 'Poems to Leonora' and *Mansus*, and coming back to England, he wrote *Epitaphium Damonis* in 1639 when Milton's earlier poetic period ended.

Milton's prose period, or his period of pamphletry, began in the middle of 1641 (May June) with the publication of his first pamphlet *On Reformation in England*. In the same year, Milton wrote two other pamphlets: *Of Practical Episcopacy* and *Animadversions upon the Remonstrant's Defence*. In the second tract he betrays his ambition of becoming 'a poet of the new age'. Next year, *i.e.* in 1642, he published *Reasons of Church Government* and *Apology for Smectymnuus*, the second being his last anti-episcopal pamphlet. The background of these two tracts is the intellectual environment of the Renaissance. It was in *Reason of Church Government* that Milton first expressed his plan of writing an Arthurian epic, but later on he changed his mind and wrote *Paradise Lost*. *Apology for Smectymnuus* is Milton's 'panegeric on the ruling majority in the Long Parliament'. His concern about education is expressed in his pamphlet *On Education* which was published in 1644. The same year he produced two other important tracts: *Judgment of Martin Bucer Concerning Divorce*, in which he justified the institution of divorce, and *Areopagitica*, in which he pleaded for free press. Next year, *i.e.* in 1645, he produced two more divorce tracts *Tetrachordon* and *Colasterion*. *Tetrachordon* is not a continuation of his earlier tract on divorce, *i.e. Doctrine and Discipline of Divorce*, as some critics seem to assume, but is altogether a new tract.

From the middle of 1645 to the end of 1648, there was a cessation of pamphlet production. During this period, Milton was busy writing the incomplete *History of Britain*, of which he wrote only four books, and collecting materials for his *De Doctrina Christiana*. In 1649, he came back to pamphleteering and wrote three major pamphlets: *Tenure of Kings and Magistrates*, *Observations upon the Articles of Peace*, and *Eikonoklastes*. Then after a gap of about one year, he wrote the Pamphlet *Defensio pro Populo Anglicano*, in 1651. Again, after a gap of three years, *i.e.* in 1654, he wrote *Defensio Secunda*, the greatest of his prose works, and in 1655 *Defensio pro Se*. Once again, there was an intermission in the production of pamphlets — from 1656 to 1659. During this period of about four years, Milton wrote some sonnets, and once again took up the writing of his *History of Britian*. But while he was engaged in writing the *History of Britain*, he produced two prose tracts: *De Doctrina Christiana* and *Defensio Prima*. Milton wrote his last pamphlets in 1659 and in 1660. Within this short period of only two years, he wrote four major pamphlets *Civil Power in Ecclesiastical Causes* (1659), *Likeliest Means to remove Hirelings out of the Church* (1659), *On the Ruptures of the Commonwealth* (1659), and *Ready and Easy Way to Establish a Free Commonwealth* (1660).

Milton's second and major poetic period began around 1660 and ended in 1671 with the completion of *Samson Agonistes*. During these eleven years, Milton produced the three great works for which he is now largely remembered, and for which he will ever be remembered: *Paradise Lost*, *Paradise Regained*, and *Samson Agonistes*. Perhaps around 1658 Milton began *Paradise Lost* — the great epic which he planned about thirty years ago (at that time the plan was to write an Arthurian epic). He completed it within seven years, in 10 Books, and published it in 1667. In 1674 (the year in which he died), *Paradise Lost* was published for the second time. It was then that the 10 Books of the epic were split up and rearranged into 12 Books, and Milton added an 'Argument' at the beginning of each Book. Immediately after the publication of *Paradise Lost*, Milton's friend, Thomas Ellwood, suggested to him the idea of writing of *Paradise Regained* which the poet did forthwith, and published it in 1671, along with his only drama *Samson Agonistes*. Before this, in 1670, Milton published his *History of*

Britain, which comprised "the whole fable of Geoffrey of Monmouth, and continued to the Norman invasion" (Johnson, 102). Dr. Johnson writes about Milton's *History of Britian* : "The style is harsh; but it has something of rough vigour, which perhaps may often strike, though it cannot please" (Johnson, 102). In the nineteen thirties, Frank Allen Patterson and others edited and published the complete works of Milton in eighteen volumes, under the title *The Works of John Milton* (New York, 1931-1938). At 47, Milton had three plans: an epic poem, a history of the country, and a dictionary of the Latin tongue. Only the third he could not produce.

2

MILTON : THE PURITAN, AND THE CHILD OF RENAISSANCE AND REFORMATION

Milton's age was an age of political and religious revolutions. Though these revolutions occurred in the seventeenth century, the seeds of these revolutions were sown much earlier, say in the eleventh or the twelfth century, when man's clouded consciousness began to brighten and the medieval faiths and superstitions had been giving way to clear thoughts, with the dissemination of rational learning, which was facilitated by the recently invented paper. In England, the credit of driving away the nagging medieval inauthentic faiths and superstitions, for the first time, should go to Roger Bacon (c. 1210-c. 1293) whose scientifico-logical attitude may be compared with that of Aristotle. Bacon's precept was : "Cease to be ruled by dogmas and authorities; look at the world" (Wells, 206). Bacon prepared the ground for the advent of new sorts of learning, culture and thought process. The actual change in the intellectual climate of England and in other European countries occurred in the 15th, 16th and 17th centuries. Even before Roger Bacon, several other rational-minded intellectuals appeared on the medieval European scene, and tried their utmost to change the prevailing mentality of the people who remained immersed in the medieval darkness. One such intellectual was Peter Abelard (1079-1142), a philosopher and poet, who challenged the authority of the Church on pains of punishment for his 'heresy' that the churchmen discovered in his book *Sic et non* (*Yes and No*) and in his other works. Abelard was a heroic lover. At 37, he fell in violent love with Heloise, his private student, and begot a child by her; but, ultimately, the lovers were forcefully separated, as their love affairs went against the Christian doctrine and tradition, and against the prevailing social mores clouded by the medieval superstitions. Their intense love may be compared with that of Tristam and Iseult or with that of Romeo and Juliet. Besides, *Sic et non*, Abelard wrote *Historia Calamitatum (History of my Calamity).* To Abelard, love was divine, and the source of humane qualities. With his writings and his exemplary love Abelard dealt a heavy blow against the medieval consciousness which had been suffering from superstitious torpor. Abelard's life and thoughts immensely influenced the people of Europe for centuries afterwards. But, generally, the influence of Abelard was ignored by the Renaissance scholars, perhaps because Bacon's influence was more proximate to the new intellectual movement, known as Renaissance, than Abelard's.

The spirit of the Renaissance, is well expressed in Dante's *Divina Comedia* : " 'Thy will is free and whole and upright and now it would be wrong to rein it in. Be thine own Emperor and thine own Pope' " (Russel, Stells, 200). The proximate cause of the Renaissance or rebirth (the meaning of the term 'renaissance' is 'rebirth') was historical. Renaissance means revival of the ancient Greek and Latin arts and letters, on the one hand, and the consequential breaking away of the modern world from the clutches of the medieval dark ages. In the middle ages, when the eastern part of the great Roman empire had Constantinople as its headquarters, scholars from all over Europe gathered at the Capital for pursuance of ancient Greek and Latin learning. For about one thousand years, this centre of high learning continued to be a great fountain of erudition and researches, away from the medieval ages' ups and downs of kings and kingdoms. But in the morning of 29 May 1453, the barbaric Turks attacked this seat of learning, broke the walls of the schools of the scholars, and were about to make a *bon fire* with the invaluable manuscripts preserved there. Like the scientists and scholars who fled from the Hitlerite Germany in the thirties of the present century, the scholars of Constantinople fled from the town, bundling up the precious manuscripts, and ran away, helter-skelter, towards different directions, but principally towards Italy. At that time, in Italy there had already been a change in the intellectual attitude of the people who began to raise diverse questions about the authenticity of the religious dogmas. The fugitive scholars from Constantinople who gathered there stimulated their urge for rational enquiry, and thus the Renaissance first began flowering in Italy. The invention of the printing press about the time of the fall of Constantinople helped the dissemination of the spirit of the Renaissance throughout Europe at a faster pace. From Italy, the spirit of the Renaissance travelled to Germany, France and England. The cause of this was the commercial and trading credo that swept over the whole of Europe and the Orient. The reciprocal lending and borrowing of knowledge among the countries of Europe brought in a new attitude towards arts and letters. Stella Pandell Russell, in her *Art in the World*, writes in this regard: "Another new force influenced art — the increased trade throughout Europe and the Orient. Its two main centres at this time were Italy and Flanders. With the rise of commercialism, Princes, merchants and bankers threatened the power of the Pope and the bishops... At the same time, intellectuals began to abandon Medieval scholasticism which had disputed such questions as how many angels could stand on the head of a pin. In its place they studied the world around them with a scientific attitude based on the readings of Aristotle, using their senses to observe and their reason to explain what they observed" (Russell, Stells, 200-201).

Some of the chief features of the Renaissance were scientifico-logical attitude towards everything : love of learning, nostalgic search for the arts and literature of the ancient Greek and Latin masters, rejection of irrational authority, and individualism. All these elements were not independent, but were mutually-influencing. The Renaissance emphasis on rationalism was so strong that it continued to be powerful over human consciousness even two centuries afterwards, when it gave rise to the Enlightenment (*Aufklärung*) in the 18th century. In England, the scientific attitude was brought in earlier, as told before, by Roger Bacon. When the waves of Renaissance broke against the shores of England, the people there preferred the ancient Greek and Latin works of art and literature to the tedious, vacant and repetitive homilies of the churches. The Aristotlean method of enquiry that belonged to the medieval ages was supplanted by Lord Francis Bacon's (1561-1626) inductive method and experimentation. The theory that all knowledge is there in the scriptures was rejected by the people who now understood that conclusions must be reached with concrete data collected through sensual experiences. Consequently, they ruled out Platonism and adopted Aristotleanism, for their enquiry. Faith, likewise, was rejected for reason; meaninglessness of this world for love of life; and other-worldliness for this-worldliness. The previously God-intoxicated people now began to feel the profundity of mundane experiences. "About 1195 Pope Innocent III had written a famous book *On Contempt for the World* (*De Contemptu mundi*); but in 1580 Montaigne, writing *On the Education of Children*, says that 'this great world' ought to be 'the book my young gentleman should study with the utmost attention.' The attitude has been completely reversed" (Brown, 381). The Renaissance imbibed in man love of beauty, imagination, music, and refined culture. It held high up human qualities and love for jovial life. But we should not forget that the Renaissance man learned all these from the ancient Greece and Italy, but principally from Greece — from *Hellen*, i.e. from the Greeks; and it is for this reason that the Renaissance is sometimes identified with Hellenism.

As told earlier, Milton was much imbued by the spirit of the seventeenth century England. Barring his last work *Samson Agonistes*, all the poetic works of Milton bear witness of the presence of the spirit of the Renaissance in him. His first substantial poetic work 'Ode on the Nativity' is the first evidence of his Renaissance spirit. The poem is romantically tuned, and is redolent of images, beautiful, lively and inspiring :

So when the sun in bed,
Curtained with cloudy red,
    Pillows his chin upon an orient wave,
The flocking shadows pale
Troop to th' infernal jail,
    Each fettered ghost slips to his several grave,
And the yellow-skirted fays
Fly after the night-steeds, leaving their moon-loved maze.

The poem was written when Milton was around twentyone. His next two major poems, 'L'Allegro' and 'Il Penseroso', that he composed within the next two years, may be called the companion poems of 'Ode on the Nativity', and these two are also full of romantic imagination and love of life. In 'L'Allegro', for instance, Milton sings (lines 25-32):

    Haste thee, Nymph, and bring with thee
Jest, and youthful Jollity,
Quips and Cranks and wanton Wiles,
Nods and Becks and wreathed Smiles,
Such as hang on Hebe's cheek,
And love to live in dimple sleek;
Sport that wrinkled Care derides,
And Laughter holding both his sides.

By the by, this poem of Milton's, or the spirit of it, reminds one of W.B. Yeats's poem 'The Stolen Child' (the refrain of it): "*Come away, O human child !/To the waters and the wild/With a faery, hand in hand,/For the world's more full of weeping than you can understand.*" In 'Il Penseroso', the Renaissance spirit of Milton is not so obvious, for it is overcast with his forthcoming Puritan sentiment. And yet there are strains in it of the Renaissance spirit, as for instance, in the following few lines of the poem (lines 131-138) :

And, when the sun begins to fling
His flaming beams, me Goddess, bring
To arched walks of twilight groves,
And shadows brown, that Sylvan loves,
Of pine, or monumental oak,
Where the rude axe with heaved stroke
Was never heard the nymphs to daunt,
Or fright them from their hallowed haunt.

Milton's Renaissance spirit was soon tempered by his Puritanism. In 1634, when he was about twentysix, he wrote *Comus* in which we find a tension between the Renaissance spirit and the Puritan spirit. The Renaissance element of *Comus* may be seen especially in its songs and dances. *Comus* is replete with scenarios of beauty and love of beauty. Of love Comus says (lines 739-742):

Beauty is Nature's coin; must not be hoarded,
But must be current; and the good thereof
Consists in mutual and partaken bliss,
Unsavory in th' enjoyment of itself.

But such love of beauty is alloyed with Puritan respect for virtues, that we especially find at the end of the mask (*Comus*) where the Spirit 'epiloguizes': "Mortals that would follow me,/Love Virtue, she alone is free." In 'Lycidas' also Milton has shown his Renaissance spirit, and his love of classicism and Puritanism. 'Lycidas', that was composed in 1637, begins with a beautiful description of natural beauty:

Yet once more, O ye laurels, and once more,
Ye myrtles brown, with ivy never sere,
I come to pluck your berries harsh and crude,
And with forced fingers rude
Shatter your leaves before the mellowing year.

The poem is full of descriptions of natural beauty, sonorous music, humane love and fellow-feeling. It also shows Milton's fascination for classical art and literature. 'Lycidas' contains pagan imagery and elaborate descriptions of natural objects too, while betraying pure love that is puritanical.

Almost along with the Renaissance movement, another movement began in England, as elsewhere, — the Reformation movement, which was complementary to the Renaissance movement. These two movements should not, perhaps, be viewed as two quite different movements, because the spirit behind both of them was the same — the spirit of freedom from the medieval theocentric consciousness. The Renaissance turned man's consciousness away from God, at least partially, and veered it towards himself, for which reason the Renaissance is rightly called humanism. The only superficial difference between the Renaissance and the Reformation is that while the Renaissance taught man to apply his free-thinking in the fields of art, philosophy and culture, the Reformation wanted that man uses his free rationality in the social and political problems. The Reformation movement, which is younger than the Renaissance movement, originated in the protestations of Martin Luther (1483-1546) against the excesses of papacy in Wittenberg, in 1517. It took different programmes and different modes in various countries. In Germany and Switzerland, it exposed itself in the shape of a civil war; but in England, as in some other European countries, many people, under the influence of it, cut off all relations with the Papacy in Italy. These people are known as non-conformists or dissidents. H.G.Wells, in his *A Short History of the World*, writes: "In England these dissidents were the Non-conformists who played a very large part in the politics of that country in the seventeenth and eighteenth centuries. In England they carried their objections to a princely head to the church so far as to decapitate king Charles I (1649), and for eleven prosperous years England was a republic under Non-conformist rule" (Wells, 214). As we have seen in the first chapter, Milton was, at the very beginning of his active life, drawn to the contemporary currents of the Renaissance and the Reformation. Since his early life, Milton was being particularly influenced by Edmund Spenser's Renaissance spirit and poetry. E.M.W.Tillyard, in his *Milton*, writes: "That Milton was very greatly influenced by details in Spenser is undoubted. The influence was life-long, and as strong in *Paradise Lost* as anywhere" (Tillyard, 389).

The Renaissance spirit of individualism, freedom, and reliance on rationalism, is strikingly embodied in the character of Satan in *Paradise Lost*, for, like the Renaissance man, he loves romance and chivalry, and aspires after freedom and individualism. In the epic, Milton lionizes and glorifies Satan, and brings into relief his exploits for the purpose of upholding his ideal of individualism. Satan's plans and exploits remind one of the adventures of the knights of Spenser's *The Faerie Queene* that is so much soaked in the Renaissance spirit. Even the central theme of the epic exudes the spirit of the Renaissance, or rather the tension between the vestigial medieval consciousness and the Renaissance consciousness; because, if we closely follow the course of the epic, we will find that it is actually not an attempt to "justify the ways of God to men" but an attempt to show the drama of conflict between reason and passion, both of which are resident only in man, not in God. Further, the rejuvenation of the literary genre called epic is itself indebted to the *Zeitgeist* of the Renaissance. It is interesting to note that most of the epics of the European countries were written in the 16th century, when the whole of Europe was being flushed with the high Renaissance spirit. The half a dozen epics of Lpoe de Vega, Ariosto's epic *Orlando furioso*, Tasso's epic *Jerusalem Delivered*, Camoën's epic *The Lusiads*, and Spenser's epic *The Faerie Queene* — all were composed in the European high Renaissance of the 16th century. It may be mentioned here that it was after the fall of the Cromwellian Republic, some critics believe, that Milton sat down to write *Paradise Lost*, and so, the same critics say, the epic should be interpreted as a rebellion against undemocratic and tyrannical authority. Perhaps such an interpretation is not quite correct, for Milton conceived the idea of writing an epic on the Arthurian theme some thirty years before he actually began *Paradise Lost*. If we agree with this, we should believe that in the epic Milton recorded the conflict between reason and passion — the conflict that the Renaissance man of England felt within his being.

The Reformation principally protested against the mediation between God and man, preached and practised by the papacy; and believed in, and advocated, direct linkage between God and man, through the medium of God's words — the Bible. This attitude to theology was shared by Protestantism that originated in the preachings of Martin Luther. The term 'protestant' was first applied to some German princes who, in the Second Diet of Speyer in 1529, protested against the decision adopted that they would not be free from religious injunctions imposed on all and sundry from time to time. Prostestantism has a long history. Though the term 'protestant' was coined later on, Protestantism actually began in the 14th century, when John Wycliffe (c 1330-1384), who subscribed to the views of the Reformation, "demanded secularization of the church's landed estates and proposed that the head of the church in England should be the king" (Progress Publishers, 610-611). In the 15th century, Jan Huss of Bohemia demanded abolition of the abject practice of simony or the practice of selling church benefits, such as pardons, preferments, etc. He also objected to the system of the Pope issuing Bulls from time to time. All these demands of Wycliffe and Huss were congurent with the Reformation spirit. It is for this and other reasons that we may say that the terms 'Reformation' and 'Protestantism' are almost equisemantic.

Protestantism was never against Christianity; what it actually objected to were the excessive church regulations and dogmatism. The Protestant spirit has gone down the history even after Milton and his age. The philosopher G.W. Leibnitz (1646-1716), though he was not concerned so much about religion, said that God is there but we need not worship him, because everything that is happening in the universe was predetermined by Him. After Leibnitz, Immanuel Kant (1724-1804), another German philosopher, said that a replica of God is there in every man's heart, and that this replica is expressed in the moral 'Categorical Imperatives' of a man. Kant believed that to obey these 'Categorical Imperatives' is the worship of God. Thus, these two and such other philosophers also reduced the supreme authority of the Church as well as that of the Bible. About two centuries later, the German poet Heinrich Heine also criticised the church, the monarchy, and philistinism, like Milton. But while Milton was God-fearing, Heine was an avowed atheist. So we see that man has always raised his voice against the excesses of the church. However, Milton was not averse to everything of the church, but he was only against the excesses of the church. That the church was once extremely dogmatic is evident from the fact that it was only as late as on 25 October, 1996, that Pope John Paul II recognised Darwin's theory of evolution.

Milton's attraction towards the spirit of Reformation was early intensified by his private tutor Thomas Young who "probably inherited the anti-prelatical animus, and carried it with him to Milton's home" (Tillyard, 1956, 371). Further, Milton's anti-clerical sentiment grew out of his knowledge of the fact that his father was a dissident, and of the fact that his grand-father had disinherited his father for his father's dissidence, and consequently his father had to undergo acute financial hardships. Milton's paternal love might have been working behind his affection for Protestantism, As the psychologists say, the first-born follows in the foot-steps of the father, and Milton was the first child of his father. The anti-clerical sentiment of Milton is obvious in *Paradise Lost* where Satan protests against the tyranny and autocephalic rule of God that seem to him irrational, inessential and excessive. But it should be pointed out here that Satan is never against God, but is always against God's 'ungodliness'. Along with the elements of the Reformation, the Renaissance humanism is also glaringly evident in *Paradise Lost.* Respect for individuality, rejection of authority, love of freedom, and rationality were the principal features of Renaissance humanism, The Renaissance humanist was not averse to beauty and love and romance — things that the radical Puritan would never admit — and all these are also evident in *Paradise Lost.*

But, whatever else Milton might have been, he was fundamentally a Puritan. Puritanism was the by-product of Protestantism that wanted to purify Christianity of all its 'drosses' or unnecessary rituals and practices. The Puritan movement in England began in the 16th century, and was spearheaded by Oliver Cromwell. Puritanism grew out of two parallel movements: the Reformation movement and the Protestant movement. "At the reformation men were told not to believe in ecclesiastical magic — the mediating saints, holy water, exorcism, relics, pilgrimages, etc. etc." (Hill, 310). And all these were insane and unceremonious particularly to the Puritans. The fulcrum of Puritanism was man's conscience. Roger Scruton, in his *A Dictionary of Political Thought*, defines Puritanism thus: "The extreme form of Protestantism in which the idea of the sovereignty of conscience is taken to require constant and scrupulous vigilance over one's every sentiment and action (and usually over everyone else's) in order to track down and extirpate all impure and irreligious thoughts and motives" (Scruton, 389).

In England, the Puritans were divided into two categories: the Separatists, who wanted to sever all ties with the Anglican Church, and the non-Separatists, who did not want separation from the Anglican Church, but only wanted to reform it. Milton was a Separatist As we have told earlier, his Puritanism is evident even in his early writings, though in seminal form. But, it may be mentioned here that in his 'L'Allegro' there are some anti-puritan passages — passages that are romantically coloured and sensuous. For instance, witness the following lines of the poem (already quoted before)

> Haste thee, Nymph, and bring with thee
> Jest, and youthful Jollity,
> Quips and Cranks and wanton Smiles,
> Such as hang on Hebe's cheek,
> And love to live in dimple sleek;
> Sport that wrinkled Care derides,
> And Laughter holding both his sides.

The poet is so much buoyed with his desire for pleasure and revelry that he tells Mirth (personified): "These delights if thou canst give,/ Mirth with thee I mean to live."

But in the companion poem, 'Il Penseroso', the puritan elements are obvious — religiosity, suavity, emotional control, and avoidance of sensuality. In this poem, Milton welcomes melancholy : 'Hail, divinest Melancholy!' Melancholy, he says, is wisdom "Whose saintly visage is too bright/To hit the sense of human sight,/And, therefore, to our weaker view/O'erlaid with black, staid Wisdom's hue". 'Il Penseroso' shows, for the first time, Milton's on-coming puritanism (lines 161-166) :

There let the pealing organ blow,
To the full-voiced quire below,
In service high and anthems clear,
As may with sweetness, through mine ear,
Dissolve me into ecstasies,
And bring all Heaven before mine eyes.

In *Comus*, the Renaissance and the romantic elements of his earlier poems are still lingering, and yet it is replete with puritan elements. The Renaissance or Hellenic elements of *Comus* is revealed in its songs and dances; but all these cannot cloud the basic puritan elements of the mask: the puritan elements or the Hebraic elements peep out through the shroud of the Renaissance elements. Puritanism is, sometimes, also called Hebraism, because the Puritans, like the Jews (Hebrews) heavily emphasise moral uprightness. The Puritans or the Roundheads (the Puritans were sometimes called Roundheads because they often used to get their hair cut close to the pate) could not tolerate moral laxity. However, Milton's puritan and anti-clerical attitude is also present in 'Lycides' in which poem the poet heavily denounces St. Peter and the corrupt Roman Catholic clergymen (lines 119-121) :

Blind mouths! that scarce themselves know how to hold
A sheep-hook, or have learned aught else the least
That to the faithful herdman's art belongs!

The puritan element in *Comus* is well expressed in the speech of Elder Brother (lines 593-597) :

But evil on itself shall back recoil,
And mix no more with goodness, when at last,
Gathered like scum, and settled to itself,
It shall be in eternal restless change
Self-fed and self-consum'd.

And again, in the epilogue of the Spirit, at the fag end of the mask *Comus*, the puritan element is glaringly evident (lines 1018-1023):

> Mortals that would follow me,
> Love Virtue; she alone is free,
> She can teach ye how to climb
> Higher than the sphery chime;
> Or, if Virtue feeble were,
> Heaven itself would stoop to her.

Paradise Lost is apparently a pot-pouri of classicism, Renaissance spirit, humanism and puritanism; but at bottom it is only puritanical. The puritanic proclamation of the epic occurs just at the beginning of it. The poet declares that his objective in the poem is: "That, to the height of this great argument,/I may assert Eternal Providence,/And justify the ways of God to men". The story of the epic is taken from the first Book of the Old Testament (of the Bible), called Genesis (1-3). *Paradise Lost* shows the conflict between reason and passion within the inner circle of the human being, and shows that the path of passion leads towards suffering (Hell) while that of reason, with God's blessings, salvages the fallen man. This is the essential message of the epic and this is purely puritanical. Nevertheless, *Paradise Lost* is not absolutely puritanical, in so far as it also contains the spirit of the Renaissance and the spirit of humanism. But Milton's last two great works, *Paradise Regained* and *Samson Agonistes* are glaring instances of his puritan stance. In *Paradise Regained* there is no craving for beauty or individualism or power, that belonged to the Renaissance spirit; instead, there is rather a blatant contempt for beauty (Book II, lines 220-224) :

> For beauty stands
> In the admiration only of weak minds
> Led captive; cease to admire, and all her plumes
> Fall flat, and shrink into a trivial toy,
> At every sudden slighting quite abashed.

Paradise Regained is basically a religious poems it urges man to know and worship God. To worship God is the only injunction imposed on mankind; it is the only meaning of life; and it is the only duty, the supreme duty of mankind: "To know, and, knowing worship God aright" (Book II, line 475). This is plain puritanism. *Samson Agonistes* is moulded in the classical Greek or Hellenic shape, but its spirit is clearly Hebraic. In his old age, Milton became a staunch puritan, and this is evident in the stern didacticism, strict morality, and austerity of *Samson*

Agonistes. In this drama, Milton's message is that man's life should be a life of dedication to God. He tells us that God is certainly just, and that truth, ultimately, must triumph, and also that though to us God sometimes seems to be insoucient about our sufferings, and about the wrongs done to us, and though the wrongs are often times triumphant. God must at the end take us back to his affectionate fold, and those wrongs must prove to be ephemeral. This conviction of Milton is evident at the end of *Samson Agonistes* where the Chorus sings (lines 1745-1750) :

> All is best, though we oft doubt
> What th' unsearchable dispose
> Of Highest Wisdom brings about,
> And ever best found in the close.
> Oft he seems to hide his face,
> But unexpectedly returns.

Samson Agonistes is the document of Milton's profound belief in God and moral uprightness, and as such it is the document of his puritanism. The whole of the drama may be summarised in just one line of the Chorus: "Just are the ways of God". The Puritans believed that there is a direct relationship between God and man, that God and truth must ultimately be victorious, that the sufferings of man are due to man's own folly or illusory passions, and that God will ultimately salvage man out of his folly. All these are the principal puritan convictions, and all these are the pillars upon which *Samson Agonistes* is built up.

3

THE PHILOSOPHY AND THE THEOLOGY OF MILTON

Milton's philosophical and theological convictions are scattered throughout most of his major writings, and so it is difficult to get a total view of his philosophy and theology. However, his Latin tract or pamphlet *De Doctrina Christiana* is generally taken to be a compendium of his philosophical, moral, theological and social beliefs and convictions. Milton began collecting materials for this tract as early as in 1645, when, perhaps, he could foresee the coming into being of a new socio-political order in England, in the near future, compatible with his avowed Puritanism. This might have been the reason behind his writing the tract: he wrote it so that it might serve as a guide for the coming socio-religio-political system. Ten years afterwards, *i.e.* in 1655, when his vision came true, he wrote *De Doctrina Christiana*. Milton's philosophy and theology was medieval, on the one hand, and eclectic, on the other. Generally, he subscribed mostly to the preachings of St. Paul of the New Testament. E.M.W.Tillyard, in his *Milton* is very perceptive when he writes: "It is remarkable how closely Milton follows St. Paul and how little weight he gives to the Gospels, in writing of Christ" (Tillyard, 1956, 232). St. Paul was one of the twelve Apostles of Christianity, and his teachings are contained mostly in 'Acts', 'Romans', 'Corinthians', 'Ephesians', 'Thessalonians', 'Timothy', and 'Philemon' of the New Testament. St. Paul (or Saul) had been a persecutor of Christians, but after Christ met him in a vision, he converted himself to Christianity. He advocated, as St. Peter did not, complete break with Judaism. St. Paul's teachings are all ethical, and only obliquely philosophical. In addition to Paulinism, Milton accepted, at least partially, the metaphysics of 'Genesis' of the Old Testament, as is apparent in *Paradise Lost*. Milton's philosophical views were coloured by the medieval scholastic philosophy, no doubt, but it must be noted that, as a child of the Renaissance and the Reformations Milton always retained his rationalistic mind while accepting adventitious ideas and beliefs of the medieval age. He looked at everything from his own rationalistic point of view. Though he declared that " 'For my own part I adhere to the Holy Scriptures alone — I follow no other heresy or sect' " (Tillyard, 1956, 214-215), we cannot take this avowal of his at face value, because, in reality, he deviated, in many places, from the Scriptures. Nevertheless, he was always generally following the spirit of the teachings of the Scriptures. His sources of truth were the Bible, works of great seers, and rationality of human beings that he called 'nature'. Milton was also much influenced by Plato. He accepted all these authorities, but never blindly; he accepted them after assaying with the touchstone of reason, which gave him flexibility of beliefs.

Milton believed in two ontological beings or primordial substances — spirit and matter — both of which can be subsumed under one ultimate substance which is God. In this regard his metaphysics may be compared with that of his contemporary French philosopher Rene Descartes who was also, like Milton, a rationalist. It may seem paradoxical to think that Milton, on the one hand, believed in the truth of 'Genesis', according to which God created everything out of nothingness, and, on the other hand, believed in the existence of matter. But Milton was never paradoxical. E.M.W. Tillyard writes about the apparent paradox in Milton's philosophy: "Discussing the Creation Milton expounds one of his most heretical and characteristic doctrines : his materialism. Even God cannot create out of nothing: the orthodox doctrine that man was created out of nothing is false. God created man out of matter, and matter is good, part of God himself" (Tillyard, 1956, 228). Therefore, Milton thought matter not to be 'material' but to be 'spiritual', for, according to him, matter is part of God who is purely spiritual. He believed that matter is of two gradations — there is a higher grade of matter and there is a lower grade of matter. The angels are of the higher grade of matter, the 'airy matter', while man is composed of the lower grade of matter. E.M.W. Tillyard writes about Milton's conviction in this regard: "If the goodness of the body is to be believed in, a kind of ladder of matter ranging from gross to tenuous was a desirable explanation: the angels were beings high up on the material ladder. The angels were created before man, and like him they possess the gift of free will" (Tillyard, 1956, 229). Matter, or for that matter the body of human beings, to Milton, was not the seat of sins, but matter was essentially good. "And it is with this belief in the essential goodness of matter that his belief in the essential goodness of the flesh is to be connected. This belief is one of those that separate him so far from St. Paul and contemporary Puritanism and makes him, as in some ways he was, so curiously modern" (Tillyard, 1956, 229).

According to Milton, God is unknowable; but he proffers at least two arguments for the existence of God. He says, *imprimis*, that the order of the world points to the existence of a Supreme Being. By 'order' he does not mean only the pattern or system or harmony obtaining among all the things and beings of the world, but also the 'order' or 'goodness' that exists in each and every thing or being of the world. In *Samson Agonistes*, therefore, the Chorus tells us: " 'Just are the ways of God' " and " 'All is best, though we oft doubt'." Milton further wrote : " 'There can be no doubt but that everything in the world, by the beauty of its order and the evidence of a determinate and beneficial purpose which pervades it, testifies that some supreme efficient Power must have pre-existed, by which the whole was ordained for a specific end' " (Tillyard, 1956, 226). After Milton, Alexander Pope also saw goodness in everything of the world. In his *Essay on Man*, Pope writes: "Whatever is, is good". However, Milton's second proof for the existence of God is the predominance of conscience over all human actions. About a century after Milton, the Prussian philosopher Immanuel Kant (1724-1804) said the same thing. However, Milton wrote : " 'The existence of God is further proved by that feeling, whether we term it conscience or right reason, which even in the worst of characters is not altogether extinguished. If there were no God, there would be no distinction between right and wrong; the estimate of virtue and vice would entirely depend on the blind opinion of men; none would follow virtue, none would be restrained from vice by any sense of shame or fear of the laws, unless conscience or right reason did from time to time convince everyone, however unwilling, of the existence of God, the lord and ruler of all things, to whom sooner or later, each must give an account of his own actions, whether good or bad' " (Tillyard, 1956, 227). It may be noted here that Milton deviates from Kant in believing that conscience is equivalent to 'right reason', because to the philosopher, conscience is something quite different from rationality. But Milton agrees with Kant in that the source of conscience or morality resides within the self itself.

Milton believed in the old cosmogony of Ptolemy (2nd century A.D.), according to which the earth did not revolve round the sun, rather the other way round, to wit, the sun revolved round the earth. It is curious enough that though over half a century before Milton's birth, the Polish astronomer Nicolas Copernicus (1473-1543) established beyond all doubts that the sun is the centre of our universe, Milton stuck to the old theory of Ptolemy, and believed that the earth was 'sedentary' (*Paradise Lost*, Book VIII, 32). He even confirms his belief in *Paradise Lost* (Book VIII) by saying that this system of heavenly motions was rightly conceived of by God, and had it been otherwise, things would go astray. At the same place of the epic, he raises a question about the matter and obliquely and implicitly gives the answer to it himself (lines 122-125) :

> What if the Sun
> Be centre to the World, and other stars,
> By his attractive virtue and their own
> Incited, dance about him various rounds?

From all these, we may conclude that in Milton, science and superstition, reason and belief, resided as neighbours.

Milton had his special theory about the relation between mind and body, and with it he believed that he could, at one stroke, solve the tangled problem of the relation between the two entities that have much baffled philosophers down the ages. He did not admit of the theory that mind is heavenly, while body, which is not spiritual like mind but is composed of only matter, is a dross; because, according to him, matter is essentially as good as mind or soul. Milton believed that man is a whole that is composed of mind and body, and that the whole is what is called soul. Therefore, according to him, soul is not something different from body. Milton wrote: " 'Man is a living being, intrinsically and properly one and individual, not compounded or separable, not, according to the common opinion, made up and framed of two distinct and different natures, as of soul and body — but the whole man is soul, and the soul-man, that is to say a body or substance, individual, animated, sensitive, and rational; and the breath of life was neither a part of the divine essence, nor the soul itself, but as it were an inspiration of some divine virtue fitted for the existence of life and reason, and infused into the organic body' " (Tillyard, 1956, 229).

As Milton believed in the inseparability of mind and body, he also believed that at the time of death, not only the body but also the soul perishes, though both the body and the mind can be resuscitated or resurrected afterwards at God's will. Therefore, Milton's conception of death differed from common man's conception of death. Milton said that death was something more than mere mortality, because in death there was " 'loss or at least obscuration of the right reason which enabled man to discern the chief good and in which consisted as it were the life of the understanding' " (Tillyard, 1956, 231). Nevertheless, Milton had the belief that " 'some remnants of the divine image still exists in us, not wholly extinguished by this spiritual death' " (Tillyard, 1956, 231). In this regard, Milton's conception of body and soul may be compared with that of Plato and Aristotle, who believed that a part, at least, of the soul is immortal. But Milton greatly differed from the two philosophers, because whereas he believed in inalienability of mind or soul and body, the two philosophers believed that at least the rational part of the soul is not destroyed with the death of the body. Yet, Milton's conception of soul is similar to Aristotle's conception of it, in at least one vital point. Aristotle said that the soul is the form of the body; and Milton believed that man was a whole composed of mind and body, and that the whole was what is called soul.

Regarding belief in the propagation of souls, Milton belonged to traducianism propounded by Tertulian (c.155-c. 222), according to which "souls are passed along the process of human generation, souls being produced from souls as bodies are produced from bodies" (Reese, 583). Milton believed in such a theory of soul-generation because he wanted to spare God of the 'servile task' of eternally generating souls, like in the philosophy of Leibnitz. He said that God created man as a free being, a being having free will; but then God sometimes interferes into the affairs of human beings when he finds that his greater plan of the whole creation is being set at naught by man, or is being tempered by man's evil actions. But God does not interfere into the actions of human beings in such a manner so that man's free will is curtailed. In *Paradise Lost*, being pursuant of their free will, Adam and Eve fell from Paradise, and in *Paradise Regained* God reclaimed them by sending instructions to them through the agency of Christ, which instructions the primordial pair could, at the instance of their free will, reject. Such is, according to Milton, the way of God's communications with human beings.

Man has a very important property: his rationality. In Miltonic philosophy, the terms 'rationality' or 'reason', and 'conscience', are interchangeable, and identical in meaning. Milton also called reason 'nature'. To him, reason or nature is supreme, in the sense that even God has not the power to set aside or nullify it. In *Tetracordon*, Milton says that " 'no ordinance, human or from heaven, can bind against the good of man' " (Tillyard, 1956, 215). Here, by 'good of man' he means man's right reason or nature. Some may discern in this statement of Milton his implicit apostasy but there is nothing apostatic here, because Milton believed that man's nature originated in God. In his *De Doctrina Christiana*, he writes: "'God's ordinary providence is that whereby he upholds and preserves the immutable order of causes appointed by him in the beginning. This is commonly, and indeed too frequently, described by the name of nature; for nature cannot possibly mean anything but the mysterious power and efficacy of the divine voice which went forth in the beginning, and to which, as to a perpetual command, all things have since paid obedience' " (italics mine) (Tillyard, 1956, 215-216). God himself is the source of reason (rationality, right thinking or conscience), and even he is, let alone man, subject to it. Therefore, there is no scope of taking Milton for a heretic: even the judge himself cannot violate his own verdict, he said.

This nature or reason exists in two modes or in two loci: in the Scriptures and in the mind of man. Milton writes: " 'The Law of God is either written or unwritten. The unwritten law is no other than that law of nature given originally to Adam, and of which a certain remnant or imperfect illumination still dwells in the heart of mankind; which in the regenerate under the influence of the Holy Spirit is daily tending towards a renewal of its primitive brightness' " (Tillyard, 1956, 216). It was because he had so great a regard for reason that Milton could not bear with the superstitious rites of the Catholic church, and could not tolerate the dictatorial injunctions of the church authority. Milton believed in an immutable causal chain or causality obtaining eternally in the whole world, the causality to which even God is subject. In this sense he may be deemed to be a precursor of the Leibnitzian philosophy of pre-established harmony in the creation. Besides, Milton admitted another kind of being in his scheme of creation, in the world; he spoke of Spirit or Holy Spirit "written in the hearts of believers, according to the promise of God" (Tillyard, 1956, 216).

When we speak of Milton's philosophy, the term 'philosophy' should not be taken in the academic connotation of the word, because his philosophy was not arrived at through any logical process, but it was rather the result of intuition. Again, Milton's philosophy cannot be separated from his theological belief system, as he was a profoundly religious soul, and so, naturally, his philosophical convictions were coloured by his religious beliefs. We have seen that Milton had absolute faith in the authority of the Bible; and so his religious convictions were not at variance with the general Christian beliefs, save that in some cases — and these are very few — he applied his neutral rationality. Milton believed in the Trinity consisting of God, his Son or Christ, and the Holy Spirit.

Throughout the history of Christianity, the Trinity has been variously interpreted. In the 3rd century, Origen held that the Father (God), Son, and the Holy Spirit formed the Trinity, in which the Son and the Holy Spirit were in relative subordination to the Father. Plotinus and other neo-Platonists believed in the Trinity of the One (God), Nous and World Soul. Sabellius believed that the Father, the Son, and the Holy Spirit were essentially of the same Substance which is manifested as the Creator, the Redeemer, and the Giver of Life. In the 4th century A.D., there was waged a fierce and long-drawn battle of arguments on the question whether the Father and the Son were of the *same* Substance, or whether the Son was of a Substance which was *similar* to that of God — whether the Son was *homoousian* or *homoiousian*. Arius (256-336) believed the Son to be *homoiousian*, and Milton subscribed to this view. Milton believed that both the Son and the Holy Spirit were created by God, and so were subordinate to God. "... Milton concludes that the Son is of a different essence from the Father, and that he did not exist from the beginning. He is the agent of the unknowable God and quite definitely inferior to him. About the Holy Ghost or Holy Spirit Milton can say little. He is definitely inferior to Son" (Tillyard, 1956, 228).

About the creation of the world and its inhabitants, Milton almost faithfully followed the account given in 'Genesis' (of the Bible). But he is not steadfast, for, in *Paradise Lost*, for instance, Raphael does not tell of the act of creation by God, though in 'Genesis', there is a detailed description of the creation by God. In 'Genesis' we hear that the creation was completed by God within the space of six days. It may be noted here that, according to 'Genesis', on the first day God created the universe and Day and Night; on the second, the sky; on the third, the sea and the earth and all kinds of plants; on the fourth, the sun and the stars; on the fifth, all kinds of creatures that live in water and in the air; and on the sixth, God said " 'And now we will make human beings; they will be like us and resemble us' ", and so God created human beings, male and female. "And so the whole universe was completed. By the seventh day God finished what he had been doing and stopped working. He blessed the seventh day and set it apart as a special day, because by that day he had completed his creation and stopped working" (Genesis, 1 and 2). But in *Paradise Lost* Milton conceived of faster creation by God, than this. In the epic, Raphael says :

> Immediate are the Acts of God, more swift
> Than time or motiont but to human ears
> Cannot without process of speech be told,
> So told as earthly motion can receive.

True to his Protestant persuasion, Milton believed in predestination: everything and every event of the world were previously determined by God; and so God knows everything and every event of the world — past, present and future. Here Milton's belief may be compared with Leibnitz's notion of 'pre-established harmony'. But Milton differs from the German philosopher to some extent. While to Leibnitz there was no free will available for man, Milton believed that God left the fate of man to his own free will. This does not mean that God never interferes in the actions and affairs of human beings. If needs be, Milton says, God interferes in the affairs of human beings, to carry out his grand purpose behind his creation well. But God interferes "in such a way as in no wise to affect human responsibility" (Tillyard, 1356, 230). Man's will is not free in the ordinary senses: man cannot be free idiosyncratically. Milton says : "But God left free the Will; for what obeys/Reason is free". Man can achieve freedom of his will only by being rational. But man's rationality or reason may be corrupted by "fair appearing good". In *Paradise Lost* (Book IX, 352-356), Milton says :

> Reason he made right,
> But bid her well aware, and still erect
> Lest, by some fair appearing good surprised,
> She dictate false, and misinform the Will
> To do what God expressly hath forbid.

Evil is not possible for one who is guarded by his rationality, and he who does not himself will harm for him will never fall into evil: "Against his will he can receive no harm" (*Paradise Lost*, Book IX, 350). This is so because God made all things as good (*Paradise Lost*, Book IX, 343-346) :

> 'Best are all things as the will
> Of God ordained them; his creating hand
> Nothing imperfect or deficient left
> Of all that he created — much less Man,'

Alexander Pope in his *Essay on Man* said almost the same thing. And Leibnitz said that the present world is the best of all possible worlds.

Milton held that miracles are not fraudulent, illusory or unscientific, but that a miracle is the power to produce an effect within the laws of nature, though the process of the miracle is not known to us, the common men. He believed that the power of producing miracles belongs to God.

One very peculiar belief of Milton was that God sometimes even abetted evil deeds, in pursuance of the grand scheme of his works; but, his abetments of evils has, of necessity, some *raison d'etre*. Milton wrote: " 'God may instigate an evil agent, without being in the least degree the cause of evil... For example, — God saw that the mind of David was so elated and puffed up by the increase of his power, that even without any external impulse he was on the point of giving some remarkable token of his pride; he, therefore, excited in him the desire of numbering the people; he did not inspire him with the passion of vain glory, but impelled him to display in this manner rather than any other that latent arrogance of his heart which was ready to break forth' " (Tillyard, 1956, 230).

One very important category in Milton's theology is the concept of sin. Milton believed in two kinds of sins the original sin that the primordial father (Adam) and mother (Eve) committed in heaven by disobeying the command of God not to taste the fruit of the Tree of Knowledge; and the private or personal sin that a man may commit in this world by disobeying God in any other way. But, in spite of the existence of sin in this world, Milton is never pessimistic; he is rather always optimistic, because Christianity is a religion of hope. And so he said that man would not be eternally condemned, howmuchever may be his sins, because he believed that everybody would ultimately receive the compunctious treatment of God, and thereby everyone would get salvation. God sent Jesus Christ to promulgate his divine truth, or his divine will, which is the same thing, and to show men the path that would lead him towards Godhead. When man will give ear to the teachings of Christ and will follow the path shown by God through the agency of Christ, he will be salvaged, *i.e.* after his death he will be regenerated and restored or brought back to the fold of God. But what will be the state of the regenerated and restored man? Milton answers: " 'The restoration of man is the act whereby man, being delivered from sin and death by God the Father through Jesus Christ, is raised to a far more excellent state of grace and glory than that from which he had fallen" ' (Tillyard, 1956, 232).

In respect of religious rites, Milton was unorthodox and liberal, though he had an absolute faith in God and in the Scriptures. He believed that many of the rites of the church were superfluous, and that the church had no special right ordained by God to perform some religious rites, but that every faithful Christian could perform them. In this regard, Milton was like the Quakers or the members of the Society of Friends (Christian). The Quakers belonged to a Protestant sect that was founded by George Fox. The Quakers did not lay so much importance on the teachings and rites of the church as on moral perfection. They regarded the Holy Scriptures as the only indisputable sources of faith and moral perfection. But there were also differences between Milton and the Quakers. For instance, whereas the Quakers believed that marriage vow was invioable, Milton, in his pamphlets, had been fiercely fighting for the right of divorce. It may be noted here that Milton was not always rational. He, for instance, believed, as is evident in *Paradise Lost*, that the world is suspended from heaven with a golden chain, and this he believed in the age of Galilio whom he met in Italy and with whom he parleyed. On the other hand, it is true that the church was sometimes extremely orthodox, when Milton was not.

In matters moral, Milton was very strict: he almost equated morality with religiosity. He said that man must be dutiful, and that to be dutiful was an act commended and commanded by God. Religion without virtue is null. It was for his laying so much importance on virtue or morality that P.B. Shelley called Milton 'sacred Milton'. Milton also respected individualism, as he did the authority of reason. This respect for individualism he showed in his literary works as well as in his own activities in society and polity. He protested against kingship because he believed that it derived its tyrannical authority only from brute force, and never from reason. And so he was a republican and a strong supporter of self-government, as against his contemporary poet John Dryden. He believed in, and practised, only the right, and to him a thing was right only when it was rational. Even in the matter of belief he was rational: he was never a bigot. This may seem strange, but this is true. It is not true that he was not aware of some criticisms about Christianity and about some potent arguments of the heretics against Christianity. Rather one may say that he was profoundly interested in the counter-arguments of Christianity. Who can otherwise believe that he had in his private possession a copy of Bodin's *Heptaplomeres* — " 'the most extensive account of those 'atheistic' ideas which circulated widely by secret and underground channels in the Renaissance society, and which, when discovered, put their adherents in danger of a burning death for heresy' " (Tillyard, 1956, 217-218).

Milton's theology is mostly and principally Augustinian. St. Augustine brought Christianity into England in 597, and since then upto the end of the medieval period his philosophy, along with Christianity, predominated men's consciousness in that country. In his *Confessions* (especially Book XI) and *The City of God*, he has expounded his philosophy. He believed that God created everything out of nothing. This is a philosophy quite different from those of Plato and Aristotle, both of whom believed that God created things out of pre-existing matter. Plato is, to some extent, mystical regarding the creation, but Aristotle is clear that God created things by impressing different forms on the pre-existing and homogenous primal matter. But Augustine, as we told before, believed that God created the world out of mere nothingness, and Milton accepted his teaching. Milton also accepted Augustine's notion of the fall of Adam and Eve, in his *Paradise Lost*. Augustine believed, as Bertrand Russell says, that "Adam and Eve, before their fall, could have had sexual intercourse without lust, though in fact they did not. Handcraftsmen, in the pursuit of their trade, move their hands without lust; similarly Adam, if only he had kept away from the apple-tree, could have performed the business of sex without the emotions that it now demands. The sexual members, like the rest of body, would have obeyed the will" (Russell, 357). Russell further writes that in his *Confessions* "St. Augustine taught that Adam, before the fall, had free will, and could have abstained from sin. But as he and Eve ate the apple, corruption entered into them, and descended to all their posterity, none of whom can, of their own power, abstain from sin. Only God's grace enables men to be virtuous. Since we all inherit Adam's sin, we all deserve eternal damnation. All who die unbaptized, even infants, will go to hell and suffer unending torment. We have no reason to complain of this, since we are all wicked.... But by God's free grace certain people, among those who have been baptized, are chosen to go to heaven; these are the elect.... No reason can be given why some are saved and the rest damned; this is due to God's unmotivated choice. Damnation proves God's justice; salvation His mercy. Both equally display His goodness" (Russell, 362). This philosophy and theology of Augustine can be found in *Paradise Lost* and *Paradise Regained*, on closer scrutiny.

Milton is said to have a Turkish contempt for women-folk. He is believed to have said that the word 'woman' derives from two syllables :

'wo', meaning 'woe', and 'man'. He is further believed to have the belief that all sorrows of man are due to woman. And, yet further, it is believed that in his estimation, woman was inferior to man. But, perhaps, this is to misconstrue his words. He had, no doubt, quite different ideals for man and woman, but he never thought the one superior to the other; rather, he thought that the two are complementary to each other — none is complete in himself or herself; and only when the two are dovetailed, both of them becomes complete, becomes fulfilled. In *Paradise Lost* (Book IV, 297-299), Milton says about the ideal man and the ideal woman :

> For contemplation he, and valour formed;
> For softness she, and sweet attractive grace;
> He for God only, she for God in him.

Milton further says about woman : "nothing lovelier found/In woman than to study household good,/And good works in her husband to promote" (*Paradise Lost*, Book IX, 232-234). But this also should not be construed as a retrogressive ideal of connubial relationship, upheld by Milton. Before we pronounce any verdict on Milton, we should take into account his age and his society. If we tend to be modernist, we should not forget that in England women got their franchise only in 1933.

However, Milton's God-fearing ideal of human life is beautifully delineated in *Paradise Lost* (Book XII, 561-571) :

> Henceforth I learn that to obey is best,
> And love with fear the only God, to walk
> As in his presence, ever to observe
> His providence, and on him sole depend.
> ....
> ......that suffering for truth's sake
> Is fortitude to highest victory,
> And to the faithful death the gate of life —

The supreme aim of life, according to Milton, should be serving God, depending on him, and obeying all his commands. If there be any suffering in the service towards God, yet none should flinch and flee from that service. Every one should have patience and fortitude while serving God. Though Milton lived the life of the intellectual, and though he thirsted for endless knowledge, yet he, in the inner regard of his heart, wished for a pastoral life and the simplicity of the rural folk, which were his ideals of life in this world: "to live/The easiest way, nor with perplexing thoughts/To interrupt the sweet of life" (*Paradise Lost*, Book VIII, 182-184). Anything in addition to this is meaningless: "what is more, is fume" (*Paradise Lost*, Book VIII, 194). For Milton, knowledge is not essential for a good life; rather he might say with Lord Byron: "Sorrow is knowledge, they who know the most,/Must mourn the deepest over the fatal truth:/The tree of knowledge is not that of life." Perhaps there was in Milton what the psychologists call enantiodromia : he did want knowledge, and yet he denied the necessity of it.

4

EARLY OR MINOR POETIC WORKS OF MILTON

1
(THE BEGINNINGS)

We shall, for convenience, call all the poems written by Milton during the period from 1624, when he was about 15, to 1634, or rather all the poems that he wrote before *Comus*, his early or minor poems. We may wonder whether Milton wrote any other valuable poem or poems during the period other than those that have come down to us, but E.M.W. Tillyard believes that "that Milton destroyed any valuable early poems seems extremely unlikely" (Tillyard, 1956, 18). The earliest verses of Milton are his paraphrasing verses of two Latin psalms : Psalms CXIV and CXXXVI of the Old Testament. When he paraphrased the two psalms, he was only about 15 and had been at St. Paul's. Milton's verse paraphrasing of Psalm CXIV along with the English version of the same Psalm, as in *Good News Bible*, published by the Bible Society of India (1983) may be quoted in full for getting an idea about the young Milton's skill in versification :

Psalm CXIV Paraphrased by Milton

When the blest seed of Terah's faithful son,
After long toil their liberty had won,
And passed from Pharian fields to Canaan land,
Led by the strength of the Almighty's hand,
Jehovah's wonders were in Israel shown,
His praise and glory was in Israel known.
That the troubled sea, and shivering fled,
And sought to hide his froth-becurled head
Low in the earth; Jordan's clear streams recoil,
As a faint host that hath received the foil.

The high, huge-bellied mountains skip like rams
Amongst their ewes, the little hill lambs.
Why fled the ocean? And why skipped the mountains ?
Why turned Jordan toward his crystal fountains?
Shake earth, and at the presence be aghast
Of Him that ever was, and any shall last,
That glassy floods from rugged rocks can crush,
And make soft rills from fiery flint-stones gush.

Psalm CXIV in the Old Testament

When the people of Israel left Egypt,
  when Jacob's descendants left that foreign land,
Judah became the Lord's holy people,
  Israel became his own possession.

The Red Sea looked and ran away;
  the River Jordan stopped flowing.
The mountains skipped like goats;
  the hills jumped about like lambs.

What happened, Sea, to make you run away?
And you, O Jordan, why did you stop flowing?
You mountains, why did you skip like goats?
You hills, why did you jump about like lambs?

Tremble, earth, at the Lord's coming,
  at the presence of the God of Jacob,
who changes rocks into pools of water
  and solid cliffs into flowing springs.

Milton's religiosity and his fascination for mythology and archaic allusions are evident in his paraphrasing of these two psalms. His propensity towards high style in poetry is also evident in the paraphrasing of these two psalms. The originals of the psalms are not rhymed, but in his paraphrasing Milton preferred rhymed verses. In Psalm CXXXVI, in original, each unrhymed line is regularly followed by a refrain, as in the first stanza of the Psalm :

Give thanks to the Lord, because he is good;
  his love is eternal.
Give thanks to the greatest of all gods;
  his love is eternal.
Give thanks to the mightiest of all lords;
  his love is eternal.

In Milton's paraphrasing of this Psalm, the verses are rhymed, and all the stanzas contain two verses each followed regularly by the two-line refrain "For His mercies aye endure,/Ever faithful, ever sure." Thus, in paraphrasing this psalm, Milton has taken more liberty than he has taken in paraphrasing psalm CXIV.

The year 1626, when Milton was about eighteen years old, was poetically very productive for him, because in this single year he wrote eleven Latin poems and one English poem. It may be mentioned here that in his early life Milton wrote a considerable number of Latin poems. In fact, he wrote more Latin poems than English, in this period. It was from the date of composition of his poem 'Nativity Ode' that Milton inclined towards English poems, though his Latin poems were as excellent as his English poems. In 1626 itself, Milton produced five elegies, only one of which was in English — 'On the Death of a Fair Infant Dying of a Cough'. This English ode was written on the death of Anne, sister to Edward Phillips who was a nephew of Milton. The poem consists of eleven stanzas, which may be divided into three groups: stanzas I-IV may be called 'separation'; V-IX 'transition'; and X - XII 'incorporation'. In 'separation', the poet expresses his sorrow for being separated from Anne on her death; in 'transition', he says that he cannot believe that Anne is really dead; and in 'incorporation' he thinks that Anne must be immortal and must be in heaven as a mediator, and so he asks her mother not to sorrow any more. This poem is Milton's first elegy in English, as told earlier. The four other elegies that he wrote in Latin in 1626 are: *Eligia Prima* that he wrote on the 'water' death of his Italian friend and class-mate Diodati; *Eligia Secunda* that was composed on the death of Esquire Bedell; *Eligia Tertia* which was composed on the death of the Bishop of Winchester; and *In Obitum Praesulis Eliensis*. In the same year, Milton also wrote two other Latin poems: *In Obitum Procancellarii Medici*, and *In Quintum Novembris* that was written on the event of the Gunpowder Plot.

Eligia Prima is not a very good poem. It is 'immature and redundant', and yet it has two points of importance: it shows the poet's quiet and happy life in London, and it shows the poet's transitory attraction to female beauty. The poem is a document of his first waking to love for the opposite sex, at a time when he was 17, *i.e.*, a time when such love is very natural. We are quoting below a few lines from Cowper's translation of *Eligia Prima* (Tillyard, 1956, 22) :

> Here many a virgin troop I may descry
> Like stars of mildest influence, gliding by.

Oh forms divine! Oh looks that might inspire
Even Jove himself, grown old, with young desire!
Oft have I gazed on gem-surpassing eyes,
Outsparkling every star that gilds the skies,
Necks whiter than the ivory arm bestowed
By Jove on Pelops, or the Milky road.
Bright locks, Love's golden snare ! These falling low,
Those playing wanton on the graceful brow!
Cheeks too, more winning sweet than after shower
Adonis turned to Flora's favourite flower.

However, the verses of the other elegies, particularly those of *In Obitum Procancellarii*, writes E.M.W. Tillyard, are as good as those of 'Nativity Ode'. Let us quote, as a specimen, three stanzas from *In Obitum Procancellarii*, below (Tillyard, 1956, 21) :

But resentful Proserpine,
Jealous of thy skill divine,
Snapping short thy vital thread
Thee too numbered with the dead.

Wise and good! untroubled be
The green turf that covers thee!
Thence, in gay profusion, grow
All the sweetest flowers that below!

Pluto's consent bid thee rest!
Aecus pronounce thee blest,
To her home thy shade consign,
Make Elysium ever thine!

All these elegies, though they are not free from diverse faults, foretell about the great poetry of Milton's mature years. We have said that early in his life, when he was just a boy, Milton took the vocation of a poet as his life's vocation. He was even confident at that time of becoming a great poet in future. Therefore, in these elegies and in his other short poems Milton had been doing exercises in the art of poetry. However, regarding the poetic beauty of these five elegies, E.M.W. Tillyard writes: "They are all of them exercises, and yet, as Longinus would say, the exercises of Milton. There is in them a sense of deliberate apprenticeship, of which Milton was clearly not in the least ashamed and of which,..., there are signs even of *Comus*. Only he varies his models, choosing the Elizabethans for the English poem, Ovid and Horace for the Latin. But all alike contain common Miltonic qualities:

an unusual assurance of tone, which might easily verge on arrogance, the beginnings generally rather blurred, of serene grandeur and of grave sweetness, and a very rigorous sense of form" (Tillyard, 1956, 19). Though most of the elegies of this period were composed on occasions of deaths, we should, perhaps, not believe that Milton was much moved by these deaths, at least more than normal. He only found occasions for writing poems in these deaths. Of the elegies Milton wrote upto November 1626, *In Obitum Novembris* is undoubtedly the best — the one that he wrote last. This may prove that Milton's poetic exercises paid him. *In Obitum Novembris* is a sort of short epic that contains two hundred odd verses. As in his English poems Milton was influenced by Spenser and by the Elizabethan poetry, so in his Latin poems he was influenced by Horace.

We have seen that even at the young age of 17, Milton dedicated his life to the vocation of a poet, and it is for this reason that we find very few instances of his amorous affairs and sensuous consciousness commensurate with his young age. Nonetheless, prompted by nature, he has left for us at least two poems where we may find his youthful attractions for female beauty: in *Eligia Prima*, that he wrote on the death of his Italian friend Diodati, and in *Eligia Septima*. We have already seen, in the few lines of *Eligia Prima* translated by Cowper and quoted above, how in his youth Milton was moved by the 'forms divine' of the female sex. The other evidence of his amorous awareness is *Eligia Septima* which he composed in May 1628, when he was 19. It is to be noted here that Milton has perhaps one and only one obviously recogniseable love poem, and that is *Eligia Septima*. In it he says that he often 'sneered at Cupid's childish weapons', but one day in May when all everywhere were flushed with the colours of spring, the 'industrious Love' stood near the poet's bed and shot his arrows at him. The god of love warned the defiant poet (in paraphrasing: lines 41-44):

> 'If Jupiter chose to turn his thunder against me,
> my barbs would stick in the sides of Jove himself.
> If doubts remain, my darts will teach better than words;
> and your heart, the target I have to hit, and hard.'

The poet soon yielded to the bidding of the god of love, and was feeling the passion of love aroused by the arrows of that god (lines 47-56) :

> 'He ended, and waving an arrow with gilded tip
> he wafted away to the warm breast of Venus.

But the sight of him fiercely thundering threats
seemed laughable
then, and I felt not the slightest fear of the boy.
And sometimes I stroll in the city where townsfolk parade,
and sometimes delight in the grounds of noble estates.
And a mighty throng with faces as lovely as goddess'
comes and goes in splendour along the paths.
And the day dazzles, its brilliance doubled by theirs —
perhaps the rays of Apollo come from here?'

And then the austere poet changes into an amorous youth and wallows in the sensuousness of love (lines 57-74) :

'I'm not so strict that I'd shun so pleasant a show,
I'm driven wherever youthful passion take me.
And reckless my gaze met theirs, my brightness their brightness,
I was quite unable to hold my eyes in check.
Then one I happened to notice, excelling the rest,
her radiance then the root of ills to come.
Venus would want to look thus, appearing to mortals;
she drew the eyes of all, like the queen of the gods.
Patient malevolent Cupid had thrust her before me,
alone he wove the snares, prepared in advance.
And the prankster was hiding nearby, with hundreds of arrows,
his torch drooping behind him, a heavy weight.

No lingering; he clings to the eyelids and mouth of the girl,
then darts between her lips, then camps on her cheek.
And wherever the agile archer roams on her person,
he wounds my helpless breast with thousands of darts.
Immediately strange emotions invaded my heart,
I burn within with love, turned wholly to flame.'

The poet enjoys the boon of love (consummate ?), and then thinks that the god of love is the highest god, and that there is no pleasure comparable with that derived from mutual love, and he vows to give offerings to the god of love. The poet tells himself (lines 97-102) :

'And I'll make your holy alters smoke with my offerings,
and call you the only chief of the gods above.
But finally take my — no, leave me my madness, I mean:
somehow, pain feels sweet to all who love.
But still, be mild with your gifts: if I love again,
let the love be mutual, one arrow piercing us both.'

But Milton, the anchorite, soon washed his hands off his own amorousness, and became repentant for his ephemeral, passing sensuousness — sensuousness that he equated with sin. In *Epilogue to the Elegies* his remorse is uncontrolable :

'In the past, with part of my mind, and perverse energy
I composed these idle trophies to celebrate vice.
I was fallen from grace, and driven by error and sin,
my corrupt master was youth, which refused to be taught:
Till Plato's shady academy offered me Socrates'
streams, and I learn to unlearn what enslaved me before.
At once my flames were extinguished, and still they are dead:
and my breast is frozen, bound with layers of ice.
So Cupid himself is afraid for the cold on his arrows,
and Venus fears my strength, Diomedes returned.'

Interestingly, even before *Eligia Septima*, Milton showed his indifference to love and amorousness, as we find in 'Epilogue to the Elegies' in his *Eligia Sexta*.

In 1628, Milton was chosen to deliver the 'Vacation Exercise', as usual at Cambridge every year. It was a great honour for him, and he rose to the occasion. His 'Vacation Exercise' consisted of his *Sixth Proclusioin*, which was in Latin prose, and a poem, 'At a Vacation Exercise', which concluded his Latin speech (*Sixth Proclusion*) — the poem being in English, and not in Latin. In this poem of 58 lines, he bade good-bye to Latin as his medium of poetry; and, save *Eligia Sexta*, he did no more write in Latin. At the beginning of 'At a Vacation Exercise' Milton expresses his debt to his mother tongue, English, and proclaims that, henceforth, he will not write in Latin, but only in English (lines 1-0) :

Hail native language, that by sinews weak
Didst move my first endeavouring tongue to speak,
And mad'st imperfect words with childish trips,
Half unpronounced, slide through my infant lips,
Driving dumb silence from the portal door,
Where he had mutely sat two years before:
Here I salute thee and thy pardon ask,
That now I use thee in my latter task:

In the poem, Milton shows his confidence that he will be able to produce good, rather excellent, verses in English: "as I did forecast,/ The daintiest dishes shall be served up last" ('At a Vacation Exercise', lines 13-14). His high ambition to become a great poet is also manifest in this poem (lines 19-24) :

Not these new-fangled toys, and trimming slight
Which takes our late fantastics with delight,
But cull those richest robes, and gayest attire
Which deepest spirits, and choicest wits desires
I have some naked thoughts that rove about
And loudly knock to have their passage out;

Milton's fascination for mythological characters and place-names is apparent even in his early poems. For instance, in his *Eligia Quinta* ('On Coming of Spring'), a poem of just 140 lines, there are some twentytwo mythological characters and place-names: Castalia, Parnassus, Pirenian spring, Apollo, Daphne, Olympus, Hymettus, Paphos, Idaean Ops, Tethys, Semele, Phaeton, Cupid, etc. Further, on a closer study, one will be able to discern the mature Miltonic 'organic voice' in his early poems, in embryonic form. For instance, in 'At a Vacation Exercise', we may find sonorous rhythm and sublimity of attitude as well as a baritone voice. E.M.W. Tillyard writes about this poem: "This poem has a double interest: it contains the earliest passage of Miltonic verse in which the rhythm is sustained with peculiar Miltonic sublimity; and it shows Milton critically aware of contemporary English poetry." (Tillyard, 1956, 30). Milton's early poems show Ovid's influence on him, and his last poem, written under Ovid's spell, is his Latin poem *Eligia Quinta*, composed in 1629 and before 'Nativity Ode'.

2
('NATIVITY ODE' AND 'THE PASSION')

Milton wrote 'Nativity Ode' or 'On the Morning of Christ's Nativity' on December 25, 1629. Though at that time he had been gradually moving away from the Italian influence, 'Nativity Ode' shows the lingering Italian influence on him, and, in fact, 'Nativity Ode' was composed in the Italian manner. The poem consists of 27 stanzas, each stanza having eight lines of varying lengths. The poem is divided into two parts: the first part comprises the first four stanzas, and the second part the rest twentythree stanzas. Stanza I speaks of the birth of Christ and his mission of rescuing mankind from the original sin ('deadly forfeit'), and of his (Christ's) works for our eternal peace:

This is the month, and this the happy morn,
Wherein the Son of Heaven's eternal king,

Of wedded Maid and Virgin Mother born,
Our great redemption from above did bring;
For so the holy sages once did sing,
That He our deadly forfeit should release,
And with His Father work us a perpetual peace.

In the next three stanzas of Part I, the poet describes the heavenly beauty of the child-Christ, and informs us of Christ's mission of sacrificing his celestial abode for the benefit of mankind. Christ, Milton says, "Forsook the courts of everlasting day,/And chose with us a darksome house of mortal clay." The poet asks the 'Heavenly Muse' (cf. *Paradise Lost*: 'Invocation') if Christ, the 'Infant God' should not be welcomed. He asks the Muse to join the choir ('Quire') of angels who are singing in praise of the 'Infant God'.

After this follows the Hymn or the second part of the poem. Here the poet says that the 'Heavenly born Child' was born very meanly, being born in a manger in a wintry weather :

It was the winter wild,
While the Heaven-born Child
All meanly wrapped in the rude manger lies;

Nature, the corrupted Nature, became frightened at the coming down of Christ to earth : "Confounded, that her Maker's eyes/Should look so near upon her foul deformities." On the alightment of Christ on earth, peace settled down in the world, and ceaseless wars ceased, and then Christ's reign began: "His reign of peace upon the earth began". Not only Nature, but even the stars and the sun felt diminished before the baby Christ. The sun thought that the brightest light had now come down to earth, and so its inferior light was no more needed now: "As his inferior flame/The new-enlightened world no more should need". The simple-minded shepherds could not recognise the 'Infant God'; they thought that the love-god Pan, and not the heavenly Christ, had come down to earth, to give them company. When the 'Infant God' came down to earth, there was so sweet music all around — perhaps the 'music of the spheres' — and such harmony prevailed everywhere that Cynthia (or Diana), the goddess of light, mountains and wood, thought that she was no more needed on earth, because more sweet music and more harmony were being bestowed on earth by this 'Infant God': "She knew such harmony alone/Could hold Heaven and Earth in happier union." Then came down 'helmed' cherubims and 'sworded' seraphims, spreading their wings, and began 'solemn quire' (solemn coir). The poet then calls upon the stars of the sky ('crystal spheres') to join the 'angelic symphony' down on earth at the advent of the 'Infant God'. In earlier times, people believed that the motion of the heavenly bodies (stars, planets, etc.) produced a harmony of eight melodies. By the 'angelic symphony', perhaps, Milton means this heavenly music. Shakespeare also spoke of such a music in *The Merchant of Venice* (V, i, 58-61) :

Look how the floor of heaven
Is thick inlaid with patines of bright gold;
There's not the smallest orb which thou behold'st
But in his motion like an angel sings,

The poet thinks that if such a symphony continues, the world will roll backward in time, and the ancient golden age will reappear: "For if such holy song/Enwrap our fancy long,/Time will run back and fetch the age of gold"; and "Hell itself will pass away". And then Truth, Justice and Mercy will prevail on earth.

But the poet knows that all these are not to occur, because Fate has something else in her plan, before all these may happen to be. Fate has ordained that this 'Infant God' must die on the cross, and thus he will glorify both himself and the human kind. And even before that the people who are in deep sleep of ignorance must first be pronounced doomed. In stanza XVI, the poet writes:

But wisest Fate says No,
This must not yet be so,
The Babe lies yet in smiling infancy,
That on the bitter cross
Must redeem our loss,
So both Himself and us to glorify:
Yet first to those chained in sleep,
The wakeful trump of doom must thunder through the deep,

The poet then speaks of the Doom's Day or the Day of Judgment when the "dreadful Judge in middle air shall spread His throne." And then "at last our bliss/Full and perfect is". On this happy and wished for day, the tyrannies of the world will begin to cease. The horrible Dragon, for instance, will ensconce itself under the ground :

But now begins; for from this happy day
Th' old Dragon under-ground
In straiter limits bound,
Not half so far casts his usurped sway,

And, wroth to see his kingdom fail,
Swings the scaly horror of his folded tail.

Stanzas 19 and 20 refer to the myth that "at the time of the Passion (the time is here changed to the Nativity) the Pilot of a ship sailing from Italy to Cyprus was bidden by a supernatural voice to proclaim, when he came to a certain island, that Pan was dead. On arriving at the place named, the ship was suddenly becalmed, until he cried out that Pan was dead; 'wherewithal was heard such piteous outcries and dreadful shrieking, as hath not been the like' " (Hughes, 200). The poet says that on this happy day of the birth of Christ, sham and deception have become futile: "The oracles are dumb,/No voice or hideous hum/Runs through the arched roof in words deceiving." That is, all black magic and superstitious beliefs are now gone, at the advent of Christ. Thus, the earth has now become 'consecrated'. Further, superstitious phenomena, belonging to paganism, have departed — superstitious phenomena such as Lars, the gods of households, Lemures or the spirits of the dead, etc. Therefore, people now will no more believe in the existence of these things. Again, with the departures of all these pagan gods, the flamens or the priests of them have also left their shrines :

In consecrated earth,
And on the holy hearth,
    The Lars and Lamures moan with midnight plaint;
In urns and alters round,
A drear and dying sound
    Affraights the Flamens at their service quaint;
And the chill marble seems to sweat,
While each particular power forgoes his wonted seat.

Other pagan gods, such as Peor, Baalim, Ashtroth, Hammon and Thammuz, have also left their respective shrines. With them have also fled Moloch, Isis, Orus and Anubis. Osiris is now no more seen in the Egyptian (Memphian) grove. In their place, the 'Infant God' is now showing his divine power, by controlling the damned troop of all these pagan gods: "Our Babe, to show His Godhead true,/Can in His swaddling bands control the damned crew."

The poet now sees that evening is coming, because the sun is going to sleep over the billows of the oriental ocean and within the red curtain of the western cloud; and that at that moment all the heathen gods are proceeding to the 'infernal jail'. And the ghosts are going to graves; and the fairies (fays) are running away, abandoning their sports in moonlight, for fear of the 'Infant God' And now, at this wonderful moment, the blessed Virgin Mary, mother of Christ, is lulling her son, the 'Infant God', to sleep. Therefore, the poet says that he should not sing any more (lest the Babe feels disturbed). He only says that the recently risen moon ("youngest teemed star") has, as if, stopped moving, and a maid is watching the moon, sitting beside the Baby Lord. And all the while beautifully dressed angels are waiting in the stable (where Christ is born and where he is lying) for any expected order from the sleeping 'Infant God':

> But see, the Virgin blest
> Hath laid her Babe to rest:
> Time is our tedious song should here have ending,
> Heaven's youngest teemed star,
> Hath fixed her polished car,
> Her sleeping Lord with handmaid lamp attending:
> And all about the courtly stable,
> Bright-harnessed angels sit in order serviceable.

Commenting on 'Nativity Ode', E.M.W. Tillyard writes: "The combination of qualities found in the *Ode* implies a state of mind in the author both desirable and rare. Milton's mind as revealed in his other poems was deep rather than varied, powerful rather than swift. But when he wrote the *Nativity Ode* he seemed to write with a pulse beating quicker, with a mind more alert, more varied, more susceptible to fancy as well as to imagination, less censorious, tender, less egoistical, than when he wrote any other poem before or since. There is much in the *Ode* that looks forward, the grandeur of language, the delight of names, the introduction of heathen gods, an apparent theological rigidity, the metrical virtuosity — all these and more have been remarked — but there is also much that Milton never repeated. We cannot help wondering what inspired him to write this poem, not his greatest but his least resembling his other compositions" (Tillyard, 1956, 38). But we do not wonder so much what prompted Milton to write this poem, because we know that religious impulse was, as if, innate in him, and the Christmastide, in which the poem was composed, was only a natural stimulation to him. But we wonder how, without much exercises, Milton could write such a beautiful poem.

'Nativity Ode' was a high success, but, unfortunately, it was followed by a great failure, by its companion poem, 'The Passion'. From the very beginning, Milton was very ambitious, and at the young age of around 21 he thought of writing an epic in future, and 'The Passion' was his first attempt in writing an epic. But after writing only 56 lines on a great epical theme, he could discern his own immaturity, and so abandoned the project, never to take it up again. 'The Passion' was written in 1630; in all probability in the season of the Lent. Apropos of the mood of the Lent, the theme of the poem is melancholic. So far as it is written, the poem contains eight stanzas, each stanza containing seven lines rhyming a b a b b c c. The poem begins with a deeply melancholic strain. Milton says that earlier there was mirth and profusion of joy at the birth of Christ, but now these are all gone :

> Ere-while of music and ethereal mirth,
> Wherewith the stage of air and earth did ring,
> And joyous news of Heavenly Infant's birth,
> My muse with angels did divide to sing;
> But headlong joy is ever on the wing,
>   In wintry solstice like the shortened light,
> Soon swallowed up in dark and long out-living night.

Consequently, dark melancholy settles over the poet's mind; and he welcomes it. He sadly tells that the Son of God had, pathetically, to undergo inhumane travails :

> For now to sorrow must I tune my song,
> And set my harp to notes of saddest woe,
> Which on our dearest Lord did seize ere long,
> Dangers and sneers, and wrongs, and worse than so,
> Which He for us did freely undergo;
>   Most perfect hero, tried in heaviest plight
> Of labours huge and hard, too hard for human wight.

In the third stanza, the poet says that Christ took his birth, and died, for the sake of the redemption of human beings; and in the fourth stanza, he simply tells us that these are the themes of his verses. In stanzas 5 and 6, he says when he cogitates over all these, he becomes melancholic. In stanza 7, the poet is confident that his present verses will be as potent and beautiful as his earlier ones: "My plaining verse as lively as before;/For sure so well instructed are my tears,/That they would fitly fall in ordered characters." But, alas! his verses could not really be as lively as before, and his present verses have had a precipitate fall in the last stanza :

> Or should I thence hurried on viewless wing,
> Take up a weeping on the mountains wild,
> The gentle neighbourhood of grove and spring

Would soon unbosom all their echoes mild,
And I (for grief is easily beguiled)
Might think th' infection of my sorrows loud
Had got a grace of mourners on some pregnant cloud.

Commenting on 'The Passion', E.M.W. Tillyard writes: "In *The Passion* Milton attempts to recapture, and in accordance with the tragic theme to deepen, the mood that prompted the *Nativity Ode*. The failure is complete. It is full of conceits as the earlier poem: but these call a dreadful attention to themselves; puerility has supplanted youthfulness. Milton seems to have forsaken the Italians and in his poverty of invention to have resorted to common stock of English seventeenth century extravagance" (Tillyard, 1956, 44).

Milton's other early poetic works after 'The Passion' are not dated. But, perhaps, the order of composition of some of these is somewhat like this: first a song, On May Morning'; then two sonnets, 'To the Nightingle' and 'On Shakespeare'; and lastly two great poems, 'L' Allegro' and 'Il Penseroso'. We shall briefly discuss only these poems, leaving out all other English and Italian poems. The song 'On May Morning' was composed probably for May Day, 1630. The song runs thus:

Now the bright morning-star, day's harbinger,
Comes dancing from the east, and leads with her
The flow'ry May, who from her greenlap throws
The yellow cowslip, and the pale primrose.
Hail bounteous May that dost inspire
Mirth and youth, and warm desire;
Woods and groves, and of thy dressing,
Hill and dale, doth boast thy blessing;
Thus we salute thee with our early song,
And welcome thee, and wish thee long.

The poem is simple and it is of no very superior quality. However, after realising that he was yet not well equipped for handling a great theme and writing a good long poem, while he was writing 'The Passion', Milton decided to do more exercises on poetic art with small themes. Consequently, he wrote some short poems, like this one, and some sonnets.

3
(THE SONNETS)

Though the Elizabethan fashion of sonneteering was not so much in vogue during (and after) the early life of Milton, the sonnet-form did not become obsolete by that time, and most of Milton's contemporary poets of that time tried their hands at sonneteering. Milton himself wrote a number of sonnets — around a score — both in Italian and in English. Some of his Italian sonnets are: 'Donna leggiadra', 'Qual in colle aspro', 'Diodati', etc. And some of his English sonnets are: 'How soon hath time', 'Lady that in the prime', 'A book was writ of late' (about his own pamphlet *Tetrachordon*), 'When faith and love', 'To the Lord General Cromwell', 'When I consider', 'To Mr. Cyriack Skinner upon his blindness', etc. Milton also wrote a few (Italian) canzoni, such as 'Ridonsi Donnee Giovani amorosi'. However, we shall briefly discuss below only a few sonnets of Milton — those which are more famous.

To the Nightingle

O Nightingle that on yon bloomy spray
Warblest at eve, when all the woods are still,
Thou with fresh hope the lover's heart dost fill,
While the jolly hours lead on propitious May,
Thy liquid notes that close thy eye of day,
  First heard before the shallow cuckoo's bill
  Portend success in love; O if Jove's will
  Have linked that amorous power to thy soft lay,
Now timely sing, ere the rude bird of hate
  Foretell my hopeless doom in some grove nigh :
  As thou from year to year hast sung too late
For my relief; yet hadst no reason why,
  Whether the Muse, or Love call thee his mate,
  Both them I serve, and of their train am I.

Milton wrote this sonnet in 1630 when he was 21. The sonnet form was imported into England from Italy in the 16th century, via Sir Thomas Wyatt and the Earl of Surrey. The particular form of sonnet that was imported into England was the Petrarchan form. In England different forms of sonnet, other than the Petrarchan, were tried by the sonneteers, and the form that was, ultimately, generally accepted was the English form or the Shakespearean form. During the first quarter of the 17th century, poets did not show much interest in the sonnet — poets neither of the Jacobean nor of the Caroline periods. It was Milton who revivified the sonnet from its doldrums. He did not write sonnet-sequences, as was the fashion during the Elizabethan period, but wrote occasional sonnets. He did not follow the English form or the Spenserian form (the form that Spenser invented) of the sonnet, but, perhaps, for his special admiration for anything Italian, he followed the Petrarchan form that varied from both the English and the Spenserian form, in rhyming pattern and in thought sequence. The rhyme-scheme of the English or the Shakespearean sonnet is: a b a b, c d c d, e f e f, g g; and that of the Spenserian sonnet is: a b a b, b c b c, c d c d, e e. But Milton deliberately followed the Petrarchan rhyme-scheme: a b b a a b b a, for the octave; and c d e c d e (as in 'To Cyriack Skinner') or c d c d c d (as in 'To Mr. Cyriack Skinner Upon his Blindness'), for the sestet. Milton did not divide the sonnet into stanzas, as for instance, Shakespeare did.

The rhyme-scheme of the above sonnet ('To the Nightingale') is Milton's favourite rhyme-scheme: a b b a a b b a c d c d c d. 'To the Nightingale' is a very beautiful sonnet with some lively images and an intense passion. Lines 6 and 7 refer to a belief "among lovers that it was a good omen to hear the nightingale earlier in the year than the cuckoo, and a bad omen to hear the cuckoo first" (Hughes, 201). At about the same time when the foregoing sonnet was composed, Milton wrote another sonnet 'On His Being Arrived to the Age of 23' (between 1631 and 1632).

How soon hath Time

How soon hath Time, the subtle thief of youth,
Stolen on his wing my three-and-twenty year!
My hasting days fly on with full career,
But my late spring no bud or blossom shew'th.
Perhaps my semblance might deceive the truth
That I to manhood am arrived so near;
And inward ripeness doth much less appear,
That some more timely-happy spirits indu'th.
Yet be it less or more, or soon or slow,
It shall be still in strictest measure even
To that same lot, however mean or high,
Toward which Time leads me, and the will of Heaven.
All is, if I have grace to use it so,
As ever in my great Task-Master's eye.

The first four lines of this sonnet may be compared with Shakespeare's Sonnets 64 and 65. But Milton does not so much bewail the destructiveness of Time as Shakespeare did. And yet Milton, like Shakespeare, calls Time a thief : "the subtle thief of youth,/Stolen on his wing my three-and-twenty year!" It may be noted here that the rhyming of the sestet or the last six lines of this sonnet does not follow any definite pattern or scheme.

On His Blindness

When I consider how my light is spent,
Ere half my days in this dark world and wide,
And that one talent which is death to hide
Lodged with me useless, though my soul more bent
To serve therewith my maker, and present
My true account, lest He returning chide;
'Doth God exact day-labour, light denied ?'
I fondly asks but patience, to prevent
That murmur, soon replies, 'God doth not need
Either man's work or his own gifts. Who best
Bear his mild yoke, they serve him best: his state
Is kingly: thousands are his bidding speed,
And post o'er land and ocean without rest;
They also serve who only stand and wait.'

As is evident from the sonnet, it was certainly not written by Milton in his early literary period: it was obviously written after he became blind. Though we do not know when exactly Milton became purblind, we know that his vision was fast getting blurred since 1652. And, in that case, the above sonnet must have been written after 1652. Yet we have quoted this sonnet only to show that as regards other poems, so also in regard to the above sonnet, we can say that Milton's poetic skill developed and matured with age. This last quoted sonnet is far superior to the other two foregoing sonnets. It is full of intense passion, free-flowing arguments, and sincerity of conviction. The conversational tone of the sonnet makes it more appealing. And all these qualities are not so much available in his earlier sonnets.

The datings of Milton's other sonnets are doubtful. However, some of his other important sonnets are: 'When the Assault was Intended to the City', 'To a Virtuous Young Lady', 'To the Lady Margaret Ley', 'On the Detraction which Followed upon My Writing Certain Treatises', another sonnet on the same theme — 'On the Same', 'To Mr. H. Lawes on His Airs', 'On the Religious Memory of Mrs. Catherine Thomsom', 'On the Late Massacre in Piedmont', 'On His Deceased Wife', 'To Mr. Lawrence', 'To Cyriack Skinner', 'On the New Forces of Conscience under the Long Parliament', 'On the Lord General Fairfax, at the Siege of Colchester', 'To the Lord General Cromwell, May 1652', 'To Sir Henry Vane the Youger', 'To Mr. Cyriack Skinner upon

His Blindness', etc. Some of these sonnets were written probably in his early poetic period, but most of them were written certainly in his later literary life. Before 1638, *i.e.* before the end of his early poetic period, besides these and other English sonnets, Milton wrote some Italian sonnets and canzoni, as we have said earlier. The English sonnets are beautiful in their ideas and in their diction. But Hazlitt liked the sonnets particularly for their sincerity, *i.e.* for the degree of the poet's own emotion and the proportional degree of emotion aroused by the appropriate words, without having any decoration, artificial emotions under-pinned, or *schwarmerei.*

4
(SOME OTHER EARLY POEMS)

In his early poetic period, *i.e.*, before he left England for Italy in 1638, Milton wrote many other poems which are not sonnets, some of which are of very high poetic quality, and we shall very briefly discuss below in this section only four out of them: 'On Shakespeare, 1630', 'On Time', 'Upon the Circumcision' and 'At a Solemn Music'. E.M.W. Tillyard writes about the dates of composition of some of these poems and also about the dates of composition of some other poems: "The dates of other poems to which I shall refer and which precede *Comus*, namely *Arcades*, *On Time*, *Upon Circumcision*, *At a Solemn Music, L'Allegro* and *Il Penseroso* are uncertain; some of them may have been written before Milton's twenty-third birthday: but they all belong to what I am calling Milton's early maturity" (Tillyard, 1956, 59).

On Shakespeare, 1630

What needs my Shakespeare for his honoured bones,
The labour of an age in piles of stones,
Or that his hallowed relics should be hid
Under a star-ypointing pyramid ?
Dear son of memory, great heir of fame,
What need'st thou such weak witness of thy name ?
Thou in our wonder and astonishment
Hast built thyself a live-long monument.
For whilst to th' shame of slow-endeavouring art,
Thy easy numbers flow, and that each heart
Hath from the leaves of thy unvalued book
Those Delphic lines with deep impression took;
Then thou, our fancy of itself bereaving,
Dost make us marble with too much conceiving;

And so repulchered in such dost lie,
That kings for such a tomb would wish to die.

In the second Folio-edition of Shakespeare (1632), this poem was printed with the title 'An Epitaph on the Admirable Dramaticke Poet, W. Shakespeare'. This is a beautiful poem in couplets. Commenting on this poem, E.M.W. Tillyard writes: "Milton's praise is indeed extremely reverential, far more so than the politeness a verse tribute absolutely demanded. To judge from his habit of generalising from the personal it is quite reasonable to think that he was modestly comparing Shakespeare's 'easie numbers' and 'Delphicke lines' with his own 'slow-endeavouring' art, his own 'late spring' which showed 'no bud or blossom'..... Displaying as it does an impassioned critical intelligence, this is the one poem of Milton that can be called metaphysical" (Tillyard, 1956, 50-51). Milton's use of the old English-style word 'star-ypointing', to make a foot, is to be noted here. The notions of 'son of memory' and 'Delphicke lines' are very interesting.

On Time

Fly envious Time, till thou run out thy race,
Call on the lazy, leaden-stepping hours,
Whose speed is but the heavy plummet's pace,
And glut thyself with what thy womb devours,
Which is no more than what is false and vain,
And merely mortal dross;
So little is our loss,
So little is thy gain.
For when as each thing bad thou hast entombed,
And last of all thy greedy self consumed,
Then long Eternity shall greet our bliss
With an individual kiss
And joy shall overtake us as a flood;
When every thing that is sincerely good
And perfectly divine,
With Truth, and Peace, and Love shall ever shine
About the supreme throne
Of Him, t'whose happy-making sight alone
When once our heavenly-guided soul shall climb,
Then, all this earthly grossness quit,
Attired with stars we shall for ever sit
Triumphing over Death, and Chance, and thee, O Time.

This poem of Milton may be read along with his two other poems, 'On His Being arrived to the Age of 23' and 'How Soon Hath Time', because in all the three poems Milton speaks of, among other things, the devastation due to Time, of which Shakespeare also spoke in his 'Time-Sonnets' (for instance his Sonnets 63 and 64). In 'On Time', Milton challenges the destructiveness of Time, because, he thinks, Time actually cannot take away from one, whose soul is guided by heaven, anything that is essentially worthy — Truth, Peace and Love — things that are eternal, and so beyond the clutch of Time. The poet says that Time can take away only 'mortal dross', and so he asks Time to take away only that 'mortal dross', because he is confident that "everything that is sincerely good/And perfectly divine,/With Truth, Peace, and Love shall ever shine". In his Sonnets 60 and 63, Shakespeare also says almost the same thing: he says that the beauty of his beloved Fair Youth will ever live in his verses. In Sonnet 60, Shakespeare says: "And yet, to times in hope my verse shall stand,/ Praising thy worth, despite his cruel hand"; and in Sonnet 63, he says : "His beauty shall in these black lines be seen,/And they shall live, and he in them still green."

Upon the Circumcision

Ye flaming powers and winged Warriors bright,
That erst with music and triumphant song,
First heard by happy watchful shepherds' ear,
So sweetly sung your joy the clouds along
Through the soft silence of the listening night;
Now mourn; and if sad share with us to bear
Your fiery essence can distill no tear,
Burn in your sighs, and borrow
Seas wept from our deep sorrow.
He who will all Heaven's heraldry whilere
Entered the world, now bleeds to give us ease;
Alas, how soon our sin
  Sore doth begin
  His fancy to seize!

O more exceeding love, or law more just?
Just law indeed, but more exceeding love!
For we by rightful doom remediless
Were lost in death, till He that dwelt above
High throned in secret bliss, for us, frail dust,

Emptied His glory, even to nakedness,
And that great cov'nant which we still transgress
Entirely satisfied,
And the full wrath beside
Of vengeful Justice bore for our excess,
And seals obedience first with wounding smart
This day; but O ere long
Huge pangs and strong
Will pierce more near His heart!

The title of the poem does not refer to the religious rite of cutting off the prepuce or the foreskin of the male sexual organ, or cutting off part of the clitoris of a female, but it means the act of spiritual purification. The poet asks 'flaming powers' and 'winged Warriors' not to rejoice but to mourn, because Christ, who had been in heaven, has now come down to earth for our happiness, but has been suffering terrible tyranny: "He who will all Heaven's heraldry whilere/Entered the world, now bleeds to give us ease". Christ has brought down with him from heaven law and love — love, more than law. And to do this, he has left behind the heavenly bliss, and he has come down nakedly, *i.e.* without any ostentation. But, ironically, man has transgressed his covenant with Christ, and this gives him excruciating pain: "Huge pangs and strong/Will pierce more near His heart!" Milton's obsessional interest with the theme of fall and redemption, with which *Paradise Lost* and *Paradise Regained* deal, is evident in this poem. His fascination for archaic words is also evident in the word 'whilere' (Line 10).

At a Solemn Music

Blest pair of Sirens, pledges of Heaven's joy,
Sphere-born harmonius sisters, Voice and Verse,
Wed your divine sounds; and mixed power employ
Dead things with inbreathed sense able to pierce,
And to our high-raised phantasy present
That undisturbed song of pure consent,
Ay sung before the sapphire-coloured throne
To Him that sits thereon,
With saintly shout and solemn jubilee;
Where the bright seraphim in burning row
Their loud uplifted angel-trumpets blow,
And the cherubic host in thousand quires
Touch their immortal harps of golden wires,

With those just spirits that wear victorious palms,
Hymns devout and holy psalms
Singing everlastingly;
That we on earth with undiscording voice
May rightly answer that melodious noise:
As once we did, till disproportioned sin
Jarred against nature's chime, and with harsh din
Broke the fair music that all creatures made
To their great Lord; whose love their motion swayed
In perfect diapason, whilst they stood
In first obedience and their state of good.
O may we soon again renew that song,
And keep in tune with Heaven, till God ere long
To his celestial consort us unite,
To live with Him, and sing in endless morn of light.

The 'argument' of this poem is very simple, like those of most of Milton's other early poems. Here the poet says that before the 'disproportion sin', *i.e.* the great sin committed by Adam and Eve by testing the fruit of the Tree of Knowledge in heaven, all the creatures used to sing in unison in praise of the Lord, making a melodious harmony. At that time, the creatures would stand before the Lord in obeisance, and that was their best state of blissfulness. The poet wishes that harmony of the voices of all the creatures once again prevails, so that we may live in the nearness of the blissful Lord. The poem foreshadows the central idea of *Paradise Lost* and *Paradise Regained*, taken together: the happy state of Man (Adam and Eve) in Paradise, his fall from Paradise, and the redemption of Man, through the agency of Christ. The terms 'disproportional sin' and 'obedience' remind us particularly of *Paradise Lost.* E.M.W. Tillyard writes about the three immediately preceding poems: "The three kindred pieces, *On Time*, *Upon the Circumcision*, and *At a Solemn Music*, are a new departure. They are experiments on high themes and in novel metres, but like the rest of the poems of Milton's early maturity they are the work of a master" (Tillyard, 1956, 60-61).

5
(L 'ALLEGRO)

Between 1632 and 1637 Milton wrote five important poems: 'L'Allegro', 'Il Penseroso' (both of which were composed some time between 1632 and 1634), 'Arcades' (written between 1632 and 1634), *Comus* (1634), and 'Lycidas' (1637). We shall discuss *Comus* in the next Chapter, and the other four poems in this and in the following three sections. We do not know when exactly 'L'Allegro' and 'Il Penseroso' were written; but commentators, generally, agree that the two poems were written, as we have said, between 1632 and 1634. We know further that the two poems were written during Milton's stay in his father's residence in the pastoral environment of the country side, the impressions of which are frequently evident in both the poems. 'L'Allegro' is bubbling in joyous mood; in it the poet is riding on the crest of mirth. Its companion poem, 'Il Penseroso' shows a contrary mood — that of melancholia. But 'Il Penseroso' is not really a melancholic poem for at least two reasons: firstly, in it the poet desires the company of melancholy not for its own sake, but because with its help the poet will be composing worthwhile verses; and secondly, the poet does not want to see melancholy simply as a particular mood, but as something divine, obviously because of its *vatic* power or for its power to inspire poets. There is a controversy as to which one of the two companion poems Milton wrote first, but it is a matter of little importance. The titles of both the poems are Italian: 'L'Allegro' means 'the cheerful man', and 'Il Penseroso' means 'the contemplative'. It may be mentioned here that during Milton's Horton period, when these two poems were written, Milton was not well acquainted with Italian, and this is evident in his using the wrong words 'Il Penseroso' for 'the contemplative' instead of the right words 'Il Pensieroso'.

In 'L'Allegro', Milton, the young poet, celebrates mirth and merriment both in the country side and in the city ("Towered cities please us than,/And the busy hum of men"). The poet bids his melancholic mood to fly away from him — the melancholic mood that is born of Cerebus, the three-headed dog that guards the doors of hell, and the 'blackest midnight', and who was delivered in the forlorn underworld cave, in the company or congregation of horrible and unholy beings (lines 1-4) :

> Hence, loathed Melancholy,
>   Of Cerebus and blackest Midnight born
> In Stygian cave forlorn
>   'Mongst horrid shapes, and shrieks, and sights unholy!

Contrarily, the poet importunes the mirthful nymph to come to him in jest and jollity and every other things that accompanies these (lines 25-32) :

Haste thee, Nymph, and bring with thee
Jest, and youthful Jollity,
Quips and Cranks and wanton Wiles,
Nods and Becks and wreathed Smiles,
Such as hang on Hebe's cheek,
And love to live in dimple sleek;
Sport that wrinkled Care derides,
And laughter holding both his sides.

These eight lines may be compared with the refrain in W.B. Yeats's (1865-1939) poem 'The Stolen Child' : "*Come away, O human child!/ To the waters and the wild/With a faery, hand in hand,/For the world's more full of weeping than you can understand.*"

The poet also wants the presence of liberty (lines 35-36): "And in thy right hand lead with thee/The mountain-nymph, sweet Liberty". With joy and liberty, the poet would like to live in an idyllic habitation, in an innocent rustic environ (lines 53-68) :

Oft list'ning how the hounds and horn
Cheerly rouse the slumb'ring morn,
From the side of some hoar hill,
Through the high hill wood echoing shrill:
Sometime walking, not unseen,
By hedgerow elms, on hillocks green,
Right against the eastern gate,
Where the great Sun begins his state,
Robed in flames and amber light,
The clouds in thousand liveries dight;
While the ploughman, near at hand
Whistles o'er the furrowed land,
And the milkmaid singeth blithe
And the mower whets his scythe,
And every shepherd tells his tale
Under the hawthorn in the dale

Such an idyllic tableau will not be devoid of the presence of human beings, and there will be musical extravaganzas and wassails and feasts, and the place will be visited by Mab, the fairy in charge of dreams (lines 91-102) :

Sometimes with secure delight,
The upland hamlets will invite,
When the merry bells ring round,

And the jocund rebecks sound
To many a youth and many a maid
Dancing in the chequered shade,
And young and old come forth to play
On a sunshine holiday,
Till the livelong daylight fail:
Then to the spicy nut-brown ale,
With stories told of many a feat,
How aery Mab the junket eat.

Hymen, the god of marriage, will also be present there, and there masks and pageants will be presented. Moreover, the plays of Jonson and 'sweetest Shakespeare' will be staged (lines 125-135) :

There let Hymen oft appear
In saffron robe, with taper clear,
And pomp, and feast, and revelry,
With mask and antique pageantry;
Such sights as youthful poets dream
On summer eves by haunted streams.
Then to the well-trod stage anon,
If Jonson's learned sock be on,
Or sweetest Shakespeare, Fancy's child,
Warble his native wood-notes wild.

Yet all these will not completely be able to satisfy our young poet: he will, in addition, desire sweet and undying verses — verses that will set free the chained harmony within the inner regard of his heart (lines 135-144) :

And ever, against eating cares,
Lap me in soft Lydian airs,
Married to immortal verse,
Such as the meeting soul may pierce,
In notes with many a winding bout
Of linked sweetness long drawn out
With wanton heed and giddy cunning,
The melting voice through mazes running,
Untwisting all the chains that tie
The hidden soul of harmony;

And only with the conglomeration or aggregation of all these sources of mirth can our young poet be full of jollity for which he is pining. And he tells Mirth that if he (Mirth) provides him (the poet) with all these things, only then he will live with him (lines 151-152): "These delights if thou canst give,/Mirth, with thee I mean to live."

The title of this poem might have been derived from the musical term 'allegro' (in English), or from the Latin term 'allagro' which means 'with brisk movement'. Both the terms derive from the Latin word 'alacer' which means 'brisk'. By briskness here in the title of the poem, Milton means jollity, for in jollity a man moves briskly, as in depression his movement slows down. Hence, by the title of the poem, the poet means 'the cheerful man' or 'the hasty man' In the poem also we find expressions indicating hastiness or briskness, such as "Haste thee, Nymph", "Come, and trip it", "In haste her bower she leaves", etc. Therefore, the title of the poem is very appropriate.

It is, frequently, said that Milton was a secluded man, an anchorite, a man of the city and never of the country. Such a charge as is often levelled against Milton was initiated by Dryden himself. Dryden said that Milton had no sympathy for nature, no eye to see her beauty; whatsoever, sprinkling of description of nature we find in Milton's works, Milton gathered from his study of books — he never felt any inclination to see the beauty of nature with his own eyes, as for instance, his successor Wordsworth did. But 'L'Allegro' is a fitting reply to this charge. 'L'Allegro' is full of pastoral images, and is resplendent with verdure and rural revelries. Nevertheless, even here Milton cannot forget his urban proclivities and intellectualism. After the revelries in the countryside, he falls asleep, being dowsed with wine, and enjoys the dreams woven by the dream-goddess Faery Mab: "Thus done the tales, to bed they creep,/By whispering winds soon lulled asleep" (lines 115-116). And, immediately, afterwards he is transported to the humdrum of the city, and there also he finds enough of revelry and enough of pleasure in the company of knights and barons and beautiful ladies (lines 117-121) :

> Towered cities please us then,
> And the busy hum of men,
> Where throngs of knights and barons bold,
> In weeds of peace, high triumph hold,
> With store of ladies,

Milton's fascination for myths, particularly, of biblical myths, is evident here — such myths as those of Cerebus, Bacchus, Zephyr, Venus and Aurora — and such myths come to him in shoals. The poem also shows Milton's love of mythopoeia or myth-making. In this poem Milton invents a new myth about the birth of Cerebus. We did not know about the parentage of the underworld being with three heads, Cerebus. But Milton says that he is the issue of Malancholy and Midnight. However, the poem is not of high quality, and yet, it is not also a drudgery, for it has some beautiful expressions and images. Some of the expressions are even catchy, such as 'Ben Jonson's learned sock' and 'sweetest Shakespeare'; 'Fancy's child'. In this poem Milton has shown enough of poetic maturity, if we consider his age. In this poem, he has followed the prosody that Chaucer, long ago, resorted to in his *House of Fame* and *The Romaunt of the Rose*. Milton has not followed the same metrical pattern throughout the poem, but has, generally, followed the iambic tetrametric rhymed couplet pattern. The resulting effect has been tripping fluency. Added to it is his choice diction. These two have given the poem the necessary and adequate vigour and enough of musical overtone.

6
(IL PENSEROSO)

'Il Penseroso' is antithetical to 'L'Allegro', as regards its theme: while in the latter the poet wants to befriend mirth and pleasure, in the former he desires the gloom of melancholy; and again, while in the latter he drives away melancholy, in the former he welcomes it. In 'Il Penseroso', the poet is contemptuous of all sorts of jollity, because joys, to him, are deluding. He spurns away joys, because he thinks that they are things or moods fittest only for idle brains (lines 1-4) :

> Hence, vain deluding Joys,
>   The brood of Folly without father bred!
> How little you bested,
>   Or fill the fixed mind with all your toys!

Instead of joy, the poet invites melancholy — melancholy that seems to him to be divine (line 12): "Hail, divinest Melancholy". He calls melancholy a 'pensive Nun' and invites her to come to him (lines 31-36):

> Come, pensive Nun, devout and pure,
> Sober, steadfast, and demure,
> All in a robe of darkest grain,
> Flowing with majestic train,
> And sable stole of cypress lawn
> Over thy decent shoulders drawn.

The poet asks melancholy to bring with her Contemplation, Silence and Philomel (nightingle) (lines 51-58) :

with thee bring
Him that yon soars on golden wing,
Guiding the fiery wheeled throne,
The Cherub Contemplation;
And the mute Silence hist along,
'Less Philomel will deign a song,
In her sweetest, saddest plight,
Smoothing the rugged brow of Night,

The poet does not want all these for their own sake, but for his own pleasure and profit. It is also for his pleasure and profit that he is desiring the presence of Contemplation. The deep melancholy will not be unpleasant to the poet if it is accompanied by Silence. Therefore, he asks Melancholy to call Silence by making a hissing sound ('hist'), in his presence. But unless ('Less') all these are not accompanied by the song of Philomel, the poet will not be able to get consumate pleasure. According to Greek mythology, Philomel was the daughter of Pandion, the king of Attica. She was raped by Tereus, husband of her sister Procne. Tereus also cut off Philomel's tongue so that she could not report the rape to anybody. Later on, at her own prayer, she was converted into a nightingle by the God, and since then she has been singing sweetest songs.

Melancholy is not intrinsically unpleasant. When it is expressed in song, it is the most sweet: Philomel, the bird that is the most melancholic, sings the most sweet songs, compared to which mirth is a folly (lines 61-62): "Sweet bird, that shunn'st the noise of folly,/Most musical, most melancholy!" For intensifying his melancholic pleasure — a sort of *Shadenfreud* — the poet wishes to enjoy tragic plays and epopees (lines 97-102) :

Sometime let gorgeous Tragedy
In sceptred pall come sweeping by,
Presenting Thebes, or Pelops' line,
Or the tale of Troy divine,
Or what (though rare) of later age
Ennobled hath the buskined stage.

The poet now wants to fall into the lap of sleep after running away from the din and bustle of the day. He, therefore, asks Melancholy to entice to him the soothing sleep (lines 141-146) :

Hide me from day's garish eye,
While the bee with honied thigh,

That at her flowery work doth sing,
And the waters murmuring,
With such consort as they keep,
Entice the dewy-feathered sleep.

The poet asks Melancholy to soothe him with sleep, and let him have mysterious dreams. But when he will wake up, he will wish to walk through the solemn spheres where the light of religion abides, and there he will enjoy religious ecstasies with the somber organ voices of the harmonius choir, and will see the face of heaven (lines 151-166) :

And, as I wake, sweet music breathe
Above, about, or underneath,
Sent by some Spirit to mortals good,
Or th' unseen Genius of the wood.

But let my due feet never fail
To walk the studious cloister's pale,
And love the high embowed roof,
With antique pillars massy-proof,
And storied windows richly dight,
Casting a dim religious light.
There let the pealing organ blow,
To the full-voiced quire below,
In service high and anthems clear,
As may with sweetness, through mine ear,
Dissolve me into ecstasies,
And bring all Heaven before mine eyes.

As the poet will grow old, he, in his melancholy, will sit looking at the stars of the sky and at the herbs that will be sipping dew-drops. And while, thus, he will be looking at the stars and at the herbs, the poet will experience a sort of 'prophetic strain' (lines 167-174) :

And may at last my weary age
Find out the peaceful hermitage,
The hairy gown and messy cell,
Where I may sit and rightly spell
Of every star that heaven doth shew
And every herb that sips the dew,
Till old experience do attain
To something like prophetic strain.

The poet believes that Melancholy is not all bad, but it can well give all these peculiar pleasures which mirth (cf. 'L'Allegro') cannot proffer.

He tells Melancholy that if it gives him all these pleasant experiences, then he will willingly choose to live with it (Melancholy), rather than with mirth (lines 175-176): "These pleasures, Melancholy, give;/And I with thee will choose to live."

As was told earlier, 'Il Penseroso' expresses a mood contrary to that of 'L'Allegro'. In 'Il Penseroso', the poet is impatient with the gaudy and glittering environment full of mirth, and the light and eccentric pleasantries. He abhors to be gay and jolly. This is so because all these are not conducive to the seriousness necessary for meditating on the higher values of life, on divinity; and for enjoying peace and the sweet but sad notes of the nightingle. It is in this sense that we can say that the poet is not actually after melancholy, but only after the melancholic condition, for some ulterior and nobler purposes. The poet only wants a situation favourable to reflection. In 'L'Allegro', he wanted to be free from any weight of contemplation, because he thought that that would mar his pleasure, but in 'Il Penseroso' he invites the melancholic and contemplative mood so that he may realise a different but deep sense of pleasure: he wants to dissolve himself in religious ecstasies.

Milton had two models of melancholy ready at hand for this poem: one in the famous song in the play *Nice Valour*, and another in the verses prefixed to Burton's *Anatomy of Melancholy*. The charge that is often labelled against Milton that he disregarded nature in his works is not tenable in this poem, as also in 'L'Allegro'. There are profuse descriptions of natural beauties in this poem, such as the "Wandering moon,/Riding near her highest noon", "Shadows brown, that Sylvan loves,/Of pine, or monumental oak", "a shower still/When the gust hath blown his fill/Ending on the rustling leaves,/With minute drops from off the Eaves", etc. The poem is written in iambic tetrametre, but there are variations. The first ten lines do not rhyme, but the rest one hundred and sixtysix lines do. In this regard, the poem may be compared with 'L'Allegro' because 'L'Allegro' is also in rhymed iambic tetrametre. Both Chaucer and Jonson used this measure, before Milton. Milton adopted this measure perhaps because it can be well adapted to musical setting. Later on, Milton employed this measure in *Comus*, as we shall soon see. But, to drive away possible monotony of the octosyllabic couplets, Milton has introduced at places a number of variations with the help of trochaic lines.

Cleanth Brooks has compared the two poems 'L'Allegro' and 'Il Penseroso' with light and shade, respectively. Perhaps, the two poems will give us more pleasure if we read them one immediately after the other, than if we read one of them, and, after an interval, the other, because successive reading will give us an added taste of the chiaroscuro. Earlier, Dr. Johnson discovered that Milton abounds in melancholy, because there is no mirth in him when he is melancholic, but there is some melancholy in him even when he is prancing in mirth. And commenting on the two poems, E.M.W. Tillyard writes : "*L'Allegro* and *Il Penseroso* are the most finished products of what I have called Milton's early poetic maturity. They have been praised lavishly and justly; and they have probably pleased more readers than anything else Milton wrote. But this popularity is not without danger to a properly proportional appreciation of Milton, for they might easily be taken, with a view either to praise or censure, as typical of him. But if typical, they are typical of only a part, and not a large part, of his mind. They are poems of escape, of fancy; and to take them too seriously is most unjust. They are delightful recreational interlude in the comprehensive studies undertaken at Horton. And it is these studies, with the ambitions that prompted them, that held the chief place in Milton's thoughts" (Tillyard, 1956, 65). However, Dr. Johnson has very truly written about the general appreciation of the two poems: "Of the two pieces, *L'Allegro* and *Il Penseroso*, I believe opinion is uniform; every man that reads them, reads them with pleasure" (Johnson, 113).

7
(ARCADES)

'Arcades' may be called a pastoral masque, or cantata, or a serenade, or a symphony, or a libretto (an Italian word meaning 'little book'). Probably, on his friend Henry Lawes' suggestion and request, Milton wrote 'Arcades' in or around 1633, in honour of the celebrated dowager-countess of Derby, and it was acted at her mansion at Harefield the same year. The masque was performed as a 'Part of the Entertainment presented to the Countess Dowager of Derby at Harefield by some Noble Persons of her family.' All the persons of this masque wear pastoral accoutrements. The masque consists of three songs, and only one character — the Genius of the Wood who has a long speech in rhymed couplets. 'Arcades' has a special importance for us in that it shows that Milton had also the genius of writing songs, and in that it also shows that he understood what drama was, for the first time. After 'Arcades', Milton shows his dramatic skill in *Comus*.

The single scene of the masque is rustic and romantic. The Countess of Derby, in whose honour the masque is presented, herself is sitting in state, and some young persons, disguised as nymphs and shepherds, sing extrolling the divine majesty of the Countess. They also speak about the wide fame of the Countess, and say that they cannot express all the worths of the Lady, because they are numerous :

Look, Nymphs, and Shepherds look!
What sudden blaze of majesty
Is that which we from hence descry,
Too divine to be mistook?
    This, this is she
To whom our vows and wishes bend:
Here our solemn search hath end.

Fame, that her high worth to raise
Seemed erst so lavish and profuse,
We may justly now accuse
Of detraction from her praise:
    Less than half we find expressed;
    Envy bid conceal the rest.

The nymphs and shepherds compare the Countess with Latona, the Roman goddess, and with Cybele, the Phrygian and Roman goddess, who is sometimes identified with the Greek goddess Rhea, the wife of Cronos, and say that the Countess is as beautiful as the two goddesses, and that she is the paragon of beautiful things.

Now the Genius of the Wood accosts them and tells them that he has understood that they have assembled there to show their fit reverence to the Countess, and further, adds that he also worships her. He tells them that it is his charge to nurse and guard the trees of the wood. The Genius of the Wood gives a description of the beautiful wood, and tells them what he does there :

All my plants I save from nightly ill
Of noisome winds and blasting vapours chill;
And from the boughs brush off the evil dew,
And heal the harms of thwarting thunders blue,
Or what the cross dire-looking planet smites,
Or hurtful worm with canker venom bites.
When evening grey doth rise, I fetch my round
Over the mount, And all this hallowed ground;
And early, ere the odorous breath of morn
Awakes the slumbering leaves, or tasselled horn
Shakes the high thicket, haste I all about,
Number my ranks, and visit every sprout
With puissant words and murmurs made to bless.

The Genius of the Wood further elaborates on his daily business, and then asks the disguised young men (disguised as nymphs and shepherds) to show their respect to the Countess by kissing the border of her robes:

> And so attend ye toward her glittering state;
> Where ye may all, that are of noble stem,
> Approach, and kiss her sacred vesture's hem.

Then the Genius of the Wood leads them into the deep forest where the Countess is sitting, and who had so far been seen only through the dark of the forest. The disguised persons follow him dancing (Song II) :

> O'er the smooth enamelled green,
> Where no print of step hath been,
> Follow me, as I sing
> And touch the warbled string:
> Under the shady roof
> Of branching elm star-proof
> Follow me.
> I will bring you where she sits,
> Clad in splendour as befits
> Her deity.
> Such a rural Queen
> All Arcadia hath not seen.

The Genius of the Wood now asks them to stop dancing, and asks them to bring their flocks to that idyllic place to live with him, and serve the Lady, *i.e.* the Countess, because none in that Arcadia has seen such an exquisite beauty as the Countess possesses (Song III) :

> Nymphs and Shepherds, dance no more
> By sandy Ladon's lilied banks;
> On old Lycaeus, or Cyllene hoar,
> Trip no more in twilight ranks;
> Though Erymanth your loss deplore,
> A better soil shall give ye thanks.
> From the stony Maenalus
> Bring your flocks, and live with us;
> Here ye shall have greater grace,
> To serve the Lady of this place.
> Though Syrinx your Pan's mistress were,
> Yet Syrinx well might wait on her.
> Such a rural Queen
> All Arcadia hath not seen.

As we have said, 'Arcades' is a pastoral masque, like *Comus*. The literary genre, called masque, originated in England and other European countries, in certain games or spectacles in which persons wore masks or 'disguises' and would dance, sometimes through streets. Masques are, generally, pastoral in nature, as it is in *Arcades*. The title of the present masque may refer to two things: the term 'arcade' and to the district in Greece known in ancient times as Arcadia. 'Arcade' is a long line of arches, open or closed, on columns, or a boulevard like path arched over with branches of trees or something else like that. In the masque, we may suppose, the thick plantation of the wood through which paths are seen, may be compared with arcades. Again, the masque reminds us of the Arcadia of ancient Greece "whose people were primitive in manners and given to music and dancing" (*Chambers Twentieth Century Dictionary*: entry: arcade). Therefore, 'Arcadia' means a primitive and pastoral tableau. Milton's *Arcades* describes one such Arcadia: its persons are of primitive habits and its locale is pastoral. *Arcades* is a short but beautiful masque with musical lilt. It is a sort of musical soiree that has the elements both of drama and of serenade. It was in this masque that Milton for the first time tried his hand at writing a play, and his skill in dramaturgy reached its apogee in *Samson Agonistes*. Commenting on *Arcades*, E.M.W. Tillyard writes: "It is very simple but very well constructed, and as a masque is quite effective. It is often read, I fancy, as an unrelated series, of a song, a speech in couplets, and two songs; but it helps much to bear in mind a picture of the setting and what slight plot can be gathered from the verses." (Tillyard, 1956, 59).

8
(LYCIDAS)

Barring *Comus*, 'Lycidas' may be called Milton's crown of success in his early poetic exploits. It presages the coming of the beauty of the great style of *Paradise Lost*, and it marks the transition from the 'early Milton' to the 'mature Milton' whom we meet after his twenty-year-long involvement in the contemporary political cross-currents, since the end of his early years. And the poem, 'Lycidas', also marks the end of the poet's fascination for the beauties of Nature — of the green pastures, the silent moon, riverines, woods, etc., as well as of the antique ditties. 'Lycidas' was written in memory of Milton's very close friend Edward King who was the son of Sir John King, Secretary to the government of Ireland under Elizabeth, James I, and Charles I. Edward King took M.A. degree in 1633 (a year afterwards Milton took his M.A.

degree) and then became a fellow and tutor in the college in which he had been a student. For about six years Milton resided with Edward. On August 10,1637, Edward was crossing the sea from Chester to Ireland, when accidentally he was drowned, as the boat capsized in the Irish seas, near the Welsh coast. After Edward's death, his friends in the Cambridge University brought out a collection of poems in his memory. The collection contained two parts: the first part was entitled 'Justa Edouardo King naufrago' (*i.e.* Rites to Edward king drowned at sea), and it contained twentythree poems in Latin and Greek; and the second part contained thirteen English poems, among which Milton's 'Lycidas' was one. 'Lycidas' was written in November, 1637, and Milton signed it simply as 'J.M.'. The second part of the collection was not published till early in 1638. 'Lycidas' was the 13th poem of the second part of that collection.

When 'Lycidas' was first published, it was not prefixed with any head note; the headnote was added later on when it was republished in 1645. The headnote runs thus : "In this Monody the Author bewails a learned Friend, unfortunately, drowned in his passage from Chester on the Irish Seas, 1637; and, by occasion, foretells the ruin of our corrupted Clergy, then in their height." In the poem, the poet says that he has come once again to the bush where he used to come with his friend Lycidas (Edward King) who is now dead. The bitter occasion, *i.e.* the demise of Lycidas, has compelled him to come to the bush, to mourn the death of his friend Lycidas. Lycidas, a peerless friend of his, died before 'his prime' (lines 1-9) :

> Yet once more, O ye laurels, and once more,
> Ye myrtles brown, with ivy never sere,
> I come to pluck your berries harsh and crude,
> And with forced fingers rude
> Shatter your leaves before the mellowing year.
> Bitter constraint and sad occasion dear
> Compels me to disturb your season due;
> For Lycidas is dead, dead ere his prime,
> Young Lycidas, and hath not left his peer.

The poet says that besides being a learned youth, Lycidas knew how to sing, and that he (Lycidas) could compose great verses (lines 10-11): "he knew/Himself to sing, and build the lofty rhyme." Such a great person and a fast friend of his must not die without drawing tears in the eyes of his friends (lines 12-14): "He must not float upon his watery bier/Unwept, and welter to the parching wind,/Without the need of some melodious tear."

As in *Paradise Lost* afterwards, or in 'The Passion' before, Milton here in this poem invokes the Muse of poetry for aid in composing the following verses in memory of Lycidas (Lines 19-22): "So may some gentle Muse/With lucky words favour my destined urn,/And as he passes turn,/And bid fair peace be to my sable shroud!" The poet remembers those bygone days when he, along with Lycidas, would tend flocks by the fountain or shade or rill. He would go to the field with Lycidas and would hear the humming of grey-flies. When night would fall, they would hear the folk-songs of the villagers. Satyrs and fauns would haunt that place and would dance gleefully. But as Lycidas is dead, everything there has changed. And now the shepherds, the woods and the forlorn caves strewn with wild thyme — all are mourning the death of Lycidas (lines 39-41): "Thee, Shepherd, thee the woods, and desert caves,/With wild thyme and the gadding vine o'ergrown,/And all their echoes, mourn." And the willow and the hazel trees now are not to be seen there. So great is the loss due to the death of Lycidas. The poet, accusingly, asks the nymphs where they had been when Lycidas was drowned. He compares Lycidas with Orpheus who was torn to pieces by the Thracian women, and whose head was thrown into the river Hebrus, and the head floated down the stream upto the isle of Lesbos; and likewise, the corpse of Lycidas floated down the stream.

Milton now meditates, or rather philosophises, on the futility of worshipping the Muse (because the Muse must have been present when Lycidas died — and Lycidas worshipped her) whom Lycidas (Edward King) worshipped by writing verses. He thinks that it is rather better to live sportingly, to live with the ordinary joys that life can proffer. It is our desire to get fame that compels us to work hard and to "scorn delight", but, after long toil, when we are about to receive our appropriate desert, our life itself is put out (lines 70-76):

> Fame is the spur that clear spirit doth raise
> (That last infirmity of noble mind)
> To scorn delights, and live laborious days;
> But the fair guerdon when we hope to find,
> And think to burst out into sudden blaze,
> Comes the blind Fury with th' abhorred shears,
> And slits the thin-spun life.

But, the poet says that Lycidas never desired fame. Then why had he to die? — the poet asks.

However, the poet says that Neptune, the Roman sea-god (identified with Greek god Poseidon) sent Triton, the sea-deity (half man and half fish), to enquire into the cause of Lycidas' death by drowning. Triton asked the waves of the seas, the winds, and the winds of the hills, but they could not say anything (about the cause of the death of Lycidas). Hippotades told Triton that when Lycidas was drowned, the sea was calm and nereids or sea-nymphs were playing in that sea. And yet the ill-fated ship accidentally capsized. Then came Camus, the god of Cam, the river at Cambridge, and mourned that Lycidas, his 'dearest pledge' was dead. And lastly came St. Peter, the 'Pilot of the Galilean Lake', and said that many poetasters tried to write verses, but pitifully failed (but Lycidas would not fail) (lines 119—129) :

> Blind mouths! that scarce themselves know how to hold
> A sheep-hook, or have learned aught else the least
> That to the faithful herdman's art belongs!
> What recks it them? What need they? They are sped;
> And when they list, their lean and fleshy songs
> Grate on their scrannel pipes of wretched straw;
> The hungry sheep look up, and are not fed,
> But, swoln with wind and the rank mist they draw,
> Rot inwardly, and foul contagion spread:
> Besides what the grim wold with privy paw
> Daily devours apace, and nothing said.

It is at this time, *i.e.* when Lycidas died, says the poet, that the long-desired parliamentary system of government was about to come to England ("that two-handed engine at the door") to smite off the tyranny of the episcopacy. Here, the phrase "two-handed engine" refers us to St. Peter "whose threat of the tow-handed engine is at once bad news for the wicked shepherds and good news for the righteous ones" (Reesing, 31). The "two-handed engine" may also refer to 'rod and staff' many times spoken of in the Bible (see, for instance, at Matthew. XXV. 32). In the poem, we had previously heard of 'A Sheep-hook' which may mean a bishop's crosier. Both the symbols, therefore, refer to sacramental rites, and so distantly refer to righteousness. However, the poet, perhaps, means to say that if the incumbent parliamentary democracy arrives, peace and happiness will return, to the state. But Lycidas is not present here; he is dead; he has gone somewhere else, and has not returned.

So Milton importunes Lycidas to come back, as the episcopal tyranny is now over, addressing him as Alpheus (a river in Arcadia) and as Sicilian Muse, so that the flowers in the vales may again bloom (lines 132-135) :

> Return Alpheus, the dread voice is past
> That shrunk thy streams; return, Sicilian Muse,
> And call the vales, and bid them hither cast
> Their bells and flowerets of a thousand hues.

The poet earnestly asks Lycidas' departed soul to come back and bid amaranthus to shed its beauty, daffodillies to fill their cups with tears, and all of them to broadcast the hearse for the dead Lycidas (lines 149-151) :

> Bid amaranthus all his beauty shed,
> And daffodils fill their cups with tears,
> To strew the laureate hearse where Lycidas lies.

But, however, the poet knows that Lycidas will never return, and yet he thinks about all these, because he presumes that such illusions as of the amaranthus shedding its beauty and daffodils filling up their cups with tears may give him some comfort, in his remorse (lines 152-153): "For so, to interpose a little ease,/Let our frail thoughts dally with false surmise." The poet does not know where Lycidas is now existing; nevertheless, he once again calls him back, addressing him, this time, as Angel. He believes that Lycidas may now be residing under water, and so he requests the dolphins to help Lycidas come out from under water (lines 163-164): "Look homeward, Angel, now, and melt with ruth:/And, O ye dolphins, waft the hapless youth."

But, immediately afterwards, the poet, once again, expresses his belief that Lycidas is not dead, and so he asks the shepherds not to mourn for him (lines 165-167) : "Weep no more, woeful shepherds, weep no more,/For Lycidas, your sorrow, is not dead,/Sunk though he be beneath the wat'ry floor." The sun now sets in the western seas, but this does not mean that it is dead, because next morning it will again rise high up in the eastern sky. In the same way, the poet believes that Lycidas has only gone down under water only to rise up to the heaven where the saints there will be wiping his tears, and be entertaining him, for ever (lines 178-181) :

> There entertain him all the Saints above,
> In solemn troops, and sweet societies,

That sing, and singing in their glory move,
And wipe the tears for ever from his eyes.

The poet believes that, henceforth, Lycidas will be the genius or the guardian spirit of the shore (of the Irish sea).

The mourning is now over, and now the sun has set in the 'western bay'. So long the poet had been speaking in the first person (see line 3: "I came to pluck your berries harsh and crude"), but now he is speaking in the third person (see lines 187,189 and 192). This is so because, in the poem, the poet identifies himself with an 'uncouth swain' who is Lycidas' friend. However, as the sun has gone down, the 'uncouth swain' (*i.e.* the poet himself) rises up, and says that he will never come back to this spot where he used to wander with Lycidas; rather, from next morrow, he will be wandering through other woods and other pastures (lines 186-193) :

Thus sang the uncouth swain to th' oak and rills,
While the still morn went out with sandals grey:
He touched the tender stops of various quills,
With eager thought warbling his Doric lay:
And now the sun had stretched out all the hills,
And now was dropt into the western bay;
At last he rose, and twitched his mantle blue :
Tomorrow to fresh woods, and pastures new.

In 'Lycidas', Milton has been able to garnar all the strength of good poetry: intense passion (sorrow for the death of Edward King, magnified several times), striking images, heart-rending music, etc. The poem was first published, as we have said, in 1638; and before its publication for the second time in 1645, Milton revised the text, and this revision added to the beauty of the poem. 'Lycidas' is a pastoral elegy. It is a pastoral, because it is situated in a pastoral surrounding relates to shepherds and flock-raising (the word 'pastoral' derives from the Latin word '*pastum*' which means 'to feed'); and it is an elegy, because it mourns the death of some close person (the word 'elegy' derives from the Latin word '*elegos*' that means 'a lament'). In the poem, Milton has followed the classical tradition of pastorals and elegies. The title of the poem does not derive from the name of Edward King, but it is a conventional name of a shepherd, used by Bion of Smyrna (fl. c. 100 B.C.) in his *Idylls* and by Theocritus (c. 310-250 B.C.) in his pastorals. Most of the devices of the pastoral elegy have been successfully employed in the poem: pastoral images, dignified and serious diction, acute grief due to loss of a close person, etc. It also follows the conventional divisions of a pastoral elegy: invocation, expression of grief, a procession of mourners, a digression, and, finally, a consolation in the thought or hope that everything has come out, or will come out, to be the best.

The charming description, in the poem, of the pastoral surround is simply unforgetable: the images are as beautiful as the diction is proper. Perhaps, only one example will suffice to illustrate the point (lines 142-151):

> Bring the rathe primrose that forsaken dies,
> The tufted crow-toe, and pale jessamine,
> The white pink, and the pansy freaked with jet,
> The glowing violet,
> The musk-rose, and the well-attired woodbine,
> With cowslip wan that hang the pensive head,
> And every flower that sad embroidery wears:
> Bid amaranthus all his beauty shed,
> And daffodillies fill their cups with tears,
> To strew the laureate hearse where Lycidas lies.

Like in his 'Arcades', Milton has in this poem betrayed enough proof of his sincere love of nature — of woods, flowers, stars, hills, fountains, etc. And, therefore, it is perhaps wrong to say that Milton had no eye for the beauty of nature. In his early poetry the beauty of nature certainly prevails, and though in his mature poetry there is conspicuous scarcity of descriptions of natural beauty, yet he has left for us some very beautiful descriptions of the decorations of nature even in his mature poetry. For instance, in *Paradise Lost* Milton has left for us a wonderful sketch of Paradise (and that while he was purblind!). Milton was never quite insensate to the beauty of nature.

Apropos of the tradition of the pastoral elegy, Milton begins the poem, of course, after a lapse of fourteen lines, with an invocation to 'some gentle Muse': "So may some gentle Muse/With lucky words favour my destined Urn". Then follows the long lamentation for Lycidas, which, in turn, is followed by a procession of mourners consisting of the woods, the caves, the echoes, Triton, 'the herald of the sea', Camus, and St. Peter, 'the Pilot of the Galilean Lake'. And then there is a brief digression in which Milton expresses his contempt for the tyrannical episcopacy. He says that the people are being guided by unworthy clergymen whom he sarcastically calls 'Blind mouths' — 'Blind', because they cannot show the people the right path, and 'mouths', because they are all mere mouths, *i.e.* gluttons. Finally, comes the consolation. The poet says that Lycidas has not actually expired; he has only gone under water soon to come out of it, and rise up to heaven. The poet, therefore, asks all to "weep no more".

There has been a long-drawn debate as to whether Milton's emotion in this poem is sincere or no — whether the emotion is external or internal; or rather, whether Milton is here expressing his personal sorrow, while Edward King's death is only an occasion for doing the same, or no. Some critics say that one thing of this poem should not be lost sight of and that is that though the theme of the poem is the mourning for the death of his dear friend, Edward King, what Milton, in the whole course of the poem says is rather more about his personal matters than about his friend. In this sense, the poem is autobiographical. Take for, instance, the fact that when Milton is speaking of the accidental death of Edward King by drowning, he is actually speaking about his possible personal fate in course of his proposed journey by sea to Italy (he went to Italy in 1638 and Edward King died in 1637, the year in which he wrote this poem). Otherwise, why should he write (lines 19-24) :

> So some gentle Muse
> With lucky words favour my destines urn,
> And as he passes turn,
> And bid fair peace be to my sable shroud!
> For we were nursed upon the self-same hill,
> Fed the same flock, by fountain, shade, and hill;

E.M.W. Tillyard paraphrases this passage thus: " 'If I die, some one will requite me with requiem, for in other ways the analogy between us was complete' " (Tillyard, 1956, 82). Tillyard further writes: "Most criticism of *Lycidas* is off the mark because it fails to distinguish between the nominal and the real subject, what the poem professes to be about and what it is about. It assumes that Edward King is the real, whereas he is but the nominal subject. Fundamentally *Lycidas* concerns Milton himself; King is but the excuse for one of Milton's most personal poems. This cannot be proved: it can only be deduced from the impression the poem leaves. Most readers agree that Milton was not deeply grieved at King's death, as they agree that the poem is great" (Tillyard, 1956, 80).

As Dr. Johnson, like John Dryden, was not very sympathetic to Milton, his criticism of 'Lycidas' has been very harsh. Dr. Johnson writes about this poem: " 'One of the poems on which much praise has been bestowed is *Lycidas*; of which the diction is harsh, the rhymes uncertain, and the numbers unpleasing' ". What beauty there is, we must therefore seek in the sentiments and images. It is not to be considered as the effusion of real passion; for passion runs not after remote allusions and obscure opinions .... " 'In this poem there is no nature, for there is no truth; there is no art, for there is nothing new. Its form is that of a pastoral, easy, vulgar, and therefore disgusting: whatever images it can supply, are long ago exhausted; and its inherent improbability always forces dissatisfaction on the mind....' " (Daiches, 242-243). Dr. Johnson further says that the poem harbours a number of unbelievable and fictious incidents. He writes: " 'This poem has a yet grosser fault. With these trifling fictions are mingled the most aweful and sacred truths, such as aught never to be polluted with such irreverent combinations. This shepherd [Lycidas] likewise is now a feeder of sheeps, and afterwards an ecclesiastical pastor, a superintendent of a Christian flock. Such equivocations are always unskilful; but here they are indecent, and at least approach to impiety, of which, however, I believe the writer not to have been conscious.... Surely no man can have fancied that he read *Lycidas* with pleasure, had he not known its author' " (Daiches, 243).

But, even if we take all these criticisms to be genuine, of course with a pinch of salt, yet we must admit that there are many things that have made the poem enjoyable; otherwise why should it have been so popular? John Reesing writes: "What ... gives Lycidas the distinguishing quality we all recognise is, I suggest, a uniquely Miltonic blend of poignance and outrage. The first is proper to the man with a strong sense that life is, specifically, *sweet*, such a sense as Adam expresses in his phrase 'the sweet of Life' and in the whole delicious passage where it occurs (*P.L.* VIII. 180-197). In *Lycidas* this keen sense of life's sweetness is everywhere in the rhythm, and occasionally explicit in the imagery (6, 59-48, 134-151, 175, 179). Outrage, which depends on a strong sense of order, is also everywhere in the poem, in imagery, rhythm, tempo, and volume; and everywhere it is qualified by the poignance" (Reesing, 27). The poem is a beautiful blend of reality and myth. Edward King does not seem to be an ordinary human being, but appears to be sort of a spirit. This is clear when we know that after the death of Lycidas, Camus, the god of the river Cam, and St. Peter, 'the Pilot of the Galilean Lake' have come to mourn his death. The poem is written against a beautiful rustic abandon, and in a mystic atmosphere, for which reason we are almost immediately compelled to forget the divide between reality and myth, and this peculiar effect Milton has created very skilfully. For all these and for many other things, 'Lycidas' is certainly a great poem. E.M.W. Tillyard, in spite of his point of criticism of this poem stated above, writes the following in praise of it: "Lycidas is the last and greatest English poem of Milton's youth. Though shorter, it is greater than *Comus*, written with newly-own but complete mastery and expressing a mental experience both valuable and profound" (Tillyard, 1956, 80). The religious atmosphere of the poem has appealed to some critics, and other critics have been attracted by the beautiful similitude drawn by the poet between Lycidas' death and the prevailing moral degeneration of England. But the greatness of the poem does not completely depend on either of the two; it depends principally on the aesthetic quality of the poem — on its intense emotion, appropriate rhythm, and appealing imagery. E.M.W. Tillyard writes: "*Lycidas* expresses a mind of the keenest sensibility and most powerful grasp acutely aware of a number of most moving sensations, but controlling these sensations so that they do not conflict but rather by contrast reinforce one another: a mind calm after struggle but keyed up to perform heroic deeds, should they need to be done" (Tillyard, 1956, 85).

'Lycidas' was written in the High Renaissance (1500-1530) style of the later half of the 16th century — the High Renaissance style that upheld loftiness, instead of cautiousness and control upheld by the Early Renaissance (1300-1500) style. The poem has been compared by some critics with Keats' 'Ode to a Nightingle'. E.M.W. Tillyard, for instance, writes: "The theme of *Lycidas* can be put in nearly the same terms as those used for the *Ode to a Nightingle*. Death, sorrow, futility of ambition, the corruption of human nature; the desire to escape them; acceptance of them in the end; and following it renewed vitality" (Tillyard, 1956, 35). Like 'Arcades', this poem is also full of mythical allusions: such mythological characters as Damaetas, Orpheus, Amaryllis, Neaera, Neptune, Hippotades, Panope, Camus, Bellerus, etc. abound in it. 'Lycidas' should remind us of another beautiful elegy of Milton — 'Epitaphium Damonis', — which he wrote in 1639, after he returned from Italy, on the death of his dear school friend, the Italian youth Diodati. Therefore, 'Epitaphium Damonis' was written two years after 'Lycidas'. 'Lycidas' is in English, but 'Epitaphium Damonis' is in Latin. 'Lycidas' was Milton's last great English poem — a great elegy — of his early period, and 'Epitaphium Damonis' was his last long Latin poem.

Perhaps, 'Epitaphium Damonis' surpasses 'Lycidas' in poetic excellence. It is approximately of the same length as 'Lycidas', but its appeal is more insistent, its sensation more poignant, and its diction more sweet. Further, it is not hindered by vicarious feeling and artificial emotion. Each stanza of 'Epitaphium Damonist' is followed by a refrain — 'Ile domum impasti, domino iam non vacat, agni' ('Go homewards hungry, my lambs, your master is busy.') — which sustains and accumulates the emotion as the poem progresses. In the poem Milton calls his friend Diodati by the name of 'Damon' ('Damon we call you'), and calls himself 'Thyrsis'. Damon and Thyrsis are two shepherd friends, and they had been pursuing the same vocation. On a business, Thyrsis went abroad, and in his absence, Damon expired. We know that Milton announced his intention of rejecting Latin and taking up English as his poetic medium in 1628 in his 'At a Vacation Exercise': "Hail, native language, that by sinews weak/Diest move my first endeavouring tongue to speak". In 'Epitaphium Damonis', the poet once again announces his intention of turning to his 'native language', and also his plan of writing an epic on some native theme (lines 168-171: in translation) :

> If I live so long,
> You'll hang from some far-off ancient pine, my pipes,
> dim in my memory, unless, transformed by my native Muse,
> You trumpt a British theme.

With 'Epitaphium Damonis' Milton ended his early poetic venture. After this poem, he did never write short poems, except a few Latin and English sonnets, because after it, he involved himself more actively in the political crisis of England, and consequently, for long twenty years he began the career of a pamphleteer. So far, we have discussed most of Milton's important works of his early poetic life, excepting *Comus*. *Comus* was written in 1634, *i.e.* before 'Lycidas' which was written in 1637, and so *Comus* must fall in his early poetic period. But, for convenience, we shall discuss the poem (*Comus*) in the next chapter.

5

COMUS

As we have said, Milton wrote *Comus* in his early poetic period. It was written in 1634 when he was around 25, *i.e.* *Comus* was written about two years before 'Lycidas' that announced the cessation of his early poetic life. *Comus* and 'Arcades' — both masques — were written at about the same time — in 1634. But some commentators say that 'Arcades' was probably written one or two years before *Comus*. Both the masques were written for special occasions. The occasion of *Comus* was the appointment of the Earl of Bridgewater in 1634, as the Lord President of Wales. "In 1634 Milton's friend, the musician Henry Lawes, who was tutor to the Earl of Bridgewater's children, asked him to write a masque to celebrate the Earl's installation as Lord President of Wales. Lady Alice Egerton, at fifteen, and her brothers, aged eleven and nine, were to perform before their parents. And in *Comus* Milton experimented with youthful profligacy" (Wordsworth Poetry Library, vi).

Comus, like 'Arcades', possesses both pastoral quality and dramatic quality of high order. In fact, Milton showed his dramatic skill, for the first time, in *Comus* — the dramatic skill that reached its apogee in *Samson Agonistes*. Milton wanted *Comus* to be a masque (or mask), *i.e.* a composition intended for staging, and a composition full of songs. *Comus* may be called a court masque, because it was composed for staging in the court-precincts, and actually it was thus staged, and was acted by persons around the court. In a court masque, generally, there are two main parts: the anti-mask that presents a problematic situation, and the mask proper that dissolves the problematic, and then presents an ideal. As has been the tradition, the anti-mask is performed by professionals, and the mask proper by members of an aristocratic family, or by officials of a court.

Comus was dedicated "To the Right Honourable John, Lord Viscount Brackley, son and heir-apparent to the Earl of Bridgewater, &c." Milton's friend Henry Lawes wrote music for the masque, and directed the performance, and also acted in it, when it was for the first time presented.

The Persons in *Comus* are:

> *Comus*, with his crew.
> *The Lady*
> *First Brother*
> *Second Brother*
> *Sabrina*, the Nymph.

The masque was first presented in 1634, the very year in which it was written, at Ludlow Castle (for which reason it is also known as Milton's Ludlow masque), the residence of the Earl of Bridgewater. In its first presentation, the masque was acted, among others, by Alice, the daughter of the Earl, who was then around fifteen and who acted the role of The Lady, and by the two sons of the Earl who were younger than Alice.

The story of the masque is short and simple, and is presented in only three scenes. The story, in brief, is this: The Lady is lost to her two brothers in a deep wood, and is duped by the lustful magician Comus. The two brothers then discuss between them whether the chastity of the Lady will be able to save her from being violated, or not. Then the Attendant Spirit descends and rescues the Lady, and the masque closes with dances and an epilogue by the Attendant Spirit. The theme of the masque is a trial of the strength of chastity. It may be mentioned here that till his late youth, Milton held celebacy and chastity as high ideals; and even after this period, he held these two properties of man in high honour. He nursed his high ideal of celebacy perhaps upto his age of 34, when he married Mary Powell in 1642. This is evident in a letter of his written to his friend, not long before 1642. In that letter he wrote about "his inclination to marriage but had chosen celebacy for the time being, in order to devote his whole attention to self-discipline" (Tillyard, 1956, 75). His inborn and deep religious sentiment coupled with his reading of *The Faerie Queene* by Spenser might have grown in him a great regard for chastity. Milton believed that both the spirit and the flesh are, in themselves, good, because both were created by God. And, therefore, if the body is not defiled any way, he believed, it must have some supernatural power, and for the reason of that chastity must have some inalienable power to protect itself from violation. In *Comus* Milton has shown just that. There might have been yet another reason with Milton for choosing the theme of chastity for the masque. As a staunch Puritan, he was averse to the prevalent licentiousness in the reign of Charles I. He, perhaps, believed that though the on-going Puritan movement was no match to the corrupted strength of the king, the tyranny of the king over the Puritans will ultimately stop.

However, the first scene of *Comus* opens in a wild wood. The Attendant Spirit 'descends' or 'enters', and delivers a speech of 92 decasyllabic lines in iambic metre. He describes the earth, and the men living there — men who are neglectful of the divine virtues. But even among such men he discovers some such men as aspire after the 'golden key' of virtue, to open the gates of the palace of eternity (lines 12-14) :

> Yet some there be that by due steps aspire
> To lay their just hands on that golden key
> That opes the palace of eternity.

The Attendant Spirit says that he has a message to deliver to one such virtuous being: "To such my errand is". He says that on this earth, a noble Peer (reference to the Earl of Bridgewater), who has much power and trust, has been entrusted with the charge of guiding the 'greatest' and 'best' 'Isle' (island: reference to Wales) whose nation is 'haughty' and 'proud in arms'. The Attendant Spirit now sees that the 'fair offspring' of the Peer (the Lady and her two brothers) are coming there through a horrible and pathless wilderness. The Attendant Spirit says that being afraid that the younglings may suffer some great peril, the 'sovran Jove' has immediately sent him for their safety (lines 36-42):

> But their way
> Lies through the perplex'd paths of this drear wood,
> The nodding horror of whose shady brows
> Threats the forlorn and wandering passenger;
> And here their tender age might suffer peril,
> But that, by quick command from sovran Jove,
> I was despatched for their defence and guard.

But why this apprehension of Jove? The Attendant Spirit narrates the reason. He says that Bacchus, the god of wine, and son of Jupiter and Semele, once landed in the territory of the sorceress Circe, daughter of Helios and Perse. Circe was attracted by the beautiful look of Bacchus, and by her charm or magic spell compelled him to lie with her. She thus got a son named Comus who resembled his father, but did more his mother. This Comus can change the countenances of human beings into those of wolves, bears, tigers, ounces, etc. by making them drink his special liquor, when their countenances will vanish (lines 68-72):

Soon as the potion works, their human count'nance,
Th' express resemblance of the gods, is changed
Into some brutish form of wolf or bear,
Or ounce or tiger, hog, or bearded goat,
All other parts remaining as they were.

When human beings are thus transformed, they think that they are more beautiful and pleasing than before, and then they forget their whereabouts, and they run after sensual pleasure. But to save these endangered younglings of the Earl, the Attendant Spirit will now change his habits and make himself look like a swain — a rustic lover. And as he has now changed himself, the Attendant Spirit hears the foot-steps of the on-coming Comus, and he instantly hides himself from the view of Comus. And then Comus enters with a train of monsters whose heads are like different beasts, but otherwise they are like ordinary human beings, male and female. Comus holds a magic wand in one hand and a glass of wine in the other. The monsters, everyone of them, bear torches and make tumultuous noises. Comus tells the human monsters that as it is late in the night, "welcome joy and feast,/Midnight shout and revelry,/Tipsy dance and jollity." (lines 102-104). He tells them that at this late hour of the night, industry and perseverance ('Rigour'), good counselling and scruple ('Advice') and instructions of old people are not to be found anywhere ('in slumber lie'). He tells the human-monsters that they are made of 'purer fire', and commands them to do morrice dance (perhaps of Moorish origin) and all such other pranks, because the night is for such revelry, and not for sleep: "What hath night to do with sleep?" He tells them that night is only for love-making and that love-making at night is no sin, because sin can be committed only by day time: " 'Tis only daylight that makes sin". Comus, therefore, invokes Cotytto, the 'goddess of nocturnal sport', and calls Hecate, the supreme god of the underworld. He then descries, in the utter darkness of the night, the Lady who has lost her path in the woods: "Some virgin sure/(For so I can distinguish by mine art)/ Benighted in these woods!" (lines 148-150). Then Comus disguises himself as a shepherd, grazing a herd, and decides to cheat the Lady with the aid of his magic art (lines 153-159) :

Thus I hurl
My dazzling spells into the sponzy air,
Of power to cheat the eye with blear illusion,
And give it false presentments, lest the place
And my quaint habits breed astonishment,

And put the damsel to suspicious flight;
Which must not be, for that's against my course.

The Lady enters, *i.e.* approaches near where Comus stands, and hears the utmost noise made by the half-beastly-half-human beings of Comus, and understands that those queer beings are dancing in praise of Pan for the benefit of their bounteous 'flocks and granges' that they received from him. She says that after a weary journey through the woods, her two brothers seated her under pine trees and went away to fetch some 'cooling fruit' for her. It is now dusk, but she cannot understand why they are not returning. It may be, she thinks, that they went too far, and at nightfall they have lost their way. In the palpable darkness of the night, the Lady recalls the memories of a thousand chimeras (lines 205-209) :

A thousand fantasies
Begin to throng into my memory,
Of calling shapes, and beck'ning shadows dire,
And airy tongues that syllable men's names
On sands and shores and desert wilderness.

Nevertheless, she is not daunted, because, she says, she is virtuous and faithful. She believes, therefore, that God will certainly send a guard for her (lines 210-220) :

These thoughts may startle well, but not astound
The virtuous mind, that ever walks attended
By a strong siding champion, Conscience.
O welcome, pure-eyed Faith, white-handed Hope,
Thou hovering angel girt with golden wings,
And thou unblemished form of Chastity !
I see ye visibly, and now believe
That He, the Supreme Good, t'whom all things ill
Are bent as slavish officers of vengeance,
Would send a glittering guardian, if need were,
To keep my life and honour unassailed.

Thus, plucking courage, she then sings a loud song to draw the attention of her two brothers. In her song, she addresses the sweet nymph Echo, and tells her that if she (Echo) has perchance hidden her brothers, who look like Narcissus, to please send them back to her.

But, yet, nothing avails; the two brothers do not return. Meanwhile, Comus descries the Lady and instantaneously feels lasciviousness within him. He determines: "I'll speak to her,/And she shall be my queen." He addresses the Lady thus: "Hail, foreign wonder!" But the Lady does not give ear to him; she says that she is only in search of her lost brothers. And then a stychomythia follows between the Lady and Comus (lines 277-290):

Comus. What chance, good Lady, hath bereft you thus?
Lady. Dim darkness and this leafy labyrinth.
Comus. Could that divide you from near-ushering guides?
Lady. They left me weary on a grassy turf.
Comus. By falsehood, or discourtesy, or why?
Lady. To seek i' the valley some cool friendly spring.
Comus. And left your fair side all unguarded, Lady?
Lady. They are but twain, and purposed quick return.
Comus. Perhaps forestalling night prevented them.
Lady. How easy my misfortune is to hit!
Comus. Imports their loss, beside the present need?
Lady. No less than if I should my brothers lose.
Comus. Were they of manly prime, or youthful bloom?
Lady. As smooth as Hebe's their unrazored lips.

Comus then tells her that he saw two human beings that seemed to be 'more than human', and that those two human beings may be her two brothers. He then proposes to her: "If those you seek,/It were a journey like the path to heaven/To help you find them." He tells her that he knows every nook and corner of the wilderness, and suggests that she may seek out her brothers with him in the dark of the night, or else — and this, he means, is better — lodge herself in his cottage for the night, and seek out the brothers in the next morning: "If otherwise,/I can conduct you, Lady, to a low/ But loyal cottage, where you may be safe/Till further quest." The gullible Lady trusts Comus and accepts his alternative offer, and having absolute faith in the Providence, asks Comus to take her to his cottage: "Eye me, blest Providence, and square my trial/To my proportional strength! Shepherd, lead on .."

Meanwhile, on the other part of the forest, the two brothers are searching for their sister, the Lady. Second Brother thinks that she is helplessly and precariously passing the night, and also that there is a possibility of her being devoured by some hungry animal or of being molested by some savage being (lines 350-358) :

But, oh, that hapless virgin, our lost sister!
Where may she wander now, whither betake her
From the chill dew, amongst rude burs and thistles?
Perhaps some cold bank is her bolster now,
Or 'gainst the rugged bark of some broad elm
Leans her unpillowed head, fraught with sad fears.
What if in wild amazement and affright,
Or, while we speak, within the direful grasp
Of savage hunger, or of savage heat!

But Elder Brother asks him to refrain from too much of thinking about the probable ill of their sister, the Lady, because the evil is uncertain, and because if evil is foredoomed, man cannot avoid it. He tells him that their sister is virtuous, and that virtue itself will tell her what to do when, and that virtue has that power : "Virtue could see to do what Virtue would/By her own radient light, though sun and moon/Were in the flat see sunk." Elder Brother then philosophises on the light of Wisdom and Contemplation (lines 381-585):

He that has light within his own clear breast
May sit i' the centre, and enjoy bright day:
But he that hides a dark foul and foul thoughts,
Benighted walks under the midday sun;
Himself is his own dungeon

Such a cogitation of Elder Brother may remind us of what Satan says in *Paradise Lost* (Book I : lines 262-263): "The mind is its own place, and in itself/Can make a Heaven of hell, and a hell of Heaven."

Second Brother agrees with him, and yet says that beauty is always the prey of incontinent assaults, and so needs a guard: "But Beauty, like the fair Hesperian tree/Laden with blooming gold, had need the guard". In spite of Second Brother's suggestion to the contrary, Elder Brother is certain that their sister is not defenceless, because, he thinks, she has a "hidden strength", and that " 'Tis chastity, my brother, chastity". Elder Brother believes that "She that has that, is clad in complete steel". He confirms and strengthens his argument with instances from "the old school of Greece" (lines 441-452) :

Hence had the huntress Dian her dread bow,
Fair silver-shafted queen for ever chaste,
Wherewith she tamed the brinded lioness
And spotted mountain pard, but set at nought
The frivolous bolt of Cupid; gods and men

Feared her stern frown, and she queen o' the woods.
What was the snaky-headed Gorgon shield
That wise Minerva wore, unconquered virgin,
Wherewith she freezed her foes to congealed stone,
But rigid looks of chaste austerity,
And noble grace that dashed brute violence
With sudden adoration and blank awe?

Elder Brother says that if chastity resides within the soul, heaven sends a "thousand angels" and purifies the remaining "sin and guilt" of the soul. Heaven then sends beams of pure light upon the body, the "temple of the mind", and converts the body into the essence of the soul, and so the body too becomes immortal (see chapter 3). He says that heaven then (lines 460-463) :

Begins to cast a beam on th' outward shape,
The unpolluted temple of the mind.
And turns it by degrees to the soul's essence,
Till all be made immortal.

Second Brother becomes bemused hearing this "divine Philosophy" of Elder Brother.

Now the two brothers hear a loud cry, and they construe it to be that of a 'night-foundered' person, like themselves, or that of an enemy. They spring to their defence. The Attendant Spirit, in a shepherd's habit, accosts them. Elder Brother cautions the Spirit, but Second Brother cognises it (the Spirit) as Thyrsis, their father's shepherd's shepherd, and asks him of the cause of his coming there. The Spirit, instead of answering, asks them: "But, oh! my virgin Lady, where is she?/How chance she is not in your company?" Elder Brother tells him that their sister is lost due to their neglect, or without their neglect (*i.e.* due to fate). The Spirit then in a long speech of 67 lines expresses his fear for the Lady, their sister. He says that in this forest Comus dwells — Comus, the inglorious beast. The Spirit tells them that he saw the place where the lady is staying, and that the Lady is now a prey of Comus' luscivousness (lines 570-574) :

I found the place
Where that damned wizard, hid in sly disguise,
(For so by certain signs I know,) had met
Already, ere my best speed could prevent,
The aidless innocent Lady, his wished prey;

Second Brother, hearing this, becomes woebegone; but Elder Brother is confident that the virtuous Lady cannot be molested, because evil is impotent when it accosts virtue (lines 589-597) :

> Virtue may be assailed, but never hurt,
> Surprised by unjust force, but not enthralled:
> Yea, even that which Mischief meant most harm
> Shall in the happy trial prove most glory.
> But evil on itself shall back recoil,
> And mix no more with goodness, when at last,
> Gathered like scum, and settled to itself,
> It shall be in eternal restless change
> Self-fed and self-consum'd.

Saying this, Elder Brother asks Second Brother to proceed to forcefully take away the Lady from the clutch of Comus: "I'll find him out,/And force him to restore his purchase back,/Or drag him by the curls to a foul death,/Cursed as his life."

But the Attendant Spirit stops him saying that the forest is charmed, and so even his mighty sword will be ineffective. The Spirit tells Elder Brother that he has an acquaintance with a certain shepherd who knows all kinds of plants and herbs, and that the shepherd loves him well. This shepherd gave him a certain outlandish plant, called haemony, that is supremely effective against all sorts of magic and certain other evils. The Spirit further tells the two brothers that it was with the help of this plant that he discovered Comus. Then the Spirit dilates on the effectiveness of the mysterious plant (lines 647-656) :

> If you have this about you
> (As I will give you when we go) you may
> Boldly assault the necromancer's hall;
> Where if he be, with dauntless hardihood
> And brandished blade rush on him, breaking his glass,
> And shed the luscious liquor on the ground,
> But seize his wand; though he and his crust crew
> Fierce sign of battle make, and menace high,
> Or, like the son of Vulcan, vomit smoke,
> Yet will they soon retire, if he but shrink.

Elder Brother takes the advice of the Spirit, whom he calls Thyrsis, and asks him to lead on: "Thyrsis, lead on apace; I'll follow thee:/And some good angel bear a shield before us!"

Here the direction of the drama runs thus: "*The scene changes to a stately palace, set out with all manners of deliciousness; soft music, tables spread with all dainties. COMUS appears with his rabble, and the LADY set in an enchanted chair: to whom he offers his glass; which she puts by, and goes about to rise.*" Now Comus is discovered — Comus who is wielding his hypnotic wand over the Lady. But the Lady, being angered, tells him that the wand will not work over her, because "Heaven sees good." But Comus tries to calm her down, saying that the place is for pleasure and fancy. He offers her a vial of julep mixed with fragrant syrups, and tells her that the julep "Is of such power, to stir up as this,/To life so friendly, or so cool to thirst." Comus then asks her with lascivious intent (lines 679-681):

Why should you be so cruel to yourself,
And to those dainty limbs, which Nature lent
For gentle usage and soft delicacy?

Comus now asks her to sip the julep for refreshment — for driving away her tiredness which is due to her long walk. He tells her that the long walk has drained away her vitality, and that this julep "will restore all soon." But the Lady refuses his offer of the julep, saying that he (Comus) has deceived her (lines 690-695):

'Twill not, false traitor!
'Twill not restore the truth and honesty
That thou has banished from thy tongue with lies.
Was this the cottage and the safe abode
Thou told'st me of? What grim aspect are these,
These ugly-headed monsters? Mercy guard me!
Hence with thy brewed enchantments, foul deceiver!

But Comus is not to give in: he persuades the Lady not to follow the path of abstinence. He argues at some length (lines 710-742):

Wherefore did Nature pour her bounties forth
With such a full and unwithstanding hand,
Covering the earth with odours, fruits, and flocks,
Thronging the seas with spawn innumerable,
But all to please and sate the curious taste?

....

List, Lady; be not coy, and be not cozened
With that same vaunted name, Virginity.
Beauty is Nature's coin; must not be hoarded,
But must be current; and the good thereof
Consists in mutual and partaken bliss,
Unsavoury in th' enjoyment of itself.

But yet the Lady spurns away the lascivous approach of Comus, in utter indignation and contempt. She says that Nature truly provided the earth with abundance, but (lines 764-767) :

> She, good cateress,
> Means her provision only to the good,
> That live according to her sober laws,
> And holy dictate of spare Temperance.

At her haughty, and repulsive but confident attitude, Comus is taken aback. He says: "I feel that I do fear/Her words set off by some superior power." And, yet, Comus does not abandon his vile project of violating her chastity. He thinks that the Lady must be suffering from acute melancholy, and so, again, he offers her the narcotic concoction, and tells her: "Be wise, and taste."

Meanwhile, "*THE BROTHERS rush in with swords drawn, wrest his [Comus's] glass out of his hand, and break it against the ground: his rout make sign of resistance, but are all driven in. The ATTENDANT SPIRIT comes in.*" The Spirit asks the two brothers not to let Comus get scot free, but to bind him. But the next moment he thinks of a novel means of punishing Comus: "Some other means I have which may be used". The Spirit then tells the brothers the story of Sabrina, the goddess of the river Severn. This 'guiltless damsel', Sabrina, was the daughter of Locrine. Once she was hotly pursued by her stepmother Guendolen, and she jumped into a stream where water-nymphs had been playing. The nymphs pitifully carried her to Nereus who made her the goddess of the river Severn. It was thus that the innocence and gentleness of Sabrina was saved. Sabrina now takes care of herds and saplings and buds in the evenings, and cures the evil pranks of elves, with her special liquor (lines 842-847):

> still she retains
> Her maiden gentleness, and oft at eve
> Visits the herds along the twilight meadows,
> Helping all urchin blasts, and ill-luck signs
> That the shrewd meddling elf delights to make,
> Which she with precious vialed liquor heals.

Sabrina can dispel charms and evil influences, and she loves virginhood. Therefore, the Attendant Spirit will now try to procure the help of Sabrina by singing a song (lines 852-858):

> she can unlock
> The clasping charm, and thaw the numbing

If she be right invoked in warbled song;
For maidenhood she loves, and will be swift
To aid a virgin, such as was herself,
In hard besetting need. This will I try,
And add the power of some adjuring verse.

In his song, the Spirit praises Sabrina's hair, and adjures her in the names of Oceanus, Neptune, Tethy, Nereus, Carpathian, Triton, Glaucus, Leucothea, Thetis, Parthenope and Ligea to come to their aid, *i.e.* to the aid of the Lady, her two brothers and himself.

In response to the Spirit's importunation, Sabrina rises (from under water), attended by a clutch of water-nymphs, and tells the Spirit, in her song, that she has come at his request: "at thy request/I am here!" The Spirit tells her that a certain virgin is in distress, and so he has implored her aid. Sabrina tells him that it is her duty to defend chastity, and she then proceeds with her remedy against the charms (wrought by Comus) on the Lady (lines 910-919):

Brightest Lady, look on me
Thus I sprinkle on thy breast
Drops that from my fountain pure,
I have kept of precious cure,
Thrice upon thy finger's tip,
Thrice upon thy rubied lip:
Next this marble venomed seat,
Smeared with gums of glutinous heat,
I touch with chaste palms moist and cold;
Now the spell hath lost his hold;

After this, Sabrina descends (under water) and the Lady, cured of the spell of Comus, "rises out of her seat." The Spirit then expresses gratefulness to Sabrina, and asks the Lady to leave the enchanted place, so that she may not be made spell-bound, once again. He asks the Lady to proceed towards her father's residence, which is not far off from that place, where revelry is going on. Their presence there, he says, will multiply the mirth. Now it is late in the night, but still the stars are shining brightly, and the moon ('Night') "sits monarch yet in the mid sky."

The next direction of the masque runs thus: "*The scene changes, presenting Ludlow Town and the President's Castle: then come in Country Dancers: after them the ATTENDANT SPIRIT, with the two BROTHERS and the LADY.*" And then two songs are sung by the

Spirit. During the second song, the Lady and her two brothers are presented to their father and mother. After the dances and the songs are over, the Spirit, in his epilogue, says that his appointed task is now over, and so he is flying to the "happy fields of the sky". He is now proceeding towards the corners of the moon ; but before he actually departs, he gives his last advice to all present, or, rather, to all human beings: Love Virtue, because only virtue can take us upto heaven (1018-1025) :

> Mortals, that would follow me,
> Love Virtue; she alone is free,
> She can teach ye how to climb
> Higher than the sphery chime;
> Or, if Virtue feeble were,
> Heaven itself would stoop to her.

Comus, in tandem with *Samson Agonistes*, proves the superb dramatic skill of Milton, beyond any shred of doubt. Of course in *Comus*, dramatic element is not so prominent, the masque being dominated rather by poetry, yet it presages about the mature dramatic skill of *Samson Agonistes*: the Milton of 25 foreshadowed the appearance of the mature dramatist Milton of 53. Milton's fascination for classicism is apparent also in *Comus*. Following the classical tradition, Milton has introduced in the masque both a prologue and an epilogue: the opening speech of the masque, *i.e.* the speech of the Attendant Spirit is the prologue, and his last speech is the epilogue, of the masque. Again, the dialogue between Comus and the Lady, when they first meet each other, is a stychomythia, and this reminds us of the Greek tragedies in which it was used far oftener than elsewhere. But in *Comus*, Milton does not only look back to the ancient past, he also does have in his mind the masque tradition of his immediately preceding age. David Daiches, in his book *Milton* writes: "*Comus* is in the Elizabethan masque tradition, one of the last English works of its kind. Book X of the *Odyssey*, Platonic and neo-Platonic philosophy, Spenser's description of the Bower of Bliss in Book II of *The Faerie Queene*, William Brown's *Inner Temple Masque* (treating Circe and Ulysses), Johnson's *Pleasure Reconciled to Virtue* (a masque where Comus figures as a glutton), Peele's *Old Wives' Tale,* Fletcher's *The Faithful Shepherdess*, each appear to have suggested some thing to Milton and Hanford has suggested that the defence of chastity in *Comus* may have been a deliberate reply on Milton's part to the libertine philosophy expounded by his fellow-student Thomas Randolph in *The Muse's Looking Glass*" (Daiches, 1968, 65).

Comus is a brilliant dramatic piece with adequate character-sketching, highly realistic concoction of crisis and enough of rhetoric -- and all these against a beautiful romantic and tell-tale background. It is full of fine poetry, and this has enormously added to the quality of the masque. E.M.W. Tillyard writes: "There is in *Comus* finer poetry than anything Milton wrote earlier" (Tillyard, 1956, 73). The characters of it are also very lively and interesting. The drama itself is so engrossing that when we enjoy it, very soon we forget everything around us and participate in the enchanting environment. The dramatic skill in *Comus* is really promising: perhaps Milton could become a great dramatic genius had there been no political predicament. E.M.W. Tillyard again writes about Milton's dramatic debut: "In *Comus* he mastered the elements of drama, and had he thought good he might later had combined them to make a great tragedy" (Tillyard, 1956, 74). Milton's journey to Italy, his long planning of writing an epic and necessary preparations for it, and the politically turbulent climate of the kingdom that compelled him to write consecutive pamphlets, etc. stood in his way of writing further dramatic pieces. However, to give an idea of the charm of *Comus* we cannot do better than quote a passage of appreciation by David Daiches: "*Comus* is a remarkable performance. Its freshness, variety, sureness of touch, mastery of different tones, show how far Milton had gone in developing high technical skill. Its variety is perhaps excessive; the different styles — including a not very successful imitation of the Greek *stichomythia* in some of the dialogue — are not always adequately subdued to the total design. But we must remember that this is a masque, meant to be sung and acted, and without the music and the somewhat stylized dramatic action it loses a great deal" (Daiches, 1968, 73).

Nevertheless, the criticisms labelled against it are not few in number, and Milton himself was aware of some of its faults. To begin with, compared to the shortness of the masque, the 'prologue' and the epilogue are inordinately and inappropriately long. The dramatic quality of it has also to a great extent been marred by the masque's direct moralising, particularly by that at the end of it. Yet another criticism of *Comus* is that the different scenes of it are not well-knitted, but are hanging loosely one from the other. This gives us the impression of some sort of artificiality on the part of its author, and makes us believe in the lack of any genuine inspiration in the author. E.M.W. Tillyard rightly says:

"The final impression I get from *Comus* viewed as a whole is that when Milton wrote it he was not inspired by any compelling mood to give it unity" (Tillyard, 1956, 72). The masque has been criticised also for several other inadequacies in it. Critics say that it is not seriously dramatic. They say that it could be so if, for instance, the Lady would actually be enticed by Comus. There is also no psychological complexity from which any of the characters suffer — in a sense, we may say that there is at all no complexity in it. Again, none of the characters develop: the characters are all flat. But there are also critics who are ready to exonerate Milton of all these charges. For instance, John Reesing in his *Milton's Poetic Art* writes: "But those qualities, virtues proper for serious drama, would be out of place here; one may grant the strictures and still regard them as virtues, not faults, in this work. For the Lady and her brothers belong to Nature..." (Reesing, 4). He further writes that according to Milton, Nature is a "standard of pure and faultless morality. What he calls Nature is the perfect physio-moral order that he looks back to as the pristine historical reality, the whole creation as God originally made it" (Reesing, 3). And thus John Reesing summarily quashes the supposedly serious charge that moralising mars the beauty of the masque.

But, the amiable adversary of Milton, Dr. Johnson, yet will not let *Comus* pass for a brilliant piece of drama. His criticisms still remain scathing: "As a drama it is deficient. The action is not probable. A Masque, in those parts where supernatural intervention is admitted, must indeed be given up to all the freaks of imagination; but, so far as the action is merely human, it aught to be reasonable, which can hardly be said of the conduct of the two brothers; who, when their sister sinks with fatigue in a pathless wilderness, wonder both away together in search of berries too far to find their way back, and leave a helpless Lady to all sadness and danger of solitude" (Johnson, 115). Dr. Johnson's imputation of foolishness certainly cannot be gainsaid, but yet we must also not forget that such occasional instances of foolishness are only part of human character. However, even Dr. Johnson was good enough not to overlook the welcome qualities of the masque. After recounting all the foregoing faults of *Comus*, he himself writes that this "is a defect overbalanced by its convenience" (Johnson, 115). After all, he has at least one grudge against *Comus* that he will never swallow. He writes : "What deserves more reprehension is, that the prologue spoken in the wild wood by the attendant Spirit is addressed to the audience; a mode of communication so contrary to the nature of dramatic representation, that no precedents can support it" (Johnson, 115). Howbeit, we cannot forget the charm *Comus* presents us with, with its beautiful images, compelling rhetoric, distancing dance and music, and fairy-land-like locale. And, to conclude this chapter, *Comus* is the most sensuous of Milton's poems. Witness, for instance, the following lines of *Comus* (lines 752-755):

> What need a vermeil-tinctured lip for that,
> Love-darting eyes, or tresses like the morn?
> There was another meaning in these gifts;
> Think what, and be advised; you are but young yet.

6

MILTON : THE PAMPHLETEER

1

(ANTI-ROYAL AND ANTI-CLERICAL PAMPHLETS)

A very pertinent question may be raised at the very beginning: is it necessary to follow the pamphlets of Milton to understand Milton the poet ? The answer should be Yes and No. No, because Milton, the poet, is in his poetry, and in his pamphlet we will find only Milton, the politician; and because the beauty of poetry cannot be discovered in the demagogic prose. And yes, because the same person is at work behind both the poetry and the prose, and because Milton's prose is a diary of his foreshadowing spirit that he expressed in his mature poetry. One further reason of reading Milton's prose is that we are here interested not only in Milton, the poet, but also in Milton, the man, *i.e.*, in brief, we are interested in the course of the poetic development of Milton. However, Milton's period of pamphleteering began a little while after his return from his journey to Italy. In April 1658, he went to Italy, his dream-land, with a plan to visit Greece and some other countries on way. But the breaking out of the Civil War at home hurriedly called him back, in August 1659. As we have seen, he was a staunch anti-royalist and anti-clericist: anti-royalist, because he was a great votary of liberty; and anti-clericist, because he despised the on-going enormously corrupting practices within the churches. His pamphlets are his philippics against Charles I and his leg-licking entourage, and against the corrupted church-men that acted also as accomplices in Charles I's perpetration of tyranny on the laity.

Milton's prose works, which are but pamphlets or tracts, fall into two categories, as regards their language: the English prose works and the Latin prose works. The second category includes such works as *Tetrachordon, Colasterion, Eikonoklasts, Defensio pro Populo Anglicano*, etc. The other works are his English pamphlets. Though the title of *Areopagitica* is latinate, it happens to be an English prose work.

Some of his pamphlets he wrote in Latin, because he wanted these pamphlets to be read by the avant-garde class at home, which class then despised English, and also because he wanted these Latin pamphlets to be distributed in some of the European countries to rouse the sympathy of the people there — people who did not understand English, but only Latin, among foreign languages. Further, Milton wrote some of his pamphlets in Latin, because though by the 17th century, Latin was no more a *lingua franca*, it was still being used for serious corpuses by such great writers and thinkers as Bacon (*Novum Organum*) and Newton (*Principia Mathematica*). However, Milton's pamphlets, again, for convenience, may be divided into three broad groups: the anti-royal and anti-clerical pamphlets, the divorce pamphlets, and the pamphlets on education and freedom of press. All the phamphlets, taken together, show us the other but congruent side of Milton, the poet.

Milton's first pamphlet, *On Reformation in England*, was published in May-June 1641, and since then the poet wrote a series of pamphlets. The first series of pamphlets was directed against the corruptions in, and under the rule of, the church. This series of pamphlets was written between May 1641 and April 1642. It may be stated here that for a considerably long time, Milton had been nursing the hope of writing some dramatic works, perhaps he being enthused at the grand success of his dramatic piece, *Comus*, and perhaps since the success of the masque. Maybe, he wanted to begin his dramatic works just after returning home from Italy, but, coming home, he painfully saw the political drama being enacted at home, and he forthwith decided to participate in it, surcharged as he was with anti-royal and anti-clerical sentiments. This was why he suspended his poetic spirit for about 20 years. His hope of writing dramatic pieces also got seared, because all the theatre-houses were closed down in 1642 by royal orders. The cause of the closing down of the theatre-houses was the fear of the king that, as the Civil War had been raging if the theatre-houses remained open, these might have been turned into buffeting arenas. As there was no hope of presenting his proposed dramatic works in the foreseeable future, Milton turned to pamphleteering, and chose prose as the medium of his pamphlets. There was yet another cause of his turning to pamphleteering. In the smoldering animosity between the royalists and the anti-royalists, Milton found an opportunity of showing, and openly upholding, his political ideology; and so he preferred the medium of prose for his pamphlets, rather than that of poetry, because poetry is not the effective medium for raising public opinion. It was also for his great political verve of this period that he temporarily abandoned his plan of writing 'Histories of Britain and Moscovia'. Of course, long after this he wrote a few chapters on *The History of Britain*, and published it in 1670 under the title *The History of Britain*. He also wrote *The History of Moscovia* that was published posthumously in 1682 (Wordsworth Reference, 625). The Civil War, therefore, made Milton's plan of a literary life temporarily go topsy turfy.

The Civil War broke out between the Royalists, who wanted to uphold Charles I as the rightful monarch, and the anti-royalists, who included the Levellers, the Ranters, the Fifth Monarchists, the Regicides, and others. In his career of a pamphleteer, Milton was much influenced by the different but complementary ideologies of the diverse groups of the anti-royalists, and particularly by their various pamphlets. "A Leveller wanted a democratic republic in which the House of Commons was superior to the House of Lords (if there was one); he wanted redistribution and extension of the franchise, legal and economic reforms on behalf of men of small property — artisans, yeomen, small merchants — but not communism.... Levellers advocated democratization guilds and City government of London, decentralization of justice, election of local governors, stability of tenure of copyholders" (Hill, 29). But the Levellers "had no distinctive religious policy, apart from wanting toleration and abolition of tithes" (Hill, 30). Walwyn, a Leveller, published his pamphlet *The Compassionate Samaritane* in 1644 in which he pleaded for religious toleration. When the Levellers were crushed by the government, the Ranters, with almost the same objectives as the Levellers fought for, came into being. Coppe, a Ranter, wrote and published the pamphlet *John the Divines Divinity*, in 1649, in which he said "Scripture is not the Word of God. Only the spirit of God 'and his working in us is our Scripture and rule of life" (Hill, 43). Coppe wrote two other influential pamphlets: *Fiery Flying Rolls* and *Coppes Return to the Ways of Truth* (in 1650 and 1651, respectively). The Fifth Monarchists pleaded that the Parliament was the voice of God. In 1643, Edmund Calamy, a Fifth Monarchist, published his pamphlet *The Soldiers Pocket Bible*, in which he wrote that the Parliament's cause was God's cause. The Fifth Monarchists' two other important pamphlets were *A Standard Set Up* (1657) and *A Door of Hope* (1661). The Regicides also produced a number of influential pamphlets, such as *Union of Hearts* (1647), *What the Independents' World Have* (1647), *A Vindication of the Law* (1648), etc. Milton was much influenced by these groups of anti-royalists and their pamphlets, and, in turn, they and their pamphlets were influenced by Milton's pamphlets. But Milton was especially influenced by a small coterie of anti-monarchists, of which Edmund Ludlow (?1617-1692) was one. Ludlow held a millenarian view of the English Revolution, to wit the Civil War, and there were some similarities between him and Milton, regarding their politico-religious views. For instance, "Like Milton, he (Ludlow) held that God's people 'were full ripe for chastisement, in that they had not freedom nor will to improve those opportunities he had put into their hands (Hill,77). There was yet another anti-royalist, William Erbery (1604-1654), with whom Milton almost identified himself, politically. However, all these people greatly inspired Milton to write consecutive pamphlets. And there were still others of whom at least two should certainly be mentioned: one was William Sedgwick (?1610-1669) and the other was John Owen (1616-1683). Sedgwick published his pamphlet *Zions Deliverance*, in which he expressed his anti-royalist views in strongest terms. He wrote: " 'The Lord is at the call of his people's prayers...., Let us resolve to lay hold on God, to wrestle with him, and not to let him go till he hath given us the blessing' " (Hill, 98). Again, in his *Some Flashes of Lightnings of Sonne of Man* (1648), he wrote: ... The kingdom must be established in this earth... The kingdom of God is within you, in every one of you... It is breaking forth in every man. God is lifting himself up in the saints (Hill, 99). John Owen, a pillar of the Commonwealth, also imbued Milton in pamphletry. Milton's *The Reason of Church Government* and *Areopagitica* bear witness to this. And last, but, of course, not the least, Oliver Cromwell's (1599-1658) personality and political views certainly made a great impact on the mind of Milton. Cromwell inspired Milton to express his religio-political views in strongly worded tracts. Milton and Andrew Marvell (1621-1678) were mutually influential, politically — both nursed the same political view. Like Milton, Marvell, Dryden and Pepys were officials of the establishment of Cromwell. Henry Stubbe (1632-1676) was, like Milton, a supporter of parliamentary form of government, and he established himself as an influential pamphleteer. His *An Essay in Defence of the Good Old Cause* (1659) and *An Account of the Rise and Progress of Mahometanism* were very effective in stirring the sentiment of the people against the monarchy. All these and other men inspired Milton, directly or indirectly, to mould his mind in anti-monarchist stance, and to produce in quick succession a spate of anti-monarchist pamphlets.

The central theme of all his pamphlets, taken together, is liberty.

Whatever might be the occasion, or the specific issues he pleaded for, and, howmuchever, emphasis he might have put on anything else, what was at the back of his mind in turning out series of pamphlets was only one thing — liberty. His concept of liberty was expressed in three modes: religious and political; domestic; and that relating to education and press. Milton desired these three kinds of liberty because, according to him, these are inalienable from three sorts of happiness, or, rather from happiness in the three speheres in the life of a man — religious, domestic and civil. This is clear from what he writes in the introduction to his pamphlets on divorce : " 'When, therefore, I perceived that there were three species of liberty, which are essential to happiness of social life — religious, domestic and civil; and as I had already written concerning the first, and the magistrates were strenuously active in obtaining the third, I determined to turn my attention to the second, or the domestic species. As this seemed to involve three material questions, the condition of the conjugal tie, the education of the children, and the free publication of the thoughts, I made them objects of distinct consideration' " (Tillyard, 1956, 109).

With these three core objectives in view, from 1641 to 1660, the year in which the Commonwealth of Cromwell was declared dissolved, Milton continued to pour out, with breaks, a number of pamphlets, the most important of them being the following:

1641 :
- i. *On Reformation in England*
- ii. *Of Practical Episcopacy*
- iii. *Animadversions upon the Remonstrant's Defence*
- iv. *Reason of Church Government*

1642 : *Apology for Smectymnuus*

1643 : *Doctrine and Discipline of Divorce* (first edition)

1644 :
- i. *Doctrine and Discipline of Divorce* (second edition)
- ii. *On Education*
- iii. *Judgement of Martin Bucer concerning Divorce*
- iv. *Areopagitica*

1645 :
- i. *Tetrachordon*
- ii. *Colasterion*

1649 :
- i. *Tenure of Kings and Magistrates*
- ii. *Observations upon the Articles of Peace*
- iii. *Eikonoklasts*

1651 : *Defensio pro Populo Anglicano*

1654 : Defensio Secunda

1655 : i. *Defensio pro Se*
ii. *De Doctrina Christiana*

1659 : i. *Civil Powers in Ecclesiastical Causes*
ii. *Likeliest Means to remove Hirelings out of the Court*
iii. *On the Ruptures of the Commonwealth*

1660 : *Ready and Easy Way to establish a Free Commonwealth.*

Milton wrote more than two dozens of pamphlets, which, as we told earlier, may conveniently be divided into three categories: political and religious, or rather, anti-monarchist and anti-episcopal pamphlets; divorce pamphlets; and pamphlets on education and freedom of press. We shall, briefly, discuss about some of his important pamphlets following this classification, in the following sections of this chapter. But, before we do this, we must repeat that Milton, by nature, was never inclined towards the lowbrow profession of a pamphleteer, he being a born poet, and from his boyhood deliberately choosing the high career of a poet. It was only the particular pressing situation that initially turned his mind towards pamphletry. E.M.W. Tillyard writes in this regard: "Critics usually assume tacitly or explicitly that Milton was diverted to prose, a medium which he acknowledges to be not fully congenial, by events of the time, and that but for them he would not have written in prose at all. Further still, some assume that these events provided Milton's mind with most of the material for his prone works" (Tillyard, 1956,108). This is largely true, and Milton himself confirmed this when he wrote "of his pamphlets hitherto published as if they were an ordered consecutive exposition of the idea of liberty in the various spheres of life" (Tillyard, 1956, 109).

Milton returned from his brisk journey to Italy in 1639, on being informed of the Bishops' War, but he did not immediately sat for writing political pamphlets. The first Bishops' War took place in 1639, and it was followed by the second Bishops' War which took place in 1641. This second Bishops' War prompted him to write a pamphlet for the first time, in 1641, — the pamphlet which he entitled *On Reformation in England*. This pamphlet and his two others — *Of Practical Episcopacy* and *Animadversions upon the Remonstrant's Defence* — were published anonymously. In 1641, Milton published yet another tract, *Reason of Church Government* and this one was the first pamphlet that he published under his own name. *On Reformation in England* is full of political deducticism. In it he says that the governance of a state demands the dedication of no common man, but that of a divine soul: " 'It is a work good and prudent to be able to guide one man; of larger extended virtue to order well one house; but to govern a nation piously and justly, which only is to say happily is for a spirit of the greatest size, and divinest mettle' " (Tillyard, 1956, 119). Commenting on this pamphlet, E.M.W. Tillyard writes : "Milton's first prose work, *Reformation in England*, is, more purely than any other, the creation of a scholar and a poet. It is in the light of his long programme of historical studies that he argues against episcopacy. He seeks to prove that the original Reformation in England remained for various reasons incomplete: now is the time for its consummation. Episcopacy would have no historical ground in antiquity, being but a corruption of the earliest Christian practice. In the poetical quality of parts of its prose this pamphlet yields to none" (Tillyard, 1956, 126).

In the two pamphlets — *On Reformation in England* and *Reason of Church Government* (1641) — the influence of the Renaissance on Milton is very much conspicuous, for, in both the tracts, he eulogises individualism. It may be pointed out here that Milton never had any great respect for the people, or, rather, for the crowd — the crowd, to him, was a cabodle. He was out and out an individualist. Witness, for instance, what he writes about the public in *Paradise Lost* (Bk. III, 49-51):

> And what the people but a herd confused,
> A miscellaneous rabble, who extol
> Things vulgar, and, well weighed, scarce worth the praise?

Of course, Milton also did not treat the public as Herdenvolk, like Her Hitler; the contempt that was there in his heart for his contemporary public was only due to the fact that it consisted mostly of the leg-licking royalists. *On Reformation in England*, *Of Practical Episcopacy* and *Animadversion* — these three tracts were directed against the corrupted episcopacy. In *The Reason of Church Government*, Milton directed his broadside both against the church and the establishment, as he did in *On Reformation in England*. In the 'Introduction' to Book II of *The Reason of Church Government*, for instance, Milton gives vent to his volcanic ire against the " 'impertinent yoke of prelatry, under whose inquisitorious and tyrannical duncery no free and splendid wit can flourish' " (Hughes, 188). It may be mentioned here that Milton's anti-episcopal sentiment crystalised long ago; even in the head-note to 'Lycidas', which he wrote in 1637, he "foretells the ruin of our corrupted

Clergy". He was not suave and gentle in attacking the clergy and the king; he was violent and invective. Even long after the publication of this tract, Milton's hosted acrimony did not abate, and so in *Paradise Lost* (Bk. X, 186-189), he writes of "Spoiled Principalities and Powers, triumphed/In open show, and with ascension bright,/Captivity led captive through the Air,/The realm itself of Satan". Milton was hopeful that the on-going popular uprising would one day certainly be able to throw off the yoke imposed upon the people by the king and the church. E.M.W. Tillyard writes: "There was in the nature of Milton's hopes, as revealed in the anti-episcopal pamphlets, something the very reverse of sober. Allowing for the exaltation natural in the years 1640 to 1642, we have to admit that Milton had an unusually sanguine temperament exaggerated by an unusual ignorance of the nature of common humanity" (Tillyard, 1956, 120-121). As to the matter of episcopacy, Milton was never against the institution of the church; he was against only the unnecessary excesses of the church regulations and the rampant corruptions of the clergy.

Milton had a utopian idea of the state, and this is evident in his tract or pamphlet *Apology for Smectymnuus* (the word 'Smectymnuus' was coined by Milton, taking the initial letters of the names of five Puritan ministers, in the names of whom he wrote this pamphlet, rebutting the arguments of Bishop Joseph Hall of Exeter, expounded in Hall's pamphlet *Humble Remonstrance to the High Court of Parliament*) where he praises the utopian ideas of Plato and others: " 'That grave and noble invention, which the greatest and sublimest wits of sundry ages, Plato in *Critias*, and our two famous countrymen, the one in his *Utopia* [of St. Thomas More 1477-1535], the other in his *New Atlantis* [of Francis Bacon 1561-1626], chose, I may not say as a field, but as a mighty continent, wherein to display the largeness of their spirits, by teaching this our world better and exacter things then were yet known or used' " (Tillyard, 1956, 121). Milton was aware that it would not be possible for his contemporary countrymen to establish a utopia in England, but he was confident that with 'proper instruction' given to them, they would be able to found a utopia even in England, in some distant future. In *The Reason of Church Government*, he expresses his utmost confidence in the capability of his countryman: " 'And verily if we look at his native towardliness in the rough-cast without breeding, some nation or other may haply be better composed to a natural civility and right judgment than he. But if he gets the benefit once of a wise and well-rectified nurture, which must first come in general from the godly vigilance of the church, I suppose that wherever mention is made of countries, manners, or men, the English people, among the first that shall be praised, may deserve to be accounted a right pious, right honest, and right hardy nation' " (Tillyard, 1956, 121). Milton was a dreamer : he believed that such a 'right pious, right honest, and right hardy nation' must be able to found a utopia in England. He was somehow confident that "a new age is at hand" and that that new age will come from the benediction of God; and that the time was not far away when the corrupted church will be cleansed of all evils. Milton was, certainly, a veritable millenarian, and he expressed his confidence in the coming into being of a time in future when the church of England would look bright. In his *Apology for Smectymnuus*, he wrote: " 'And whereas at other times we count it ample honour when God vouchsafes to make man the instrument and subordinate worker of his gracious will, such acceptation have their prayers found with him, that to them he hath been pleased to make himself the agent and immediate performer, dissolving their difficulties when they are thought inexplicable, cutting out ways for them where no passage could be seen; as who is there so regardless of divine Providence, that from late occurances will not confess?... Whence only it is that I have not feared, though many wise men have miscarried in praising great designs before the utmost event, because I see who is their assistant, who their confederate, who hath engaged his omnipotent arm to support and crown with success their faith, their fortitude, their just and magnanimous actions, till he has brought to pass all that expected good which, his servants trust, is in his thoughts to bring upon this land in the full and perfect reformation of his church' " (Tillyard, 1956, 122-123).

Milton, fervently, appealed to God, or, rather invoked the power of God for bringing into England that state of utopia. In *Animadversion upon the Remonstrant's Defence*, he worte: "'O perfect and accomplish thy glorious acts! for men may leave their works unfinished, but thou art a God, thy nature is perfection: shouldst thou bring us thus far onward from Egypt to destroy us in this wilderness, though we deserve, yet thy great name would suffer in the rejoicing of thine enemies, and the deluded hope of all thy servants. When thou hast settled peace in the church and righteous judgment in the kingdom, then shall all thy saints address their voices of joy and triumph to thee, standing on the shore of that Red Sea into which our enemies had almost driven us' " (Tillyard, 1956, 123). Milton aspired to be a great poet of the new age, by the grace of God, and so he prayed to him to grant him the power of a great poet, so that he could sing his (God's) praise for generations to come. In the same tract, to wit, in *Animadversions upon the Remonstrant's Defence*, he again wrote : " 'And he [Milton himself] that now for haste snatches up a plain ungarnished present as a thank-offering to thee [God], which could not be deferred in regard of thy so many late deliverances wrought for us one upon another, may then perhaps take up a harp, and sing thee an elaborate song to generations' " (Tillyard, 1956, 123). However, in this pamphlet, Milton fiercely attacked Joseph Hall who strongly supported the episcopal cause.

Milton was also an out and out anti-monarchist, and he never did budge even an inch from his anti-monarchist stance. He was an anti-monarchist because he believed in democracy, and because he hated tyranny : he could not tolerate the idea that a single man would govern over a multitude of men. In *Paradise Lost* (Book XII, lines 69-70) he says that God did not want that a man be a lord to another: "but man over men/ He made not lord". A few lines afterwards, in the same epic, Milton alludes to the lack of moral uprightness and liberty in his contemporary England, due to the corrupt reign of Charles I (lines 97-101):

> Yet sometimes nations will decline so low
> From virtue, which is reason, that no wrong,
> But justice, and some fatal curse annexed,
> Deprives them of their outward liberty,
> Their inward lost;

And, once again, in the same Book (lines 517-518) of the same epic, Milton speaks of the spiritual coloration of the corrupt rule of the king: "Secular power, though feigning still to act/By spiritual". However, after the execution of Charles I, the people, in general, revised their opinion about the executed king, and turned sympathetic to him, but Milton, without swerving from his earlier stand, boldly supported the execution, and, further, pooh-poohed the soft sentimentality of the people. For instance, in *The Tenure of Kings and Magistrates*, he strongly vituperated the people for revising and softening their opinion about the executed king: " 'But certainly, if we consider who and what they are, on a sudden grown so pitiful, we may conclude their pity can be no true and Christian commiseration, but either *levity and shallowness of mind, or else a carnal admiring of that worldly pomp and greatness from whence they see him* [Charles I] *fallen*' " (emphasis added) (Tillyard, 1956, 181). It may be mentioned here that some critics have found a parallel to the phrase 'levity and shallowness of mind' in the characters of Adam and Eve in *Paradise Lost* — 'levity and shallowness of mind' are the causes of their Fall. The opposition to tyranny that we find in the same epic may also be found in this tract: " 'If men within themselves would be governed by reason and not generally give up their understanding to a double tyranny, of custom from without and blind affection from within, they would discern better what it is to favour and uphold the tyrant of a nation' " (Tillyard, 1956, 181).

After the Commonwealth was established in 1649 under the leadership of Cromwell, Milton was appointed Secretary for Foreign Tongues to the Council of State. At that time, the people of Ireland and, particularly, the Ulster royalists could not see the Commonwealth as a justifiable institution, and so they grumbled. Milton, vehemently, attacked the recalcitrancy of these people in his pamphlet *Observation upon the Article of Peace with the Irish Rebels*. Milton was a devoted worshipper of liberty, and he attacked these people because they stood in the way of liberty. Whatever went to suppress liberty Milton deeply hated. This sentiment of Milton is also expressed in his *Areopagitica*, about which we shall discuss in the last section of this chapter. Here we only say that in *Areopagitica* Milton felt nostalgic about the old England, and wrote that once in the olden days England led the whole of Europe in the fields of arts, science and theology, but now " 'as our obdurate clergy have with violence demeaned the matter, we are become hitherto the latest and the backwardest scholars, of whom God offered to have made us the teachers' " (Hughes, 177-178). So, even in *Areopagitica* which was intended principally for freedom of the press, we find that Milton inveighed the clergy for ruining the country. In the same tract, Milton, perhaps, summarised the whole argument of the tract in one single term — liberty: " 'Give me the liberty to know, to utter, and to argue freely according to conscience, above all liberties' " (Hughes, 182). This sentiment of Milton dominates at least the earlier Books of *Paradise Lost*, through the agency of Satan.

This venerating sentiment of Milton towards liberty — and this time the sentiment was even more intense — was expressed in *Defensio Secunda* that was published in 1654, three or four years before Milton began his first epic. According to E.M.W. Tillyard, *Defensio Secunda* is "one of the greatest of the world's rhetorical writings" (Tillyard, 1956, 192-193). Concerning the similarity of tone and argument between *Defensio Secunda* and *Paradise Lost*, Tillyard again writes: "None can be more precise and say that *Defensio Secunda* and the first two books or so of *Paradisė Lost* are closely akin in their temper. *Paradise Lost* as a whole is pervaded by a pessimism not found in the prose work, a pessimism which resulted (to anticipate a little) from the course of political events leading up to the Restoration. But the earlier books are less pervaded by this spirit than the latter. I feel confident from internal evidence that they were shaping themselves in Milton's mind about the time of *Defensio Secund*, and that, howover modified, they never quite lost the original brightness of the time of reviving hopes. But there is external evidence too connecting *Defensio Secunda* with *Paradise Lost*, nor is the internal evidence confined to a general similarity of tone" (Tillyard, 1956, 194). Saura and Tillyard further think that the 'theme' of overcoming oneself is present in both the works. That Milton held Cromwell very hing in estimation is to a large extent due to the fact that Cromwell could "conquer himself" (Tillyard, 1956, 196). However, the beauty of the Latin prose of *Defensio Secunda* is captivating. E.M.W. Tillyard writes about this: "The way Milton makes the Latin language obey him, rousing it to eloquence, subduing it to plainness, hushing it to a poetical serenity, or goading it to the brutalities of his satire, is astonishing" (Tillyard, 1956, 198). The tract *Defensio Secunda* is great not only for its beautiful prose but also for its convincing arguments. In it Milton argues for the continuance of the liberty achieved after the execution of Charles I, with all pusillanimity: " 'Do you then, sir, continue your course with the same unrivalled magnanimity; it sits well upon you; — to you our country owes its liberties; nor can you sustain a character at once more momentous and more august than that of the author, the guardian, and the preserver of our liberties; and hence you have not only eclipsed the achievements of all our kings, but even those which have been fabled of our heroes....; and lastly, revere yourself; and, having endured so many sufferings and encountered so many perils for the sake of liberty, do not suffer it, now it is obtained, either to be violated by yourself, or in any one instance impaired by others' " (Tillyard, 1956, 199).

Milton was, perhaps, to an extent, like the legendary hero Robin Hood who committed thefts for benefits of the poor. Robin Hood, the outlawed hero only "triumphed over the corrupt forces of law and order" (Wordsworth Reference, 789), as Milton fought only against the corruptions of the church, and never against the sacred church itself. Milton's anti-episcopal verve was not exhausted in his anti-episcopal tracts, but it split into *Paradise Lost*, where his aversion and sarcastic attitude towards the on-going corrupt practices of the church is obliquely expressed. For instance, in *Paradise Lost* (Book IV, lines 187-192), where Satan jumps over the palisade around Eden, the dwelling place of Adam and Eve, the poet compares Satan with a thief, and thus gives us a picture of the social condition of his time in England as well as of the churchmen who, he says, were no better than thieves:

> Leaps o'er the fence with ease into the fold;
> Or as a thief, bent to unhoard the cash
> Of some rich burgher, whose substantial
> Cross-barred and bolted fast, fear no assault,
> In the window climbs, or o'er the tiles;
> So climb this first grand Thief into God's fold :

In achieving what he wanted to achieve — puritanism and liberty — Milton was always ready, if need arose, to resort even to hatred. In *De Doctrina Christiana*, he said that some amount of hatred was necessary even for one who wanted to be religious. He wrote in *De Doctrina Christiana* : " 'some hatred... is a religious duty, as when we hate the enemies of God and of the Church' " (Hall, 315). This conviction of Milton, that religion also asks us to hate, — to hate God's enemies — is well evident in *Paradise Lost* (Book VI, lines 734-735) where Christ tells God: "whom thou hat'st I hate, and can put on/Thy terrors, as I put thy mildness on".

2
(THE DIVORCE PAMPHLETS)

As we have said, Milton married his first wife, Mary Powell, very hastily in May-June 1643, and in July or August of the same year Powell left her husband's house for her father's house, with the intention never to return. Milton was as much shocked as he had never been, and his first divorce tract *Doctrine and Discipline of Divorce* was anonymously published on August 1, 1643. The near simultaneity of these two events has prompted some commentators to hazard the assumption that Milton's shock from his unconsummated first marriage caused him to find reasons in divorce, and to write the pamphlet *Doctrine and Discipline of Divorce*. There is reason, no doubt, in such an assumption. According to Pattison, Milton was not quite happy with his first marriage, because Mary refused Milton "the consummation of marriage" (Tillyard, 1956, 141). Saurat goes further. He writes: " 'But the young woman's refusal gave Milton the first great shock of his life. He saw at once his irreparable mistake. He found himself placed in a dilemma intolerable both to his purity and his pride. Psychical passion had been roused in him, and then thwarted; he was not really married, and he was now forbidden to get married. His highest ideal, that of love as a harmony between body and spirit, was at once shattered and soiled. And the cause of this painful degradation was the blind impulse of the flesh. Hence, the anger against the mistrust of the flesh which remained, under his more liberal general ideas, all through his life. The flesh will play an essential part in the Fall [of Paradise Lost]' " (Tillyard, 1956, 141). But other commentators refuse to come to the same conclusion. They say that to Milton liberty was something next only to God, and he wanted liberty not only in the political sphere, but also in two other vital spheres : religious and domestic. They say that Milton supported the institution of divorce with cool rationality: he believed that neither the wife should be a bond slave to her husband, nor *vice versa*. These commentators believe that Mary Powell's running away from Milton's home was not the reason of his writing *Doctrine and Discipline of Divorce*, because they, like E.M.W. Tillyard, believe that he wrote the tract even while Mary Powell had been "still in his house" (Tillyard, 1956, 140)

However, in *Doctrine and Discipline of Divorce* Milton argued for two things: man's superiority over women, and the superiority of the spiritual over the physical in a marriage tie. The former view he, perhaps, got from the Hebrew tradition and belief system. According to Milton, the chief aim of marriage should be refreshment — physical, but principally mental — of the husband by the wife: " 'the apt and cheerful conversation of man with woman to comfort and refresh him against the evil of solitary life' " (Tillyard, 1956, 148). The third point Milton argued for in this pamphlet was concerning the mode of marriage. He had all contempt for arranged marriage, for, in it, he argued, the freedom of the couples is attenuated, or sacrificed altogether. And forced marriage he forcefully denounced. In *Doctrine and Discipline of Divorce*, he wrote: " 'As for the custom that some parents and guardians have of forcing marriages, it will be better to say nothing of such a savage inhumanity, but only this; that the law which gives not all freedom of divorce to any creature endued with reason so associated, is next in cruelty' " (Tillyard, 1956, 148).

Milton sometimes faced difficulties when he upheld the 'nature' or 'rationality' of human beings over and above the prescriptions and proscriptions of the Scriptures. But when he faced such difficulties, he stuck to his supreme ideal of humanity, a worshipper of humanity as he had been. In *Doctrine and Discipline of Divorce*, he wrote: " 'Yet thus much I shall insist on, that whatever the institution wore, it could not be so enormous, nor so rebellious against both nature and reason, as to exalt itself above the end and person for whom it was instituted' " (Tillyard, 1956, 149). In another passage of the same tract, Milton also said that even the supernatural injunctions of Christ, as these were ordinarily expounded, were not binding upon human beings — injunctions regarding continuity of marriage tie in disregard of the non-existence of real love in the couple, and in disregard of all reasons: " 'This saying of Christ, as it is usually expounded, can be no law at all, that a man for no cause should separate but for adultery, except it be a supernatural law, not binding us as we are now. Had it been the law of nature, either the Jews, or some other wise and civil nation, would have pressed it: or let it be so, yet that law, Deut. XXIV. 1, whereby a man hath leave to part, when as for just and natural cause discovered he cannot love, is a law ancienter and deeper engraven in blameless nature than the other' " (Tillyard, 1956, 149). Milton, sometimes, seems to take the side of the Scriptures, and, sometimes the side of 'nature' or 'reason', but, ultimately, he reconciles the two extremities by believing that the two are complementary, and not antagonistic. However, in *Doctrine and Discipline of Divorce*, to tell it briefly, Milton said that marriage tie should continue only as long as love between the partners continued, and so when love disappeared, it was better to dissolve the marriage knot. He deemed the marriage knot to be a 'covenant' and thought that the strength or force of the covenant did not rest on 'forced cohabitation' or on 'counterfeit performance of duties', but only on 'unfeigned love and peace'. And so a loveless matrimony was, to him, an 'empty husk' and a 'kind of hypocrisy'.

As we have said, *Doctrine and Discipline of Divorce* was written and published in 1643. The popularity of this pamphlet can be guessed from the fact that it had its second edition just in the next year, when virtually no change was made in the matter of the tract. In the same year, *i.e.* in 1644, Milton wrote another divorce tract, *Judgment of Martin Bucer concerning Divorce*. It is a minor tract having almost nothing new than in the former tract. Milton's last two important divorce tracts are: *Tetrachordon* and *Colasterion*. Both of these two tracts were written in March, 1645. The word 'tetrachordon' derives from two Greek words: 'tetra', meaning 'four', and 'cordon', meaning 'cords' or 'strings'. Hence, by the title of the tract *Tetrachordon*, Milton, perhaps, meant 'closely woven' (marriage knot). When published, the tract found prospective buyers standing askance at its queer title. Milton observed this and indignantly wrote a sonnet, 'A book was writ of late' :

A book was writ of late called *Tetrachordon*;
And woven close, both matter, form and style;
The subject new: it walked the town awhile,
Numbering good intellects; now seldom pored on.
Cries the stall-reader, Bless us ' what a word on
    A title-page is this ' And some in file
    Stand spelling false, while one might walk to Mile-
    End Green. Why is it harder sirs than Gordon,
Colkitto, or Macdonnel, or Galasp?
    Those rugged names to our like mouths grew sleek
    That would have made Quintilian stare and gasp.
Thy age, like ours, O soul of Sir John Cheke,
    Hated not learning worse than toad or asp;
    When thou taught'st Cambridge, and King Edward Greek.

However, in *Tetrachordon*, Milton spoke with sighs about 'the very joys of harmonious wedlock' which his fate denied him. The beauty and joy of a perfect wedlock Milton again narrates in *Paradise Lost* (Book IV, lines 300-311) :

His fair large front and eye sublime declared
Absolute rule; and hyacinthine locks
Round from his parted fore-lock manly hung
Clustered, but not beneath his shoulders broad:
She, as a veil down to the slender waist,
Her unadorned golden tresses wore
Dishevelled, but in wanton ringlets waved
As the vine curls her tendrils, which implied
Subjection, but required with gentle sway,
And by her yielded, by him best received,
Yielded with coy submission, modest pride,
And sweet, reluctant, amorous delay.

In *Tetrachordon*, Milton proved the injustifiability of the existing divorce provisions which permitted separations of the couple only on grounds of physical disharmony between them, ignoring grounds far more potent and, therefore, far more justifiable: the grounds relating to mental disharmony between the spouses. In this tract, Milton's arguments were very strongly put forth: " 'This I amaze me at, that though all the superior and nobler ends both of marriage and of the married persons be absolutely frustrate, the matrimony stirs not, loses no hold, remains as rooted as the centre but if the body bring but in a complaint of frigidity, by that cold application only this adamantine Alp of wedlock has leave to dissolve; which else all the machination of religious or civil reason at the suit of a distressed mind, either for divine worship or human conversation violated, cannot unfasten. What courts of concupiscence are these, wherein fleshy appetite is heard before right reason, lust before love or devotion? They may be pious Christians altogether, they may be loving and friendly, they may be helpful to each other in the family, but they cannot couple; that shall divorce them, though either party would not. They can neither serve God together, nor one be at peace with the other, nor be good in the family one to other; but live as they were dead, or live as they were deadly enemies in a cage together: it is all one, they can couple, they shall not divorce till death, no, though this sentence be their death. What is this besides tyranny, but to turn nature upside down, to make both religion and the mind of man wait upon the slavish errands of the body, and not the body to follow either the sanction or the sovereignty of the mind, unspeakably, wronged, and with all equity complaining? what is this but to abuse the sacred and mysterious bet of marriage to be the compulsive sty of an ungrateful and malignant lust, stirred up only from a carnal acrimony, without either love or peace, or regard to any other thing holy or human?' " (Tillyard, 1956, 163-164).

In *Tetrachordon*, to emphasise the rationality and necessity of divorce, Milton partially denied the biblical story that the woman was created by God out of a rib of the man — the story which he himself enshrined in *Paradise Lost* (Book VIII, lines 465-471) :

> From thence a rib, with cordial spirits warm,
> And life-blood streaming fresh; wide was the wound,
> But suddenly with flesh filled up and healed.
> The rib he formed and fashioned with his hands;
> Under his forming hands a creature grew,
> Man-like, but different sex,

In *Tetrachordon*, Milton wrote : " 'That there was a nearer alliance between Adam and Eve, than could be ever after between man and wife, is visible to any. For no other woman was ever moulded out of her husband's rib' " (Tillyard, 1956, 165). And thus Milton revised the precept of St. Paul: "wives, be subject to your husbands." Hereby Milton emancipated the wife from the tyranny of the husband, as he released the husband from the slavish bond of tyrannical wedlock that was not sanctified with heavenly love and peace. Milton's another divorce tract, *Colasterion*, had nothing new to say than in *Tetrachordon* :

it is only a "dreary piece of invective" against unholy, unwanted, and tyrannical wedlock.

In his divorce tracts, Milton vowed to be all rational, but in fact he was always swayed by the intensity of his sentiment and by his half-opinionated judgments. Again, in his divorce tracts or pamphlets, he wanted to believe in the rationality of human beings, but he actually believed against his beliefs. He knew that human beings were not so rational, and yet, in his pamphlets he continued to argue very rationally. This self-deception made him disillusioned, as is evident in his sonnet 'On the detraction which followed upon my writing certain treatises' where he writes :

I did but prompt the age to quit their clogs
 By the known rules of ancient liberty,
 When straight a barbarous noise environs me
Of owls and cuckoos, asses, apes and dogs.

3
(ON EDUCATION AND FREEDOM OF PRESS)

Milton's pamphlet *Of Education* was addressed to his friend Hartlib, and was published in June 1644. Unlike the majority of his pamphlets on other topics, *Of Education* is suave. We have seen that in the divorce tracts, for instance, he banked for his messages or ideas upon the rationality of man, but there, in fact, he was deceiving himself, because the rationality was to him only a thing to be wished for. But in *Of Education*, Milton had firm conviction in the rationality of man. However, about the ideal of education, he wrote : " 'I call, therefore, a complete and generous education, that which fits a man to perform justly, skilfully, and magnanimously all the offices, both private and public, of peace and war' " (Tillyard, 1956, 153). In this tract, Milton showed his hatred for the existing educational system. E.M.W. Tillyard writes: "There is the same hatred of mere antiquarianism, of irrelevant dialectical subtleties, of unrelated fact in general, and of the state of learning at the Universities. His contempt for mere linguistic knowledge is typical of his whole way of thinking" (Tillyard, 1956, 153-154). Milton formed his ideal of education out of his studies at school (St. Paul's) and his brief experience as a private tutor. He "advocated a remarkably extensive regimen for the religious, intellectual and physical training of boys as responsible citizens" (Wordsworth Reference, 624). In *Of Education*, the influence of the Renaissance on Milton is quite evident. According to E.M.W. Tillyard, "Of all the prose works [of

Milton] *On Education* is the only one that could be called charming" (Tillyard, 1956, 155).

Areopagitica was Milton's reaction to the Printing Ordinance of 1643, which was intended for ruthless censoring and banning of books. In the tract, Milton wrote: " 'Many man lives a burden to the earth; but a good book is the precious life-blood of a master spirit, embalmed and treasured up on purpose to a life beyond life' " (Hughes, 174). *Areopagitica* is pithy, and at the same time vibrant and mature in its arguments. It is Milton's 'chief song of hope' and is "a definite development of ideas towards *Paradise Lost*". Like *Of Education*, this tract also shows the influence of the Renaissance on Milton. E.M.W. Tillyard writes about this tract: "*Areopagitica* is the best of Milton's English prose works, because it expresses more of his mind than of any other. It is also the summit of one period of his development, comparable to *Lycidas* which was at once the crowning poem of Milton's youth and the promise of what aught to have followed" (Tillyard, 1956, 156). In *Areopagitica*, we see the on-going controversy between the Republicans and the Royalists. In this tract or pamphlet, Milton speaks in the person of Isocrates (436-358 B.C.), the Platonic philosopher, and successor and contemporary of Plato. Not only Isocrates' but also Plato's influence on Milton is evident here. The tract was occasioned, as we have said, by the passing of the bill in the Parliament requiring that all publications must be censored by a specially constituted body. In violation of this Act, Milton published a tract, and consequently he was called upon to justify his behaviour. It was in reply to this call of the Parliament that Milton wrote *Areopagitica*. And it was for this reason that he, in this tract, addressed the 'Lords and Commons of England' (of the Parliament). After the submission of *Areopagitica*, why we do not know, the Parliament dropped the case against Milton. The full title of this tract is *Areopagitica, a Speech of John Milton for the Liberty of Unlicensed Printing, to the Parliament of England*. The purpose and the theme of the tract is conspicuous in the full title of the tract. In it, Milton very puissantly supported the cause of freedom of thought and expression. A paragraph of the tract may be quoted below, to partially show the strength of the argument, the rhetorical skill, and the beauty of the language of the tract: "What should ye do then, should ye suppress all this flowery crop of knowledge and new light sprung up and yet springing daily in this city, should ye set an oligarchy of twenty engrossers over it, to bring a famine upon our minds again, when we shall know nothing but what is measured to us by their bushel? Believe it, Lords and Commons, they who counsel ye to such a suppressing do as good as bid ye suppress yourselves; and I will soon show how. If it be desired to know the immediate cause of all this free writing and free speaking, there cannot be assigned a truer than your own mild and free and human government; it is liberty, Lords and Commons, which your own valorous and happy counsels have purchased us, liberty which is the nurse of all great wits; this is that which hath rarefied and enlightened our spirits like the influence of heaven; this is that which hath enfranchised, enlarged and lifted up our apprehensions degrees above themselves. He cannot make us now less capable, less knowing, less eagerly pursuing of the truth ye first make yourselves, that made us so, less the lovers, less the founders of our true liberty. We can grow ignorant again, brutish, formal, and slavish, as ye found us; but you then must first become that which ye cannot be, oppressive, arbitrary, and tyrannous, as they were from whom ye have freed us. That our hearts are now more capacious, our thoughts more erected to the search and expectation of greatest and exactest things, is the issue of your own virtue propagated in us; ye cannot supress that unless ye reinforce an abrogated and merciless law, that fathers may dispatch at will their own children. And who shall then stick closest to ye, and excite others? Not he who takes up arms for coat and conduct and his four nobles of Danegelt. Although I despise not the defence of just immunities, yet love my peace better, if that were all. Give me the liberty to know, to utter, and to argue freely according to conscience, above all liberties." This is a fine piece of rhetorical speech and the rest of the tract is no less attractive than this. Hardin Craig writes about *Areopagitica*: "*Areopagitica* is Milton's greatest prose work and has become in Britain and America the original document on the subject of the freedom of speech and the press. His [Milton's] style in at least part of the address is the acme of the prose style of that eloquent age; not Browne or Taylor or Donne or Bacon ever surpassed it" (Craig, 244). Frederick B. Artz has found not only *Areopagitica* full of beautiful prose passages, but all the prose tracts of Milton containing these. Artz writes about the prose period or pamphleteering period of Milton: "The prose of this period is polemical and uneven, but full of passages of a soaring eloquence, as in *Areopagitica*, where he combines the loftiest majesty of style with real exultation of spirit" (Artz, 197). However, besides these pamphlets, Milton's prose works include also some other political and religious tracts and a few non-descript tracts. These political tracts include *Defence of Himself* (1655) and *Of True Religion* (1673). In

1670, Milton published his *The History of Britain*, and his *The History of Musocovia* was posthumously published in 1682. Milton's political and religious pamphlets once raised a great controversy, and this may prove the great influence of his pamphlets. But he himself had no great opinion about the worth of his own pamphlets: "He considered his pamphlets works of his 'left hand' merely" (Wordsworth Reference, 625).

7

PARADISE LOST

1
(INTRODUCTION)

It is, generally, agreed that it was during his visit to Italy that Milton thought of writing an epic; but he dithered for a long time, and then vacillated between an Arthurian theme and a biblical theme for his epic; and then only at long last, when his wished-for Republic proved a fiasco and he became purblind (his blindness began to grow around 1652), he, finally, chose a biblical theme for his long-awaited epic, *Paradise Lost.* The signs of loosing the Republic and his sight might have prompted him to think about something precious but lost. When, actually, Milton began writing this epic we do not know for certain. According to Christopher Hill, "Milton started *Paradise Lost* in about 1658 and finished it in 1665" (Hill, 15). But he planned writing an epic long ago. E.M.W. Tillyard writes: "Taken together, the passages from the *Sixth Elegy* and the *Apology for Smectymnuus* make it highly probable that about Christmas 1629 Milton made a mental dedication of himself to the high calling of epic poet" (Tillyard, 1956, 40). Or, if we like, we may say that even at the very young age of 19 (in 1628), Milton thought of writing an epic, and expressed this wish in his 'At a Vacation Exercise': "Such as the wise Demodocus once told/In solemn songs at king Alcinous' feast."

When this great English epic, *Paradise Lost*, was published in 1667, it contained 10 Books, *i.e.* the epic was divided into 10 Books, and not 12, and then, no Book of it was preceded by an 'Argument', as we find it today. In 1674, the second edition of the epic was brought out, and this time it was divided into 12 Books, and each Book was preceded by an 'Argument', supposedly written by Milton himself. The philosophy, ethics and religious consciousness of the epic, as well as the 'mentality' of the poet while composing it can be traced out in his earlier writings — poetic and prose — particularly in *Defensio Secunda*.

E.M.W. Tillyard writes: "... *Defensio Secunda* is very largely the mentality of *Paradise Lost*. One can be more precise and say that *Defensio Secunda* and the first two books or so of *Paradise Lost* are largely akin in their temper" (Tillyard, 1956, 194).

Milton chose the story of Genesis (of the Bible) as the theme of *Paradise Lost* the story that includes the great design of God, the disobedience shown to him by Satan, the tempting of Eve by Satan as an act of revenge towards God, and the Fall of Man. Through the narration of the story, Milton wanted to "justify the ways of God to men." The theme of the epic is enormously vast, and it includes heaven, hell, the whole creation of the universe, and, perhaps, everything conceivable. More than three centuries before Milton, Dante Alighieri (1265–1321) dared to handle so vast a theme, in his *Divine Comedy* (Dante himself simply called it *La Commedia* or *The Comedy*). In his epic, Milton wanted to rival the Greek poet Homer's (probably 8th c. B.C.) *Iliad* and *Odyssey*, and the Roman epic poet 'Virgil's (70–19 B.C.) *Aeneid*, though, in his epic he followed their footsteps. He got from them such techniques as of invocation, elaborate similes, flash-back, involved expression, etc. that went to enrich his epic very highly. It is, really, awe-inspiring and pathetic to think that, being purblind, Milton had to depend completely on his unwilling daughters', and sometimes on his wife's, help in taking down his dictations of the epic. How many emendations were necessary, how many references he had to look for, how many sittings with unwilling hands were necessary during a period of over seven years, and yet Milton was relentless! It was really a very hard and difficult task for him, even if we forget the tension of a poet during the time of the composition of such a great poetry, but Milton succeeded greatly.

It may not be out of place to think here over what actually makes a poem an epic. What makes a poem an epic is difficult to say, because the concept of the epic has undergone a number of metamorphoses. Further, critics and commentators are sometimes sharply divided among themselves as to the essential qualities of a poem that may go into making it an epic. Some of them emphasise those qualities which are related to the content of the poem, such as the vastness of its theme, the loftiness of its ideals, the complexity of its plot, the length of the poem, the supernatural elements, the prophecy innuendoed in it, etc. On the other hand, some give more emphasis on its style: the heroic metre (the hexametre or, as in later epics, the pentametre), beginning *in media res* (*i.e.* beginning from about the middle of the story or the plot, and then narrating earlier episodes by flash-back method), presages (narrating later episodes by flash-forward method), epic similes, mythological references, etc. However, according to F.L. Lucas, the 'essential epic qualities' are: " 'Unity of action, rapidity, the art of beginning in the middle; the use of the supernatural, of prophecy, of the underworld; the ornamental simile, the recurrent epithet; and above all, a nobility truthful, unstrained, incomparable except at moments in the sages of the north' " (Merchant, vii). But some critics are not happy with only these qualities of the epic: they say that the epic must chronicle some principal events, customs, traditions, and the *geist* or spirit of some race, as *Iliad* and *Odyssey* have done, in addition to having all the above qualities. It is for the reason that the epic deals with some principal events, customs, of a race that the epic is sometimes also called 'book of the tribe'.

The definition of epic, as we have said, has changed down the ages, and yet, even today, the chronicling feature of the epic is maintained to be its principal feature. Ezra Pound, for instance, in his *A B C of Reading*, has defined epic thus: " 'An epic is a poem including history' " (Merchant, 1). Paul Merchant has identified two vital features of an epic: 'surpassing the dimension of reality' (as it is an imaginative art of the highest degree) and 'including history' (as Pound demands). But Paul Merchant points out three more characteristic features of an epic: 'scale', 'mass', and 'weight'. The epic must be of a very vast scale or dimension, *i.e.* its scope of movement must be enormous. For instance, the scale of *Paradise Lost* ranges from heaven to hell, and includes the world and even the Chaos. Secondly, the epic contains a huge amount of the 'mass' of great incidents; for instance, *Paradise Lost* narrates the battle of Satan with God, birth of Adam and Eve, Satan's tempting of Eve, etc. And thirdly, the epic has the heavy 'weight' of sublime thoughts and emotions; for instance, *Paradise Lost* arouses within us the sublime thoughts of the greatness of God, the justifiability of the apparently incongruent acts of him, the ideals of good life, etc.

The epic originated in the antiquity. It originated at a time when it was not possible even to write it down, and so it continued to be handed down to successive generations through oral tradition, through songs of minstrels, scopes, etc. The blind poet Homer, for example, used to sing his epic *Iliad* from door to door, they say, for earning a living. Such epics are known as 'oral', 'primitive' or 'primary' epics. The Babylonian epic *Gilgamesh* (c 2700 B.C.), Homer's *Iliad* and *Odyssey*, *Beowulf*, etc. are primary epics (it was only long after their origination or composition that these were written down). On the other hand, those epics which are modelled on the old or primary epics, are known as secondary or literary epics. This is one difference between the primary epic and the secondary epic. There is another difference between the two. The primary epic was first orally transmitted; it was not written down as soon as it was composed. On the other hand, the secondary or literary epic is written down from the very beginning of its composition. Ovid's *Metamorphoses*, Lacan's *Pharsalia* (1 A.D.); Vyasa's *Mahabharata*; Valmiki's *Ramayana*; Dante's *Divina Commedia* (c. 1310), Langland's *Piers Plowman* and Chaucer's *Canterbury Tales* (if these two can be treated as epics); Spenser's *Faerie Queene*; and Milton's *Paradise Lost* and *Paradise Regained* are instances of secondary or literary epics. By the by, we may, if we choose, call *Paradise Lost* and *Paradise Regained* oral epics, in as much as the blind poet dictated the two epics. Paul Merchant has called *Paradise Lost* an 'oral epic' (Merchant, 58), and by the same token, *Paradise Regained* may also be called an 'oral epic'. The primary epics have some common features, such as : they deal with heroic figures of supernatural calibres; they use supernatural elements for embellishments and heightening; they employ epic or Homeric or extended similes, kennings, long speeches, digressions; and they maintain althrough a lofty tone; and all these are shared by the secondary epics as well.

Nevertheless, the primary epics have some special features. C.S. Lews, in his *A Preface to Paradise Lost*, writes : "The most obvious characteristic or technique is its continual use of stock words, phrases, or even whole lines.... In 103 lines of the parting between Hector and Andromache (justly regarded as one of the peaks of European poetry) phrases, or whole lines, which occur again and again in Homer are twentyeight times employed (*Il.* VI, 390-493). Roughly speaking, a *quarter* of the whole passage is 'stock'. In Beowulf's last speech to Wiglaf (Beow. 2794-820) 'stock' expressions occur six times in twentyeight lines — again there are about a quarter of the whole" (Lews, 20). The primary epics had some distant advantages in drawing the attention of the people: the special robes of the minstrels, the solemn atmosphere in which those epics were sung, the occasional feats along with the singing of the epics, etc. All these added to the favourable mood of the audience of the epic. But as the secondary epic, which was first began by Virgil, in the European countries, lacks in all these helpful ancillaries, the poet of the secondary epic has to depend largely on imaginative substitutes to achieve the favourable mood as well as also 'grandeur' and 'elevation'. The poet of the secondary epic also uses some other techniques, and most of these techniques or means have been used by Milton in his *Paradise Lost*. C.S. Lews writes about Milton's techniques of achieving 'grandeur' and 'elevation': "As far as Milton is concerned (...) this grandeur is produced mainly by three things: (1) The use of slightly unfamiliar words and constructions, including archaisms. (2) The use of proper names, not solely nor chiefly for their sound, but because they are the names of splendid, remote, terrible, voluptuous, or celebrated things. They are there to encourage a sweep of the reader's eye over the richness and variety of the world — to supply that *largior aether* which we breathe as long as the poem lasts. (3) Continued allusion to all the sources of heightened interest in our sense experience (light, dark storm, flowers, jewels, sexual love, and the like), but all over-topped and 'managed' with an air of magnanimous austerity. Hence, comes the feeling of sensual excitement without surrender or relaxation, the extremely tonic, yet also extremely rich, quality of our experience while we read. But all this you might have in great poems which were not epic. What I chiefly want to point out is something else — the poet's unremitting *manipulation* of his readers — how he sweeps us along as though we were attending an actual recitation and nowhere allows us to settle down and luxuriate on any one line or paragraph. It is common to speak of Milton's style as organ music. It might be more helpful to regard the reader as the organ and Milton the organist. It is on us he plays, if we will let him" (Lews, 40-41).

However, the epics are, generally, divided into two other categories: folk epic and art epic. The subject-matter of a folk epic is a folk Saga or myth, and the folk epic involves the particular folk-traditions associated with that saga or myth. On the other hand, the subject-matter of an art epic, though, generally, based on some saga or myth, is created by the fancy of the poet, or at least decorated and enriched by the fancy of the poet. The folk epic follows the mores of a particular folk, but the art epic rises above that mores, and upholds an ideal standard of morality. The art epic is more complex and sophisticated than the folk epic. Milton's *Paradise Lost*, like Virgil's *Aeneid*, is an art epic; and *Beowulf, Iliad* and *Odyssey* are folk epics.

Previously, it was held that the epic must be in verse form, but in the modern age the connotation of the epic has been extended so that if only the theme of a literary piece be of epic dimension, it may be called an epic. It is for this reason that such novels as Cervantes' *Don*

Quixote (1615), Henry Fielding's *Tom Jones*, Herman Melville's *Moby Dick*, Tolstoy's *War and Peace*, Thomas Mann's *The Magic Mountain*, Ivo Andric's *Bosnian Story*, etc. are called epics. Again, for the identical reason, such plays as Bartolt Brecht's *Mother Courage and her Children*, written against the back drop of World War II, Goethe's *Faust*, Thomas Hardy's *The Dynasts*, written against the background of the Napoleonic Wars, etc. are called epic dramas. Paul Merchant even says that Shakespeare's *Troilus and Cressida* "contains in a single play most of the essential elements of epic" (Merchant, 81). The modern or contemporary epic has moved far away from the traditional epic in other respects too. For instance, the traditional hexametre and pentametre have been replaced by collage in verse. Thus, the modern epic has become more varied, in both content and form.

To come back to Milton. He had acquired a good amount of knowledge about the form of the epic before he sat down to write one. He was much influenced by the form of the classical Greek and Latin epics, and by the sweetness of the epic of Spenser — *The Faerie Queene*. For a long time Milton had been gestating the idea of writing an epic, as we have said, on the Arthurian theme. This is evident in *Paradise Lost* (Book I, lines 580-581) where the poet says: "In fable or romance of Uther's son,/Begirt with British and Armoric knights". He wanted to write his epic on the theme of this 'Uther's son' — Arthur. Paul Merchant here writes: "The reference to Arthur (Uther's son) and Lancelot, the Armoric knight, acts as a reminder that Milton had originally intended his epic to have king Arthur as its hero" (Merchant, 57). But, as his wished-for Commonwealth became crest-fallen, for one reason or another, Milton began to change his mind, and while he was touring Italy, he ultimately decided to write an epic on some biblical theme. An epic on some theme of the Bible was not absolutely new in the 17th century. In 1656, Abraham Cowley, the metaphysical poet, wrote his epic *Davideis*, in 12 Books, on the biblical theme of David. Perhaps Milton's deeply religious sentiment was also to some extent responsible for his preference for some biblical theme for his epic. At the beginning, he thought of using the biblical theme of the Fall of Adam, in a drama to be entitled *Adam Unparadised*. Further, on the authority of Dr. Johnson, we know that Milton, at first, was thinking of writing a 'Mistry' play on the theme of *Paradise Lost*, employing such characters as Justice, Mercy, Faith, etc. He thought of two plans for the projected Mistry play, and these two plans are still kept in the library of the university of Cambridge. In the first plan, he wanted to entitle the projected play *Paradise Lost*, and thought of dividing the play into five Acts. In the second plan, he changed the episodes of the projected play, and wanted to entitle it *Adam Unparadised.* However, long afterwards, he used the same theme in his *Paradise Lost*, after much painful vacillation as to whether he should write a drama or an epic on this theme. Milton's long vacillation and his final decision in this regard can be discerned at the beginning of Book IX of *Paradise Lost* (lines 25-26): "Since first this subject for heroic song/Pleased me, long choosing and beginning late". The epic poet, as Homer did, must deal with a single action, said Aristotle in his *Poetics*, and in Milton's single action in *Paradise Lost* is the Fall of Man. Curious enough, *Paradise Lost* could not easily find a kind publisher, and only after some quest one was ultimately found in Aldersgate, and that only on condition of a paltry royalty. The agreement between Milton and Aldersgate is still today preserved in the national museum of England. According to the agreement, "The author received £ 5 down, was to receive a second £ 5 when the first edition should be sold, a third £ 5 when the second, and a fourth £ 5 when the third edition should be gone. Milton lived to receive the second £ 5 and no more: £ 10 in all, for *Paradise Lost*" (Sutherland, 39). The epic did not receive immediate public acclaim. About the readership of that time, Dr. Johnson writes: "To prove the paucity of readers, it may be sufficient to remark that the nation had been satisfied, from 1623 to 1664, that is, fortyone years, with only two editions of the work of Shakespeare, which probably did not together make one thousand copies" (Johnson, 101). By this measuring rod of readership, we may say that Milton's *Paradise Lost* was not very coldly received by the public either, because three thousand copies of the epic was sold in eleven years.

Milton had a grand preparation before beginning to write *Paradise Lost.* He assiduously read, in depth, the epics and other poetic works of Homer, Virgil, Boiardo, Ariosto, Tasso and others, and even the Portuguese epic *Os Lusiadas* by Luis de Camoes (c. 1524-1580), through translation, and was much influenced by these epic poets. He also thought much over the story of the Fall of Man from different angles. Milton not only read the epics of different poets but also borrowed from them. C.V. Wedgwood writes: "Milton borrowed from the Duchman Vondel, from the Italian Andreini, and from many others in his epic [*Paradise Lost*]" (Wedgwood, 114). Wedgwood further writes that the theme of the Fall of Man was very much popular in the 17th century, and many poets were inspired by the theme: "Satan and the aweful gloom of Hell had inspired some of the finest works of Phineas Fletcher, Crashaw, and Cowley; the theme of *Paradise Regained* had been treated by Giles Fletcher in his beautiful epic *Christ's Victorie*" (Wedgwood, 114). In *Paradise Lost* Milton conceived of an ideal life in an ideal place. The Spanish poet Gongora (1561-1627), who dominated Spanish verse throughout the 17th century, in his famous poem *Soledades*, describes "an ideal society, materially primitive but morally rich, viewed through the eyes of a wanderer from the outside world. It is a backward glance at the golden age of mankind, a hymn to the splendours of nature, a thesis about the harmony in which man once lived with nature, and a sermon about materialistic attitudes in the Spain of Philip II" (Thorlby, 323). It is not unlikely that Milton read *Soledades* and was influenced thereby, as it may be evident from his conception of Eden and the ideality of the life of Adam and Eve before their Fall. In the conception and execution of *Paradise Lost*, Milton might also have been inspired and guided, at least to a little extent, and that only indirectly, by *Genesis* (B) or *Later Genesis* presumably written by Caedmon (fl. 670-680), which is now preserved as Junius Manuscript. This presumption is supported by the fact that the Junius Manuscript was collected by the philologist Francis Junius (1589-1677) who was a friend of Milton. *Genesis* (B) deals with the same materials as are contained in *Paradise Lost*. It deals with Satan's tempting of Adam and Eve and their Fall. Like in *Paradise Lost*, in *Genesis* (B) also Adam's Fall is due to his tenderness towards Eve. And, again, as in *Paradise Lost*, in *Genesis* also Satan is the heroic figure (Height, 29). Nevertheless, *Paradise Lost* is something unique in its conception and execution: it is never a collage. In the Invocation of the epic, Milton himself announces that he is going to sing about such a thing as has not yet been attempted by anybody: "unattempted yet in prose or rhyme." Long before this, in *Comus* (lines 44-45), Milton said the same thing: "What never yet was heard in Tale or Song/From old, or modern Bard in Hall, or Bowr."

It may be said in passing that the word 'paradise' derives from the Greek word 'paradeisos' which means 'a park', or from the Old Parsian word 'pairidaeza' which also means 'a park' (*Chambers Twentieth Century Dictionary*; entry: paradise). But Milton did not only think of an ideal life and an ideal habitation, but also thought of a 'Paradise of Fools'. In Book III of *Paradise Lost* (lines 489-496), he describes this 'Paradise of Fools':

then might ye see
Cowls, hoods, and habits, with their wearers tossed

And fluttered into rags; then reliques, beads,
Indulgences, dispenses, pardons, bulls,
The sport of winds: all these, upwhirled aloft,
Fly o'er the backside of the World far off
Into a Limbo large and broad, since called
The Paradise of Fools;

The description of the 'Paradise of Fools' is the bitterest attack by Milton on the episcopacy and the decadent church.

In ancient times it was believed that the poetic inspiration is a sort of divine *afflatus*, for which reason the poet was deemed as a *vates* or prophet. Whether Milton actually received any divine *afflatus* we do not know; but Milton himself says in *Paradise Lost* (Book IX, lines 20-24) that he wrote the epic having received inspiration from some spirit; and so he wrote it without any premeditation :

If answerable style I Can obtain
Of my celestial patroness, who deigns
Her mighty visitation unimplored,
And dictates to me slumbering, or inspires
Easy my unpremeditated verse;

In *Paradise Regained* also Milton says that he was inspired by some supernatural power (Book I, lines 8-12) :

Thou Spirit, who led'st this glorious Eremite
Into the desert, his victorious field
Against the spiritual foe, and brought'st him thence
By proof th' undoubted Son of God, inspire,
As thou art wont, my prompted song,

But, Milton's confessional dispositions may not be taken at face value, because such confessions may be a poet's feigning, or these may be simply traditional.

Milton wrote *Paradise Lost* "in parcels of ten, twenty, or thirty verses at a time" (Johnson, 95), *i.e.* at one sitting. Dr. Johnson reports, he himself being reported, that Milton " 'would sometimes lie awake whole nights, but not a verse could he make; and on a sudden his poetical faculty would rush upon him with an *impetus* or *oestrum*, and his daughter was immediately called to secure what came. At other times he would dictate perhaps forty lines in a breath, and then reduce them to half the number' " (Johnson 97). However, the break-up of the total 10,565 lines of *Paradise Lost* is as follows : BK I 798 lines; BK II 1,055; BK III 742; BK IV 1,015; BK V 907; BK VI 912; BK VII

640; BK VIII 653; BK IX 1,189; BK X 1, 104; BK XI 901; and BK XII 649 lines.

2
(SUMMARY OF THE TWELVE BOOKS OF *PARADISE LOST*)

Book I

As we have said, each Book of *Paradise Lost* opens with an Argument which is, in fact, a brief summary of the whole Book. The Argument of Book I reads thus: "This First Book proposes, first in brief, the whole subject, — Man's disobedience, and the loss thereupon of Paradise, wherein he was placed; then touches the prime cause of his fall — the Serpent, or rather Satan in the Serpent; who, revolting from God, and drawing to his side many legions of Angels, was, by command of God, driven out of Heaven, with all his crew, into the great Deep. Which action passed over, the Poem hastens into the midst of things; presenting Satan, with his Angels, now fallen into Hell — descried here not in the Centre (for heaven and earth may be supposed as yet not made, certainly not yet accursed), but in a place of utter darkness, fittiest called Chaos. Here Satan, with his Angels lying on the burning lake, thunderstruck and astonished, after a certain space recovers, as from confusion; calls up him who, next in order and dignity, lay by him: they confer of their miserable fall. Satan awakens all his legions, who lay till then in the same manner confounded. They rise: their numbers; array of battle; their chief leaders named, according to the idols known afterwards in Canaan and the countries adjoining. To these Satan directs his speech; comforts them with hope yet of regaining Heaven; but tells them, lastly, of a new world and new kind of creature to be created, according to an ancient prophecy, or report, in Heaven — for that Angels were long before this visible creation was the opinion of many ancient Fathers. To find out the truth of this prophecy, and what to determine thereon, he refers to a full council. What his associates thence attempt. Pandemonium, the palace of Satan, rises, suddenly built out of the Deep, the infernal Peers there sit in council." And then begins the twentysix-line Invocation in which the poet implores the 'Heavenly Muse' to sing about how in the beginning heaven and earth were created out of Chaos, so that he may get 'aid' or assistance or inspiration from that song. The poet invokes the 'aid' of the 'Heavenly Muse', because he does not want to sing a commonplace song, but a highly elevated one: he does not desire a 'middle flight'. The poet also implores the Spirit to teach him how the earth was populated with flora and fauna, and to raise his poetic faculty so that he may prove that whatever God does is good :

> Of Man's first disobedience, and the fruit
> Of that forbidden tree, whose mortal taste
> Brought death into the World, and all our woe,
> With loss of Eden, till one greater Man
> Restore us, and regain the blissful seat,
> Sing, Heavenly Muse, that on the secret top
> Of Oreb, or of Sinai, didst inspire
> That Shepherd who first taught the chosen seed
> In the beginning how the heavens and earth
> Rose out of Chaos: or, if Sion hill
> Delight thee more, and Siloa's brook that flowed
> Fast by the oracle of God, I thence
> Invoke thy aid to my adventurous song,
> That with no middle flight intends to soar
> Above th' Aonian mount, while it pursues
> Things unattempted yet in prose or rime.
> And chiefly Thou, O Spirit, that dost prefer
> Before all temples th' upright heart and pure,
> Instruct me, for Thou know'st; Thou from the first
> Wadt present, and, with mighty wings outspread,
> Dove-like sat'st brooding on the vast Abyss,
> And mad'st it pregnant: what in me is dark
> Illumine, what is low raise and support;
> That, to the height of this great argument,
> I may assert Eternal Providence,
> And justify the ways of God to men.

After the Invocation, Milton very imperceptively moves away from his prayer to the Spirits to his own narration, and this is a device that is very interesting. Milton says that Satan (earlier, *i.e.* before his fall, he was known as Lucifer — the angel of light), the Archangel, revolted against God (Milton here does no say why, but later on we will know that Satan revolted against God's supposed tyranny), and in retaliation, Satan was thrown by God down to the pit of hell, along with his (Satan's) comrades who fought on his side against God. The hell being very far down from heaven, Satan and his comrades fell through the vast Abyss for long nine days, after which they fell unconscious in the lake of liquid fire of hell. After a while, Satan collects his consciousness and views the damnable region of hell (lines 59-69):

At once, as far as Angel's ken, he views
The dismal situation waste and wild;
A dungeon horrible, on all sides round,
As one great furnace flamed; yet from those
No light, but rather darkness visible
Served only to discover sights of woe,
Regions of sorrow, doleful shades, where peace
And rest can never dwell, hope never comes
That comes to all, but torture without end
Still surges, and a fiery deluge, fed
With ever burning sulphur unconsumed.

While floating and rolling in the liquid fire, Satan finds his adjutant and next in strength only to him, Beelzebub, who has also banished from heaven, and tells him that that they are still existing proves that their strength is not lost completely. Satan tells him that he has still his unconquerable will and his 'study of revenge' and also his courage and 'immortal hate', and that with all these he will certainly be able to vanquish God, though in the battle of the recent past he was defeated by him (lines 105-109) :

What though the field be lost?
All is not lost — the unconquerable will,
And study of revenge, immortal hate,
And courage never to submit or yield:
And what is else not to be overcome.

Beelzebub recalls that they wanted to see whether God held his powers "by strength, or chance, or fate". Beelzebub tells Satan that they should not undergo "eternal punishment" as they are still keeping their strength undiminished. Satan replies that they must either revolt once again, or will-nilly suffer: "Doing or suffering". But how to revolt against God, this time? Satan elaborates: "To do aught good never will be our task,/ But ever to do ill our sole delight,/As being the contrary to his high will/ Whom we resist." Then, with Beelzebub, the hugely-framed Satan escapes "the Stygian flood" of the liquid fire, and reaches another part of hell which consists of solid fire which is no less horrible than their former place. Satan is never mentally lost; he is as iron-willed and stoic as he had been in heaven. He says that he is not repentant for losing heaven, because it is actually the mind that creates either heaven or hell: "The mind is its own place, and in itself/Can make a Heaven of Hell, a Hell of Heaven." So what if heaven be lost? He still nurses within his heart his will of becoming a ruler, even if in hell : "To reign is worth ambition, though in Hell:/ Better to reign in Hell than serve in Heaven."

Beelzebub now advises Satan to call the host of other fallen angels who also fought on Satan's side in heaven against God, and who met with the same fate as befell him. Then Satan approaches the innumerable fallen angels who are half-unconsciously floating on the lake of liquid fire of hell, and reproaches them in his leader-like voice "Awake, arise, or be ever fallen!" And "to their General's voice they soon obeyed/ Innumerable." First comes Moloch, the "horrid king, besmeared with blood/Of human sacrifice, and parent's tears." Next comes Chemos, "th' obscene dread of Moab's sons." After Chemos, comes Thammuz "Whose annual wound in Lebanon allured/The Syrian damozels to lament his fate/In amorous ditties all a summer's day." Next comes Dagon — a "sea-monster, upward man/And downward fish". And then come Osiris, Isis and Orus and their followers. The poet says that these are the most renowned of the followers of Satan who promptly responded to his call. And all these are followed by a long line of their followers: "These were the prime in order and in might/The rest were long to tell, though far renowned,/Th' Ionian gods". And "All these and more came flocking". Azazel, the tall cherub, then unfurled the "imperial ensign" of rebellion, and "A shout that tore Hell's Conclave, and beyond/ Frightened the region of Chaos and old Night." Satan is now feeling proud, but his pride is overcast by some gloom. Milton beautifully describes the features of Satan, at this moment (lines 589-599) :

> Their dread Commander: he above the rest
> In shape and gesture proudly eminent,
> Stood like a tower: his form had yet not lost
> All her original brightness, nor appeared
> Less than Archangel ruined, and the excess
> Of glory obscured as when the sun new-risen
> Looks through the horizontal misty air
> Shorn of his beams, or, from behind the moon,
> In dim eclipse, disastrous twilight sheds
> Half the nations, and with fear of change
> Perplexes monarchs.

However, Satan now gathers his shattered strengths and addresses the mustered host of fallen angels thus: " 'O myriads of immortal Spirits! O Powers/Matchless, but with th' Almighty!' " Addressing them thus, Satan tells them (lines 645-649) :

our better parts remains
To work in close design, by fraud or guile,
What force effected not; that he no less
At length from us may find, who overcomes
By force hath overcome but half his foe.

And maddened by his own ferocious speech, Satan drew thousands of swords from the waists of the spirits, and threw them high up in the air. Soon Mammon leads a band of the spirits upto the pick of a nearby hill in whose womb an immense amount of gold was stored, which the multitude of the spirits dig up. With that gold and other precious metals and jewels the fallen angels, under the direction of Mammon, build up a huge structure, since called Pandemonium (a term coined by Milton by conjoining two Latin words — 'pan' meaning 'all', and 'demonium' meaning 'place for demons'; and hence the word means 'a place for all demons') which is "the high capital/Of Satan and his peers." Now all the fallen spirits are summoned, and they, reducing themselves into smallest forms, assemble in the Pandemonium in huge numbers. Only the Seraphic Lords and Cherubim sit in the hall (central part) of Pandemonium without reducing their normal forms. And then, under the presidentship of Satan, a great consultation begins, after a silence for a short while: "After short silence then,/And summons read, the great consult began."

Book II

The 'Argument' of the second Book runs thus "The consultation began, Satan debates whether another battle be to be hazarded for the recovery of Heaven: some advise it, others dissuade. A third proposal is preferred, mentioned before by Satan, to search the truth of that prophecy or tradition in Heaven concerning another world, and another kind of creature, equal, or not much inferior, to themselves, about this time to be created. Their doubt who shall be sent on this difficult search: Satan, their chief, undertakes alone the voyage; is honoured and applauded — The council thus ended, the rest betake them several ways and to several employments, as their inclinations lead them, to entertain the time till Satan returns. He passes on his journey to Hell-gates; finds them shut, and who sat there to guard them; by whom at length they are opened, and discover to him the great gulf between Hell and Heaven; with what difficulty he passes through, directed by Chaos, the Power of that place, to the sight of this new World which he sought."

In the Pandemonium, Satan seats himself "on a throne of royal state", and orders deliberations to begin. Moloch rises first and says: ' " 'My sentence is for open war...' " After him, Belial speaks. Milton describes Belial's person and personality thus (lines 108-117) :

On th' other side up rose
Belial, in act more graceful and humane;
A fairer person lost not heaven; he seemed
For dignity composed, and high exploit.
But all was false and hollow; though his tongue
Dropped manna, and could make the worse appear
The better reason, to perplex and dash
Maturest counsels: for his thoughts were low;
To vice industrious, but to nobler deeds
Timorous and slothful.

Belial begins by saying " 'I should be much for open war...' ", but he dissuades himself and others from 'open war' against the Almighty, because he believes that all might and guiles are ineffectual in frustrating God : " 'War, therefore, open or concealed, alike/My voice dissuades; for what can force or guile/With him, or who deceive his mind, whose eye/Views all things at one view?' " Finally, Belial submits that if they continue to suffer, as they are doing, the wrath of God will, in course of time, slacken (lines 208-214) :

This is now
Our doom; which if we can sustain and bear,
Our supreme Foe in time may much remit
His anger, and perhaps, thus far removed,
Not mind us not offending, satisfied
With what is punished; whence these raging fires
Will slacken, if his breath stir not their flames.

Thus Belial with seeming logic tried to persuade the assemblage to refrain from war — war that he first dissemblingly proposed. He now proposes to keep inactive, and to ignobly bear with the exeruciating pain of hell, for the cause of peace — peace which is not peace in actuality: "Thus, Belial, with words clothed in reason's garb,/Counselled ignoble ease and peaceful sloth,/Not peace". After Belial, Mammon stands to speak. He says that it is impossible to overcome the adverse power of God, and so it is better to try to better their lot in hell. He further says that hell has everything that are necessary for making a heaven out of it: he says that hell has "gems and gold". In accordance with his nature, Mammon thinks that only "gems and gold" can make a heaven; and these two are available in plenty in hell : " 'This desert soil/Wants not her hidden lustre, gems and gold;/Nor want we skill or art from whence to raise/Magnificence; and what can Heaven show more?' " Mammon's proposal for peace is highly applauded by all. He further proposes : "To found this nether empire, which might rise,/By policy and long process of time,/In emulation opposite to Heaven."

Then Beelzebub rises with a grave mien and denounces the proposal of Mammon, and then submits his own proposal. He prophetically says that another world soon be created by God for a new race, which will be called the race of man. He persuades the assemblage to capture that world by force to subtlety. He says that man will be the best and the most favoured creation of God, and so it will be strategically the most advantageous to seduce man, and thus, indirectly, to inflict pain on the Almighty. He says that when man will be seduced, he will commit treachery towards God, and consequently God will destroy his (God's) own creation. Beelzebub says (lines 368-386) :

Seduce them to our party, that their God
May prove their foe, and with repenting hand
Abolish his own works. This would surpass
Common revenge, and interrupt his joy
In our confusion, and our joy upraise
In his disturbance; when his darling sons,
Hurled headlong to partake with us, shall curse
Their frail originals, and faded bliss—
Faded so soon!

At last Beelzebub's proposal is accepted by the house, and then Beelzebub asks the house to decide who should first try to re-enter heaven to try to seduce man. Satan forthwith rises on his feet, and tells the house that he is ready to undergo the hazard of re-entering heaven alone, because he wants to reign, and because the enterprise is of public moment. Satan, then, adjourns the 'Stygian council', and the host of the fallen angels disperse.

According to his own design, Satan now with 'swift wings' soars up to the gates of hell. Milton describes the gates of hell thus (lines 643-648):

At last appear
Hell bounds, high reaching to the horrid roof,
And thrice threefold the gates; threefolds were brass,

Three iron, three adamantine rock,
Impenetrable, impaled with circling fire
Yet unconsumed.

There near the hell-gate, Satan sees a 'formidable Shape' sitting on either side of the hell-gate. One of the two horrid Shapes seems to be half-woman and half-snake (lines 650-653):

The one seemed woman to the waist, and fair,
But ended foul in many a scaly fold,
Voluminous and vast, a serpent armed
With mortal sting.

This horrid Shape is the mother of Sin and Death. The other Shape seems to be indistinguishable from the first. The two Shapes, fierce 'as ten Furies' stand before Satan, but the Archfiend stands unterrified, and fights with the two horrid Shapes. One of the gate-keepers is the daughter of Satan, called Sin, and the other is his son, called Death. While fighting with them, Satan recognises both the Shapes, as they disclose their identities to him. Sin, Satan's daughter, then opens the gates of hell with the key that she always keeps with herself (lines 871-879) :

from her side the fatal key,
Sad instrument of all our woe, she took;
....
...... then in the key-hole turns
Th' intricate wards, and every bolt and bar
Of massy iron or solid rock with ease
Unfastens.

As the gates open, huge fire and smoke gushes out, and the anarchy of hell comes to view. Satan now comes out of hell and "Stood on the brink of Hell and looked a while,/Pondering his voyage". And then he begins his voyage upwards towards heaven (lines 1011-1016) :

glad that now his sea should find a shore,
With fresh alacrity and force renewed
Springs upward, like a pyramid of fire,
Into the wild expanse, and through the shock
Of fighting elements, on all sides round
Environed, wins his way;

After he has traversed a long way, Satan sees the light of heaven, and then the heaven itself as well as the newly created world to which he speeds forth (lines 1047-1055) :

Far off th' empyrean Heaven, extend wide
In circuit, undermined squire or round,
With opal towers and battlements adorned
Of living sapphire, once his native seat;
And fast by, hanging in a golden chain,
This pendent World, in bigness as a star
Of smallest magnitude close by the moon.
Thither, full fraught with mischievous revenge
Accursed, and in a cursed hour, he hies.

Book III

The 'Argument' of Book III goes like this: "God sitting on his throne, sees Satan flying towards this World, then newly created; shows him to the Son, who sat at his right hand; foretells the success of Satan in perverting mankind; clears his own justice and wisdom from all imputation, having created Man free and able enough to have withstood his Temper; yet declares his purpose of grace towards him, in regard he fell not of his own malice, as did Satan, but by him seduced. The Son of God renders praises to his Father for the manifestation of his gracious purpose towards Man: but God again declares that grace cannot be extended towards Man without the satisfaction of Divine Justice; Man hath offended the majesty of God by aspiring to Godhead, and therefore, with all his progeny, devoted to death, must die, unless some one can be found sufficient to answer for his offence, and undergo his punishment. The Son of God freely offers himself a ransom for Man: the Father accepts him, ordains his incarnation, pronounces his exaltation above all names in Heaven and Earth; commands all the Angels to adore him: they obey, and, hymning to their harps in full quire, celebrate the Father and the Son. Meanwhile, Satan alights upon the bare convex of this World's outermost orb; where wandering he first finds a place since called the Limbo of Vanity; what persons and things fly up thither : thence, comes to the gate of Heaven, described ascending by stairs, and the waters above the firmament that flow about it. His passage thence to the orb of the Sun: he finds there Uriel, the regent of that orb, but first changes himself into the shape of a meaner Angel, and, pretending a zealous desire to behold the new Creation, and Man whom God had placed here, inquires of him the place of his habitation, and is directed: alights first on Mount Niphates."

Sitting on his throne, God now casts his glance downwards and views the beauty of this newly created world. About him are sitting "all the Sanctities of Heaven", and on his right side is sitting 'His only Son'

(Jesus Christ). Now God also sees our grand parents (Adam and Eve) who were recently created by him. Of our grand parents, or rather of Man (man in general), God says (lines 124-134) :

'.... I formed them free, and free they must remain
Till they enthrall themselves: I else must change
Their nature, and revoke the high decree
Unchangeable, eternal, which ordained
Their freedom; they themselves ordained their fall.
The first sort by their own suggestion fell,
Self-tempted, self-depraved; Man falls, deceived
By the other first: Man, therefore, shall find grace
The other none: in mercy and justice both,
Through heaven and Earth, so shall my glory excell;
By mercy, first and last, shall brightest shine.'

Then Christ, the compassionate Son of God, who is sitting beside God, begins to plead for his grace for Man, so that the fallen Man, God's youngest son, may be saved and be united with Godhead. In turn, God assures Christ (lines 173-177):

Man shall not quite be lost, but saved who will;
Yet not of will in him, but grace in me
Free vouchsafed. Once more I will renew
His lapsed powers, though forfeit, and enthralled
By sin to foul exorbitant desires:

Satisfied by the assurance of God, Christ says that he is ready to die for the salvation of Man: "me for him, life for life, I offer". God therefore asks Christ to descend to earth in carnation, as the son of Adam, to save the whole of human race (lines 283-289) :

'... And be thyself Man among men on Earth,
Made flesh, when time shall be, of virgin seed,
By wonderous birth; be thou in Adam's room
The head of all mankind, though Adam's son.
As in him perish all men, so in thee,
As from a second root, shall be restored
As many as are restored; without thee none...'

As God ceases, a multitude of angels make a 'loud hosannas', and the huge expanse of heaven is filled with the sacred song of the angels — the song that they sing due to the 'unexampled love' of God for mankind.

Meanwhile Satan ('Fiend'), who was flying towards the earth, through Chaos and preternatural darkness, "alights upon the bare convex of this World's outermost orb". To Satan, the earth now seems bigger but inclement (lines 422-430):

> Satan alighted walks. A globe far off
> It seemed; now seems a boundless continent,
> Dark, waste, and wild, under the frown of Night
> Starless exposed, and ever-threatening storms
> Of Chaos blustering round, inclement sky,
> Save on that side which from the wall of Heaven,
> Though distant far, some small reflection gains
> Of glimmering air less vexed with tempest loud:
> Here walked the Fiend at large in specious field.

The earth is, Satan observes, devoid of any creatures, living or dead; and so he walks lonely: "Alone, for other creature in this place,/Living or lifeless, to be found was none;—". He sees the earth full of "superstition and blind zeal" and full of papal "Indulgences, dispenses, pardons, bulls"— reasons for which the earth since then is called "Paradise of Fools". Now, at a distance, Satan sees a staircase from the earth upto heaven (lines 501-512):

> Far distant he descries,
> Ascending by degrees magnificent
> Upto the wall of Heaven, a structure high;
> At top whereof, but far more rich, appeared
> The work of a kingly palace-gate,
> With frontispiece of diamond and gold
> Embellished; thick with sparkling orient gems
> The portal shone, inimitable on Earth
> By model, or by shading pencil drawn.
> The stairs were such as whereon Jacob saw
> Angels ascending and descending, bands
> Of guardians bright,

From the lower stair of the flight towards heaven, Satan looks downwards and sees the magnificence of the world, surrounded by bright stars. And now he thinks of entering the Paradise on earth — "the happy seat of Man". Before entering the Paradise, Satan changes his countenance by putting on the appearance of a 'stripling Cherub'. On entering the Paradise, Satan finds Uriel, the guardian of tho sun and "one of the seven/Who in God's presence, nearest to his throne,/Stand ready at command". Satan expresses to Uriel his wish to observe the wonderful things created by God, but particularly Man "Unspeakable desire to see and know/All these his wonderous works, but chiefly Man,/His chief delight and favour". Uriel gives complement to Satan for his being interested in the glorious creations of God. Uriel also gives him a fast and brief history of the creation of the world, at the bidding of the Almighty (lines 710-721) :

> Confusion heard his voice, and wild Uproar
> Stood ruled, stood vast Infinitude confined;
> Till, at his second bidding, Darkness fled,
> Light shone, and order from disorder sprung.
> Swift to their several quarters hasted then
> The cumbrous elements, Earth, Flood, Air, Fire;
> And this ethereal quintessence of Heaven
> Flew upward, spirited with various forms,
> That rolled orbicular, and turned to stars
> Numberless, as thou seest, and how they move:
> Each had his place appointed, each his course;
> The rest in circuit walls this Universe.

Then Uriel shows Satan Paradise, the place of Adam, and turns to move away. Satan bows to him in gratitudes, and stoops post-speed towards Paradise, and alights on the pick of the hill called Niphates.

Book IV

Milton's 'Argument' to this Book runs thus: "Satan, now in prospect of Eden, and nigh the place where he must now attempt the bold enterprise which he undertook alone against God and Man, falls into many doubts with himself and many passions, fear, envy, and despair; but at length confirms himself in evil; journeys on to Paradise, whose outward prospect and situation is described; overlaps the bounds; sits, in the shape of a cormorant, on the Tree of Life, as highest in the Garden, to look about him. The Garden described; Satan's first sight of Adam and Eve; his wonder at their excellent form and happy state, but with resolution to work their fall; overhears their discourse; thence gathers that the Tree of Knowledge was forbidden them to eat of under penalty of death, and thereon intends to found his temptation by seducing them to transgress; then leaves them a while, to know further of their state by some other means. Meanwhile Uriel, descending on a sunbeam, warns Gabriel, who had in charge the gate of Paradise, that some evil Spirit had escaped the Deep, and passed at noon by his Sphere, in the shape of a good Angel, down to Paradise, discovered after by his furious gestures in the mount. Gabriel promises to find him out ere morning. Night coming on, Adam and Eve discourse of going to their rest: their bower described; their evening worship. Gabriel, drawing forth his bands of night-watch to walk the round of Paradise, appoints two strong Angels to Adam's bower, lest the evil Spirit should be doing some harm to Adam or Eve sleeping: there they find him at the ear of Eve, tempting her in a dream, and bring him, though unwilling, to Gabriel: by whom questioned, he scornfully answers; prepares resistance; but, hindered by a sign from Heaven, flies out of Paradise."

The poet says that the coming of Satan near Paradise is the omen of sorrow to the inhabitants of the earth: "*Woe to the inhabitants on Earth*!" He says that our first parents were well warned, well in advance, of the coming of Satan onto the earth. However Satan, with a hideous heart, comes to the earth. But he despairs because conscience arises even within the evil heart of his, as now he remembers his former state of existence while in heaven. Satan moans (lines 50-61) :

> I 'sdained subjection, and thought one step higher
> Would set me highest, and in a moment quit
> The debt immense of endless gratitude,
> So burdensome, still paying, still to owe;
> Forgetful what from him I still received;
> And understood not that a grateful mind
> By owing owes not, but still pays, at once
> Indebted and discharged; what burden then?
> Oh, had his powerful destiny ordained
> Me some inferior Angel, I had stood
> Then happy; no unbounded hope had raised
> Ambition.

Thus, Satan repents for his past acts of ingratitude shown to the Almighty. But immediately afterwards he controverts his state of mind, and boasts that he has all the parts necessary for being right ambitious. And again he falls into deep despair and feels miserable : "Me miserable! which way shall I fly/Infinite wrath and infinite despair?/ Which way I fly is Hell; myself am Hell". In this wise Satan is undulated by hopes and despairs, and moves from one passion to another, and back again — "ire, envy, and despair". The beauty and peace and glory of the earth are the cause of the undulatings of Satan's passions.

Meantime, Satan comes near Paradise, in the Garden of Eden. Milton describes Paradise thus (lines 134-159) :

> As with rural mound, the champaign head
> Of a steep wilderness, whose hairy sides

With thicket overgrown, grotesque and wild,
Access denied; and overhead up-grew
Insuperable height of loftiest shade,
Cedar, and pine, and fir, and branching palm,
A sylvan scene, and, as the ranks ascend
Shade above shade, a woody theatre
Of stateliest view, Yet higher than their tops
The verdurous wall of Paradise up-sprung;

....

And higher than that wall circling row
Of goodliest trees, loaden with fairest fruit,
Blossoms and fruits at once of golden hue,
Appeared, with gay enamelled colours mixed;
On which the sun more glad impressed his beams
Than in fair evening cloud, or humid bow,
When God hath showered the earth: so lovely seemed
That landscape; and of pure, now purer air
Meets his approach, and to the heart inspires
Vernal delight and joy, able to drive
All sadness, but despair. Now gentle gales,
Fanning their odoriferous wings, dispense
Native perfumes, and whisper whence they stole
Those balmy spoils.

Satan now enters Paradise through the western gate of it, the gate "that looked east",— Satan, the "first grand Thief into God's fold". He then sits on the Tree of Life — "The middle tree and highest there that grew"— and sat there on the tree "like a cormorant"— a web-footed and voracious sea-bird. To Satan, Paradise seems "A Heaven on Earth". Next to the Tree of Life, there comes to Satan's view the Tree of Knowledge which signifies that knowledge of good is possible only through knowledge of evil : "Knowledge of good, bought dear by knowing ill." However, Milton describes the exquisite beauty of Eden as follows (lines 223-268) :

Southward through Eden went a river large,
Nor changed his course, but through the shaggy hill
Passed underneath ingulfed; for God had thrown
That mountain, as his garden-mould, high raised
Upon the rapid current, which through veins
Of porous earth with kindly thirst updrawn
Rose a fresh fountain, and with many a rill

Watered the garden; thence united fell
Down the steep glade, and met the nether flood,
Which from his darksome passage now appears,
And now, divided into four main streams,
Runs diverse, wandering many a famous realm
And country whereof here needs no account;
But rather to tell how, if Art could tell
How, from that sapphire fount the crisped brooks,
Rolling on orient pearl and sands of gold,
With mazy error under pendent shades
Ran nectar, visiting each plant, and fed
Flower worthy of Paradise, which not nice
Art in beds and curious knots, but Nature boon
Poured forth profuse on hill, and dale, and plain,
Both where the morning sun first warmly smote
The open field, and where the unpierc'd shade
Embrowned the noontide bower. Thus was this place,
A happy rural seat of various view:
Groves whose rich trees wept odorous gums and balm;
Others whose fruit, burnished with golden rind,
Hung amiable — Hesperian fables true,
If true, here only — and of delicious taste.
Betwixt them lawns, or level downs and flocks
Grazing the tender herb, were interposed,
Or palmy hillock; or the flowery lap
Of some irreligious valley spread her store,
Flowers of all hue, and without thorn the rose.
Another side, umbrageous grots and caves
Of cool recess, o'er which the mantling vine
Lays forth her purple grape, and gently creeps
Luxuriant; meanwhile murmuring waters fall
Down the slope hills, dispersed, or in a lake,
That to the fringed bank with myrtle crowned
Her crystal mirror holds, unite their streams.
The birds their quire apply; airs, vernal airs,
Breathing the smell of field and grove, attune
The trembling leaves, while universal Pan,
Knit with the Graces and the Hours in dance,
Led on th' eternal Spring.

There, in Eden, Satan sees all sorts of creatures, including two human beings: Adam and Eve, who are in mutual love. To Satan, Adam and Eve appear thus (lines 288-311):

> Two of far nobler shape, erect and tall,
> God-like erect, with native honour clad
> In naked majesty, seemed lords of all,
> And worthy seemed; for in their looks divine
> The image of their glorious Maker shone,
> Truth, wisdom, sanctitude severe and pure —
> Severe, but in true filial freedom placed;
> Whence true authority in men: though both
> Not equal, as their sex not equal seemed;
> For contemplation he and valour formed,
> For softness she and sweet attractive grace;
> He for God only, she for God in him.
> His fair large front and eye sublime declared
> Absolute rule; and hyacinthine locks
> Round from his parted forelock manly hung
> Clustering, but not beneath his shoulders broad:
> She, as a veil down to the slender waist,
> Her unadorned golden tresses wore
> Dishevelled, but in wanton ringlets waved
> As the vine curls her tendrils, which implied
> Subjection, but required with gentle sway,
> And by her yielded, by him best received,
> Yielded with coy submission, modest pride,
> And sweet, reluctant, amorous delay.

Both Adam and Eve are naked, and yet they are not ashamed; because shame grows out of Nature when simplicity and 'spotless innocence' are banished, and Adam and Eve are still simple and innocent. They walk about Eden which is full of necterine fruits and 'compliant boughs' and have flowers galore. There are also all sorts of fauna (lines 343-350):

> Sporting the lion ramped, and in his paw
> Dandled the kid; bears, tigers, ounces, pards,
> Gambolled before them; th' unwieldy elephant,
> To make them mirth, used all his might, and wreathed
> His lithe proboscis; close the serpent sly,
> Insuating, wove with Gordian twine
> His braided train, and of his fatal guile
> Gave proof unheeded.

Now, Satan becomes jealous of the beauty and happiness of Eden, and, particularly, of the divine love between Adam and Eve, and so he is determined to wreck the beauty and happiness and love of Eden, by inveigling the two innocent human creatures to their destruction, in order to inflict pain upon their creator, the Almighty. At this moment, Adam tells Eve that they are free to share all sorts of joy of Eden, but they should "not taste that only Tree/Of knowledge, planted by the Tree of Life", because the fruits of the Tree of knowledge is interdicted by God. Eve then very beautifully narrates how one day she came by Adam (lines 449-462) :

> That day oft I remember, when from sleep
> I first awaked, and found myself reposed,
> Under a shade, on flowers, much wondering where
> And what I was, whence thither brought, and how.
> Not distant far from thence a murmuring sound
> Of waters issued from a cave, and spread
> Into a liquid plain, then stood unmoved,
> Pure as th' expanse of Heaven. I thither wont
> With unexpected thought, and laid me down
> On the green bank, to look into the clear
> Smooth lake, that to me seemed another sky.
> As I went down to look, just opposite,
> A shape within the wat'ry gleam appeared,
> Bending to look at me.

It was the 'shape' of Adam whose "beauty is excelled by many grace/ And wisdom". Adam then "pressed her matron lip/With kisses pure." Satan sees this celestial love-lock, and burns within himself in hatred and jealousy, and plans to bring ruin upon Adam and Eve. He decides to instigate them to have the taste of the fruit of the Tree of knowledge — to know more than what they do, in contravention of the command of the Almighty: "Hence, I will excite their minds/With more desire to know, and to reject/Envious commands, invented with design/To keep them low, whom knowledge might exalt/Equal with gods." Meanwhile, Uriel cautions Gabriel, chief of the angelic guards, that "This day at height of noon came to my sphere/A spirit, Zealous, as he seemed, to know/More of the Almighty's works, and chiefly Man,/God's latest image." Now night comes, and Adam and Eve, hand in hand, walk towards a bower, and enter into it, and lay there side by side. And then they make pure and mutual 'connubial love' (lines 741-747):

> Straight side by side were laid; nor turned, I wean,

Adam from his fair spouse, nor Eve the rites
Mysterious of connubial love refused:
Whatever hypocrites austerity talk
Of purity, and place, and innocence,
Defaming as impure what God declares
Pure, and commands to some, leaves free to all.

God approves of such 'connubial love', Milton says, because the Almighty wants increase of his creatures: "Our maker bids increase; who bids abstain/But our destroyer, foe to God and Man ?"

Now it is midnight. Cherubims have for long been acting as night-watches. Gabriel asks Uzziel, next in power to him, to keep strict vigilance all around along with other spirits. He gives Ithuriel and Zephon the special charge of searching the garden of Eden where Adam and Eve have been sleeping entwined to each other, because (lines 792-796) :

'...
This evening from the Sun's decline arrived
Who tells of some infernal Spirit seen
Hitherward bent (who could have thought No), escaped
The bars of Hell, on errand bad, no doubt:
Such, where ye find, seize first, and hither bring.'

Saying so, Gabriel led on his troops of spirits, and in the garden of Eden found Satan (partially recognisable) sitting like a toad, close to Eve (lines 799-802):

Him there they found
Squat like a toad, closest the ear of Eve,
Assaying by his devilish art to reach
The organs of her fancy,

At the grisly sight of Satan, Ithuriel and Zephon are, at first, taken aback, but then they accost him; and then there ensues an altercation between Zephon and Satan, and at last the two bright angels, Ithuriel and Zephon, being angered at the effrontery and suspected evil design of Satan, bind the Archfiend (Satan) with 'iron curb', and conduct him to Gabriel who has been waiting at the western gate of Eden with his band of watchful angels. Gabriel asks Satan why he has broken into Eden, and Satan, in reply, tells him that he has not done any harm to anybody thereby. Satan, further, tells him that he has come here "in hope to find/Better abode, and my afflicted Powers/To settle here on Earth, or in mid Air". The warrior angel Gabriel then threatens Satan with dire consequences if he does not leave the place. Satan pays no heed to the threat of Gabriel, and then Gabriel tells him that his lot will be decided by the power up above the world, if he does not obey to leave the place. Intimidated, Satan then flies out of Eden: "The Fiend looked up, and knew/His mounted scale aloft; nor more; but fled/ Murmuring; and with him fled the shades of Night."

Book V

The 'Argument' of Book V runs thus: "Morning approached, Eve relates to Adam her troublesome Dream; he likes it not, yet comforts her; they come forth to their day labours: their morning hymn at the door of their bower. God, to render Man inexcusable, sends Raphael to admonish him of his obedience, of his free estate, of his enemy near at hand, who he is, and why his enemy, and whatever else may avail Adam to know. Raphael comes down to Paradise; his appearance described; his coming discerned by Adam afar off, sitting at the door of his bower; he goes out to meet him, brings him to his lodge, entertains him with the choist fruits of Paradise, got together by Eve; their discourse at table. Raphael performs his message, minds Adam of his state and of his enemy; relates, at Adam's request, who that enemy is, and how he came to be so, beginning from his first revolt in Heaven, and the occasion thereof; how he drew his legions after him to the parts of the North, and there incited them to rebel with him, persuading all but only Abdiel, a seraph, who in argument dissuades and opposes him, then forsakes him."

At break of morning, Adam wakes and romantically views the celestial beauty of Eve who is still lying asleep beside him "He, on his side/Leaning half raised, with looks of cordial love/Sung over her enamoured, and beheld/Beauty which, whether waking or asleep,/Shot forth peculiar graces." At the whispering of Adam, Eve wakes, embraces him, and tells him about the dream she had during the previous night. She narrates her dream to him thus (lines 35-93):

'... Methought
Close at mine ear one called me forth to walk
With gentle voice; I thought it thine it said,
"Why sleep'st thou, Even now is the pleasant time
The cool, the silent, save where silence yields
To the night-warbling bird, that now awake
Tunes sweetest his love-laboured song; now reigns
Full-orbed the moon, and, with more pleasing light,
Shadowy sets off the face of things — in vain,

If none regard. Heaven wakes with all his eyes;
Whom to behold but thee, Nature's desire,
In whose sight all things joy, with ravishment
Attracted by thy beauty still to gaze ?"
I rose as at thy call, but found thee not:
To find thee I directed then my walk;
And on, methought, alone I passed through ways
That brought me on a sudden to the tree
Of interdicted knowledge Fair it seemed,
Much fairer to my fancy than by day;
And as I wondering looked, beside it stood
One shaped and winged like one of those from Heaven
By us oft seen his dewy locks distilled
Ambrosia. On that tree also gazed;
And, "O fair plant," said he, "with fruit surcharged,
Deigns none to ease thy load, and taste thy sweet,
Nor God, nor Man? Is knowledge so despised?
Or envy, or what reserve forbids to taste?
Forbids who will, none shall from me withhold
Longer thy offered good, why else set here?"
This said, he paused not, but with vent'rous arm
He plucked, he tasted. Me damp horror chilled
At such bold words vouched with a deed so bold;
But he thus, overjoyed: "O fruit divine,
Sweet of thyself, but much more sweet thus cropped,
Forbidden here, it seems, as only fit
For gods, yet able to make gods of men
And why not gods of men, since good, the more
Communicated, more abundant grows,
The author not impaired, but honoured more?
Here happy creature, fair angelic Eve!
Partake thou also: happy though thou art,
Happier thou may'st be, worthier canst not be.
Taste this, and be henceforth among the gods
Thyself a goddess; not to Earth confined,
But sometimes in the Air, as we; sometimes
Ascend to Heaven, by merit thine, and see
What life the gods live there, and such live thou."
So saying, he drew nigh, and to me held,
Even to my mouth, of that same fruit held apart
Which he plucked: the pleasant savoury smell

So quickened appetite that I, methought,
Could not but taste. Forthwith upto the clouds
With him I flew, and underneath beheld
The Earth outstretched immense, a prospect wide
And various: wandering at my flight and change
To this high exaltation, suddenly
My guide was gone, and I, methought, sunk down,
And fell asleep; but O, how glad I waked
To find this but a dream!

So long Adam was apprehensively listening to Eve's narration of her dream, and as she now has ceased, he tells her that the dream was brought by some evil power, and he, further, explains to her the cause of the dream (lines 100-116) :

But know that in the soul
Are many lesser faculties, that serve
Reason as chief. Among these Fancy next
Her office holds; of all external things,
Which the five watchful senses represent,
She forms imaginations, aery shapes,
Which Reason, joining or disjoining, frames
All what we affirm or what deny, and call
Our knowledge or opinion; then retires
Into her private cell when Nature rests.
Oft in her absence, mimic Fancy wakes
To imitate her; but, misjoining shapes,
Wild work produces oft, and most in dreams,
Ill matching words and deeds long past or late.
Some such resemblances, methinks, I find
Of our last evening's talk in this thy dream,
But with addition strange.

Adam now consoles Eve for her grief due to seeing such a grisly dream, and then a tear rolls down her cheek. The couple then goes out into the field to do their "morning's rural work". God sees them working and feels pity. He calls Raphael and asks him to caution Adam of the plotting of Satan. He tells him that Satan is conspiring to make Adam fall from the state of bliss, for fault of some one else's: " '... This let him know,/Lest, wilfully transgressing, he pretend/ Surprisal, unadmonished, unforewarned.' " And accordingly Raphael hies downward towards earth.

Adam sees the glorious shape of Raphael and calls Eve to come near him. The couple takes Raphael for a guest, and Eve collects diverse fruits to entertain him. Raphael tells them that God is one, and that he created everything as perfect. Raphael, further, tells them that everything, as created by God, will remain perfect, as long as, it is not adventitiously corrupted. But, says Raphael, the creation of the world vary in degrees of perfection., and that every creation of the world is continually aspiring to spirituality. And so, Raphael also says, man may become like angels, if he obeys the commands of God (lines 482-503):

flowers and their fruit,
Man's nourishment, by gradual scale sublimes,
To vital spirits aspire, to animal,
To intellectual; give both life and sense,
Fancy and understanding; whence the Soul
Reason receives, and Reason is her being,
Discursive, or intuitive: discourse
Is oftest yours, the latter most is ours,
Differing but in degree, of kind the same.
Wonder not, then, what God for you saw good
If I refuse not, but convert, as you,
To proper substance. Time may come when Men
With Angels may participate, and find
No inconvenient diet, nor too light fare;
And from these corporeal nutriments, perhaps,
Your bodies may at last turn all to spirit,
Improved by tract of time, and winged ascend
Ethereal, as we, or may at choice
Here or in heavenly paradises dwell,
If we ye be found obedient, and retain
Unalterably firm his love entire
Whose progeny you are.

Now, at the request of Adam, Raphael narrates to him the history of the creation. Raphael says that before this creation, there was no world, and that there was only Chaos. God first made the orbs or the circular celestial bodies, and then created his Son (Jesus Christ) and asked all the innumerable angels to show obeisance to the Son (lines 600-615):

'Hear, all ye Angels, Progeny of Light,
Thrones, Dominations, Princedoms, Virtues, Powers,
Hear my decree, which unprovoked shall stand !

'This day I have begot whom I declare
My only Son, and on this holy hill
Him have appointed, whom ye now behold
At my right hand. Your head I him appoint,
And by myself have sworn to him shall bow
All knees in Heaven, and shall confess him Lord.
Under his great vicegerent reign abide,
United as one individual soul,
For ever happy. Him who disobeys
Me disobeys, breaks union, and, that day,
Cast out from God and blessed vision, falls
Into utter darkness, deep engulfed, his place
Ordained without redemption, without end....' "

All the angels are pleased at this pronouncement of God and so they rejoice. After this, as night approaches, they fall asleep. But Satan (who is the Archangel and till now is known by the name of Lucifer) cannot sleep due to his envy towards the Son of God. He, therefore, arouses jealousy in the breasts of numerous sleeping angels, and thus raises the standard of rebellion against God. God, the 'Eternal Eye' comes to know of this plot of Satan, and cautions his Son about this. In response, the Son tells his father that he (God) justly derides Satan. Satan, then, with all the rebellious angels flies to the northernmost region, and takes his royal seat on top of a hill, made of "diamond quarries hewn and rocks of gold —" which is the "place of great Lucifer". Lucifer (now, Satan) now addresses the congregation of the rebellious spirits or angels as "Thrones, Dominations, Princedoms, Virtues, Powers —", and asks the congregation to devise means of casting off the yoke of slavery (under the Son of God) put on all of them by God (lines 787-802) :

"..
Will ye submit your necks, and choose to bend
The supple knee ? ye will not, if I trust
To know you right, or if ye know yourselves
Natives and Sons of Heaven possessed before
By none, and, if not equal all, yet free,
Equally free; for orders and degrees
Jar not with liberty, but well consist.
Who can in reason, then, or right, assume
Monarchy over such as live by right
His equals — if in power and splendour less,
In freedom equal? or can introduce

Law and edict on us, who without law
Err not? much less for this to be our Lord,
And look for adoration, to th' abuse
Of those imperial titles which assert
Our being ordained to govern, not to serve!"

From among the angels, Abdiel then stood up and opposed the proposal of Satan and the consenting mood of the congregation (lines 809-825):

" 'O argument blasphemous, false, and proud
Words which no ear ever to hear in Heaven
Expected; least of all from thee, ingrate,
In place thyself so high above thy pears!
Canst thou with impious obloquy condemn
The just decree of God, pronounced and sworn,
That to his only Son, by right endued
With regal sceptre, every soul in Heaven
Shall bend the knee, and in that honour due
Confess him rightful king? Unjust, thou say'st,
Flatly unjust, to bind with laws thee free,
And equal over equals to let reign,
One over all with unsucceeded power!
Shalt thou give law to God? shalt thou dispute
With him the points of liberty, who made
Thee what thou art, and formed the Powers of Heaven
Such as he pleased, circumscribed their being?...' "

Abdiel delivers this speech with zeal, but he is supported by no one, and so Satan gladly rejects this plea of Abdiel, and declares that he and all the other rebel angels were not created by God : "We know no time when we were not as now;/Know none before us, self-begot, self-raised". As Satan stops, his speech is highly applauded by all the rebellious angels (except Abdiel). Lastly, Abdiel warns Satan : "I see thy fall".

Book VI

Milton's 'Argument' of Book VI runs thus: "Raphael continues to relate how Michael and Gabriel were sent forth to battle against Satan and his Angels. The first fight described: Satan and his Powers retire under night. He calls a council; invents devilish engines, which, in the second day's fight, put Michael and his Angels to some disorder; but they at length, pulling up mountains, overwhelmed both the force and machines of Satan. Yet, the tumult not so ending, God, on the third day, sends Messiah his Son, for whom he had reserved the glory of that victory. He, in the power of his Father, coming to the place, and causing all his legions to stand still on either side, with his chariot and thunder driving into the midst of his enemies, pursues them, unable to resist, towards the wall of Heaven; which opening, they leap down with horror and confusion into the place of punishment prepared for them in the Deep. Messiah returns with triumph to his Father."

The narration of the pre-history of the creation, that was began by Raphael at the end of Book V, continues. Raphael tells Adam and Eve that Gabriel and Michael continue to pursue Satan, and a supernatural voice from a golden cloud encourages the two angels in their pursual (lines 44-50):

> " '... Go, Michael, of celestial armies prince,
> And thou, in military prowess next,
> Gabriel; lead forth to battle these my sons
> Invisible; lead forth my armed Saints,
> By thousands and by millions ranged for fight,
> Equal in number to that godless crew
> Rebellious....' "

At this moment, the host of Satan's rebellious spirits are marching towards the Mount of God. Abdiel accosts Satan and rebukes him: " 'Fool' not to think how vain/Against th' Omnipotent to rise in arms;/ Who, out of smallest things, could without end/Have raised incessant armies to defeat/Thy folly...' " Then altercation between Abdiel and Satan follows. Satan says that he is bent on achieving freedom: "Servility with freedom to contend". Abdiel contradicts him: he says that God's command and inclination of Nature are one; therefore, obeying God is equivalent to obeying one's Nature, which is always good (lines 172-181):

> " 'Apostate! still thou err'st, nor end wilt find
> Of erring, from path of truth remote.
> Unjustly thou deprav'st it with the name
> Of servitude, to serve whom God ordains,
> Or Nature: God and Nature bid the same,
> When he who rules is worthiest, and excells
> Them whom he governs. This is servitude —
> To serve th' unwise, or him who hath rebelled
> Against his worthier, as thine now serve thee,
> Thyself not free, but to thyself enthralled;...' "

Saying thus, Abdiel strikes at Satan, and Satan becomes amazed under the impact of the heavy stroke. Soon battle ensues between the armies of Abdiel and Satan, and at the clash of the two armies, heaven and earth shake. Ultimately, Satan is subdued, and is taken a captive. Nevertheless, Satan is not daunted; he challenges Abdiel in another battle (lines 293-295): " '... Meanwhile thy utmost force—/And join him named Almighty to thy aid—/I fly not, but have sought thee far and nigh...' " Another battle ensues, and this time Michael cuts off the right side of Satan, and Satan writhes in pain, for the first time (lines 320-327):

> But the sword
> Michael from the armoury of God
> Was given him tempered so that neither keen
> Nor solid might resist that edge; it met
> The sword of Satan, with steep force to smite
> Descending, and in half cut sheer; nor stayed,
> But, with swift reverse, deep entering, sheared
> All his right hand. Then Satan first knew pain,

In the other front of the battle, Gabriel fiercely fights with Moloch and breaks into pieces his battle-array. In yet another front, Uriel and Raphael vanquish Adramelech and Asmadai. Thus thousands of evil angels are defeated. Then night falls, and Michael, with his angels, begins to guard one part of Eden. But, on the other part of Eden, Satan calls a council of the rebellious and fallen angels, and addresses it. He tells the evil angels that they have fought for only one day against the powers of God; and so asks them if they can fight for one day more. No, he asks them why they cannot fight for eternity. Satan tells them that they are ethereal and so immortal beings; and so they have no fear of death. Satan thus urges them to fight another battle (lines 433-442):

> " 'Since now we find this our empyreal form
> Incapable of mortal injury,
> Imperishable, and, though pierced with wound,
> Soon closing, and by native vigour healed.
> Of evil, then, so small as easy think
> The remedy; perhaps more valid arms,
> Weapons more violent, when next we meet,
> May serve to better us and worse our foes,
> Or equal what between us made the odds,
> In nature none....' "

Nisroch, a fallen angel, agrees with Satan, and urges upon him to arrange for another battle with the powers of God. Satan ratifies Nisroch's proposal and declares that this time he will employ an (perhaps cannon-like) engine in the battle — a firespitting engine : " 'Which, into hollow engines long and round/Thick-rammed, at th' other bore with touch of fire/Dilated and infuriate, shall send forth/From far, with thundering noise, among our foes/Such implements of mischief as shall dash/To pieces and o'erwhelm whatever stands/Adverse,....' "

Now, as morning begins to show, the victorious angels, God's powers, blow trumpets as a sign of their victory; but seeing that the fallen angels are bent on renewed quarrel, prepares for battle. Fierce fight begins again and continues for two days, and then God tells his Son that for two days past the war has continued "Since Michael and his Powers went forth to tame/These disobedient." God predicts the perpetuity of the war, and suspends the doom of the fallen angels: "I suspend their doom:/Whence in perpetual fight they needs must last/Endless, and no solution will be found." After this, Urim, Michael and thousands of saintly angels go up towards heaven. On the other hand, seeing this, Satan prepares for renewed war with "hope conceiving from despair." On the third day of the war, Satan musters all his forces for final battle: "To final battle drew". Meanwhile, Messiah, the Son of God, to wit Jesus Christ, also orders his powers to get prepared for the final battle. The poet says that as the Son of God orders his forces, his countenance becomes ferocious: " 'So spoke the Sons, and into terror changed/ His count'nance, too severe to be beheld,/ And full of wrath bent on his enemies....' " Now Messiah, the Son of God, himself fiercely attacks the enemy ranks, and soon the rebellious spirits fall down into the deep pit of hell, like terrified goats (lines 856-866):

> " '... The overthrown he raised, and, as a herd
> Of goats or timorous flock together thronged,
> Drove them before him thunderstruck, pursued
> With terrors and with furies to the bounds
> And crystal wall of Heaven; which, opening wide,
> Rolled inward, and a spacious gap disclosed
> Into the wasteful Deep. The monstrous sight
> Struck them with horror backward; but far worse
> Urged them behind: headlong themselves they threw
> Down from the verge of Heaven: eternal wrath
> Burnt after them to the bottomless pit....' "

The sound of their fall is so reverberating that hell is shaking to its foundation. The beaten warriors thus fell for long nine days. " '...Hell at last,/Yawning, received them whole, and on them closed —/Hell, their fit habitation, fraught with fire/Unquenchable, the house of woe and pain....' " Messiah, the Son of God, now returns triumphantly to heaven. This is an example of the punishment God inflicts upon those who disobeys him.

Book VII

The 'Argument' that prefaces this Book is very short. It reads: "Raphael, at the request of Adam, relates how and wherefore this world was first created:— that God, after the expelling of Satan and his Angels out of Heaven, declared his pleasure to create another world, and other creatures to dwell therein; sends his Son with glory, and attendance of Angels, to perform the work of creation in six days: the Angels celebrate with hymns the performance thereof, and his reascension into Heaven." At the beginning of Book VII, the poet once again importunes the Goddess to tell him the story of the creation of the world, and Raphael, being commended by her, narrates the story of the creation of the world, the multitude of the inhabitants of the earth, and of the flora and fauna, and Adam and his 'consorted Eve' listen to him with all attention. Raphael tells them that he will impart them only 'knowledge within bounds', and asks them to know no more, because overmuch of knowledge may be a matter of harm (lines 120-130):

' . . . beyond abstain
To ask, nor let thine own inventions hope
Things not revealed, which th' invisible king,
Only omniscient, hath suppressed in night,
To none communicable in Earth or Heaven.
Enough is left besides to search and know;
But knowledge is as food, and needs no less
Her temperance over appetite, to know
In measure what the mind may well contain;
Oppress else with surfeit, and soon turns
Wisdom to folly, as nourishment to wind...'

Raphael continues his narration. He says that after the defeat of the evil design of Satan, God thought of creating a new world (lines 154-161):

" '...and in a moment will create
Another world; out of one man a race
Of men innumerable, there to dwell,

Not here, till, by degrees of merit raised,
They open to themselves at length the way
Up hither, under long obedience tried,
And Earth be changed to Heaven, and Heaven to Earth,
One kingdom, joy and union without end....' "

Now God asks the 'Word' or the 'begotten Son' or 'the Filial Godhead' to create that new world, and as 'the Filial Godhead' pronounces a word, the particular object corresponding to that word, is created. After this, God goes to retirement, but henceforth what God will will will be Fate (lines 163-173):

'... And thou, my Word, begotten Son, by thee
This I perform; speak thou, and be it done !
My overshadowing Spirit and might with thee
I send along; ride forth, and bid the Deep
Within appointed bounds be heaven and earth;
Boundless the deep, because I am who fill
Infinitude, nor vacuous the space,
Thou I, uncircumscribed, myself retire,
And put not forth my goodness, which is free
To act or not, Necessity and Chance
Approach not me, and what I will is Fate...'

God ordains that the new world be such that there good may be created even out of evil: " 'Good out of evil to create' ". The Word now orders the abyssal Chaos to stop the discord within it : " 'Your discord end!' " It then pronounces : " 'Thus, far extend, thus, far thy bounds;/ This be thy just circumference, O World!' " Then further creations proceed at the command of God, or, better, of the Word :

'... Thus God the Heaven created, thus the Earth,
Matter unformed and void. Darkness profound
Covered th' abyss; but on the wat'ry calm
His brooding wings the Spirit of God outspread,
And vital virtue infused, and vital warmth,
Throughout the fluid mass, but downward purged
The black, tartarous, cold, infernal dregs,
Adverse to life; then founded, then conglobed
Like things to like, the rest to several place
Disparted, and between spun out the air,
And Earth, self-balanced, on her centre hung....'

God next commands that there be light, and light appears there, all around. And God, through the agency of the Word, creates the sun, day and night, sky and water. All these are created on the first and the second days. On the next day, God wishes that there be flora on earth and the flora appears on earth, and now earth "Seemed like to Heaven". On the following day, God creates stars, the moon, etc. also. On the fifth day, he ordains that creatures of water and air be formed, and these are formed. On the sixth day, or the last day of the creation, God says: " 'Let th' Earth bring forth soul living in her kind,/Cattle, and creeping things, and beast of the earth,/Each in their kind!' " And, lastly, on the same sixth day, God asks his Son, the Word, to create Man (lines 519-523):

'... Let us make now Man in our image,
Man In our similitude, and let them rule
Over the fish and foul of sea and air,
Beast of the field, and over all the earth,
And every creeping thing that creeps the ground.'

This saying, God, through the medium of his Son, the Word, creates Man out of earth, and infuses life into him, and calls him Adam. And God tells Adam that he can enjoy the tastes of all the fruits around him, but he must not taste the fruit of the Tree of knowledge, on pain of death (lines 541-544) :

'... All sorts are here that all th' earth yields,
Variety without end; but of the tree
Which, tasted, works knowledge of good and evil
Thou may'st not; in the day thou eat'st thou diest.

Thus, within the space of only six days, God creates everything, including Man. He says that he "will deign/To visit oft the dwellings of just men Delighted, and with frequent intercourse/Thither will send his winged messengers/On errands of supernal grace.' " And, lastly, on the seventh day, Gad takes rest, ceasing all his works, and the seventh day is called Sabbath.

Book VIII

In this Book, Raphael is still narrating the story of the creation. Here we may note that Raphael, the 'divine Historian' began his narration in Book V, continued the narration through Books VI and VII, and now completes the narration here in this Book. However, Milton's 'Argument' of this Book runs thus: "Adam inquires concerning celestial motions, is doubtfully answered, and exhorted to search rather things more worthy of knowledge. Adam assents, and, still desirous to detain Raphael, relates to him what he remembered since his own creation — his placing in Paradise; his talk with God concerning solitude and fit society; his first meeting and nuptials with Eve. His discourse with the Angel thereupon: who, after admonitions repeated, departs." Adam and Eve, so long, have been listening to Raphael's narration of the 'history' of the creation with raft attention. Though Raphael has said much about the creation, yet they seem to be eager to know more about it. But Raphael forbids them, as he once ago did: " '... the rest/From Man or Angel the great Architect/Did wisely to conceal...' " And yet Raphael does not cease talking to them, and from what he tells them, it is clear that the sun is the centre of the universe, and that the world is a static planet, and not a rotating thing: " '... Earth sitting still...' ". Adam learns from Raphael that the ideal life (of man) is that life which is sweet (happy) without ostentation of intricate knowledge and thoughts, and that too much of knowledge and complicated thought are meaningless (lines 191-194):

> '... not to know at large of things remote
> From use, obscure and subtle, but to know
> That which before us lies in daily life,
> Is the prime wisdom: what is more is fume,...'

Now, Raphael, in turn, asks Adam to tell him the story of his (Adam's) being created, because he (Raphael) was absent on the day on which God created him (Adam). And Adam tells him (lines 253-261):

> '...As new-waked from soundest sleep,
> Soft on the flowery herb I found me laid,
> In balmy sweat, which with his beams the Sun
> Soon dried, and on the reeking moisture fed.
> Straight toward Heaven my wandering eyes I turned,
> And gazed a while the ample sky, till, raised
> By quick instructive motion, up I sprung,
> As thitherward endeavouring, and upright
> Stood on my feet....'

After being created, Adam wandered all about and now falls asleep, and in a dream sees God standing before him. God warns Adam of the dire consequences of tasting the fruit of the Tree of Knowledge — the tree that stands by the Tree of Life. Adam, in reply, tells God that all the creatures of the world except man are created in pairs — pair of a male and a female, for instance, 'lion with lioness'. Adam further tells God that unlike him (God), who is perfect, though single, man has imperfection through his having no mate (lines 416-426):

> '............... not so is Man,
> But in degree —— the cause of his desire
> By conversation with his like to help
> Or solace his defects. No need that thou
> Should'st propagate, already infinite,
> And through all numbers absolute, though One;
> But Man by number is to manifest
> His single imperfection, and beget
> Like of his like, his image multiplied,
> In unity defective, which requires
> Collateral love, and dearest amity...'

The compassionate God understands the argument of Adam and creates Eve out of Adam's breast bone. Adam narrates how it all was done (lines 460-477):

> '... Mine eyes he closed, but open left the cell
> Of fancy, my internal sight; by which,
> Abstract as in a trance, methought I saw,
> Though sleeping, where I lay, and saw the Shape
> Still glorious before whom awake I stood;
> Who stooping, opened my left side, and took
> From thence a rib, with cordial spirits warm,
> And life-blood streaming fresh; wide was the wound,
> But suddenly with flesh filled up and healed.
> The rib he formed and fashioned with his hands;
> Under his forming hands a creature grew,
> Man-like, but different sex, so lovely fair
> That what seemed fair in all the world seemed now
> Mean, or in her seemed up, in her contained,
> And in her looks, which from that time infused
> Sweetness into my heart, unfelt before,
> And into all things from her air inspired
> The spirit of love and amorous delight....'

Adam tells Raphael that to him Eve represents everything desirable, and much more, and that he is all happiness for getting her beside him. But he complains that Nature has given her much more outward show of beauty than inward excellence of wisdom. Nevertheless, Adam admits that whenever he accosts her, it seems to him that she is quite perfect in all aspects, inward and outward (lines 537-559) :

'... on her bestowed
Too much ornament, in outward show
Elaborate, of inward less exact.
For well I understand in the prime end
Of Nature her th' inferior, in the mind
And inward faculties, which most excel;
In outward also her resembling less
His image who made both, and less expressing
The character of that dominion given
O'er other creatures. Yet when I approach
Her loveliness, so absolute she seems
And in herself complete, so well to know
Her own, that what she wills to do or say
Seems wisest, virtuousest, discreetest, best.
All higher knowledge in her presence falls
Degraded; Wisdom in discourse with her
Loses, discount'nanced, and like
Folly shows; Authority and Reason on her wait,
As one intended first, not after made
Occasionally; and, to consummate all,
Greatness of mind and nobleness their seat
Build in her loveliest, and create an awe
Above her, as a guard angelic placed.'

In reply, Raphael advises Adam regarding connubial relationship. He tells Adam that he should not undervalue Nature that has created Eve. Raphael says that Adam represents wisdom, while Eve represents Nature, and that the perfect balance of wisdom and Nature will give perfect happiness, and also that such perfect balance should be the ideal of marital relationship. Raphael further says (lines 561-578):

'Accuse not Nature! she hath done her part;
Do thou but thine! and be not diffident
Of wisdom; she deserts thee not, if thou
Dismiss not her, when most thou need'st her nigh,
By attributing overmuch to things
Less excellent, as thou thyself perceiv'st.
For what admir'st thou, what transports thee so ?
An outside; fair, no doubt, and worthy well
Thy cherishing, thy honouring, and thy love;

Not thy subjection: weigh with her thyself;
Then value: oft-times nothing profits more
Than self-esteem, grounded on just and right
Well managed. Oft that skill, the more thou know'st,
The more she will acknowledge thee her head,
And to realities yield all her shows —
Made so adorn for thy delight the more,
So aweful that with honour thou may'st love
Thy mate, who sees when thou art seen least wise....'

Raphael continues his speech, and now advises Adam about the ideal sex relationship and love relationship between the husband and the wife. He says (lines 579-594):

'... But, if the sense of touch, whereby mankind
Is propagated, seem such dear delight
Beyond all other, think the same vouchsafed
To cattle and each beast; which would not be
To them made common and divulged, if aught
Therein enjoyed were worthy to subdue
The soul of Man, or passion in him move.
What higher in her society thou find'st
Attractive, human, rational, love still:
In loving thou dost well; in passion not,
Wherein true love consists not. Love refines
The thoughts, and heart enlarges — hath his seat
In Reason, and is judicious, is the scale
By which to heavenly love thou may'st ascend,
Not sunk in carnal pleasure; for which cause
Among the beasts no mate for thee was found.'

Adam, in reply, says that he is more interested in non-carnal love than in carnal (lines 596-604) :

'Neither her outside formed so fair, nor aught
In procreation, common to all kinds
(Though higher of the genial bed by far,
And with mysterious reverence, I deem),
So much delights me as those graceful acts,
Those thousand decencies, that daily flow
From all her words and actions, mixed with love
And sweet compliance,

Milton here shows his preference for sexual abstinence and his passion for abstract or pure love. But he also, sometimes, betrays his ambivalence towards physical love. For instance, before parting from Adam, Raphael tells him that in the fullness of love both the spirits and the bodies of a couple should be united, and that only from such consummate union, happiness can come, and this goes against his general preference for sexual abstinance. However, Raphael further tells Adam that even the heavenly spirits or angels enjoy both spiritual and physical love: " '... if spirits embrace,/Total they mix, union of pure with pure/Desiring, nor restrained conveyance need/As flesh to mix with flesh, or soul with soul...' " After all this, Raphael and Adam part company : "the Angel to Heaven/From the thick shade, and Adam to his bower."

Book IX

In Book IX, Milton tells us about the Fall of Man — of Adam and Eve — from Paradise. As a result of the sin committed by tasting the fruit of the Tree of Knowledge, the couple become aware of shame and guilt, and dissension ensues between them — dissension that was absent between them, earlier. The punishment of their sin comes down upon them in the form of the immortal couple's turning into mortals, and in the shape of their Fall from Paradise. However, Milton's 'Argument' of this Book runs thus: "Satan having compassed the Earth, with meditated guile, returns as a mist by night into Paradise; enters into the Serpent sleeping. Adam and Eve in the morning go forth to their labours, which Eve proposes to divide in several places, each labouring apart: Adam consents not, alleging the danger lest that enemy of whom they were forewarned, should attempt her found alone. Eve, loth to be thought not circumspect or firm enough, urges her going apart, the rather desirous to make trial of her strength; Adam at last yields. The Serpent finds her alone: his subtle approach, first gazing, then speaking, with much flattery extolling Eve above all other creatures. Eve, wandering to hear the Serpent speak, asks how he attained to human speech and such understanding not till now; the Serpent answers that by tasting of a certain tree in the garden he attained both to speech and reason, till then void of both. Eve requires him to bring her to that tree, and finds it to be the Tree of knowledge forbidden: the Serpent, now grown bolder, with many wiles and arguments induces her at length to eat. She, pleased with the taste, deliberates a while whether to impart thereof to Adam or not; at last brings him of the fruit; relates what persuaded her to eat thereof. Adam, at first amazed, but perceiving her lost, resolves, through vehemence of love, to perish with her, and, extenuating the trespass, eats also of the fruit. The effects thereof in them both; they seek to cover their nakedness; then fall to variance and accusation of one another."

In this Book, Milton is going to narrate how 'a world of woe' comes down to this earth of ours. As an *obiter dictum*, he says that he is writing this epic with the inspiration got from his 'celestial patroness', the Muse. Before this, for more than one occasions, the poet begged inspiration from the Muse. However, he tells us that he is not so much intent upon writing an epic as he is inclined to speak about a 'higher argument'. Saying this, Milton resumes his narration. He says that now night comes, and Satan, being ordered out of Eden by Gabriel, meditates upon 'fraud and malice' as instruments of the destruction of Man. Then, Satan, for long seven nights in tandem, revolves round earth, and on the eighth night returns to earth (lines 62-67):

> Thence full of anguish driven,
> The space of seven continued nights he rode
> With darkness — thrice the equinoctial line
> He circled, four times crossed the car of Night
> From pole to pole, traversing each colure —
> On the eighth returned,

And then, Satan descends at the foot of Paradise and near the Tree of Life, and then metamorphoses himself into a mist, and enters into the body of a sleeping serpent, through its mouth. On the other hand, at breaking of dawn, Eve tells Adam that they should begin their day's work — the pruning of the garden of Eden — separately. Adam very happily accepts her proposal, saying "nothing lovelier can be found/In woman than to study household good,/And good works in her husband to promote." If they part company, Adam will feel lonely; but he says: "solitude sometimes is best society". Eve knows beforehand that an evil spirit is somewhere around, who may ruin both of them: "we have a foe/May tempt". And, therefore, she prays to earth to protect her. Adam tells her that there is nothing evil in the creation of God (lines 343-346):

> '... best are all things as the will
> Of God ordained them; his creating hand
> Nothing imperfect or deficient left
> Of all that he created — much less Man,...'

Adam further tells her that without one's wishing for, no harm can reach him : "Against his will he can receive no harm." He tells her that everything of the universe obeys, and works according to the dictates of God, save Will and Reason, which are free: " '... But God left free the Will; for what obeys/Reason is free...' ". But free reason sometimes may be corrupted by 'fair appearing good', and then one may do sacrilegious deeds (lines 352-356) :

'... Reason he made right,
But bid her well beware, and still erect,
Lest, by some fair appearing good surprised,
She dictates false, and misinform the Will
To do what God expressly hath forbid...'

Satan, in an ambush, finds the two lonely human beings, pruning the garden and doing such other jobs. He then approaches Eve, admires her beauty, and then in submission licks the ground. All these done, Satan flatteringly addresses Eve as 'Empress of this World' and as 'resplendent Eve', and tells her, tongue in cheek, that he is a lowly creature and that one day he saw a beautiful tree, out there, a laden with delicious fruits (lines 576-583) :

A goodly tree far distant to behold,
Loaden with fruit of fairest colours mixed,
Ruddy and gold: I nearer drew to gaze;
When from the boughs a savoury odour blown,
Grateful to appetite, more pleased my sense
Than smell of sweetest fennel, or the teats
Of ewe or goat dropping with milk at even,
Unsucked of lamb or kid, that tend their play.

Satan tells her that he tasted the fruit of that tree — the Tree of Knowledge — and that the fruits being on the high-rise branches of that tree, other creatures could not have that delectable taste. He further tells Eve that as a result of tasting of that fruit, he became all wise: " '... Thenceforth to speculations high or deep/I turned my thoughts, and with capacious mind/Considered all things visible in Heaven,/Or Earth, or Middle, all things fair and good...' ". At this, Eve unwarily becomes curious about the fruit of that tree near which, after Satan, she approaches. Even at this perilous moment, she is not oblivious of the fiat of God: " '... But of this tree we may not taste or touch;/God so commanded...' ".

Without even an iota of doubt of defeat in his malicious design, Satan now doubles his effort in tempting Eve, addresses the tree as 'Mother of Science' and Eve as 'Queen of this Universe', and falsely assures Eve that the taste of the fruit will never make her mortal. And with superb rhetoric, he persuades her thus (lines 679-732):

'O sacred, wise, and wisdom-giving Plant,
Mother of Science! now I feel thy power
Within me clear, not only to discern
Things in their causes, but to trace the ways
Of highest agents, deemed however wise.
Queen of this Universe! do not believe
Those rigid threats of death; ye shall not die.
How should ye ? by the fruit it gives you life
To knowledge; by the Threatener? look on me,
Me who have touched and tasted, yet both live,
And life more perfect have attained than Fate
Meant me, by venturing higher than my lot.
Shall that be shut to Man which to the beast
Is open? or will God incense his ire
For such a petty trespass, and not praise
Rather your dauntless virtue, whom the pain
Of death denounced, whatever thing Death be,
Deterred not from achieving what might lead
To happier life, knowledge of good and evil?
Of good, how just? of evil — if what is evil
Be real, why not known, since easier shunned?
God, therefore, cannot hurt ye, and be just;
Not just, not God; not feared then, nor obeyed:
Your fear itself of death removes the fear.
Why, then, was this forbid? Why but to awe?
Why but to keep ye low and ignorant,
His worshippers? He knows that the day
Ye eat thereof your eyes, that seem so clear,
Yet are but dim, shall perfectly be then
Opened and cleared, and ye shall be as Gods,
Knowing both good and evil, as they know.
That ye should be as Gods, since I as Man,
Internal Man, is but proportion meet;
I, of brute human; ye, of human, Gods.
So ye shall die perhaps, by putting off
Human, to put on Gods — death to be wished,
Though threatened, which no worse than this can bring
And what are Gods, that Man may not become
As they, participating godlike food
The Gods are first, and that advantage use

On our belief, that all from them proceeds.
I question it; for this fair Earth I see,
Warmed by the Sun, producing every Kind;
Them nothing. If they all things, who enclosed
Knowledge of good and evil in this tree,
That whose thereof forthwith attains
Wisdom without their leave ? and within lies
Th' offence, that Man should thus attain to know ?
What can your knowledge hurt him, or this tree
Impart against his will, it all be his?
Or is it envy? and can envy dwell
In heavenly breasts? These, these and many more
Causes import your need of this fair fruit.
Goddess humane, reach, then, and freely taste!'

It is now noon, and Eve is feeling intense pang of hunger. Therefore, she is thinking of tasting the interdicted fruit. She now ponders over the prohibition of God. She asks how is it that God prohibits the tasting of the fruit which makes one wise? She thinks that man is thereby being stunted by God so that he may not become wise: "In plain, then, what forbids he but to know,/Forbids us good, forbids us to be wise?" And she decides: "Such prohibition bind not." She, further, considers: knowledge is 'intellectual food'. How is it that God ordained that subhuman creatures, like the snake (actually, Satan in the form of it), could taste it without any harm done to him, and man is prohibited to taste it ? On thus cogitating, she determines to eat the fruit: "What fear I, then?" In this way, her reason being clouded by her will, "Forthreaching to the fruit, she plucked, she eat". And at once "Earth felt the wound, and Nature from her seat,/Sighing through all her works, gave signs of woe/That all was lost." And, his malicious design being fructified, Satan sleeked away. To Eve, the taste of the fruit was inordinately delectable, and after tasting it she felt tipsy and jocund, and expressed extreme wonder about the fruit : " O sov'ran, virtuous, precious of all trees/In Paradise". Elated by the sweet taste of the fruit of the Tree of Knowledge, Eve henceforth decided not to obey the command of God, but to depend on her own newly gained knowledge and experience (lines 803-810) :

I grow mature
In knowledge, as the Gods who all things know.
....
Experience, next to thee I owe,

Best guide: not following thee,
I had remained in ignorance; thou open'st Wisdom's way,
And giv'st access, though secret she retire.

Eve now thinks of asking Adam to taste the same fruit, but she dithers. At last, she thinks that after eating the fruit, she has become mortal, and in the event of her death, the immortal Adam may marry another woman. She, therefore, feels jealous and decides to make Adam taste the fruit, to make him mortal, too (lines 827-831):

And death ensue? Then I shall be no more;
And Adam, wedded to another Eve,
Shall live with her enjoying, I extinct!
A death to think! Confirmed, then, I resolve
Adam shall share with me in bliss or woe.

Eve now goes to Adam and with her womanly wiles draws Adam's sympathetic attention. She tells him that the Tree of knowledge is not bad, and that those who have tasted the fruit of it have become god-like. She admits that Satan and herself have also tasted the fruit. Therefore, she will like Adam partake of the fruit, so that both of them may remain equal as before (lines 881-884) :

Thou, therefore, also taste, that equal lot
May join us, equal joy, as equal love;
Lest thou not tasting, different degree
Disjoin us,

Adam instantly becomes aghast at the frailty of Eve: "How art thou lost! how on a sudden lost,/Defaced, deflowered, and now to death dovote!" But, being blind with sympathy for Eve, Adam decides to die along with her, and does not prefer his present immortality by not tasting the fruit: " '... Certain my resolution is to die./How can I live without thee?...' " He tells Eve that it may be a falsity that the taste of the fruit will make an immortal creature mortal, and that God cannot destroy his best creations, which they themselves are, because that will be foolish, for in the case of their ruin, God's foe will become triumphant. Adam, therefore, tells Eve that God cannot unmake what he has made. Adam concludes his arguments by expressing his wish of following the fate of Eve: " 'we are one,/One flesh; to lose thee were to lose myself...' " Eve returned: " '...On my experience, Adam, freely taste,/ And fear of death deliver to the winds.' " Eve tells Adam all this and weeps in extreme joy, because he is ready to eat the fruit. She now reaches out the fruit to her husband, and Adam, being fascinated by the beauty and nagging supplication of Eve, loses all his rationality, and tastes the fruit: "He scrupled not to eat,/Against his better knowledge, not deceived,/But fondly overcome with female charm."

As soon as Adam tastes the fruit, he feels an amorous impulse of the fleshy kind, and his carnal invitation of Eve is reciprocated by her (lines 1008-1015):

> As with new wine intoxicated both,
> They swim in mirth, and fancy that they feel
> Divinity within them breeding wings
> Wherewith to scorn the Earth: but that false fruit
> For other operations first displaced,
> Carnal desire inflaming; he on Eve
> Began to cast lascivious eyes; she him
> As wantonly repaid; in lust they burn,

Adam now asks Eve to go to a 'shady bank' for the carnal consummation of their love (lines 1037-1043):

> Her hand he seized, and to a shady bank,
> Thick overhead with verdant roof embowered,
> He led her, nothing loth; flowers were the couch,
> Pansies, and violets, and asphodel,
> And hyacinth — Earth's freshest, softest lap
> There they their fill of love and love's disport
> Took largely,

Out of this carnal love, shame grows in them, and to cover their shame, they sew fig-leaves and wear these on themselves. But the whole of their shame is not covered by the fig-leaves, and so they weep. Along with shame, there also grows in them anger, hate, mistrust, suspicion and discord. Adam now repents that had Eve not strayed away from him, this Fall might not occur. Hearing this, Eve accusingly retorts: " '... why didst not thou, the head,/Command me absolutely not to go,/ Going into such danger, as thou saidst?...' " At this, Adam flies into a rage and says: " '... Thus, it shall befall/Him who, to worth in woman overtrusting,/Lets her will rule: restraint she will not brook;/And, left to herself, if evil thence ensue,/She first his weak indulgence will accuse.' " Thus, in frequent discords, they continue living together.

Book X

The 'Argument' of Book X runs thus: "Man's transgression known, the guardian Angels forsake Paradise, and return up to heaven to approve their vigilance, and are approved; God declaring that the entrance of

Satan could not be by them prevented. He sends his Son to judge the transgressors; who descends, and gives sentence accordingly; then, in pity, clothes them both, and reascends. Sin and Death sitting till then at the gates of Hell, by wonderous sympathy feeling the success of Satan in this new World, and the sin by Man there committed, resolve to sit no longer confined in Hell, but to follow Satan, their sire, up to the place of Man to make their way easier from Hell to this World to and fro, they pave a broad highway or bridge over Chaos, according to the track that Satan first made; then, preparing for Earth, they meet him, proud of his success, returning to Hell; their mutual gratulation. Satan arrives at Pandemonium; in full assembly relates with boasting his success against Man; instead of applause is entertained with a general hiss by all his audience, transformed, with himself also, suddenly into Serpents, according to his doom given in Paradise; then, deluded with a show of the Forbidden Tree springing up before them, they, greedily reaching to take of the fruit, chew dust and bitter ashes. The proceedings of Sin and Death: God foretells the final victory of his Son over them, and the renewing of all things; but, for the present, commands his Angels to make several alterations in the Heavens and Elements. Adam, more and perceiving his fallen condition, heavily bewails, rejects the condolement of Eve; she persists, and at length appeases him: then, to evade the curse likely to fall on their offsprings, proposes to Adam violent ways; which he approves not, but, conceiving better hope, puts in mind of the late promise made them, that her seed should be revenged on the Serpent, and exhorts her, with him, to seek peace of the offended Deity by repentance and supplication."

In this Book we will find that God is seeing the Fall of Man, from Heaven, but he does not intercept the evil doings of Satan, because he left Man free with his free will. After the Fall, the angels, incharge of protecting Adam and Eve, report the Fall to God, and God decides that his Son (Jesus Christ) will be sent to earth to redeem Adam and Eve. God tells his Son (lines 58-62) :

'... I intend
Mercy colleague with justice, sending thee,
Man's friend, his Mediator, his designed
Both ransom and Redeemer voluntary,
And destines Man himself to judge Man fall'n.'

The Son assures God that he will descend down to earth, according to his order, to judge the transgression of Man: " '...I go to judge/On Earth these thy transgressors...' ". He says that he will lessen the inevitable ruin of Adam and Eve, which is due to their recently committed sin, and will show them both justice and mercy. The Son then 'descended straight' on earth in the evening. The Son (who is also God, says Milton) calls Atam and Eve, and asks them why they are in their fallen condition. Adam replies that it was due to Eve that he fell from the neighbourhood of God. Then, the Son admonishingly asks Adam why he did obey the entreaty of Eve, instead of the commandments of God: " 'Was she thy God, that thou didst obey/ Before his voice?...' " And, after this, the Son asks Eve: " 'Say, Woman, what is this which thou hast done?' " Eve succinctly replies: " 'The Serpent me beguiled, and I did eat.' " Hearing this, Lord God pronounces death on Satan, the Serpent (lines 175-181) :

> 'Because thou hast done this, thou art accursed
> Above all cattle, each beast of the field;
> Upon thy belly grovelling thou shalt go,
> And dust shalt eat all the days of thy life.
> Between thee and the Woman I will put
> Enmity, and between thine and her seed;
> Her seed shall bruise thy head, thou bruise his heel.'

When the Son of God, "Jesus, son of Mary, second Eve", tells this (from his grave), Satan falls from heaven like a thunder. The Son of God then (rises from his grave and) pronounces wrought wreck upon all the evil powers: "Spoiled Principalities and Powers". He also warns Eve of dire consequences for her sin, and, further, warns her progeny of the same dire consequences (lines 193-196):

> 'Thy sorrow I will greatly multiply
> By thy conception; children thou shalt bring
> In sorrow forth, and to thy husband's will
> Thine shall submit; he over thee shall rule.'

Adam is not spared of the consequences, because he was driven by passion to accepting Eve's suggestion of tasting the fruit of the Tree of Knowledge, The Son awards Adam his dire verdict (lines 198-208) :

> 'Because thou hast hearkened to the voice
> And eaten of the tree concerning which
> I charged thee, saying, *Thou shalt not eat thereof*,
> Curs'd is the ground for thy sake; thou in sorrow
> Shalt eat thereof all the days of thy life;
> Thorns also and thistles it shall bring forth
> Unbid; and thou shalt eat th' herb of th' field;

> In the sweat of thy face shalt thou eat bread,
> Till thou return unto the ground; for thou
> Out of the ground wast taken: know thy birth,
> For dust thou art, and shalt to dust return.'

Jesus, the Son of God, now clothes the primal couple with skin of beasts to cover up their shame, and he clothes their inward nakedness with righteousness. So long Sin, the daughter of Satan, and Death, the son of him, were waiting in hell for arriving on earth. Now Sin proposes to Death to fly up to earth where, she presumed, her father, Satan, has been ruling supreme: " '... let us try/Adventurous work, yet to thy power and mine/Not unagreeable! to found a path/Over this main from Hell to that new world/Where Satan now prevails...' " Death, the shadow of Sin, agreed; and they two fly towards earth like 'ravenous fowl', because they have smelt 'mortal change on Earth'. The two meet their father, Satan, who has so long been observing the consequences of the Fall of Adam and Eve. Sin admires her father for the 'magnific deeds' he has done in Paradise. She tells Satan: " 'Thine now is all this world' ". Sin and Death then construct a broad highway between earth and hell. Through that highway, Satan descends down to Pandemonium, and sits in a council, and he is given a standing ovation by all the evil spirits there.

In the council, Satan addresses all as 'Thrones, Dominations, Princedoms, Virtues, Powers' and narrates before the evil spirits all his exploits in heaven and on the newly created earth. As he finishes his long speech, he hears a long and 'dismal universal hiss' — the sound of snakes — resembling the sound that issues from people while they propagate scorn among themselves in *soto voce*. Then Satan sees that he himself and all the other evil spirits are instantaneously metamorphosed into snakes: "punishes in the shape he sinned". And this transmogrification of their bodies occurs according to their fate (lines 572-577) :

> Thus they were plagued,
> And, worn with famine, long and ceaseless hiss,
> Till their lost shape, permitted, they resumed —
> Yearly enjoined, some say, to undergo
> This annual humbling certain numbered days,
> To dash their pride, and joy for Man seduced.

During all this while, Adam and Eve had been waiting under the spell of Sin and Death. God now pronounces his further orders. He says that till now he permitted everyone (of the creatures) to do whatever it pleased, and now he ordains that the jaws of hell will be shut and "then Heaven and Earth, renewed, shall be made pure/To sanctify that shall receive no stain". The heavenly bodies cry halleluiah at this joyful pronouncement of the Almighty. After this Adam gloomily soliloquises that he has to bear his misery silently, and says that he will do that though painfully (lines 726-732):

> I deserve it, and would bear
> My own deservings; but this will not serve:
> All that I eat or drink, or shall beget,
> Is propagated curse. O voice, once heard
> Delight fully, '*Increase and multiply*,'
> Now death to hear! for what can I increase
> Or multiply but curses on my head ?

In this long lamentation, Adam shows a ray of hope in his heart: he says that his 'mortal coil' may be destroyed at death, but his spirit, which was inspired by God himself, cannot die (lines 783-786):

> '... I cannot die;
> Lest that pure breath of life, the Spirit of Man
> Which God inspired, cannot together perish
> With this corporeal clod...'

He, therefore, concludes : "Both Death and I/Am found eternal, and incorporate both:/Nor on my part single; in me all/Posterity stands cursed."

Eve now gloomily approaches Adam, and Adam, seeing her, flies into a rage: " 'Out of my sight, thou serpent!....' " Adam repents for his being unable to discern the 'female snares'. Eve prays to him that he may not leave her in the lurch. She, too, repents for her wrongs and sins (lines 931-936) :

> '... I against God and thee,
> And to the place of judgement Will return,
> There with my cries importune Heaven, that all
> The sentence, from thy head removed, may light
> On me, sole curse to thee of all this woe,
> Me, me only, just object of His ire.'

Saying this, Eve begins to weep, and Adam feels commiseration with her. He tells her that he has forgiven her of her loose character : "Thy frailty and infirmer sex forgiven". Eve proposes to Adam not to propagate human beings, *i.e.*, not to bring forth children, because their issues will be heir to their own sorrow and repentance. Contrarily, if they do not propagate and multiply, Death will find no more victims besides themselves (lines 989-991):

'... Childless thou art; childless remain; so Death
Shall be deceived his glut, and with us two
Be forced to satisfy his ravenous maw.

Eve suggests to Adam that they put an end to their suffering or destruction by destroying themselves: " '... Destruction with destruction to destroy...' ". But Adam argues that even their own doom may not end their death; rather their self-destruction may abet the Almighty's ire. However, Eve heaves a hope by thinking that their issues, as predicted by the Son of God, will destroy snakes, the heinous forms of Satan, and she ejaculates to Adam : " '... thy seed shall bruise/The Serpent's head: piteous amends! ...' ". Adam now advises Eve to genuflex before God, confess their sins, and pray for his mercy. Adam is confident that if they do so, God will show mercy to them (lines 1086-1096):

' . . . What better can we do than, to the place
Repairing where he judged us, prostrate fall
Before him reverent, and there confess
Humbly our faults, and pardon us, with tears
Wat'ring the ground, and with our sighs the air
Frequenting, sent from hearts contrite, in sign
Of sorrow unfeigned and humiliation meek?
Undoubtedly he will relent, and turn
From his displeasure; in whose look serene,
When angry most he seemed and most severe,
What else but favour, grace, and mercy shone?'

And the first couple now does accordingly.

Book XI

Book XI shows the possibility of retrieval of Adam and Eve by God, and of their restoration in their happy state. In this Book, the poet tells that Adam and Eve sees in vision the future course of events. However, Milton's 'Argument' of this Book runs thus: "The Son of God presents to his Father the prayers of our first parents now repenting, and intercedes for them. God accepts them, but declares that they must no longer abide in Paradise; sends Michael ,with a band of Cherubim to dispossess them, but first to reveal to Adam future things: Michael's coming down. Adam shows to Eve certain ominous signs: he discerns Michael's approach; goes out to meet him: the Angel denounces their departure. Eve's lamentation. Adam pleads, but submits : the Angel leads him up to a high hill; sets before him in vision what shall happen till the Flood."

While Adam and Eve have been repenting for their sin, and begging for God's mercy, the Son of God intercedes between them and God, and pleads before the Almighty that they (Adam and Eve) are repentant, and so he may permit them to live in bliss (though the Son pleads for only Adam, he means to plead for both Adam and Eve) (lines 38-44) :

> '... let him live,
> Before thee reconciled, at least his days
> Numbered, though sad, till death, his doom (which I
> To mitigate thus plead, not to reverse),
> To better life shall yield him, where with me
> All my redeemed may dwell in joy and bliss,
> Made one with me, as I with thee am one.'

God grants the prayer of his Son, but says that Adam and Eve will not be allowed to dwell in Paradise: " '... But longer in that Paradise to dwell/ The law I gave to Nature him forbids...' " However, God allows them second life, after their death, should they purge themselves of their sin. Thus, God postpones his verdict of final death upon them (Adam and Eve), and orders that they be allowed to taste the fruit of the Tree of Life and till the soil; but, he repeats, they must be driven out of Paradise (lines 84-98) :

> 'O Sons, like one of us Man is become
> To know both good and evil, since his taste
> Of that defended fruit; but let him boast
> His knowledge of good lost and evil got,
> Happier had it sufficed him to have known
> Good by itself and evil not at all.
> He sorrows now, repents, and prays contrite —
> My motion in him; longer than they move,
> His heart I know how variable and vain,
> Self-left. Lest, therefore, his now bolder hand
> Reach also of the Tree of Life, and eat,
> And live for ever, dream at least to live
> For ever, to remove him I decree,

And send him from the Garden forth, to till
The ground whence he was taken, fitter soil...'

God now asks Michael to see that his orders have been perfectly executed, and, accordingly, Michael, the 'Archangelic Power', descends to earth. Meanwhile Raphael also comes down to earth in the shape of man, and tells Adam and Eve that it is his duty, by order of God, to drive them away from Paradise and upto earth : " '... to remove thee I am come,/And send thee from the Garden forth, to till/The ground whence thou was taken, fitter soil.' " Both Adam and Eve are full of sorrow for leaving Paradise. Adam tells Raphael that what affects him most is that he will no more be able to be in the neighbourhood of God: " '...This most afflicts me — that departing hence,/As from his face I shall be hid, deprived/His blessed count'nance...' ". Raphael comforts him by saying that God's presence is everywhere. He, Adam and Eve then ascend, God observing their flight, upto the top of the highest hill in Paradise, being borne by Tempest 'Our second Adam'. Reaching there, Michael removes the 'film' from the eyes of Adam — the 'film' that settled on the eyes of Adam as a result of his tasting the interdicted fruit (lines 412-416):

Michael from Adam' eyes the film removed,
Which that false fruit that promised clear sight
Had bred; then purged with euphrasy and rue
The visual nerve, for he had much to see,
And from the well of life three drops instilled.

And as a result of this surgery, Adam gets 'mental sight', and now, when he opens his eyes, he sees the effects of his original sin. First, he sees a vast field, half tilled and half fallow. Next, he sees a meek shepherd and his folk. The shepherd sacrifices one of his firstlings of the flock and strows the guts and fat of it before the altar that stands in the middle of that field. The offerings of the shepherd is soon consumed by a heavenly fire. There is another shepherd there who also likewise makes sacrifies, but his offering is not accepted by that heavenly fire. Being thereby enraged, the second shepherd kills the first. Trembling at the sight of this ghastly deed, Adam asks Michael to tell him the meaning of this vision, and Michael tells him that the two shepherds are two brothers (Abel and Cain, respectively, born out of Adam's loin), and that (lines 455-458) —

'... th' unjust the just hath slain,
For envy that his brother's offering found

From Heaven acceptance; but the bloody fact
Will be avenged,...'

This is the first time that Adam sees the sight of death — gory death — and he shudders at the sight (lines 462-465):

'... But have I now seen Death? Is this the way
I must return to dust? O sight
Of terror, foul and ugly to behold,
Horrid to think, how horrible to think!

Michael tells him that there are other various horrible ways of death, and, for instances of such various other horrible deaths, Adam is shown lazars, and patients of epilepsy, catarrhs, etc. Adam now asks Michael to tell him if there is any being who is out of such horrible things, and Michael tells him (lines 530-537):

'There is', said Michael, 'if thou well observe
The rule of *Not too much*, by temperance taught
In what thou eat'st and drink'st, seeking from thence
Due nourishment, not gluttonous delight,
Till many years over thy head return:
So may'st thou live, till ripe fruit, thou drop
Into thy mother's lap, or be with ease
Gathered, not harshly plucked, for death mature:...'

Hearing this, Adam decides : " 'Henceforth, I fly not death, nor would prolong/Life much,... ...' ". Michael further advises him; " 'Nor love thy life, nor hate; but what thou liv'st/ Live well;...' "

Adam now, for the first time, makes tools out of molten ore. He sees a group of men and women dancing, and singing amorous songs, and soon these men and women get married — one man with one woman. It is now that Adam, for the first time, knows what marriage is, and feels what delight it gives, and thinks that marriage makes one blessed. But Michael cautions him: " 'Judge not what is best/By pleasure,...' " Michael tells him that some of those women are 'fair atheists' who indulge in shameful and lustful 'appetence' and so they are doomed to weeping. Adam understands this, and says: " '...But still I see the tenor of Man's woe/Holds on the same, from Woman to begin' ". And Michael forthwith adds: " 'From Man's effeminate slackness it begins'/Said th' Angel, 'who should better hold his place/ By wisdom, and superior gifts received...' ". And now Michael invites Adam to see another sight, and Adam sees cities and villages drowned in factitious and bloody wars and oppressions. Michael tells him:

" 'These are the product/Of those ill-mated marriages thou saw'st,/ Where good with bad were matched;...' ". After this, Adam turns his eyes elsewhere and sees (lines 713-718):

> The brazen throat of war had ceased to roar;
> And now was turned to jollity and game,
> To luxury and riot, feast and dance,
> Marrying or prostituting, as befell,
> Rape or adultery, where passing fair
> Allured them; thence from cups to civil broils,

Adam, next, sees the great purging flood in which all the creatures of the world are destroyed, save "the sire and his three sons/With their four wives", and "Of every beast, and bird, and insect small,/Came sevens and pairs" — all these being rescued on a bark or ship (this is the Flood in which Noah and his train of birds and animals were saved with a boat) (lines 747-752) :

> all dwellings else
> Flood overwhelmed, and them with all their pomp
> Deep under water rolled; sea covered sea,
> Sea without shore; in their palaces,
> Where luxury late reigned, sea-monsters whelped
> And stabled: of mankind, so numerous late,
> All left in one small bottom swum embarked.'

As Adam is seeing all this, he is weeping, and Michael tells him (lines 754-758) :

> How didst thou grieve then, Adam, to behold
> The end of all thy offspring end so sad,
> Depopulation 'thee another flood,
> Of tears and sorrow a flood, thee also drowned,
> And sunk thee as thy sons;

Adam is now shuddering in fear. He is averse to the vision of the future, and says (lines 770-776) :

> '... Let no man seek
> Henceforth to be foretold what shall befall
> Him or his children evil, he may be sure,
> Which neither his foreknowledge can prevent,
> And the future evil shall no less
> In apprehension than in substance feel,
> Grievous to bear...'

Adam now asks Michael whether human kind will, thus, be forever destroyed, and Michael replies that that certainly will not occur, but the universal wreckage will partially be retrieved by one just man (Jesus Christ) (lines 808-821):

> '... One man except, the only son of light
> In a dark age, against example good,
> Against allurement, custom, and a world
> Offended; fearless of reproach and scorn,
> Or violence, he of their wicked ways
> Shall then admonish, and before them set
> The path of righteousness, how much more safe
> And full of peace, denouncing wrath to come
> On their impenitence, and shall return
> Of them derided, but of God observed
> The one just man alive: by his command
> Shall build a wondrous ark, as thou beheld'st,
> To save himself and household from amidst
> A world devote to universal wrack...'

Michael now shows Adam, in a vision, how that one true man (Jesus Christ) will save a few members of each species (in pairs male and female), including human species, from the great flood. He describes the great event thus (lines 822-838):

> '... No sooner he, with them of man and beast
> Select for life, shall in the ark be lodged
> And sheltered round, but all the cataracts
> Of heaven set open on the Earth shall pour
> Rain day and night; all fountains of the deep,
> Broke up, shall heave the ocean to usurp
> Beyond all bounds, till inundation rise
> Above the highest hills: then shall this Mount
> Of Paradise by might of waves be moved
> Out of his place, pushed by the horned flood,
> With all his verdure spoiled, and trees adrift,
> Down the great river to the opening a Gulf,
> And there take root, an island salt and bare,
> The haunt of seals, and orcs, and sea-mews' clang
> To teach thee that God attributes to place
> No sanctity, if none be thither brought
> By men who there frequent or therein dwell...'

Adam sees the vision of universal wreckage and the providential retrieval of specimens of all species, as foretold by Michael, and rejoices. Michael assures him that God never means universal and eternal wrackage. He says that God only wants a covenant from Man to the effect that Man shall never disobey him (God), and that God will show Man this covenant from time to time: " '... when he brings/Over the Earth a cloud, will therein set/His triple-coloured bow, whereon to look/And call to mind his cov'nant....' " Michael tells him that there will be various courses of the nature; but whatsoever they may be, the just man must live untouched by the vagaries of nature (lines 898-901) :

'...Day and night,
Seedtime and harvest, heat and hoary frost,
Shall hold their course, till fire purge all things new,
Both Heaven and Earth, wherein the just shall dwell.'

Book XII

Adam and Eve are still in Paradise, and Adam is listening to Michael who is continuing his narration of the events of the future. At the end of this Book, we will find that Adam and Eve are driven out of Paradise, as ordained by the Almighty. However, Milton, in his 'Argument' of this Book, writes: "The Angel Michael continues, from the Flood, to relate what shall succeed; then, in the mention of Abraham, comes by degrees to explain who that Seed of the Woman shall be which was promised Adam and Eve in the Fall: his incarnation, death, resurrection, and ascension; the state of the Church till his second coming. Adam, greatly satisfied and recomforted by these relations and promises, descends the hill with Michael; wakens Eve, who all this while had slept, but with gentle dreams composed to quietness of mind and submission. Michael in either hand leads them out of Paradise, the fiery sword waving behind them, and the Cherubim taking their stations to guard the place." The Book opens with Michael telling Adam that so far he (Adam) has seen "one world begin and end", and now he (Michael) is beginning to narrate what is going to happen in future. Michael predicts that those human beings, who will survive the universal destruction by the huge flood, will continue to live and "spend their days in joy unblamed". But after that one human being will be born who will not be content with the prevailing peace, amity and equality, and so will be tyrannous. He will claim "second sovranty" from the Almighty, and will be insouciant towards both good and evil, and his works will be known as *Confusion*. At this point, Adam feels remorse on thinking that it will be his own son who will be tyrannous. Adam says to himself that God did never mean that man would have no authority; God, certainly, ordained that man would rule over all the creatures, except man: " 'He gave us only over beast, fish, fowl,/ Dominion absolute; that right we hold/By his donation: but man over man/He made not lord — such title to himself/Reserving, human left from human free...' ". Michael tells him that since his (Adam's) original lapse, true liberty and reason have been lost.

Michael narrates that from that single corrupt man, a race will come up : a race in which each one will be "servant of servants". And then this new world will be drowned in corruption and idol-worship: " '... To worship their own work in wood and stone/For gods! ....' ". God, therefore, will turn his attention away from such a nation, for some time, and then he will again turn his gaze towards the fallen state of man, and arrange for retrieval of this nation. Here we come across Michael's longest speech in which he says (lines 120-127) :

'... — yet him God the Most High vouchsafes
To call by vision from his father's house,
His kindred, and false gods, into a land
Which he will show him, and from him will raise
A mighty nation, and upon him shower
His benediction, so that in his seed
All nations shall be blessed; he straight obeys;
Not knowing to what land, yet firm believes....'

That seed is none else but the great Deliverer, the '*faithful Abraham*' — the 'patriarch blessed'. Michael now narrates how the descendants of this Abraham will move from Canaan to Egypt, increase in number through propagation, and will be enthralled by a certain Pharaoh there. He says that God will then send Moses and Aaron to reclaim them, and to bring them back to their promised land (lines 151-172) :

'... This patriarch blessed,
Whom *faithful Abraham* due time shall call,
A son, and of his son a grandchild, leaves,
Like him in faith, in wisdom, and renown.
The grandchild, with twelve sons increased, departs
From Canaan to a land hereafter called
Egypt, divided by the river Nile;
See where it flows, disgorging at seven mouths
Into the sea: to sojourn in that land
He comes, invited by a younger son

> In time of dearth, a son whose worthy deeds
> Raise him to be the second in that realm
> Of pharaoh: there he dies, and leaves his race
> Growing into a nation, and now grown
> Suspected to a sequent king, who seeks
> To stop their overgrowth, as inmate guests
> Too numerous; whence of guests he makes them
> Inhospitably, and kills their infant males:
> Till, by two brethren (those two brethren call
> Moses and Aaron) sent from God to claim
> His people from enthralment, they return,
> With glory and spoil, back to their promised land...'

God will then ordain, continues Michael, civil and religious laws so far unknown to that race or society of men, and following those laws mankind will be delivered from their sins (lines 227-235):

> '... God, from the mount of Sinai, whose grey top
> Shall tremble, he descending, will himself,
> In thunder, lightning, and loud trumpet's sound,
> Ordain them laws — part, such as appertain
> To civil justice; part, religious rites
> Of sacrifice, informing them, by types
> And shadows, of that destined Seed to bruise
> The Serpent, by what means he shall achieve
> Mankind's deliverance...'

But, before all this, says Michael, " 'Some blood more precious must be paid for Man,/Just for unjust,...' ".

At this, Adam feels joyous — joyous at the prospect of Man's ultimate deliverance. He tells Michael (lines 375-385):

> 'O prophet of glad tidings, finisher
> Of utmost hope! now clear I understand
> What oft my steadiest thoughts have searched in vain —
> Why our great Expectation should be called
> The Seed of Woman. Virgin Mother, hail!
> High in love of Heaven, yet from my loins
> Thou shall proceed, and from thy womb the Son
> Of God Most High; so God with Man unites.
> Needs must the Serpent now his capital bruise
> Expect with mortal pain: say where and when
> Their fight, what stroke shall bruise the Victor's heel.'

Michael tells Adam that this fight will not be a bloody one; it will be a different kind of fight. This fight will be against one's own self for self-imposed obedience to God, and in this war man will fight by suffering the sufferances of life and death, which are due to transgression of God's will by tasting the interdicted fruit (lines 386-401):

'Dream not of their fight
As of duel, of the local wounds
Of head or heel:....................
....
Not by destroying Satan, but his works
In thee and in thy seed: nor can this be,
But by fulfilling that which thou didst want,
Obedience to the law of God, imposed
On penalty of death, and suffering death,
The penalty to thy transgression due,
And due to theirs which out of thine will grow:
So only can high justice rest appaid...'

Michael further tells Adam that then death will be only " 'A gentle wafting to immortal life...' ", and then the earth will become a Paradise.

Hearing this, Adam rejoices, but asks Michael when the Deliverer (Jesus Christ) will return to heaven, his appropriate place, after he will have executed the command of God — the Deliverer who will guide those few faithful human beings that will be left behind on earth after the execution of the command of God. Michael tells him that then God will send a Comforter (lines 487-492) —

'... who shall dwell,
His Spirit, within them, and the law of faith
Working through love upon their hearts shall write,
To guide them in all truth, and also arm
With spiritual armour, able to resist ...
Satan's assaults, and quench his fiery darts — '

But, yet, says Michael, the general society of humans will be drowned in concordance of evils, and then " 'Truth shall retire/Bestruck with sland'rous darts, and works of Faith Rarely be found:...' ", and thus the world will go on — with goodness rare but evils galore. Nevertheless, Michael assures Adam, the world will ultimately be restored to righteousness by the 'Woman's Seed'; and then new heavens will be established on earth: " '... New Heavens, new Earth, Ages of endless date/Founded in righteousness and peace and love,/To bring forth fruits, joy and eternal bliss' " And hearing this, Adam, once again, becomes full of joy, and vows that he will henceforth obey the will of God. He will love God with fear, walk in his presence, and solely depend on him. And when he will die, he will think that he has gained a new life, because he will then remain in the neighbourhood of God (lines 561-571) :

'... Henceforth I learn that to obey is best,
And love with fear the only God, to walk
As in his presence, ever to observe
His providence, and on him sole depend.
Merciful over all his works, with good
Still overcoming evil, and by small
Accomplishing great things — by things deemed
Subverting worldly-strong, and worldly-wise
By simply meek; that suffering for Truth's sake
Is fortitude to highest victory,
And to the faithful death the gate of life — ...'

Lastly, Michael tells Adam that only this much wisdom he should acquire, or hope to acquire, and "hope no higher". But to this much of wisdom, Michael further advises Adam, he (Adam) should add faith, virtue, patience, temperance, love, and charity, and when he will do this, he will find a Paradise within his own self (lines 582-587):

'....add faith;
And virtue, patience, temperance; and love,
By name to come called Charity, the soul
Of all the rest: then wilt thou not be loth
To leave this Paradise, but shalt possess
A Paradise within thee, happier far....'

Michael now asks Adam to come down from the top of the hill on which they were conversing, along with the angel, because the time of parting has arrived. All this while, Eve has been sleeping. Michael tells Adam that he has shown the coming of goodness in future to her also, through her dream. Adam now meets Eve who has, meanwhile, arisen from her sleep. She tells him that God has shown her in a vision that all her future seeds will be restored to the land which is promised to them by God: " '...By me the Promised Seed shall all restore.' " At last, Michael holds Adam by one hand, and Eve by another, and leads them towards "the subjected plain", away from Paradise, and then disappears. Adam and Eve look back for once and take the last view of Paradise, and shed "some natural tears". But, soon, they recover themselves from this silent sorrow, and look forward to the new world they are ordained to enter into and lead their lives (lines 464-469) :

> The world was all before them, where to choose
> Their place of rest, and Providence their guide:
> They, hand in hand, with wandering steps and slow,
> Through Eden took their solitary way.

And, thus, Paradise is lost to Adam and Eve, and, for the reason of that, also to their future seeds.

3
(PRINCIPAL CHARACTERS IN *PARADISE LOST*)

The story of *Paradise Lost* being based on *Genesis*, all the characters of the epic are mythological, and the characters of Satan, Adam and Eve are the leading ones. In the first four Books of the epic, the character of Satan is certainly predominant; but as the epic progresses, the character of Satan diminishes in importance. On the other hand, Adam and Eve are absent in the first three Books, but since Book IV, they begin to progressively dominate the course of events of the epic. Some commentators believe that Satan is the projection of the rebellious character of Milton himself, but this is debatable (we will concern ourselves with this debate in section IV, below). Nevertheless, we must admit that Satan is the greatest creation of Milton: it seems that Milton employed almost all his energy to shape out the character of Satan. This is, one of the reasons, why some commentators surmise that Satan is the embodiment of the ideals of Milton — the ideals of love, of liberty, of pride, of courage, of leadership, of self-respect, and of uncompromising attitude — though sometimes some evil means are employed by him (Satan) to sustain and fructify these ideals — evil means such as envy, revenge, meanness, hideousness, selfishness, sensuality, etc. Satan is a pot-pouri of high ideals and abominable evils — the evils always being the means of achieving the high ideals. Satan is very much passionate: his is, as if, the other name of passion. Milton trusted only rationality, but, personally, he was much passionate. Thus, in him there was what depth-psychologists call enantiodromia, *i.e.* coexistence of two divergent forces, rationality and passion. Milton says that Adam and Eve had their fall due to their lack of rationality; but, all the same, he portrayed the character of Satan as his ideal hero, as the supreme example of passionate beings.

As told earlier, Satan dominates the earlier Books of the epic; his absence is felt only at the last quarter of the epic. He is the dominant figure in *Paradise Lost*, just as Achilles is the dominant character in *Iliad*, and Odysseus in *Odyssey*. The vast and unabating agony of Satan is perhaps the perfect expression of the agonising consciousness of the human race that ceaselessly aspire after freedom. In *Paradise Lost*, the character of Satan is elaborately and beautifully delineated by the poet with all possible care, skill and toil. In the first and the second Books of the epic, Milton sings of the grandeur of Satan, but from the third Book, the grandeur begins to fade away. Though Milton portrays the character of Satan throughout almost the whole of the epic, actually his character is nearly full-blown in the very first Book itself. Satan is like a huge monster, 'huge in bulk' like Briareos who fought against Uranus, or like Typhon who battled Jove. The sprawling body of Satan is compared with the mythical sea-monster Leviathan: "which God of all His works/ Created hugest that swim the ocean-stream." The stature of Leviathan is so enormous that while sometimes it had been "slumbering on the Norway foam", it seemed to be an island. The comparison of Satan's body with that of Leviathan is enough to give us an impression of the hugeness of Satan's stature. This huge monster that Satan is was once a cherub, but now he is the arch-fiend. For his disobedience shown to God — disobedience born of his extreme pride and ambition —, he has been banished by God from heaven. But even after his fall, his pride and insolence have not diminished even an iota, and so he will not beg to God for mercy :

To bow and sue for grace
With suppliant knee, and deify his power
Who, from the terror of his arm, so late
Doubted the empire — that were low indeed;

Satan is very much ambitious, too. As we have said, it was his vaulting ambition that caused his fall from the grace and bliss of heaven. He wanted to be equal to the Almighty; nay, he wanted even to supersede his creator, in might and privileges. Again, he is very courageous. After his fall, dejected though he was for a while, he soon collected his courage and prepared for a renewed battle to regain his lost glory that he enjoyed in heaven: " 'What though the field be lost? All is not lost.' " Satan's indomitable courage and perseverance may perhaps be expressed through a single line of Tennyson's *Ulysses*: "To strive, to seek, to find, and not to yield." Satan's vaulting ambition has its adamantine will and studied courage. He denies the lawful acts of God, and determines to take revenge on as mighty a being as the Almighty.

He has the guts for doing effrontery and hitting back at God himself. He does not shrink back from doing any dreadful deed to reclaim his former status. He is ready to stoop too low, if needs be, or to resort to any sort of guile, to pursue his one-directional end. For all these, Milton very rightly calls him the infernal Serpent. This is no wonder, therefore, that Satan very courageously welcomes his second dwelling place, in hell (Book I):

> Farewell, happy fields,
> Where joy for ever dwells! Hail, horrors! hail,
> Infernal world!

Satan has enormous amount of jealousy. When Adam and Eve are caressing each other, in Paradise, he feels extreme jealousy. In Book IV, we find Adam kissing Eve in amorous affection : "as Jupiter/On Juno smiles when he impregns the cloud/That shed May flowers, and pressed her matron lip/With kisses pure." And observing this rightful amorous acts of affection, Satan burns in jealousy and suffers from heart-rending agony. He utters in pain :

> 'Sight hateful, sight tormenting! Thus these two,
> Imparadised in one another's arms,
> The happier Eden, shall enjoy their fill
> Of bliss on bliss; while I to Hell am thrust,
> Where neither joy nor love, but fierce desire,
> Among our other torments not the least,
> Still unfulfilled, with pain of longing pines !...'

Satan is so much prone to jealousy that even such slight events as Adam's escaping the snare laid by him arouses jealousy in him. We find an instance of Satan's jealousy for such slight things at the beginning of Book IV. Book IV begins with Satan's cursing the earth where Adam and Eve have escaped from his snare " '*Woe to the inhabitants on Earth*!' " Satan is also the meanest of all beings. Though once he had been the archangel, he, without any qualm of conscience or without any hesitation, now metamorphoses himself into the meanest of creatures — a cormorant, *i.e.* a web-footed sea-bird of great voracity; and then, after some time, infuses himself into the abominable body of a snake, only to materialise his abject and immoral design of corrupting Eve, and, through her, Adam. Satan is also a liar. He tells Eve that the fruit of the Tree of knowledge will not harm her; rather, it will make her wise; and so she should not abide by the interdiction of God:

> '... In plain, then, what forbids he but to know,
> Forbids us Good, forbids us to be wise?
> Such prohibitions bind not...'

Contrary to the Christian and humanitarian ideal of being of service to others, Satan worships the ideal of being a dictator. He prefers to be the ruler of even of hell to being a servant in heaven:

> '... To reign is worth ambition, though in Hell
> Better to reign in Hell than serve in Heaven...'

Satan wants power, and only power, and that by any means, fair or foul: he is the supreme example of the Nietzschean hero.

Thus, Milton has painted the character of Satan in pitch black. But, as Satan is his ideal hero or his *döppelganger*, he has not forgotten to betray Satan's saving graces, very sympathetically. Milton frequently reminds us that Satan once had been the archangel of heaven, possessing all the superior and beatific qualities ever imaginable and available only in heaven. This is confirmed by the fact that even after his fall from heaven or Paradise, the train of the fallen angels holds him in high esteem. A great leader is one whom his followers do not desert in either weal or woe; and, by that criterion, Satan is certainly a great leader. On the other hand, he has all sympathy for his fellow rebels. After he has reached the solid ground, or, rather, the ground of solid fire, where he finds a negligible amount of relief, he is anxious to transport the innumerable other fallen angels there. His feeling for his fellows, his humaneness, his sense of duty — all are obvious here. After the other fallen angels gather on the solid fire, Satan infuses those fallen angels with courage, brushing aside their despair, and help them shake off their utter dejection. He possesses courage, determination, skill in stratagems, etc. in abundance — parts that are rare indeed. He has enough adjustability: he can bear with any situation whatsoever, with astonishing aplomb, or, otherwise, he would not be able to survive in the pressing gloom and excruciating fire of hell.

Astonishingly, Satan is almost as wise as Nestor, in spite of the blackest evil resident in him. He can well philosophise on life and happiness, and thus can console himself as well as others, like Boethius did in his *The Consolation of Philosophy*. For instance, instead of being dejected after his fall from the bliss of heaven, and instead of being even a little morose, in the hell pit, he astonishingly cants on peace and bliss (Book I):

> The mind is its own place, and in itself
> Can make a Heaven of Hell, a Hell of Heaven.

And last but not the least, Satan has the heroic quality of having *fortezza* or fortitude, of both body and mind, — a quality which, in the tradition of the epic, has always been held to be a virtue *par excellence*. Even in his fallen state, Satan has enough *fortezza*.

However, C.S. Lews writes about the character of Satan: "What we see in Satan is the horrible coexistence of a subtle and incessant intellectual activity with an incapacity to understand anything.... throughout the poem [*Paradise Lost*], all his torments come, in a sense, at his own bidding, and the Divine judgement might have been expressed in the words 'thy will be done'." (Lews, 99). Lews further writes: "...Satan in his speech shows complete inability to conceive any state of mind but infernal. His argument assumes as axiomatic that in any world where there is any good to be envied, subjects will envy their sovereign. The only exception is Hell, for there, since there is no good to be had, the sovereign cannot have more of it, and therefore cannot be envied. Hence, he concludes that the infernal monarchy has a stability which the clestial lacks" (Lews, 98). So we see that gubernatorial instinct is predominant in Satan. He is certainly a heroic character, but he is a false-heroic character (not anti-heroic), in the sense that he always shows his proclivity towards evil, and never towards good. Such false-heroic characters are no modern inventions, but they are available in classical literature and even in the Scriptures. John M. Steadman writes "the pseudoheroism of Satan, Harapha, and the secular conquerors — derives from both classical and Scriptural tradition" (Steadman, xvii).

However, perhaps, every one will admit that in *Paradise Lost* Satan's is the best character drawn, and for this Milton should certainly be accredited. But what C.S. Lews says in this regard is very interesting, and what he says is not perhaps wholly incorrect. He says: "Of the major characters whom Milton attempted he [Satan] is comparatively the easiest to draw. Set a hundred poets to tell the same story and in ninety of the resulting poems Satan will be the best character. In all but a few writers the 'good' characters are the least successful, and every one who has ever tried to make even the humblest story ought to know why. To make a character worse than oneself it is only necessary to release imaginatively from control some of the bad passions which, in real life, are always straining at the leash; ..." (Lews, 100). Nevertheless, we must once again say that Satan is a magnificent character. But what do we mean when we say that Satan is a magnificent character? C.S. Lews says: "It may mean that Milton's presentation of him [Satan] is a magnificent poetical achievement which engage attention and excites the admiration of the reader. On the other hand, it may mean that the real being (if any) whom Milton is depicting, or any real being like Satan if there were one, or a real human being in so far as he resembles Milton's Satan, is or ought to be an object of admiration and sympathy, conscious or unconscious, on the part of the poet or his readers or both. The first, so far as I know, has never till modern times been denied; the second, never affirmed before the times of Blake and Shelley — for when Dryden said that Satan was Milton's 'hero' he meant some-thing quite different. It is, in my opinion, wholly erroneous" (Lews, 94).

Next to Satan, comes Beelzebub, the adjutant of the archangel and arch-fiend Satan, whose character has also been very sympathetically drawn by Milton. We come across Beelzebub only at lines 128 to 282 of Book I, and after this he disappears for good. But within this short space, Milton has been able to draw a three-dimensional picture of Beelzebub. Beelzebub is the 'bold compeer' of Satan. Like Satan, he too had been an angel of great importance in heaven, and enjoyed all the enviable privileges of the celestial sphere. He loves freedom and justice, as Satan does, and it is for this reason that he stood by Satan, arms in hand, and fought against the tyranny of God. Along with Satan and his long train of rebellious angels, Beelzebub was also vanquished and kicked off heaven by the forces of the Almighty. Like Satan, Beelzebub is very courageous; for even after his fall he did not lose his heart. He is therefore optimistic, like his general Satan. Beelzebub is also trustworthy and loyal. He fell from heaven, which is quite due to Satan's instigating him, and yet, even after his fall, he is as loyal to Satan as he had been earlier. After undergoing a state of coma, in the sulpherous fire of hell, Satan searches Beelzebub out, and addresses all the fallen angels, and delivers a demagogy of encouragement: "What though the field be lost?/All is not lost". In reply to Satan's address, Beelzebub also delivers a speech of encouragement to all the fallen angels. But, before that, he addresses Satan very obediently as 'Prince' and 'Chief of many throned powers'. Beelzebub's sense of loyalty, comradeship and faithfulness are well attested by this speech of his.

Again, like Satan, Beelzebub has enough *fortezza* or fortitude: he is non-pareil in bearing hardship. Even in the excruciating pain of hell fire, he is not daunted, not cowed down or dejected or broken down. He believes that his mind and spirit are as strong, after the fall, as these had been before :

> '... for the mind and spirit remains
> Invincible, and vigour soon returns,
> Though all our glory extinct,...'

But, unlike Satan, Beelzebub is a realist. Satan always overestimates his qualities and merits; he is a dreamer and an egotist. In overestimating himself, he thinks himself to be superior even to God. Contrarily, Beelzebub never overestimates himself, and knows that God is more powerful than all the fallen angels put together. Therefore, he frankly admits that God is the most mighty one: "(... since no less,/Than such could have o'erpowered such force as ours)".

Beelzebub is no less wise than Satan; rather, in some cases he is more wise than him, for he can read the mind of God, which Satan cannot do. Beelzebub knows the motive of God behind his throwing down the revolting angels into the pit of hell: "That we may suffer his vengful ire;/Or do him mightier service, as his thrall". Beelzebub is a fast friend and comrade of Satan, and is second only to Satan, in physical strength. He is Satan's 'next mate' and trustworthy partner. So when Satan rose for the second time against God, with 'rallied arms', Beelzebub obediently followed him. Beelzebub well understands the minds of his innumerable fallen angels, and that is why he can assure Satan that the fallen angels will respond to his (Satan's) call for the second battle against God:

> '... If once they hear that voice, their liveliest pledge
> Of hope in fears and dangers, heard oft
> ....
> .... they will soon resume
> New courage and revive,............................'

Here we find Beelzebub's wisdom and intuitive faculty — qualities that are essential for a leader and master general that he is. He is as democratic minded and as great a hater of tyranny as his superior is. Though a fallen angel, he possesses these and some other admirable qualities. He is a trustworthy comrade, and a faithful friend both in time of peace and in time of adversity. He has enough respect for his superior. He pays tribute to Satan in glorious terms when he, after the fall, first accosts him :

> 'O Prince, O Chief of many throned powers,
> That led that embattled Seraphim to war
> Under thy conduct, and, in dreadful deeds
> Fearless, endangered Heaven's perpetual king,...'

Beelzebub, therefore, does not ungratefully forgets the past. Such qualities of his betray the partial nobleness of his heart — partially, because he rose against God in collusion with Satan, and so his heart certainly harbours sin and ignominy. However, in short, Beelzebub is a rare Samaritan to Satan, and a very resourceful one at that. Though Milton has overtly lionised Satan in the epic, the immensity of the arch-fiend has not been able to completely overshadow the personality of his comrade-in-arms, Beelzebub.

Adam and Eve are God's finest and dearest creations, endowed with the rare property — freedom of will. God said of them: "I formed them free, and free they must remain/Till they enthrall themselves". They were habilitated in the finest and happiest abode ever conceivable — Paradise: "Paradise, the happy seat of Man". They were created as innocent and sinless beings, and they were created in the image of God himself. God, first, created Adam, and allowed him to rule over all other creatures of the world. God said: " 'Let us make now Man in our image, Man/In our similitude, and let them rule/Over the fish and fowl of sea and air,/Beast of the field, and over all the earth,/And every creeping thing that creeps the ground.' " "Man is God's latest image", and so Adam and Eve are God-like in appearance. In Scandinavian mythology, Adam and Eve lived in *Midgard* which is between *Asgard* or the celestial abode, and Utgard or the abode of the giants (*Chambers's Compact English Dictionary*). But Milton took the mythology of Adam and Eve from *Genesis* of the Bible. However, Adam relates his faint memory of his being crested by God thus :

> 'As new-waked from soundest sleep,
> Soft on the flowery herb I found me laid,
> In balmy sweat, which with his beams the Sun
> Soon dried, and on the reeking moisture fed.

Adam was created by God out of dust which is a conglomeration of four primal elements: earth, water, fire and air. On the other hand, Satan was created by him out of pure fire. Elementally, therefore, Satan, is superior to Adam. This is one of the causes why Satan feels jealous of Adam. But Adam was endowed with God's image, *i.e.* he was given all the godly qualities, though in reduced quantities, to be exact, and in this sense, Adam is certainly superior to Satan. God gave Adam free will and rationality, but this rationality could be obliterated should will predominate over it :

> But God left free the Will; for what obeys
> Reason is free; and Reason he made right,
> But bid her will beware, and still erect,
> Lest, by some fair appearing good surprised,

She dictate false, and misinform the Will,
To do what God expressly hath forbid.

Adam had his fall only when his reason was blurred by his will. So, though he was created in the image of God, he has his quantum of weakness of character.

Seeing the gloomy solitariness of Adam, God devised to create his female mate, Eve. God took a rib out from Adam's breast, and therewith created the beautiful Eve: God

'... took
From thence a rib, with cordial spirits warm
And life-blood streaming fresh; wide was the wound,
But suddenly with flesh filled up and healed.
The rib he formed and fashioned with his hands;
Under his forming hands a creature grew,
Man-like, but different sex, so lovely fair
That what seemed fair in all the world seemed now
Moan, or in her summed up, in her contained,...'

There is no difference, therefore, between the innate nature of Adam and that of Eve, save the case that Adam is a man and Eve is a woman. But this innate difference, later on, gave rise to several associated differences. To begin with, though both of them are exquisitely beautiful, they are diversely so :

His fair large front and eye sublime declared
Absolute rule; and hyacinthine locks
Round from his parted forelock manly hung
Clustering, but not beneath his shoulders broad:
She, as a veil down to the slender waist,
Her unadorned folden tresses wore
Dishevelled, but in wanton ringlets waved
As the vine curls her tendrils which implied
Subjection,

Adam has, the poet says, the proclivity of ruling over others, while Eve always tends to submit. Adam and Eve are also different from each other regarding the purposes for which they were created: Adam is a strong and contemplative person, made for worshipping only God; but Eve is soft and fair, and was created for worshipping the image of God within Adam: "For contemplation he and valour formed,/For softness she and sweet attractive grace;/He for God only, she for God in him."

Before their fall, Adam and Eve did not know amorous passion, and, consequently, shame was unknown to them. At that time, they were absolutely rational, and their will was absolutely free. But after some time, Eve's will slackened the strength of her rationality, as a result of which she was swayed by the temptation of Satan, and she committed sin by tasting the fruit of the Tree of Knowledge. Soon, Adam, knowing that Eve was to suffer banishment from Paradise, willingly, elected to taste that fruit, and thus both of them suffered banishment. Here, Milton has shown the generous character of Adam. Adam is very fond of Eve, and is true to their marriage vow. He tells Eve "Should God create another Eve, and I/Another rib afford, yet loss of thee/Would never from my heart." Milton here means to say that this generosity and honesty is lacking in Eve, because she corrupted Adam not for her love of him, but for her jealousy of some imaginary substitute of herself:

> '... And Adam, wedded to another Eve,
> Shall live with her enjoying, I extinct!
> A death to think! Confirmed, then, I resolve
> Adam shall share with me in bliss or woe.

Perhaps Eve is more gullible than Adam, because she is less rational than he, and that was why, Satan chose Eve first as his prey. Eve is also more proud than Adam, and that was why Satan, in the shape of a snake, flattered her beauty :

> 'Wonder not, sovran mistress (if perhaps
> Thou cants who art sole wonder), much less arm
> Thy looks, the heaven of mildness, with disdain,
> Displeased that I approach thee thus, and gaze
> Insatiate, I thus single, nor have feared
> Thy awful brow, more awful thus retired
> Fairest resemblance of thy Maker fair,
> Thee all things living gaze on, all things thine
> By gift, and thy celestial beauty adore,
> With ravishment beheld — there best beheld
> Where universally admired.

In *Paradise Lost*, it is only Adam and Eve who undergo metamorphosis of their characters, and none else. They were unware of 'civilisation': they went nakedly and yet they felt no shame. They had no awareness about individuality, though they were two quite different individuals. They had no selfishness — selfishness that originates in individuation. But, as a result of their fall, they felt ashamed of their nakedness, became aware of their individuality, and became selfish. Earlier, they were immortals, but after the fall, they were doomed to die. Before the fall, they were innocent, but after it they became full of frailties : carnal attractions, garrulousness, etc. And after the fall Adam, too, became "overcome with female charm", as Eve became attracted towards Adam's sinewy strength, and

> As with new wine intoxicated both,
> They swim in mirth, and fancy that they feel
> Divinity within them breeding wings
> Wherewith to scorn the Earth: but that false fruit
> Far other operations first displayed,
> Carnal desire inflaming; he on Eve
> Began to cast lascivous eyes; she him
> As wantonly repaid; in lust they burn,

The evanescent carnal pleasure being had, they soon began mutual bickerings, and they since then became garrulous. Eve accused Adam of going away from her, keeping her in insecurity, for which reason, she said, she was inveigled by Satan, and consequently tasted the false fruit :

> 'Would thou hadst hearkened to my words, and stayed
> With me, as I besought thee, when that strange
> Desire of wandering, this unhappy morn,
> I know not whence possessed thee! We had then
> Remained still happy — not, as now, despoiled
> Of all our good, shamed, naked, miserable !....'

Eve further accuses him sometime afterwards, thus: " '.... why didst not thou, the head,/Command me absolutely not to go,/Going into such danger, as thou saidst?...' " And, astonished at the effrontery of the first sinner Eve, Adam retorted in dejection:

> '... women overtrusting,
> Lets her will rule : restraint she will not brook;
> And left to herself, if evil thence ensue,
> She first his weak indulgence will accuse.'

Adam and Eve are, in Milton's view, representative models of manhood and womanhood, and in our view, the representation is realistic. Milton's ideal manhood may be found in the character of Adam, before his fall. Likewise, his ideal of womanhood may be discerned in the character of Eve, before her fall. Milton's ideal of the relation of a woman to her husband is apparent in the following lines:

> '... nothing lovelier can be found
> In woman than to study household good,
> And good works in her husband to promote....'

And, Milton's ideal of the relationship between man and woman in wedlock is well expressed by him in one single line of the epic: "He for God only, she for God in him." Milton has conceived of the ideal manhood and womanhood as complementary. He says that when this complementareity is perfect, the wedlock is the most blissful; and when any one of the couple is overpowering, the wedlock is the most painful. Adam and Eve, in their heavenly abode, were the most innocent, the most God-fearing, and the most loving of creatures; but, as Eve's passion — and she was full of passion — dominated over Adam's rationality or reason — and Adam represents reason — they fell from the bliss of heaven, and became not very different from other ordinary creatures of the earth.

4
(THE HERO IN *PARADISE LOST*)

It can, perhaps, be expected that one will, after reading *Paradise Lost*, but not going deeper into the matter of it, say that Satan is the hero of the epic. Not only that this is the case, but even some great critics have come to the same conclusion. Certainly, they have some cogent arguments behind their judgments. Firstly, for long Milton had been contemplating over the idea of writing an epic on the Arthurian theme in imitation of Vergil's *Aeneid*, but he postponed the execution of the idea, as he engaged himself in urgent pamphleteering. But, while he had been touring Italy, he decided to write an epic on the theme or story of *Genesis* of the Bible. For his fierce anti-establishment sentiment of this period, he was looking for an iconoclastic hero, and that was why he abandoned the Arthurian theme, and turned to *Genesis* where Satan is such a hero. As a child of Renaissance and Reformation, Milton sought after knowledge of each and every thing, and all at the same time wanted to strike at the overlordship of the church. Satan, in *Paradise Lost*, is also after knowledge of each and every thing, and, further, he wants Eve knows about everything — life, death, sin, etc. — by tasting the interdicted fruit. Again, Satan disobeys God and wants that both Adam and Eve disobey the Almighty. Secondly, Milton has obviously lionised the character of Satan, particularly in the first three Books of the epic. This amply speaks for the surmise that Satan is the hero of the epic. Further, the hero of an epic or drama is one on whose character the author concentrates, or is one round whose character the story of an epic or drama revolves, and Satan, certainly occupies the central position in the pattern of the story of the epic. Thirdly, Satan pervades almost the whole space of the epic For all these reasons, Satan may seem to be the hero of the epic.

In support of the thesis that Satan is the hero in *Paradise Lost*, we may, in addition, say that the epic may be construed as the narration of a long-drawn battle between God, who is mostly invisible in the epic, and the arch-fiend Satan, like the battle between Aeneas and the Trojans, in *Aeneid.* So, either God or Satan may be recognised as the two candidates for being the hero of the epic, and not either Adam or Eve. But God cannot be the hero because he is invisible and almost absent in the epic. Therefore, the lone candidate for being the hero remaining is Satan. Objections may be raised here that Satan is a diminutive figure beside God, but this is not quite true, because regarding courage, determination, perseverance, etc. Satan is of course not a whit inferior to God. Rather, in his *Defence of Poetry*, P.B. Shelley says that in moral strength, magnificence and energy, Satan is certainly superior to God. In epics, of course, it sometimes occurs that some relatively inferior character seems to occupy a place of prominence and demands the most energy of the author, perhaps in spite of the poet's contrary intention. In Vergil's *Aeneid*, for instance, Dido is no match for Aeneas, and yet the poet Vergil painted her character with so much devotion and skill that she seems to be the heroine of *Aeneid*. But this is not the case in *Paradise Lost*. Milton certainly poured out his heart into the character of Satan, and it was for this reason that William Blake said that Milton was "the Devil's [Satan's] party without knowing it". Satan is not a minor character: he may be compared even with God but only for a few additional divine qualities. Some critics are of the opinion that so Mephistophelean a character as that of Satan cannot be the hero of the epic. But it must be borne in mind that Satan is not only evil personified, he also possesses some admirable qualities, such as generosity, fellow-feeling, self-sacrifice, prudence, etc. After his fall from heaven, he searches out his fellow fallen angels, and feels for their pathetic plight, and also strives to ameliorate their condition. Such humane qualities also tempt us to believe that Satan is the hero of *Paradise Lost*.

Further, Satan was actually a heroic personality in heaven, and was known by the name of Lucifer or light: he was the archangel among innumerable angels. It was only after his fall that his name was tarnished and he was renamed Satan. In Book VII, Raphael tells Adam:

'... Know then, that after Lucifer from Heaven
(So call him, brighter once amidst the host
Of angels then that star the stars among)...'

Satan was the first of created beings. He is very rational: he can never tolerate tyranny or irrational commands. He has the courage to protest against the tyranny of God — tyranny, because God thinks that whatever he commands must be right. To Satan, who worships the democratic spirit, God is autodidactic. Satan is ready to suffer for establishing the rule of the many, and to uproot the rule of the whimsical one. All these fine qualities of Satan prompted William Hazlitt to conclude that Satan is the hero of the epic. Hazlitt writes: "Satan is the most heroic subject that ever was chosen for a poem; and the execution is as perfect as the design is lofty. He was the first of created beings, who, for endeavouring to be equal with the highest, and to divide the empire of heaven with the Almighty, was hurled down to hell. His aim was no less than the throne of the universe; his means, myriads of angelic armies bright, the third part of heaven, whom he lured after him with his countenance, and who durst defy the Omnipotent in arms. His ambition was the greatest, and his punishment was the greatest; but not so his despair, for his fortitude was as great as his sufferings. His strength of mind was matchless as his strength of body; the vastness of his designs did not surpass the firm, inflexible determination with which he submitted to his irreversible doom, and final loss of all good. His power of action and of suffering was equal. He was the greatest power that was ever overthrown, with the strongest will left to resist or to endure. He was baffled, not confounded. He stood like a tower; or

' — As when Heaven's fire
Hath scathed the forest oaks or mountain pines' " (Hazlitt, 63).

In brief, Satan had been above the average regarding almost all qualities. He fell for his *hamartia* of choosing to rise against the Almighty; and so his fall is a tragic one. So, even as per the Aristotlean standard, Satan may be called the hero of *Paradise Lost*. But, all the same, Satan is a different kind of hero, as Milton has been able to show us, and for this reason John M. Steadman says that *Paradise Lost* may be deemed to be a 'Copernican Revolution' in the sphere of the epic, in the sense that Milton has altogether changed the traditional concept of the hero. Steadman writes: "Unlike the usual heroic poem, it [*Paradise Lost*] does not propose a victory, but a defeat. Its action is not some illustrious 'set of benefit', but a crime. Its hero is not a paragon of heroic virtue, but the archetypal sinner. The results of this conflict are not glory but shame, not dominion or deliverance, but servitude and death." (Steadman, v).

But this is not quite so: Satan cannot be deemed to be the hero of the epic, and this for, at least, three reasons. Firstly, because the character of Satan is not an ideal one. Satan may have some humane qualities — those that we have already come across — but these good qualities are nullified by some of his heinous attributes: he has the effrontery of fighting against God; he is very jealous of his creator's *i.e.* God's, supremacy, and of the happy nuptial affection between Adam and Eve; and he is a seducer, a liar, and deceiver. Secondly, for the same reasons, Satan's fall does not evoke pity and fear in us, rather, we feel hilarious at his fall. Thirdly, Satan stoops too low to achieve his abject objective. For instance, in Book IV, we find him sitting on a tree of Paradise like a cormorant or a gluttonous bird "Thence, up he flew, and on the Tree of Life,/The middle tree and highest there that grew,/Sat like a cormorant". Again, in the same Book, we find him assuming the shape of a toad to deceive and corrupt Eve's faculty of imagination, while she was asleep: "Squat like a toad, close at the ear of Eve,/Assaying by his devilish art to reach/The organs of her fancy". Further, before that, in the same Book, Satan entered into the garden of Eden by leaping over the palisade around it, like a thief :

> Leaps o'er the fence with ease into fold;
> Or as a thief, bent to unhoard the cash
> Of some rich burgher, whose substantial doors,
> Cross-barred and bolted fast, rear no assault,

And lastly, to entice Eve, Satan inserted himself into the mouth of an abject creature — a snake. And since then, Satan has been progressively diminished in stature — both physically and mentally: "From hero to general, from general to politician, from politician to secret service agent, and thence to a thing that peeps in at bedroom or bathroom windows, and thence to a toad, and finally to a snake — such is the progress of Satan" (Lews, 99). Now, if even then he is to be called a hero, he should be called a 'vicious hero'. Steadman writes "As a heroic *eidolon*, Satan displays the vicious modes of the conventional formulae — a fortitude that is really rashness, a prudence that is folly and fraud, a leadership that misleads, a magnanimity that strives for unmerited honours, accomplishes acts of destruction instead of 'acts of benefit', and turns out to be vainglorious ambition and pride. Milton has invested his Archfiend with the ethos of the 'vicious hero'." (Steadman, 17).

The two other principal characters of *Paradise Lost* that may be candidates for being the hero or the heroine of the epic, are Adam and Eve. But Eve cannot be the heroine, because she is but a shadow of Adam, and moreover, she was even created out of a rib of Adam. So she owes her mental and physical being to Adam, and therefore, she cannot claim to be the heroine of the epic. Consequently, the only character that can claim to be the hero is Adam. Though he does not appear in the first two Books of the epic, he is present throughout the rest of it. However, the following arguments may be offered for the candidature of Adam for being the hero of the epic. Firstly, Adam predominates the last ten Books of the epic, *i.e.* he is the principal character in the Books III to XII, as Satan is the principal character in only the first two Books. Secondly, the theme of the whole epic actually revolves round the character and destiny of Adam. As we have said, for his epic Milton chose the theme of *Genesis*, *i.e.* the fall of humanity from its state of perfection, and bliss, symbolically presented as the fall of Adam from Paradise. The great actions of the archangel Satan are only means of bringing down Adam from his heavenly seat, and so Satan is simply instrumental in the fall of Adam, *i.e.* in the fall of Man. Thirdly, Adam is not a simple being, in so far as he represents the whole humanity. Fourthly, though Adam is not so huge in physical stature as Satan is, and though he was created out of earth, and not out of fire, as Satan was created, it is only he, among all the creatures of God, who was created in God's image, and therefore, he is, at least in this sense, superior to Satan. Fifthly, Adam is more humane than Satan: he is more sensitive and more rational than Satan. It is for this reason that we are moved by the fall of Adam and not by that of Satan who, we think, deserved his fall.

Therefore, we may say that the hero of *Paradise Lost* is Adam. The reason of the fact that to some critics Satan seems to be the hero is that Milton of necessity had to lionise the character of Satan to make him an appropriate foil to the Almighty (or Adam, he being the image of God) — because a weak combatant would not do; it would rather indirectly diminish the greatness of God. Hardin Craig writes that it was the intention of Milton to make Adam the hero of the epic, ant not Satan "it was his [Milton's] manifest intention to make Adam the hero of *Paradise Lost* — Adam and his progeny down to us who are living today. One would attribute the excellence of Milton's picture of Satan not to his sympathy with the heart of the arch-fiend, but to his great knowledge of the nature, even the power and attractiveness, of evil."

(Craig, 251). C.M. Bowra is also of the opinion that Adam and not Satan is the hero of the epic "Adam is the central figure of *Paradise Lost*; his actions give unity to it, his fate is its chief subject. He takes the place of Aeneas. Like him he is not perfect, and like him, when he errs, his errors lead to grave results" (Bowra, 200).

We should remember here that the concept of the hero has changed from time to time throughout the ages. Homer's hero was martial, bent on winning wars. To Virgil, the martial spirit of the hero must concern itself with the prospect of the hero's own nation : the hero must be extremely nationalistic, *i.e.*, to him love of nation and heroism must be interchange terms. To Tasso, on the other hand, one who fought for the cause of religion, was a hero. But there is something common among all these three types of the hero : all the heroes are extraverts and action-oriented. Contrarily, Milton's hero is introvert and contemplative. His hero has the most capability of bearing with pain, and not inflicting pain — he is more of the masochist than of the sadist. Again, Milton's hero has absolute faith in God, and for God's cause he is ready to suffer to any extent. M.V. Rama Sharma writes: "In Book IX [of *Paradise Lost*] Milton particularly draws our attention to the fact that his concept of heroism should not be equated with one available in romances where elaborate descriptions of tournaments and trophies will be found. He is not prepared to

> describe Races and Games,
> Or tilting Furniture, emblazon'd Shields" (Sharma, 13).

Milton's hero is God-fearing, meek, innocent, submissive, rational and humane; and his Strength lies not in his sinews but in endurance of pain, rightly suffered. He as enough *fortezza*, an essential quality of the hero. Satan has also this property, but Adam's *fortezza* is quite different from his. Satan, after his fall, well keeps his physical and mental strength for rebellion against God; and Adam has his *fortezza* for bearing with the punishment inflicted upon him by God. This *fortezza* is an essential quality of Milton's hero. Milton was, perhaps, influenced, in this regard, especially by the Portuguese poet Luis de Camoes's epic *Os Lusiadas*, in which the poet adulated the *fortezza* of his hero Lusiadas. To conclude this section, we should, perhaps, take Adam, and not Satan, for the hero of *Paradise Lost*.

5
(IS *PARADISE LOST* AUTOBIOGRAPHICAL?)

Before considering the question whether the epic *Paradise Lost* is autobiographical or not, we should keep in mind that the epic contains many contradictory elements: religiosity and atheism, spirituality and gross materialism, innocence and sinfulness, obedience and rebelliousness, pessimism and optimism, crime and punishment, reason and passion, love and hatred, mercy and abhorrence, pride and lowliness or humiliation, purity and corruption, paradisaical bliss and hellish suffering, etc. Milton, personally, had express positive as well as negative attitudes towards these properties or elements, and his personal attitude towards these things is obvious in the epic. This is one of the reason why some of the critics are of the opinion that the person Milton is obviously present in the poem *Paradise Lost.* These critics say that Milton is a very subjective poet, and that this subjectivity is a drawback of the epic, because the epic is an objective genre of literature. Milton inherited his religiosity particularly from his father. He was brought up in the environ of his father's love of puritanism, innocence, spirituality and rationality. The quality of showing obeisance to the Almighty he acquired through showing deference to his loving father. Pride was his inborn trait, which was enhanced by his knowledge of his superiority over his friends, in respect of academic excellence. Pessimism he tasted through his wedlock; passion was his natural gift; respect for rationality he learned from his study of the classics; and the knowledge of the paradisical bliss and the hellish torture he gathered from the Bible. And all these are conspicuous in *Paradise Lost.* Again, Milton had, in his mind, two aspects of a man the private and religious, and the public and political. As a private person, he had firm belief in God and in God's righteousness. He believed that whatever God does is rational and just, though to evil and irrational eyes (like those of Satan) he seems to be wayward, whimsical and tyrannical. It is for this reason that in the invocatory part of the epic, the poet wants to "justify the ways of God to men." He believed that the essence of God and that of man is rationality, and so God cannot be tyrannical. Milton believed in the inviolability of the fiat of God, and he believed that God will punish any disobedience shown to him. In *Paradise Lost*, therefore, Satan has to bear the brunt of God's ire aroused by his disobedience. Adam and Eve, the dearest creatures of God, also had to suffer the punishment inflicted upon them by God for their disobedience. But God is also merciful; of course only to those who repent for their sins, like Adam and Eve. This strong sentiment of religiosity of Milton was nourished by his devoted study of the Bible. In *Paradise Lost*, Book XII, Adam expresses, in clear terms, Milton's sentiment of religiosity:

> '... Henceforth I learn that to obey is best,
> And love with fear the only God, to walk
> As in his presence, ever to observe
> His providence, and on him sole depend.
> Merciful over all his works, with good
> Still overcoming evil, and by small
> Accomplishing great things — by things deemed weak
> Subverting worldly-strong, and worldly-wise
> By simply meek; that suffering for Truth's sake
> Is fortitude to highest victory,
> And to the faithful death the gate of life — ... '

Milton's experiences in his early life may be found in *Paradise Lost*. The memory of the idyllic Horton, where his father lived, may have influenced his description of Paradise, as, later on, W.B. Yeats's boyhood memory of Sligo coloured his descriptions of pastoral scenes of his poems. In Book IV, Milton writes about Eden that it is situated in a hilly region with profusion of tall trees, punctuated by fast-running brooks, and then he further writes :

> Thus was this place,
> A happy rural seat of various view:
> Groves whose rich trees wept odorous gums and balm;
> Others whose fruit, burnished with golden rind,
> Hung amiable —

Milton's learning and love of Latin is also evident in the latinate words and syntaxes of *Paradise Lost*. Such words as 'sov'ran', 'Pandemonium' etc. show the poet's profound knowledge and love of Latin. Milton, in his youth, was very fond of archaic geographical names and the natural features of particular regions. He was also much interested in the mythologies of different nations. His knowledge of all these things is clearly evident in the epic. In no other poem in the English language do we find so many archaic place-names and mythological characters. Milton's extensive study of ancient geography and mythologies has certainly left its mark in the epic. His father was a music composer, and hence the poet had a life-long love and respect for music, and hence the 'organ voice' of *Paradise Lost*. Again, his mother was full of charity, and hence God's charity in the epic. In Book III of the epic, God says: " '...But mercy, first and last, shall brightest shine....' ".

Milton's practical experiences in the company of the fair sex and his experiences of wedlock may also be found in the epic. Early in his life, before he took B.A. degree, Milton fell in love with an Italian singer, the gentle Emilia, and later on, composed some sonnets about her. Glimpses of his first experiences of the feeling of love in the presence of the beloved, and his vision of the beloved may be discerned in the description of Eve, who is in love with Adam, in Book IV of the epic:

She, as a veil down to the slender waist,
Her unadorned golden tresses wore
Dishevelled, but in wanton ringlets waved
As the vine curls her tendrils, which implied
Subjection, but required with gentle sway,
And by her yielded, by him best received,
Yielded with coy submission, modest pride,
And sweet, reluctant, amorous delay.

Or this may be the reflection of Milton's first nuptial amorous meeting with his first wife Mary Powell. Milton's bitter relationship with Mary Powell is certainly and indelibly written down in Book IX of *Paradise Lost* where Adam and Eve accuse each other for the first great sin of humanity. The fault was really Eve's, and yet she scolds Adam: " 'why didst not thou, the head,/Command me absolutely not to go,/Going into such danger, as thou saidst?' " And, despairing, and wondering at her effrontery, Adam concludes: " 'woman overtrusting,/Lets her will rule: restraint she will not brook;/And, left to herself, if evil thence ensue,/ She first his weak indulgence will accuse.' " But from this, one should certainly not conclude that Milton was a misogynist: he had every respect for admirable women, and he had his kind of high ideal of womanhood in wedlock. The bickerings between himself and Mary Powell was due only to the fact that Mary could not rise upto his high ideal of womanhood. However, C.M. Bowra writes about Milton's admiration for womanhood, as is evident in *Paradise Lost*: "Into Eve Milton has thrown much of his own deep admiration for womanhood. She is not only beautiful, but until Satan tempts her, she is almost all that a wife ought to be" (Bowra, 203). Again, Powell's repentant returning to her husband's fold, soon after she deserted him, may be found in *Paradise Lost* (Book X, lines 914-917), as we find the same also in *Samson Agonistes*. At the place of the epic referred to above, Eve tells Adam in entreating words :

'Forsake me not thus, Adam! witness Heaven

What love sincere and reverence in my heart
I bear thee, and unwitting have offended,
Unhappily deceived !...'

While, thus, apologising to Adam, Eve was continually weeping with a crest-fallen mien. Milton describes her picture at this dramatic moment thus (Book X, lines 909-913) :

He added not, and from her turned; but Eve,
Not so repulsed, with tears that ceased not flowing,
And tresses all disordered, at his feet
Fell humble, and, embracing them, besought
His peace, and thus proceeded in her plaint:-

And, as we know, Mary Powell, while she had been begging Milton's pardon after her returning to his fold, appeared like Eve at this dramatic situation.

In his private life, Milton was almost, orthodoxically, religious-minded. He was morally very pure, was proud, and was of a rebellious nature; and all these traits of the poet are sprinkled throughout the epic. To begin with, as we have said earlier, Milton at first thought of writing an epic on the Arthurian theme, but later on he switched over to the story of *Genesis*. The former theme, if executed, would make an ethical poem; and the latter, as it is executed, has made a religious poem. As a perfect puritan, Milton was averse to the prejudicial and adventitious rituals of the church; and for this reason we do not find any reference to such rituals in the epic. The puritans believed in simplicity of religious life with purity of mind. They believed that obedience to God was the only path of salvation. Accordingly, we find in the epic that love of, and obedience to, God are the only means of reaching the neighbourhood of God. Again, Milton was by nature very proud — even in his boyhood. This may be due to his superiority over his fellows, regarding academic achievements and other talents. Unlike his fellows, he deeply thought of becoming a poet of great worth. This sense of superiority grew in him, in turn, a sense of pride. And this sense of superiority and pride we find in Satan. Further, in his young age, Milton was once reportedly beaten by his tutor, one Mr. Chappell, in his undergraduate class, for which reason he was wounded in his personality, and he could not swallow this insult, and so he grumbled. To Chappell's treatment, Milton "became exasperated and told his tutor what he thought of the Cambridge educational method" (Tillyard, 1956, 16). Milton could never bear with wounded pride, lying supine. And this aspect so his character we may find also in the character of Satan.

Milton was certainly a staunch puritan, but he was never an ascetic. He believed that the body, as it is created by God, cannot be sinful or evil or immoral — and this was in contravention of the prevailing Christian mores. However, this belief in the purity of the body is evident in Book IV of *Paradise Lost* where he comments on the 'connubial love' between Adam and Eve:

> Whatever hypocrites austerely talk
> Of purity, and place, and innocence,
> Defaming as impure what God declares
> Pure, and commands to some, leaves free to all.

And lastly, Milton was innately rebellious: he could never tolerate tyranny and oppression. He was quick to attack, if attacked. When at Cambridge, some rough pupils frequently taunted him by calling him 'Lady' for his lack of sociableness and sense of fun and lack of interest in wine, as they wrongly perceived him, Milton bitterly wrote about them: " 'Some people have lately nick-named me the Lady. But why do I seem to them too little of a man? I suppose because I have never had the strength to drink off a bottle like a prize-fighter; or because my hand has never grown horny with holding a plough-handle; or because I was not a farm hand at seven, and so never took a midday nap in the sun — last perhaps because I never showed my virility in the way these brothellers do. But I wish they could leave playing the ass as readily as I the woman' " (Tillyard, 1956, 29). This rebellious and anti-tyrannical attitude of Milton is also obvious in the character of Satan.

As told earlier, there were two aspects in Milton's personality: private and public. Nonetheless, he was true to himself. We have already seen him as a private man, and now let us see his public life, and see whether his public life is reflected in *Paradise Lost*. In his public life he fought for democracy and freedom as fiercely as he fought for nothing else. This aspect of his public life or his political philosophy is well borne out by his political pamphlets or tracts as well as by *Paradise Lost*. In fact, Milton's religious and political thoughts in the epic were earlier rehearsed in his religious and political tracts. In his tract *Reason of Church Government*, which he wrote well ahead of *Paradise Lost*, to wit in 1642, Milton wrote about the Englishman : " 'And verily if we look at his native towardliness in the rough-cast without breeding, some nation or other may haply be better composed to a natural civility and right judgment then he. But if he get the benefit once of a wise and well-rectified nurture, which must first come in general from the godly vigilance of the Church, I suppose that wherever mention is made of countries, manners, or men, the English people, among the first that shall be praised, may deserve to be accounted a right pious, right honest, and right hardy nation.' " Here, Milton's pride in his being an Englishman is obvious — and pride was an element of his personality — and this pride Satan too possesses enormously. Again, Milton conceived of some sort of paradise well ahead of his writing *Paradise Lost*. He probably got the idea of a paradise or utopia from his reading of the writings of Plato, Bacon and Sir Thomas More. And he perhaps got the idea of the 'loss' or 'wasteage' or 'fall', to which human beings are heirs, — the 'loss' of , or 'fall' from, some utopia — from his study of their writings and also from his study of *Genesis*. Inklings of this idea of his is available in his tract *Apology for Smectymnuus*, in which also he suggests, as in *Paradise Regained*, how to retrieve or reclaim the former blissful state of human beings. In the tract, he writes: " 'that grave a and noble invention, which the greatest and sublimest wits in sundry ages, Plato and Critius, and our two famous countrymen, the one in his Utopia, the other in his New Atlantis, chose, I may not say as a field, but as a mighty continent, wherein to display the largeness of their spirits, by teaching this our world better and exacter things than were yet known or used.' " Like Plato, Bacon (*New Atlantis*) and Sir Thomas More (*Utopia*), Milton found his utopia, and it is not different from the paradise in *Paradise Lost*.

Milton was a devoted and unflinching votary of liberty and freedom — of maximal freedom allowable to citizens of a society. He always fought for freedom of thinking, of speech, and of conscience. In his politico-pedagogic tract *Areopagitica*, he writes: "Give me the liberty to know, to utter, and to argue freely according to conscience, above all liberty." And what did Satan want? He wanted liberty: freedom to know, freedom to think, freedom to speak, and freedom to do — all according to one's own unbiased judgment and according to one's own conscience. Right to knowledge he would never part with. This devotion of his towards knowledge we find also in Satan. In Book IV of *Paradise Lost*, Satan meditates upon the Tree of Knowledge and its fruits thus: " 'O fair plant', said he, 'with fruit surcharged,/Deigns none to ease thy load, and taste thy sweet,/Nor God, nor Man? Is Knowledge so despised?' " Again, in Book V, Satan adulates knowledge while he inveigles Eve to taste the fruit of the Tree of Knowledge. He tells her that it is only knowledge which can open before our eyes the mystery of the life on earth and in heaven. Satan persuades Eve thus :

... Partake thou also: happy thou art,
Happier thou may'st be, worthier canst not be.
Taste this and be hanceforth among the gods
Thyself a goddess; not to Earth confined,
But sometimes in the Air, as we; sometimes
Ascend to Heaven, by merit thine, and see
What life the gods live there, and such live thou.'

The taste of the fruit of the Tree of knowledge will, Satan tells Eve, metamorphose a mortal into a god. Such a high opinion or valuation of knowledge we find also in *Areopagitica*. And along with his thirst and respect for knowledge, Milton had a craving for authority. He was quite independent minded: he was never going to servilely imitate anybody; rather, he wanted to set examples for others. He wanted to rule. And this gubernatorial tendency also we find, of course in its diabolical form, in Satan : " 'To reign is worth ambition, though in Hell:/Better to reign in Hell than serve in Heaven' " (*Paradise Lost*, Book I).

It should be mentioned here that the freedom or liberty that Milton demanded was bot universal or allowable to all men: he did not demand freedom or liberty for men and women equally. Milton did not hold man and woman on identical footing, but only on equal footing. He held that man has his own privileges and duties as woman has hers; the duties and the privileges are not identical, but are equal. Notice what he says in *Paradise Lost* (Book IV): "For contemplation he and valour formed,/For softness she and sweet attractive grace;/He for God only, she for God in him." Milton thought that manhood and womanhood are complementary attributes that can be equal but never identical. And, nonetheless, we must say that Milton believed in the superiority of man over the fair sex ("He for God only, she for God in him."). In this regard, he differed from the Cavaliers who believed in the equality, or rather in the identity, between man and woman. Milton's belief in the non-identity between man and woman is well expressed in his tract *Doctrine and Discipline of Divorce*. E.M.W. Tillyard writes about such beliefs of Milton as expressed in that tract: "The passage concerning man's rights over woman, the exaltation of companionship over mere physical satisfaction, and his protest against forced and arranged marriages, were probably founded on earlier thought. It is now fairly widely recognised, I should guess, that Milton tempered a Hebraic belief in the superiority of man with ideas remarkable in his day for their enlightment. If Milton has no sympathy with the adoration, sincere or feigned, current among the Cavaliers for their womankind, at least he believes that the chief end of marriage is 'the apt and cheerful conversation of man with woman to comfort and refresh him against the evil of solitary life" (Tillyard, 1956, 148). In *Paradise Lost*, we find that Eve was created out of Adam's rib, which means that Eve is dependent on Adam, even for her existence. In Book IV of the epic, Eve accepts this position of woman when she tells Adam: " 'My author and disposer, what thou bidd'st/Unargued I obey; so God ordains:/ God is thy law, thou mine: to know no more/Is woman's happiest knowledge, and her praise....' ". And, before this, she had already accepted Adam as her guide: " '.... my guide/And head !....' " Woman is inferior to man, and nature herself (or God himself) has made her inferior. The woman may boast of her beauty, but before man's wisdom, that beauty fades. In Book IV of the epic, Eve herself admits of the inferiority of her beauty compared with the wisdom that belongs to Adam. She says: " 'How beauty is excelled by manly grace/And wisdom, which alone is truly fair.' " Again, in Book I, Adam abuses Eve for her frailty — frailty which, he means to say, is inelactably given only to womankind: " 'Oh, why did God,/Creator wise, that peopled highest Heaven/With Spirits masculine, create at last/This novelty on Earth, this fair defect/ Of nature,...' " Lastly, and curiously, Milton's description of Adam's physical beauty includes at least one feature of his physical appearance — his locks of hair. To add yet another point: can we not find Milton's morbid pain due to his blindness and his fancy of getting back his sight in the following lines of *Paradise Lost* (Book XI, lines 412-416)?

> Michael from Adam's eyes the film removed,
> Which that false fruit that promised clearer sight
> Had bred; then purged, with euphrasy and rue
> The visual nerve, for he had much to see,
> And from the well of life three drops instilled.

Thus, we find a number of ideals and beliefs which are common between Milton's personal and familial life and experiences, on the one hand, and what he has written in *Paradise Lost* and some of his tracts, on the other. And so *Paradise Lost* may be taken as an autobiographical poem, or may be, as a confessional document of the poet. But we should be very cautious in calling the epic autobiographical. Because, firstly, no poet can remain absolutely neutral to his works, and in this sense every piece of literature is, to a degree, autobiographical, and hence *Paradise Lost* should not specially be called an autobiographical epic. Secondly, Milton took for his epic the story of *Genesis*, and so he had to depend heavily on the Christian philosophy and teachings.

So, whatever, we may find in the epic should be treated as primarily belonging to the Christian teachings and philosophy, and not always, and necessarily, as coinciding with Milton's personal ideals and views. Thirdly, for Milton's alleged political views in *Paradise Lost*, it may be said that such hazards may not be found to be warranted. It is further to be noted that the tragic element that we find in the epic is, perhaps, in no way related to the poet's personal tragic life, save, may be, to his tragic blindness; for, even in his youth the poet planned to write a tragic drama on some aspect of the fall of man or the loss of paradise. In the epic, Milton's principal objective was to "justify the ways of God to men", and this justification also he found in his beloved book, the Bible. So, C.V. Wedgwood is, perhaps, quite correct in believing that *Paradise Lost* is not so much influenced by the affairs of his own life. Wedgwood rather believes that the epic shows us the culmination of the poet's creative faculty. He writes: "It is easier to explain the development of genus by itself than by reference to outside circumstances, and *Paradise Lost* is more the outcome of *Comus* than it is of the outside circumstances of Milton's life" (Wedgwood, 111). And it is for this his belief that Wedgwood says that Milton's productive life should not be divided into three periods — the period of early poems, the period of pamphletry, and the great period of epic poetry — because, he further says, there is an unbroken thread running through the three consecutive periods.

6

(THE EPIC SIMILES IN *PARADISE LOST*)

In both *Paradise Lost* and *Paradise Regained*, Milton has cultivated what is known as grand style. His precursors in the extensive use of epic or extended similes were Homer (c. 850 B.C.), Virgil (70-19 B.C.) and Dante (1265-1321). The epic simile is a great component of the grand style that comprises sublimity, grandeur, broad descriptions, high sonority, classical allusions, latinised expressions, archaism, etc. as well. Certainly, the loftiness and majesty of an epic is reinforced by the cumulative force of the epic similes. A simple or ordinary simile is a comparison of one thing with another, announced by such words as 'like', 'as', etc. But an epic simile compares between one complex action or relation with another complex action or relation. In *Iliad*, for instance, the Greek host led by Ajax is compared to a storm-cloud, citing the similarities between the two things. T.S. Eliot, in his essay 'Dante', says that the epic similes "make us see more definitely the scene."

Milton has employed the epic similes in *Paradise Lost* rather profusely, and this has boosted up the quality of his grand style. He has used expanded or epic similes that go beyond superficial comparison between two grand images. In lines 194-207 of *Paradise Lost*, Book I, Milton compares the person of Satan with that of the huge mythological sea-monster Leviathan :

.... his other parts besides
Prone on the flood, extended long and large,
Lay floating many a rood, in bulk as huge
As whom the fables name of monstrous size,
Titanian or Earth-born, that warred on Jove,
Briaroes or Typhon, whom the den
By ancient Tarsus held, or that sea-beast
Leviathan, which God of all his works
Created hugest that swarm th' ocean-stream.
Him, haply slumbering on the Norway foam,
The pilot of some small night-foundered skiff
Deeming some island, oft, as seamen tell
With fixed anchor in his rind,
Moors by his side under the lee,

Again, in lines 284-291 (Book I), of the epic, when Satan moves towards the edge of the solid fire of hell to call forth the innumerable fallen angels, who are lying unconscious in the wavy liquid fire, Milton compares the huge shield of Satan with the enormous circumference of the moon :

............his ponderous shield,
Ethereal temper, massy, large, and round,
Behind him cast. The broad circumference
Hung on his shoulders like the moon, whose orb
Through the optic glass the Tuscan artist views
At evening, from the top of Fesole,
Or in Valderno, to descry new lands,
Rivers, or mountains, in her spotty globe.

Satan's spear, like his shield, is also enormous: it is much more elongated than the tallest pine available in the hill-tops of Norway. Milton compares Satan's spear with the tallest pine of Norway, in lines 292-294 of Book I :

His spear, to equal which the tallest pine
Hewn on Norwegian hills, to be the mast
Of some great ammiral, were but a wand,

In Book I of *Paradise Lost*, Milton gives us many such beautiful epic similes. Here, as Homer compared Ajax's army with a storm-cloud, Milton compares Satan's legion with the innumerable 'autumnal leaves' that float on the brooks in Vallombrosa (Book I, lines 301-304):

> His legions, Angel forms, who lay intranced
> Thick as autumnal leaves that strow the brooks
> In Vallombrosa, where th' Etrurian shades
> High over-arched embower;

Next, Satan's army is compared with locusts and 'pitchy cloud' in lines 340-341 of Book I: "up called a pitchy cloud/Of locusts". The rebel army of Satan is a multitude which is like the invaders from the north on the 'Lybian sands' (Book I, lines 351-355) :

> A multitude, like which the populous North
> Pour'd never from her frozen loins, to pass
> Rhene or the Danaw, when her barbarous sons
> Came like a deluge on the South and spread
> Beneath Gibralter to the Lybian sands.

Again, in lines 535-539 of Book I, Milton beautifully compares Azazel's 'imperial ensign' with a meteor

> ....the glittering stuff unfurled
> The imperial ensign which, full high advanced,
> Shone like a meteor streaming to the wind,
> With zems and golden lustre emblazed
> Seraphic arms and trophies;

Satan orders the fallen angels to prepare for battle against the Almighty. But when they are in battle array, Satan, in his faded glory, looks like the sun seen through a mist (Book I, lines 594-597) "as when the sun new-ris'n/Looks through the horizontal misty air/Shorn of his beams". Not only Satan, but all other fallen angels also stood crest-fallen. Milton compares them with a forest of oaks or pines that have lost their foliage due to fire (Book I, lines 612-614) "as, when Heaven's fire/Hath scathed the forest oaks, or mountain pines,/With singed top their stately growth". Again, when the Pandemonium is built up and the council of the innumerable rebel angels is summoned, the angels make a mess of things, and chaos prevails, which Milton compares with a clutch of bees busy in spring-time (Book I, lines 769-773) "As bees/In spring-time, when the Sun with Taurus rides,/Pour forth their populous youth about the hive/In clusters; they among fresh dews and flowers/Fly to and fro".

Book I of *Paradise Lost* is packed up with epic similes or extended similes, but the rest eleven Books of the epic are not so: there Milton employs such similes rather sparingly. In Book II, we find Satan's 'Stygian council' begins and ends. After the council is over, multitudes of fallen angels disband and wander about. Milton compares the scene created by all these scattered angels with the scenes at Olympus and Pythia (lines 528-538) :

> Part on the plain, or in the air sublime,
> Upon the wing or in swift race contend,
> As at th' Olympian games or Pythian fields;
> Part curb their fiery steeds, or shun the goal
> With rapid wheels, or fronted brigades form:
> As when, to warn proud cities, war appears
> Waged in the troubled sky, and armies rush
> To battle in the clouds; before each van
> Prick forth the aery knights, and couch their spears,
> Till thickest legions close; with feats of arms
> From either end of heaven the welkin burns.

In Book IV, Satan "Squat like a toad, close at the ear of Eve" and begins to fire the imagination of Eve, in her sleep, with abjectly evil intention. Ithuriel, the right angel, sees this and touches Satan with his spear, and Satan, perceiving Ithuriel, stands aghast. Milton draws a very beautiful picture of the startled archangel, with the help of an extended simile (Book IV, lines 815-819) :

> Up he starts,
> Discovered and surprised. As when a spark
> Lights on a heap of nitrous powder, laid
> Fit for the tun, some magazine to store
> Against a rumoured war, the smutty grain,
> With sudden blaze diffused, inflames the air:
> So started up, in his own shape, the Fiend.

In Book V, God tells Raphael how Satan is plotting to corrupt Eve, and through her, all humanity; and he warns Raphael to be on intense guard against such plottings. Raphael then goes up to heaven from where it seems to him that the earth is in no way different from other planets of the firmament. Raphael observes the earth (Book V, lines 261-266):

> .... as when by night the glass
> Of Galilio, less assured, observes

Imagined lands and regions in the Moon;
Or pilot from amidst the Cyclades
Delos or Samos first appearing kens,
A cloudy spot.

Again, in Book VII, we come across another beautiful extended simile. God creates the world by his command, within the space of only six days. On the third day God creates huge-rise hills, and then commands that water-falls be created, and these get created. Milton compares these water-falls with huge armies (lines 295-298): "As armies at the call/Of trumpet (for of armies thou hast heard)/Troops to their standard, so the wat'ry throng,/Wave rolling after wave, where way they found —"

These are only some of the epic or extended similes that Milton has employed in *Paradise Lost*. Now the question is: what purposes do these similes serve in the epic? It is obvious that these similes are serving some very important purposes in the epic. To begin with, some of these similes explain, clarify, or bring into relief some distant, vague or unfamiliar images or things or events. For instance, Milton brings into relief and thus makes life-like his description of Satan's 'Stygian council' of the innumerable fallen angels (Book II, lines 488-495):

As when from mountaintops the dusky clouds
Ascending, while the north wind sleeps, o'erspread
Heaven's cheerful face, the louring element
Scowls o'er the darkened landscape snow, or shower,
If chance the radiant sun, with farewell sweet,
Extend his evening beam, the fields revive,
The birds their notes renew, and bleating herds
Attest their joy, that hill and valley rings.

Secondly, there is a very small coterie of characters in the epic with only which it would be very difficult for the poet to deal with so vast a subject of the epic had he not resorted to a number of extended similes, through which he has been able to introduce occasions for dealing with colossal events in detail, or with archaic philosophy, politics, mythology, etc. in detail. By employing similes, the poet has been able to refer us to archaic events and allusions, and thereby to superbly handle so extended a subject, and to enrich the whole epic. Thirdly, Milton has introduced into the epic even some contemporary events and situations with the help of extended similes. In Book IV, for instance, Satan journeys towards Paradise, leaps over the pallisade around Eden, and thus enters into the celestial garden, like a thief. While narrating the event of Satan's burghlery in Paradise, Milton is, indirectly, describing the condition of his contemporary society, infested with thieves and 'lewd hirelings' (Book IV, lines 183-193) :

As when a prowling wolf,
Whom hunger drives to seek new haunt for prey,
Watching where shepherds pen their flocks at eve,
In hundred cotes amid the field secure,
Leaps o'er the fence with ease into the fold;
Or as a thief, bent to unhoard the cash
Of some rich burgher, whose substantial doors,
Cross-barred and bolted fast, fear no assault,
In at the window climbs, or o'er the tiles
So climb this first grand thief into God's fold:
So since into his Church lewd hirelings climb.

Fourthly, sometimes through some of the similes, Milton finds occasions for introducing beautiful images, as when he describes the beauty of Paradise, he brings before our view the beauty of the spicy islands and that of 'Araby'. In Book IV, when Satan first views Paradise, it seems to him an uncomparable sight which Milton describes with the help of an extended simile (lines 152-165):

....................so lovely seemed
That landscape; and of pure, now purer air
Meets his approach, and to the heart inspires
Vernal delight and joy, able to drive
All sadness but despair. Now gentle gales,
Fanning their odoriferous wings, dispense
Native perfumes, and whisper whence they stole
Those balmy spoils. As when to them who sail
Beyond the Cape of Hope, and now are past
Mozambic, off at sea north-east winds blow
Sabean odours from the spicy shore
Of Araby the Blest, with such delay
Well pleased they slack their course, and many
Cheered with grateful smell old Ocean smiles;

A few lines afterwards, Milton further narrates the beautiful aspects of Paradise, and while so narrating, he brings in a plethora of mythological characters as *obiter dicta* (Book IV, lines 268-290) :

Not that fair field
Of Enna, where Proserpin gathering flowers,

Herself a fairer flower, by gloomy Dis
Was gathered — which cost Ceres all that pain
To seek her through the world — nor that sweet grove
Of Daphne, by Orontes and th' inspired
Castalian spring, might with this Paradise
Of Eden strive; nor that Nyseian isle,
Girt with the river Triton, where old Cham,
Whom Gentiles Ammon call, and Lyban Jove,
Hid Amalthea, and her florid son,
Young Bacchus, from his stepdame Rhea's eye;
Nor, where Abassin kings their issue guard,
Mount Amara (though this by some supposed
True Paradise) under the Ethiop line
By Nilus' head, enclosed with shining rock,
A whole day's journey high, but wide remote
From this Assyrian garden, where the Fiend
Saw undelighted delight, all kind
Of living creatures, new to sight and strange
Two of far nobler shape erect and tall,
God-like erect, with native honour clad
In naked majesty, seemed lords of all
And worthy seemed;

Thus, with the help of epic or extended similes, Milton has brought before us diverse mythologies, histories, ancient wars and civilisations, ancient places, beautiful places, etc., and thus has enriched his epic *Paradise Lost* to a great extent.

7
(THE GRAND STYLE OF *PARADISE LOST*)

In his Oxford lectures *On Translating Homer*, Matthew Arnold coined, in 1861, the term 'Grand Style'. Such a phrase arises, he said, "when a noble nature 'poetically gifted, treats with simplicity or with severity a serious subject' " (Cuddon, 291). By poetically gifted persons Arnold here meant such persons as Homer, Virgil, Dante and Milton, and he believed that the style of all these great poets were grand. According to him, the grand style is a lofty and grave style, suitable for epopes. Arnold himself attempted this style in his epic narrative *Sohrab and Rustum*.

'O thou young man, the air of Heaven is soft,
And warm and pleasant; but the grave is cold.

Heaven's air is better than the cold dead grave.
Behold me: I am vast, and clad in iron,
And tried; and I have stood on many a field
Of blood, and I have fought with many a foe;
Never was that field lost, or that foe sav'd.
O Sohrab, wherefore wilt thou rush on death?
Be govern'd: quit the Tartar host, and come
To Iran, and be as my son to me,
And fight beneath my banner till I die.
There are no youth in Iran brave as thou.'

Unfortunately, Arnold did not elaborate on the features of the grand style; and, perhaps, he was helpless in this regard; for, in his *Last Words*, he writes that " 'grand style is the last matter in the world for verbal definition to deal with adequately' " (Preminger, 325). Not only that, but even the exact meaning of the word 'style' is hard to be explicated. Style has been variously defined or explained; but, without going into the controversy about the meaning of the word 'style', we may regard style as variation in expressions of the same meaning content, or "saying the same thing in different words and ways" : "*Smokers are requested to occupy rear seats*; *Smokers please sit at the back*; *If you smoke, sit at the back; Smokers must sit at the back; Smokers at the back.*" (McArthur, 994). Style has generally been divided into three categories: plain or low, middle, and high or grand. However, Arnold divided the grand style into two categories: 'grand style simple' and 'grand style severe'. "In the 'grand style severe', of which Milton is perhaps the best model, a thing is said 'with a kind of intense compression, or in an allusive, brief, almost haughty way, as if the poet's mind were charged with so many and such grave matters, that he would not deign to treat any one of them explicitly" (Preminger, 325). The softer variety of the grand style is the 'grand style simple'. Arnold coined the term 'grand style', of course, but he was not the first to employ this style; because, before him, besides the ancient masters mentioned earlier, Reynolds and Ruskin, among others, employed this style in their poetry.

The grand style did not come to Milton as a windfall, but he had to learn the use of it, exercise it, and refine his version of it. In his 'L'Allegro' and 'Il Penseroso', Milton used sonorous octosyllabic couplets, and in his *Comus* he employed sounding blank-verse. These may be taken as the prelude or prolegomena to his employment of the grand style in *Paradise Lost.* The blank-verse of *Comus* is particularly stately in its diction, and it is sonorous and splendid. By the time he wrote *Comus*, Milton almost reached the apogee of perfection of the grand style, and when he wrote *Paradise Lost*, his grand style was a full-blown flower. John Reesing writes about the style of *Paradise Lost*: "a wonderfully alert and supple responsiveness which, in holding together all the varied materials of the poem, contributes importantly to the achievement of the distinctive quality we all feel" (Reesing, 107). Reesing further writes about *Paradise Lost* and particularly, about the technique of the poem that has contributed to the grandeur of its style : "The narrator's is the first voice we hear in the poem, and the last. He is a persona, not Milton..... He speaks a little more than a third of the poem (34.95 per cent of the total 10,565 lines). He is thus a part of the poem's total economy, one among many means for so distributing the energies of response that the mind of Milton the poet, and of us who follow him, may achieve an order of a very definite and distinctive quality" (Reesing, 107). However, Arnold's praise of the style of Milton in the epic under consideration is more than inspiring. In his address delivered in St. Margaret's Church, Westminster, on the 13th of February, 1888, at the ceremony on the occasion of the unveiling of a Memorial Window presented by Mr. Geroge W. Childs of Philadelphia, in memory of Milton, Arnold wrote about Milton's style in profusion of praise, calling the poet a prophet. In the written address Arnold said: "If to our English race an inadequate sense of perfection of work is a real danger, if the discipline of respect for a high and flawless excellence is peculiarly needed by us, Milton is of all our gifted men the best lesson, the most salutary influence. In the sure and flawless perfection of his rhyme and diction he is as admirable as Virgil or Dante, and in this respect he is unique amongst us. No one else in English literature and art possesses the like distinction." Perhaps, there can be no more encomium for a poet for his art than this. And yet, as to the quality of the poetry in *Paradise Lost*, Arnold further wrote in the same address: "Shakespeare is divinely strong, rich and attractive. But sureness of perfect style Shakespeare himself does not possess. Milton, from one end of *Paradise Lost* to the other, is in his diction and rhythm constantly a great artist in the great style. Whatever may be said as to the subject of his poem, as to the conditions under which he received his subject and treated it, that praise, at any rate, is assured to him." Arnold, in the same address, again, also compared Milton's style with the styles of the great poets of ancient Greece and Rome. He wrote : "In our race are thousands of readers, presently there will be millions, who know not a word of Greek and Latin, and will never learn those languages. If this host of readers are given to gain any sense of power and charm of the great poets of antiquity, their way to gain it is not through translations of the ancients, but through the original poetry of Milton, who has the like power and charm because he has the like great style."

Milton's grand style, like most of others', consists of several components or aspects: sublimity, grandeur, description of images, epic or extended similes, organic sonority, use of classical proper names, and place names, classical allusions, latinised expressions and syntax, etc. Let us briefly discuss these, one by one. The first quality that is to be noted in Milton's grand style is the note of sublimity that comprises majesty, grandeur, grace and simplicity. To take a few lines, for instance, from Book I :

> Of Man's first disobedience, and the fruit
> Of that forbidden tree, whose mortal taste
> Brought death to the World, and all our woe,
> With loss of Eden, till one greater Man
> Restore us, and regain the blissful seat,
> Sing, Heavenly Muse,....................

This is sublime, of course, but what sublimity is, is difficult to define or, at least, difficult to convey. It is supposed that the term 'sublime' or 'sublimity' (from Latin word '*sublimis*', meaning 'in a high position' or 'exalted') was first used by Cassius Longinus (3rd century A.D.) in his great fragmentary work of literary criticism, *On the Sublime*. By sublimity Longinus meant excellence of language; but he thought that this sublimity or excellence of language was impossible without grandeur of thought and intensity of feeling, both of which were dependent principally on the native endowments of the author, and secondly on the author's training and exercise. According to Longinus, sublimity depended on the quality (nobleness) of diction, skilful composition, and rhetorical excellence. Following Longinus, some other critics and thinkers also tried, though vainly, to identify the necessary elements and the nature of sublimity. Edmund Burke, in his *A Philosophical Inquiry into the Origin of our Ideas of the Sublime and the Beautiful* (1757), contributed substantially to the understanding of sublimity. The philosopher Immanuel Kant also wrote about sublimity. According to him, sublimity could be equated with infinity, as beauty could be equated with finitude. However, sublimity is, perhaps, that quality of a poem that disentangles us from our earthly moorings and wafts us to the unearthly plane of greatness. It widens our vision, deepens our feeling, and reassures our existence. Milton's style, both in *Paradise Lost* and in

Paradise Regained, is grand and sublime, and this is due to the several particular components of the poems: their characters are no ordinary mortals but are God, Christ, Satan, Gabriel, Michael, Adam and Eve — the first progenitors, etc.; and their themes are also great — fall of Man, and his rehabilitation, respectively. Actually, Milton could never come down to the paltry. Even in some of his other great poems, the themes are sublime. For instance, the theme of his poem 'Nativity Ode' is the birth of Christ, the saviour; and the theme of *Comus* is the insuperable strength of moral rectitude.

The verse of *Paradise Lost* has the stamp of grandeur: it has stately diction, magnificence of thought, and great flow of phrases appropriate for hightened emotion. Mark what Satan says at the beginning to Book II:

> Powers and Dominions, Deities of Heaven!
> For, since no deep within her gulf can hold
> Immortal vigour, though oppress'd and fall'n,
> I give not Heaven for lost: from this descent
> Celestial Virtue rising will appear
> More glorious and more dread than from no fall,
> And trust themselves to fear no second fate! ....'

The descriptions in *Paradise Lost*, again, are broad, sweeping and impressive. Milton never describes the mean, but he has always broad perspecrives, and is always concerned with the big and the broad. In Book I of the epic, for instance, when Satan raises himself from the vale of liquid fire, Milton describes his movements thus :

> Forthwith upright he rears from off the pool
> His mighty stature; on each hand the flames
> Driven backward slope their pointing spires and rolled
> And billows, leave in the midst a horrid Vale.

Likewise, in the same Book, Milton describes the view of Chaos in stately diction and with majestic touches.

Milton's epic or extended similes have added a great deal to his grand style, in *Paradise Lost*. The things with which some characters or actions or conditions are compared are always supranormal in features, astronomical in number, and boundless in spatiality. For instance, in Book I, of the epic, he compares Satan's spear with the tallest pine available in the hill-tops of Norway, and says that even that tallest pine will seem to be but a wand, beside Satan's spear :

His spear, to equal which the tallest Pine
Hewn on Norwegian hills, to be the Mast
Of some great Ammiral, were but a wand.

Again, the sonority and musicality of Milton's verse is simply superb. The sound of the verse is baritone, robust, organic. The organic voice of Milton can be compared only with the sound that is produced by the billows of the sea that break against the shingles of the shore. It does not move imperceptibly, but rolls. The orchestration of different pitches and timbers of the verses produce majestic notes. But this is not admitted by all the critics. T.S.Eliot, for instance, in his essay 'A Note on the Verse of Milton', calls Milton's verse a sort of 'noise'. Eliot writes in the 'Note' : " 'It is at least more nearly possible to distinguish the pleasure which arises from the noise, from the pleasure due to other elements, than with the verse of Shakespeare, in which the auditory imagination and the imagination of the other senses are more nearly fused, and fused together with the thought.' " (Ricks, 68). But such a scathing attack is perhaps not justifiable. Christopher Ricks will never agree with Eliot. Ricks writes about Milton's poetry, in spite of Eliot's poignant criticism: "The poetry is superb, and it is quite without superbia [pride]" (Ricks, 70). Again, Frederick B. Artz says that in *Paradise Lost, Paradise Regained* and in *Samson Agonistes*, Milton has produced 'sublime verse': "Hence, Milton, writing in sublime blank verse, tried to do for English poetry what Virgil had done for Latin verse. He shows everywhere an unrivaled grasp of the intricacies of metrical music, and in trying 'to justify the ways of God to men' he renders the infinite in terms of the finite. Milton's poetry is very scholarly, but it is scholarship distilled into poetry......He was steeped in classical mythology, philosophy, and poetry, and in literature of the Italian and French Renaissance. Likewise, he was familiar with English poetry from Chaucer through Spenser, whom he especially admired, to Donne. Out of these rich stores, he created his own lofty and majestic style with the vigour of a Baroque architect." (Artz, 197). But, perhaps, the most glowing panegeric for Milton's style in verse is to be found in the Address of Matthew Arnold from which we have already quoted. In that Address, Arnold praised Milton' a style in absolute terms. He wrote that the power of Milton's poetry "resides chiefly in the refining and elevation wrought in us by the high and rare excellence of the great style."

The use of the proper names of some splendid, terrible, voluptuous or elevated mythological beings has also contributed to the grandeur of Milton's style. Such proper names as Satan (Lucifer), Beelzebub,

Moloch, Mammon, Babel, Mulciber, Soldan, Paynim, Belus, Serapis, Azazel, Baalim, Ashtatoth, Thammuz, etc. bring before our mind's eye a world of boundless horror and awe. Milton has also used, to the same effect, certain place names, such as Gehenna, Hinnom, Sodom, Olympus, 'Delphian cliff', Dodona, Adria, 'Hesperian fields', etc. He had a passion for such strange and sonorous names even in his young years. "In a passage of youthful bravura (stanzas XIX-XXV) we see the young poet indulging in the passion for strange sonorous names which colours so much of *Paradise Lost*, as he pictures pagan deities and prophets of Syria, Egypt and ancient Greece retreating before the conquering light of Christian truth" (The Wordsworth Poetry Library, v-vi). In his youth Milton was very much interested in the history, mythology, and geographical features of diverse climes. And with the help of extended similes, he has amply been able to bring before us those things, and thus his similes have greatly enriched the epic. Further, to add to our horror, Milton has also used numerous awe-inspiring classical and biblical allusions, such as the fall of man, the hell-fire, the inveigling of man by Satan, etc. To uphold the tenor of his grand style, the poet has introduced some other techniques in his epic, such as use of latinism, archaism, inversions, condensed phrases, epithets, metaphors, omission of words; use of words in different forms; punning; etc. Milton is very fond of, and apt in, latinism, as is evident in *Paradise Lost*. The use of latinism has added to the dignity and charm of the poem. In his latinism, Milton does not say 'Pharaoh and his Egyptian horse-men' but says "Busiris and his Memphian chivalry". He avoids the common idiomatic style by using bold metaphors; for instance, 'spangled with eyes', 'imparadised in one another's arms', etc. Again, sometimes he brings about inversions, *i.e.* he changes the normal order of words, in a sentence, and this emphasises the effect of his verse to a great extent. For example, he even begins the epic with an inversion:

> Of Man's first disobedience, and the fruit
> Of that forbidden tree, whose mortal taste
> Brought death into the World, and all our woe,
> With loss of Eden, till one greater Man
> Restore us, and regain the blissful seat,
> Sing, Heavenly Muse,....................

The poet has also used many archaic words, such as 'emprise' for 'enterprise', and 'frore' for 'frozen'. His compound epithets have also contributed substantially to the beauty of his grand style. He has employed such beautiful compound epithets as 'Heaven-banished host', 'night-warbling bird', etc. The cumulative forces of all these devices, adopted by Milton, have made his style grand and majestic and beautiful. Milton's style is at once lofty and impressive; it is a style that soars high and surpasses every other style that poets generally may devise.

In his grand style, Milton might have been influenced by what is known as Gongorism — a term that derived from the name of the Spanish writer Luis de Gongora (1561-1627). Gongorism is "baroque and affected style whose chief characteristics are : latinistic vocabulary and syntax, intricate metaphors, excessive hyperbole, rich colour images, mythological allusions and a general strangeness of diction" (Cuddon, 288). Milton also used all these devices, and hence he might have been influenced by Gongorism, we may presume. Again, Milton might have been influenced by the Spanish *culteranismo*, in his latinised expressions,— *culteranismo* that had a tendency to follow the Latin syntax in languages other than English language is subject-predominant, while Latin is predicate-predominant : in English the subject, as a rule, comes first, but in Latin the object generally comes first. To take an example of the Latin synrax or of latinism of Milton from *Paradise Regained*: " 'This is my Son belov'd, in him am pleased' ". However, Gongorism is a wider term that may include the style of *culteranismo*. The style of Milton is not oppressively monotonous, as is sometimes alleged: it is not all the while sombre, brooding and meditative, but it allows for occasions for light, ironic or comic strains, for spicing the style with variety, or to bring into relief the seriousness that pervades the whole poem. John Reesing writes: "The flexibility and variety of Milton's responsiveness in *Paradise Lost* have not always received their full due. For one thing, comic notes, though decorously subordinated always to more grand and epic concerns, are often firmly registered. There is a pervasive delight in puns and other forms of verbal wit, as critics have recently been noticing. There is awareness, grim and sardonic and contained in fear, yet still genuine awareness of comic inflation in the characters of Hell. There is an attitude childlike and playful — and wistful — towards the antics of Adam and Eve's domestic zoo; in the last book there is a sense of mild and benevolent amusement at Adam's impulsiveness. There is even a sense for the comically enigmatic in the representation of the good angels looking at the new cannon, which Raphael so painstakingly describes — something of the impulse to chuckle that we manage to suppress as we watch a naive but clever child try to puzzle out a suspicious situation. There is also a rich and continuous responsiveness to the physical world, to the enormous bliss of nature's abundance, and more particularly, to sensations of muscular action and of light and taste ('bright' and 'delicious' are very potent words). But the joyous feeling for the world of nature, a sense so largely and variously physical, is also largely a delight in nature as the creation of God." (Reesing, 114-115). Therefore, Milton, in *Paradse Lost*, is not always monotonous and somber. However, C.M. Bowra has written the following in praise of Milton's grand style: "Of all grand styles it is the grandest, and that not merely in its sustained sonority and its distance from the speech of every day. It has a more than Latin solidity; in comparison with the language of Camoes or of Tasso it is cold and even inhuman. No conclusions are made to human weakness; all topics are raised to the same sublime level" (Bowra, 1967, 198).

In *Paradise Lost* (as also in *Paradise Regained*), Milton has not used rhyming, and has given the reason thereof in an adjunct to his 'Argument' for the epic: "The measure is English heroic verse without rime, as that of Homer in Greek, and of Virgil in Latin — rime being no necessary adjunct or true ornament of poem or good verse, in long works espicially, but the invention of a barbarous age, to set off wretched matter and lame metre; graced indeed since by the use of some famous modern poets, carried away by custom, but much to their own vexation, hindrance, and constraint to express many things otherwise, and for the most part worse, than else they would have expressed them. Not without cause, therefore, some both Italian and Spanish poets of prime note have rejected rime both in longer and shorter works, as have also long since our best English tragedies, as a thing of itself, to all judicious ears, trivial and of no true musical delight; which consists only in apt numbers, fit quantity of syllables, and the sense variously drawn out from one verse into another, not in the jingling sound of like endings — a fault avoided by the learned ancients both in poetry and all good oratory. The neglect then of rime so little is to be taken for a defect, though it may seem so perhaps to vulgar readers, that it rather is to be esteemed an example set — the first in English — of ancient liberty recovered to heroic poem from the troublesome and modern bondage of riming." Andrew Marvell, in his poem 'On *Paradise Lost*', says that Milton was quite right in rejecting rhyming in *Paradise Lost*: "Thy verse created like thy theme sublime,/In number, weight, and measure, needs not rhyme." But, it is not true that Milton never used rhymes, or that he wanted the skill of rhyming. In his 'Lycidas' and in his sonnets, for instance, he has very skilfully used rhymes.

The poet, Robert Bridges, published his commandable study of Milton's prosody, *Milton's Prosody*, in 1921. In this book, Robert Bridges has dealt at some length with the features, variety and beauty of Milton's verse. Milton has composed *Paradise Lost* in five-stressed decasyllabic lines. Take, for instance, the five beginning lines of the epic :

Of Mán's | first dís | o bé | dience, ánd | the frúit
Of thát | for bíd | den trée, | whose mór | tal táste
Bróught | déath | into the Wórld, | and áll | our wóe,
With lóss | of É | den, tíll | one gréat | er Mán
Restóre | us, ánd | regáin | the blíss | ful séat,

But, Robert Bridges has sorted out several sort of variations in Milton's generally adopted prosody (Bridges, 1-45). A few of these variations are being cited below.

I. *Exceptions to the number of syllables being* ten. This sort of variation may be of two types:

i. The number of syllables being less than ten. There is no such variation in *Paradise Lost.*

ii. The number of syllables being more than ten: Examples:

(a) Of rébel ángels, bý whose aíd aspíring (I, 38).

(b) For sólitude sometímes is bést socíety, (IX, 249).

II. *Exceptions to the number of stresses being five.* This sort of variation is, again, of two sorts.

i. Lines with only four accents. Examples:

(a) As from the céntre thríce to th' útmost póle (I,74).

(b) And in lúxuríous cíties, where the noíse (I, 498).

ii. Lines with only three full stresses. Examples:

(a) His mínisters of véngence and pursúit (I,170).

(b) The sójourners of Góshen, who behéld (I, 309).

(c) Transfíx us to the bóttom of this gúlf ? (I, 329)

III. *Exceptions in the position of the stress.* Bridges writes about this type of variations: "Blank verse is typically in rising rhythm, *i.e.* the metric accent is regularly on the even syllables, but the rhythm is sometimes falling; *i.e.* the accent may be shifted on to the odd syllable in any place in the line; it is then described as inverted." (Bridges, 40). There are many such inverted rhythms in *Paradise Lost*. Examples are :

a. Régions of sórrow, dóleful shádes, where péace (I, 65).

b. A mind nót to be chánged by pláce or tíme. (I, 253).

c. Which, tásted, wórks knówledge of góod and évil (VII, 543).

d. Beyónd all pást exámple and fúture — (X, 840).

8
(CLASSICAL, OR HELLENIC, AND HEBRAIC INFLUENCES ON *PARADISE LOST*)

We are aware of Milton's voracious reading of classical literature, among so many other things, in his young days. He had had a very good training in Greek and Latin languages and literatures, and so he could well furbish himself with the poetic essences and metrical technicalities of the literatures in those two languages. He was also very much interested in the mythologies of Greece and Rome, as he was in those of some other countries, and he devoured and retained for long in his prodigious memory the inventory of so many mythological characters and their stories. He was so much interested in Greece and Rome that immediately after finishing his academic studies, he sailed for these two countries: the lands of his heart's desire. Milton's love of ancient Greece and Rome, and in things Grecian and Roman is very much conspicuous in *Paradise Lost*. Among all English poets, Milton was the most influenced by classical Greece and Rome. But the tradition of Rome itself was inspired by Greece, or Hellene or Hellas, and it is for this reason that the classical traditions of Greece and Rome are sometimes collectively known as Hellenic. The Hellenic influence on Milton, particularly in *Paradise Lost*, is pervading.

Milton was no less influenced by the tradition and religion of ancient Israel. He was much interested in, and was much attracted by, the monotheism and the ethical consternity of the ancient Israilities or the Hebrews. He was well-versed in the religion, mores, folk-tales, literature and mythology of the Hebrew society. Consequently, his theological concepts bore the imprint of Hebraism, and this is conspicuous in *Paradise Lost*. The oneness of God, the strict moral injunctions, the lordliness of the husband over the wife, etc. that we find in the epic were certainly inspired by Hebraism. We have said that Milton was a child of both Renaissance and Reformation. Renaissance grew in man a nostalgic love of beauty and humanism — things that once dominated the hearts of the people of ancient Greece and Rome. On the other hand, Reformation gave rise to the Puritanism of Milton's age, that generated an urge to uplift the moral standard of men — an urge that originated in the Hebraic tradition. The beauty of the human form — of Adam and Eve — and the beauty of nature that we come across in *Paradise Lost* may remind us of the Hellenic influence on Milton. Notice the description of the beautiful physical forms of Adam and Eve in *Paradise Lost* (Book IV, lines 300-307) :

> His fair large front and eye sublime declared
> Absolute rule; and hyacinthine locks
> Round from his parted forelock manly hung
> Clustering, but not beneath his shoulders broad:
> She, as veil down to the slender waist,
> Her unadorned golden tresses wore
> Dishevelled, but in wanton ringlets waved
> As the vine curls her tendrils,

This is Greek — the Hellenic ideal of human forms: male and female. In the same way, the Hellenic love of the beauty of nature is also evident in the epic. Consider, for instance, the description of the plush verdancy of Paradise an its surround, given in Book IV (lines 132-170). Had Milton not been moved by the Hellenic love of the beauty of nature, he might not have spent about 38 lines in the description of Paradise. Take just a few lines out of those 38, for an instance of Milton's beautiful description of the captivating charm of nature:

> ....delicious Paradise,
> Now nearer, crowns with her enclosure green,
> As with a rural mound, the champaign head
> Of a steep wilderness, whose hairy sides
> With thicket overgrown, grotesque and wild,
> Access denied;

J.A.K.Thomson, in his *Classical Influences on English Poetry*, has enumerated several influences of classical techniques of the epos, or rather the features of the epos, on Milton, as is conspicuous in *Paradise Lost*. To begin with, Milton invokes the aid of the Muse and the Spirit at the beginning of the epic, and here he imitates Homer. Secondly, following Homer, he begins the epic *in media res*, i.e. from the middle of the story, and then with the flash-back technique narrates the past events. Thirdly, some characters of the epic have the power of prediction.

In Book VII, for instance, Raphael "had forewarned/Adam, by dire example, to beware/Apostasy", and in Book X "God foretells the final victory of his Son" (see 'Argument, to Book X), and God further prophesises that after the evil ones will receive their stern guerdon, "Then Heaven and Earth, renewed, shall be made pure/To sanctify that shall receive no stain". Here also Milton has followed the classical tradition. Fourthly, in Homer's and Virgil's epics we find many 'councils', and in *Paradise Lost* Satan also sits in council several times. Fifthly, a description of Hell or Hades was almost a *sine qua non* of the classical epic tradition. In *Paradise Lost*, Milton has also described Hell, following, particularly, Dante and Ariosto. J.A.K. Thomson writes in this regard : "A description of Hell or Hades came to be thought almost a necessary part of any heroic epic. Milton knew, of course, the *Inferno* of Dante, and other medieval and more recent descriptions of Hell; he borrows something even from Ariosto" (Thomson, 54). Sixthly, it is generally held that Milton took the concepts of Sin and Death from the Bible, but J.A.K.Thomson says that "Sin at least is imagined by Milton on the model of Ovid's Scylla in the *Metamorphoses*" (Thomson, 54). Seventhly, Satan's journey from hell to the Garden of Eden and elsewhere was perhaps conceived of by Milton following the narration of the journeys of Odysseus and Aeneas. And lastly, in classical epics, we find that divine personages frequently change their physical shapes. In the same way, we see that in *Paradise Lost* Satan now changes himself "into the shape of a meaner Angel" and then into the shape of a cormorant, and then again into the body of a toad, and lastly he injects his own body into that of a snake. However, from all these and some other evidences, J.A.K.Thomson has come to the conclusion that "Both in its general structure and in its separate episodes *Paradise Lost* is formed with careful and learned fidelity upon the model of the ancient epic" (Thomson, 61).

Further, Milton followed the ancient masters even in the matter of the style of *Paradise Lost*. He followed, particularly, the style of Virgil. As we know, Milton acquired a mastery of the Latin language and literature, and so he could well follow the style of Virgil in his own epic with abundant skill. Of course he never sacrificed his originality while imitating the masters. J.A.K.Thomson writes: "a principal charm of Virgil's style resides in a very subtle alteration or deflection of the normal meaning of quite common words. Milton no doubt felt this charm, but in his own style he sought it, not by varying the normal connotation of words, but by using them in their original meaning when that had been altered by time or ignorance" (Thomson, 64). There being fundamental characteristic or structural differences between the Latin and the English languages, it was no easy task for Milton to follow the blank verse of the classical masters; but Milton followed the classical blank verse, there being no English model of the blank verse used in *Paradise Lost*, with commendable skill. In his epic, Milton followed, particularly, the blank verse of *Aeneid* J.A.K.Thomson writes: "The blank verse of *Paradise Lost* had no English model; it is a wonderful and successful effort to reproduce the metrical effects of the Aeneid" (Thomson, 66).

Milton's verse has marvellous musicality that is produced by variation of pauses, and modulation of vowel and consonant sounds. He learned this technique of producing musicality, we may guess, from Virgil, because musicality is to be found more in Virgil than in any other poets. Again, like Virgil, Milton frequently uses enjambment, where the flow of a line continues into the next line. To take an instance of enjambment from *Paradise Lost* :

> So saying, a noble stroke he lifted high,
> Which hung not, so swift with tempest fell
> On the proud Crest of Satan, that no sight,
> No motion of swift thought, less could his Shield
> Such ruin intercept;

Milton was indebted to Virgil for yet other things. He has written blank verse in paragraphs. In fact, he was the first English poet to do so, and in this matter also he followed Virgil. Milton's paragraphs are so constructed that the sense of the lines in a paragraph, becomes complete and clear only with the last line. An example of blank verse in paragraphs, from *Paradise Lost*, may be given below :

> High on a Throne of Royal State, which far
> Outshine the wealth of Ormus and of Ind,
> Or where the gorgeous East with richest hand
> Showers on her kings Barbaric Pearl and Gold,
> Satan exalted sat, by merit rais'd
> To that bad eminence; and from despair
> Thus high uplifted beyond hope, aspires
> Beyond thus high, insatiate to pursue
> Vain war with Heaven, and by success untaught
> His proud imaginations thus displaid.

Milton not only learnt some techniques of the grand style from

Virgil, he even, at places of *Paradise Lost*, borrowed ideas and words from Virgil's *Aeneid*. Take, for instance, Satan's lines with which he addresses his compeer Beelzebub :

> If thou beest he—but oh, how fall'n! how changed
> From him who, in the happy realm of light,
> Clothed with transcendent brightness, didst outshine
> Myriads, though bright!

"This is a deliberate quotation of the words in which Aeneas described the ghost of Hector:

> Ah, how he looked 'how changed from his old self,
> the Hector who brought back Achilles' armour!" (Height, 156).

Therefore, we find that a great influence of the classical masters on Milton is undeniable. Gilbert Height, in his *The Classical Tradition*, justiy writes about *Paradise Lost* and *Paradise Regainod*: "Classical influences in these poems, in every one of them, is all-pervading. It is not predominant in them all; but it is one of the main presuppositions without which they cannot be understood" (Height, 147). The English literature before Milton's days cannot be said to become mature enough in all its genres, particularly regarding the genre of epic, and so Milton was wise enough to unashamedly borrow from the classical masters. In fact, English literature was growing up to maturity only with constant borrowings from those ancient poets of Greece and Rome. P.B. Shelley, in the Preface to his lyrical drama *Hellas*, is quite right when he writes: "We are all Greeks. But for Greece, Rome the instructor, the conqueror, or the metropolis of our ancestors, would have spread no illumination with her arms, and we might still have been savages and idolators; or what is worse, might have arrived at such a stagnant and miserable state of social institutions as China and Japan." Therefore, Milton may be said to be one of the pioneers who enriched English literature through borrowings from the ancient masters.

9

(A GENERAL DISCUSSION ON *PARADISE LOST*)

Paradise Lost was conceived of, as we have said, on the myth of the Fall of man, as enshrined in the story of *Genesis* of the Bible. J.M. Evans writes that the story of the Fall of man has for over two thousand years been of absorbing interest and curiosity to the Western mind: "Few stories have worked so powerfully or so continuously on the imagination of Western Man as that of the Fall of Adam and Eve. It has been one of the dominant themes of our theology, literature, and art for nearly two thousand years, the subject of commentaries by every major Christian and Jewish thinker from Prudentius to Dietrich Bonhoeffer, of poems and plays by writers from Prudentius to Bernard Shaw, and of pictures by artists from the anonymous painter who decorated the crypt of San Gennaro in Naples to Marc Chagall. The reasons for its enduring vitality are many, but perhaps the most potent of them is to be found in its nature as a myth" (Evans, 9). The concept of man, as expounded in *Genesis* (the first book of the Old Testament), was hardly explained in the Jewish theology, and it was explained, later on, in the Christian theology, particularly in the Epistles of St. Paul. Yet the explanation of the concept of man did not end there, but ever newer and newer interpretations of the phenomenon of man came in along the course of time. In the same way, the meaning of the Tree of Life, the Tree of Knowledge, the Fall of Adam, etc., as we conceive of them today, has had gradual and almost imperceptible accretions down the ages. The accretions were supplied by the rest of the Old Testament, particularly by its Apocrypha and Pseudoepigrapha, rabbinic tractates, Christian tradition, neo-classical treatments of the myths, scholastic treatments of the myths, etc.

Even in a particular society, interpretations of myths vary from one section of the society to another section. After the Fall of Adam and Eve, it is believed, their eyes were opened. According to some Jewish interpretation, the opening of their eyes means that they now became aware of "the repercussions of their disobedience" (Evans, 50), as a result of which their rationality came back to them. But Maimonides (real name is Moses Ben Maimon: 1135-1204) does not agree with this interpretation, and, in his main philosophical tract *A Guide for the Perplexed*, Maimonides gives his own interpretation of the myth. He says that Adam and Eve cannot receive rationality as a result of their Fall. He writes in the work just now referred to: " 'It appears strange that the punishment for rebelliousness should be the means of elevating man to a pinacle of perfection to which he had not attained previously' " (Evans, 50-51). After thus rebutting the interpretation of his opponents, Maimonides gives his own interpretation of the story of Adam's and Eve's eyes being opened. He writes: "......... before the Fall Adam's purely intellectual knowledge was complete. His gain in moral knowledge was made only at the expense of a large part of his other philosophical powers: 'Then he fully understood the magnitude of the loss he had sustained, what he had forfeited, in what situation he was thereby placed' " (Evans, 51). Again, there is a disagreement among interpreters as to why the Serpent, or Satan in the body of the Serpent, chose Eve for temptation, and not Adam. One interpretation is that the female sex is more prone to be inveigled than the male sex, and Satan chose the easier way. But the other interpretation is that Satan saw Adam and Eve in amorous entertainment, and so felt sexually attracted to Eve, and so went to her first to cajole and tempt her.

In the Christian exegetics also the original story of *Genesis* had been variously interpreted, and the hermeneutics are so varied — and sometimes so widely varied — that consensus explication is not yet reached. In one explication, or, rather, in one version of the story, for instance, it is held that Christ himself persuaded Adam and Eve to eat the interdicted fruit. Those who accept such version of the story, say that both Adam and Eve ate the fruit and, consequently, Eve gave birth to Cain and Abel — Cain representing evil, and Abel representing goodness. Before tasting the fruit, Adam and Eve were ignorant of their divine qualities, and also of the existence of God, they being engrossed in the abundant sensual enjoyment of heaven. And it was to arouse in them the knowledge of their spirituality that Christ himself persuaded them to eat of the fruit of the Tree of Knowledge. The Tree of Knowledge, here, is the forbidden Tree which is different from the Tree of Life. But, according to *Acta Archelai*, the forbidden tree is rather the Tree of Life that bestows upon the eaters of its fruits lust and other evils: " 'Now, with respect to paradise, it is not called a cosmos. The trees that are in it are lust and other seductions, which corrupt the rational powers of those men. And that tree in paradise, by which men know the good, is Jesus Himself, (or) the knowledge of Him in the world. He who partakes thereof discerns the good and the evil'. " (Evans, 67). The philosopher Philo interpreted the Fall of man keeping within the Christian tradition : "The foundation of Philo's interpretation of the Fall story was his equation of Eden with the rational soul, with what a present-day psychologist might call the psyche. In this region lived the passions, represented by the animals, and the virtues and opinions, represented by the plants : 'Moses evidently signifies by the plesaunce of the ruling power of the soul which is full of countless opinions, as it might be of plants; and by the tree of life he signifies reverence toward God, the greatest of the virtues, by means of which the soul attains to immortality; which by the tree that is cognisant of good and evil things he signifies moral prudence, the virtue that occupies the middle position, and enables us to distinguish things by nature contrary the one to the other' " (Evans, 71-72). J.M. Evans writes that according to Philo "Eve stood for the soul's sense or sense-perception of the physical world .....Adam's recognition of Eve, then, constituted the beginning of the Fall, revealing that the mind was ready to abandon its natural authority for the sake of physical sensation. And the Fall itself took just this form. The Serpent, which symbolized pleasure, attacked the mind via the senses: 'Pleasure does not venture to bring her wiles and deceptions to bear on the man, but on the woman, and by her means on him. This is a telling well-made points for in us mind corresponds to man, the senses to woman.' Here lay the key to the serpent's prior approach to Eve!" (Evans, 72).

Another Christian philosophical interpretation of the fall and its associated notions is available in the writings of Clement of Alexandria (d. before 215). Clement writes: " 'The Tree of Knowledge itself was good, and its fruit was good. For it was not the tree, as some think, but the disobedience, which had death in it. For there was nothing else in the fruit than only knowledge; but knowledge is good when one uses it discretely. But Adam, being yet an infant in age, was on this account as yet unable to receive knowledge worthily. For now, also, when a child is born it is not at once able to eat bread, but is nourished first with milk, and then, with the increment of years, it advances to solid food. Thus, too, would it have been with Adam; for not as one who grudged him, as some suppose, did God command him not to eat of knowledge. But He wished also to make proof of him, whether he was submissive to His commandment' " (Evans, 79-80). In support of Clement's argument, we may say that God himself admits that by tasting the interdicted fruit, man (Adam) has become almost one of his (God's) kind, if not almost equal to himself: " 'O Sons, like one of us Man is become/To know both good and evil, since his taste/Of that defended fruit' ". Knowledge and experience are certainly godly. Eve, after tasting the fruit, says to Adam: "Experience, next to thee I owe,/ Best guide". So knowledge and experience cannot be bad, in themselves. Only the disobedience shown to God's command is bad and highly sacrilegeous. However, so much about the different interpretations of the various elements of the story of the Fall. Milton has not orthodoxically followed any one of the interpretations, but has relied on the consensual interpretation. But he has, for the most part, narrated the bare, unadorned and simple story of *Genesis*, in *Paradise Lost*, and he is wise enough here. Nevertheless, at places he is certainly bold enough to differ from the traditional interpretations. For instance, in *Paradise Lost*, he differs from the previous explanations of the Tree of Knowledge. As a humanist, he believed that knowledge is an essential element of an ideal man. But the biblical interpreters generally held knowledge to be the cause of man's Fall. Milton found a middle course: he thought that the Tree of Knowledge did not represent all sorts of knowledge, but only the knowledge of good and evil. Again, according to J.M. Evans, Milton held the view that "by releasing Adam and Eve from the sterile confines of ignorance in which their envious and malign Creator had originally imprisoned them the Tempter [Satan] opened up the way to the 'Paradise within' " (Evans, 243) Thus, Milton's view of Satan also differed from the traditional view of the arch fiend. Though Milton heavily depended upon *Genesis* for the story of *Paradise Lost*, he was, perhaps, influenced by the Anglo-Saxon poems concerning the same story of the fall of man in his narration of the story. Some of the Anglo-Saxon poems that might have influenced him are: 'Christ', 'Christ and Satan', and 'Guthlac'. He was, perhaps, also influenced by the medieval *Bestiary*, in which we find the story of Adam, Christ and a tree (a foreshadow of the Tree of Knowledge) All these things helped him form his own opinion about some of the concepts concerning the fall of man.

Another point deserves our consideration. In the invocatory part of the epic *Paradise Lost*, Milton declares that he is going to sing an 'adventurous song' about "Things unattempted yet in prose or rime." This declaration is apt to be misunderstood: why 'adventurous', why 'unattempted yet'? It is true that different exegetical, literary and even philosophical interpretations and commentaries of the theme of the Fall of man were galore by the time of Renaissance. Therefore, Milton does not claim any originality, regarding the interpretation of the theme. What he means by his adventure is that "his epic would outdo all previous treatment of the story in the sheer comprehensiveness of its vision, that it would explore the 'ways of God to Man' on a scale never before conceived by a Christian poet" (Evans, 219). It may be mentioned here, in passing, that Milton has not included all the elements of the story of the fall, but he has selected most of them to be treated in his epic. Further, he has also employed in *Paradise Lost* some extra-biblical elements, for enriching the literary quality of the epic. J.M. Evans writes in this regards "... however interested Milton may have been in doctrinal questions, the principle which determined his selection from and manipulation of the mass of extra-Biblical amplification at his disposal was essentially literary" (Evans, 221).

Some points of criticism as to some concepts contained in *Paradise Lost* may be mentioned here. For one thing, if we agree with the line of argument, as in the epic, that Adam and Eve fell from heaven for tasting the interdicted fruit, then we suffer hesitation in calling God benevolent. Acquisition of the knowledge of good and evil, itself, can, or at least should, never be a sin. Even if we think that God used that ukase as a ploy for testing how much obedient Adam and Eve were, yet we cannot approve of God's imposition of severe punishment upon the couple for a supposed sin of lighter degree. In fact, Eve was simply inveigled by Satan, and so the wrong should belong to Satan, and not to Eve who tasted the fruit unawares. On the other hand, Adam tasted the fruit knowing fully that he was thereby disobeying God, and so only Adam should fall for tasting the fruit, and not Eve, too. But if we agree that Eve should also fall, then we should say that she should fall not for tasting the fruit, but for bringing Adam into the trap of tasting the fruit. But we hear in the epic that both of them fell for tasting the fruit. In any case, God does not seem to be benevolent when He imposes a heavy punishment upon Adam and Eve for a sin of lighter degree : they simply ate a certain fruit. Even if we think that by tasting the fruit, Adam and Eve committed a great sin, because thereby they spurned away the command of God, yet we would like to see that God, the omnipotent, excused the first erring of the first couple. We may recall here A.E. Housman's (1859-1936) banter about the supposed justice in *Paradise Lost* : "Malt does more than Milton can/To justify God's ways to man."

Secondly, B. Willey says that though Milton describes paradise as a 'happy garden', it is certainly not a genuinely a happy garden, because here Adam and Eve have to do menial and char jobs, such as mending fences. E.M.W. Tillyard also expresses such an opinion: " 'Reduced to the ridiculous task of working in a garden which produces of its own accord more than they will ever need, Adam and Eve are in the hapless position of Old Age pensioners enjoying perpetual youth' " (Evans, 244). Thirdly, the garden of Eden seems to be charmless, drab and boring, because there is no change, no development, and so no variety — variety that is the spice of life : "The state of perfection in which they [Adam and Eve] are generally held to have been created admitted of no development, no growth, no challenge, nor even any change, except possibly for the worse" (Evans, 244). Fourthly, we would like to see Adam and Eve, naturally, mutually, drawn to each other, like, for instance, Ferdinand and Miranda in Shakespeare's *The Tempest*, they being ideal prototypes of man and woman in an ideal state of existence. But surprisingly we find in Book IV that Eve, at first, is not interested in Adam (lines 477-480):

> Till I espised thee, fair, indeed, and tall,
> Under a platan; yet methought less fair,
> Less winning soft, less amiably mild,
> Than that smooth wat'ry image. Back I turned;

It is only after Adam convinces her that manly grace and wisdom are fairer than the physical beauty of a woman that Eve turns to him. Adam tells her: "beauty is excelled by manly grace/And wisdom, which alone is truly fair." We do not expect such a love relationship between a man and a woman that depends on persuasion and not on instinct.

C.S. Lewis has discovered 'a grave structural flaw' in *Paradise Lost*. He writes : "Milton, like Virgil, though telling a short story about remote past, wishes our minds to be carried to the results of that story. But he does this less skilfully than Virgil. Not content with following his master in the use of occasional prophecies, allusions, and reflections, he makes his two books into a brief outline of sacred history from the Fall to the Last Day. Such an untransmuted lump of futurity, coming in a position so momentous for the structural effect of the whole work, is inartistic. And what makes it worse is that the actual writing in this passage is curiously bad" (Lewis, 129). Lewis is also not happy with Milton's depiction of the character of God : "infinite sovereignty *de jure*, combined with infinite power *de facto*, and love which, by its very nature, includes wrath also — it is not only in poetry that these things offend" (Lewis, 130). Lewis finds a further fault in the structure of the story of *Paradise Lost.* A great story, Lewis says, is that which is not closed, which is not *sui generis*, which does not happen only once — but that may occur in future. *Paradise Lost* fails here: it is a closed story — the Fall will not be repeated.

Critics have raised a very pertinent question regarding the Fall of Adam and Eve: is the Fall due to tasting the interdicted fruit, which is tantamount to showing disobedience of God, or due to the couple's concupiscence? It is generally held that the tasting of that fruit was the cause of their Fall. But if we closely follow the text of the epic, we find that before tasting the fruit, Adam and Eve had mutual sensual pleasure, that is ever forbidden in heaven. In Book IV (lines 492-502), we find the couple engaged in amorous play :

> So spake our general mother, and, with eyes
> Of conjugal attraction unreproved,
> And meek surrender, half-embraced leaned
> On our first father; half her swelling breast

Naked met his, under the flowing gold
Of her loose tresses hid. He, in delight
Both of her beauty and submissive charms,
Smiled with superior love, as Jupiter
On Juno smiles when he impregns the clouds
That shed May flowers, and pressed her matron lip
With kisses pure.

It is only after such sensuous enjoyments that Eve tastes the interdicted fruit, and then Adam follows her in her footsteps. Therefore, we may perhaps say that the disobedience shown to God by tasting the fruit was rather a consequence of the sensual enjoyment which should be identified as the prime cause of the Fall. But we may look at the matter from another angle, too. Though Adam and Eve had fleshy enjoyment, in Book IV, Milton connives at this as pure enjoyment — pure and untainted. He says in the same Book that such cohabitation is pure and innocent, because "Our Maker bids increase; who bids abstain/ But our destroyer, foe to God and Man?" But, after the tasting of the fruit, the same cohabitation becomes 'amorous' (Book IX): "So said he, and forbore not glance or toy/Of amorous intent, well understood/Of Eve, whose eye darted contageous fire./Her hand he seized, and to a shady bank,/Thick overhead with verdant roof embowered,/He led her". Only after this, the couple feels shame, and becomes anxious to "girt their waist". 'This is the real fall from heaven, though the couple is not yet physically driven out of heaven. But here all the critics are not unanimous: some still hold that the tasting of the fruit is the cause of the Fall and that the fall means loosing Paradise, physically. Perhaps, Milton is a little bit obscure here.

As we have said, there has been much controversy regarding the significance of the interdicted fruit. Does Milton want to say that God wanted to keep men in ignorance, by denying them the taste of the fruit of the Tree of Knowledge? Milton never upheld ignorance, and, in *Areopagitica*, he even rejected a 'cloistered virtue'. He himself was profoundly interested in the acquirement of knowledge, as we have already said. Then what sort of knowledge was it that God forbade man to acquire? It was, perhaps, the knowledge of 'discrimination among ideas' — it was discursive knowledge or analytic (not synthetic) knowledge, that shows us diversity, and not unity. Milton thought that it was with such knowledge that man thinks himself equal to God. Further, he thought that such knowledge sows the seeds of dissension and discrimination, and so such knowledge initiates destruction. Hardin

Craig writes : "If we ask what interpretation shall be given to the fact that the eating of the forbidden fruit brought death into the world, we may find at least a partial answer in the destruction that comes from lawlessness — individual, national, and international" (Craig, 255).

Though Milton has utilised a variety of themes in his principal poetic works, the central point of the themes is always religion, and he being a deeply religious person, this is not unexpected. And so *Paradise Lost* is expectedly a religious poem. L.A. Cormican, in his article 'Milton's Religious Verse', justly writes about *Paradise Lost*: "The poem is, among other things, a prayer addressed to the Deity from all mankind,... If the ways of God can be justified, it must be through a purification of the heart rather than by the reasonings of the intellect" (Ford, 175). Further, Milton is always concerned with goodness, evil, and salvation through God's grace. John Reesing writes in this regard: "Milton typically chooses as his subject for a poem a situation in which a human being encounters some evil from which he cannot escape through his own unassisted powers. Sometimes the evil involves supernatural enemies (as in the *Ludlow Mask* and *Paradise Lost*), sometimes more or less natural calamities which the victim may or may not have brought upon himself (as in *Samson Agonistes* and *Lycidas*, respectively). Always the evil is complex, involving both moral and physical dimensions, though the predominant mode of affliction may shift from moment to moment. But even the physical evils (premature death by violence in *Lycidas,* slavery and blindness in *Samson Agonistes*) are always perceived in a moral and religious context which shows that if in any way the protagonist is to transcend them, he must do so by being rescued. Divine grace is seen as ultimately the only answer for whatever evils man may suffer; and Christianity itself is understood as, very precisely, the religion of a Saviour" (Reesing, 123-124). Milton's religion is not simply soteriological; it is also concerned with our daily life, with everyday moral problems. The philosophy of *Paradise Lost* is not an abstract philosophy; it is very much pragmatic. "In approaching *Paradise Lost* it is to be remembered, first of all, that Milton was not a child telling a tale with naive credulity. *Paradise Lost* is not an historical epic; it is a modern poem with religious content. Its chronology is the life of every man, of every day. Adam and Eve are man and woman, as they live in the world. This fact is elemental, and it means that in *Paradise Lost* we have to do with one of the broadest studies of religion and ethics ever undertaken. Its story is symbolic and one of immediate daily application, or it is nothing" (Craig, 250). Further,

Milton was not interested in any abstract religion : he believed that religion touched everything and everyday. The pivotal point of his religion is Man, with a capital M — the concrete man in his earthly and worldly affairs. In *Paradise Lost*, he has attempted to produce a justification of the unfortunate predicaments of this concrete man's life, and to show him the way to salvation. The condition of man was a perpetual concern to Milton, and not only in *Paradise Lost*. M.V. Rama Sharma very rightly says: "Milton's interest in the story of Man can be traced back to the days of writing *Areopagitica* where he discusses the justness of God's action in punishing Man" (Sharma, 20). And this same human interest is there in *Paradise Lost*. And here Johnson is quite erronous when he says that *Paradise Lost* "comprises neither human actions nor human manners" (Patrides, 15). Johnson's criticism of *Paradise Lost* is reverberated in Joseph H. Summers's comment on the same epic: "The major characters of the great English poem [*Paradise Lost*] are neither English nor, until the final books, even fully what we know as human beings .... No heroic poem was ever less a glorification of a nation or a civilisation" (Patrides, 67-68). But, like Johnson, Summers also fails to see the human drama of destiny in the epic. In fact, like all other literary genres, the epic also deals with human problems, and not merely with gods and angels; of course the human problems may sometimes be deeply laid in the epic, under the surface actions of gods and goddesses and angels; and *Paradise Lost* is no exception.

In *Paradise Lost*, Milton has borrowed much, and imitated no less. His guide has, perceptively, been Virgil, as regards material and even as regards technique, as told earlier. C.S. Lewis, in his *A Preface to Paradise Lost,* has interestingly called the materials of an epic — the experiences and emotions — the mother, and the form of it the father. If these be so, Milton found both the father and the father of his epic in Virgil. But such borrowings should not be a reason for devaluing *Paradise Lost.* If we believe in T.S. Eliot's theory, as expounded in his essay 'Tradition and Individual Talent', that there can be no literary work of some worth without elements of tradition in it, Milton is rather right than wrong in imitating the ancient masters. And in imitating the masters, or in borrowing from them, Milton has not shown his weakness, but has rather proved his competence, because he has borrowed not as a slave, but as a compeer. He has seen a sleight in Virgil, for instance, and has shown us that he can produce another such. William Hazlitt, in his essay 'On Shakespeare and Milton', rightly says: "Milton has borrowed more than any other writer, and exhausted every source of imitation, sacred or profane; yet he is perfectly distinct from every other writer.... In reading his works, we feel ourselves under the influence of a mighty intellect, that the nearer it approaches to others, becomes more distinct from them."

Milton was as indebted to the exegetics of St. Augustine, for the story of *Paradise Lost*, as he was indebted to Virgil and other classical epic poets, for the form of, and the technique used in, the epic. According to C.S. Lewis, "Milton's version of the Fall story is substantially that of St. Augustine, which is that of the Church as a whole" (Lewis, 66). Lewis, in his *A Preface to Paradise Lost*, has enumerated the principal points of St. Augustine's philosophy, which may very briefly be stated below (Lewis, 66-72) :

i. God created everything as good.

ii. 'Bad, means 'good' perverted.

iii. Therefore, 'good' can exist without 'bad', but 'bad' cannot exist without 'good'.

iv. Though God created everything as good, yet he foreknows that some of the creations will turn bad.

v. God wanted men inhabit earth and not heaven; hence, the Fall. But all the same, he wanted all men ultimately restored, by instalments.

vi. Women are more vulnerable and gullible than men.

vii. Adam had his fall willingly, because he believed in the sacred institution of marriage (Milton here added concupiscence to Adam as another cause of his Fall).

viii. The Fall was due to Disobedience shown to God. The Fruit had nothing intrinsically bad in it. God only wanted to teach Man obedience through the tasting of the Fruit.

ix. "But while the Fall *consisted* in Disobedience it *resulted*, like Satan's, from Pride (...). Hence, Satan approaches Eve through her Pride; first by flattering of her beauty (*P.L.* IX, 532-48).... and secondly (this is more important) by urging her selfhood to direct revolt against the fact of being subject to God at all" (Lewis, 69).

x. "Since the Fall consisted in man's Disobedience to his superior, it was punished by man's loss of Authority over his inferiors; that is, chiefly, over his passions and his physical organism" (Lewis, 69).

xi. The Disobedience, therefore, ultimately led man especially to sexuality.

In *Paradise Lost*, for the most part, Milton has vary faithfully followed the exegesis of the Fall given by St. Augustine; but, of course, he has at places differed from the saint, as indicated once above, for instance.

C.S. Lewis further observes that *Paradise Lost* involves the conception of hierarchy. He writes: "According to this conception degrees of value are objectively present in the universe. Everything, except God has some natural superior; everything except unformed matter has some natural inferior. The goodness, happiness, and dignity of every being consists in obeying its natural superior and ruling its natural inferiors. When this fails in either part of this two-fold task we have disease or monstrosity in the scheme of things until the peccant being is either destroyed or corrected" (Lewis, 73-74). It may be mentioned here that though Milton expounded such a philosophy of hierarchy in *Paradise Lost*, in his own life, he himself revolted against this scheme of hierarchy.

Christopher Ricks has found a very interesting thing in *Paradise Lost.* He says that like Shakespeare, Milton had a fascination for the word 'light'. In Milton's case, this might have been due to his blindness. In his book *The Force of Poetry*, Ricks has enumerated a number of lines, in *Paradise Lost* , where Milton's fascination for the word 'light' is evident. A few of such lines are being quoted below (Ricks, 1984):

i. This horror will grow mild, this darkness light; (Book II, line 220).

ii. Veiled with his gorgeous wings, unspringing light, (Book V, line 250)

iii. Looked round, and scouts each coast light-armed scour, (Book VI, line 529).

iv. Light as the lightning-glimpse they rant, they flew; (Book VI, line 642).

v. On me, as on their natural centre, light (Book X, line 740)

Moreover, Book III of *Paradise Lost* even begins with a line where the word 'light' appears prominently "Hail, holy light, offspring of Heaven first-born!"

But the analogy between Milton and Shakespeare, says Ricks, ends here, because the poetic genius of the two bards are poles apart. Ricks says that "Milton's genius was radically un-Shakespearean" (Ricks, 65) in that while Shakespeare's poetry works on us from inside, Milton's does so from outside. This means that Milton's poetry inspires the generality of human hearts, and not any specifically tuned heart; *i.e.* Milton's poetry works on the objective dimension of the heart, and not on the subjective dimension. And for this reason, F.R. Leavis has even accused Milton. But Ricks exonerates Milton by saying that "although the highest art is the dramatic inwardness of Shakespeare, or that which accommodates such inwardness while not limiting itself to even that, it is not true that no great poetry can be external or can work from outside" (Ricks, 66). Ricks further says about the diction of Milton's poetry: "Though the words do indeed work externally, they are not unfelt; what is alive in them is not the feeling of a fleshy heart but the heart-felt aspiration towards a spiritual heart" (Ricks, 67).

Some critics, for instance T.J.B. Spenser, call *Paradise Lost* an anti-epic, because in it Milton, instead of lionizing the exploits of an ideal hero, has introduced an unheroic hero — be he Satan or Adam. Spenser further says that *Paradise Lost* is an anti-epic, because in it Milton has not followed the old or classical formula of a hero, but has introduced his own conception of a hero. If we take Satan to be the hero of the epic, he is an abominable being; and if we take Adam to be the hero, yet, he is too meek a person to be accounted as hero, as per the classical formula. In fact, Milton did not agree with the classical masters that the hero of an epic must be a war-hero who has the supreme power of the sinews as well as the indomitable strength of the mind in subduing opposing forces. He thought that the hero might not be as strong in body as in mind, but then the strength of his mind would not show itself in giving pains, but would show its strength in suffering the pain. In short, while the hero of the classical epics was sadistic, in psychological terms, that of Milton's epics is mesochistic. Not only this much, Milton even ridiculed the epic tradition, regarding the war-heroism of the epic hero, as is evident in *Paradise Lost* (Book IX, lines 27-43):

> Not sedulous by Nature to indite
> Wars, hitherto the only argument
> Heroic deemed, chief mastery to dissect
> With long and tedious havoc fabled knights
> In battles feigned (the better fortitude

Of patience and heroic martyrdom
Unsung), or to describe races and games,
Or tilting furniture, emblazoned shields,
Impresses quaint, caparisons and steeds,
Bases and tinsel trappings, gorgeous knights
At joust and tournament; then marshalled feast
Served up in halls with sewers and seneschals:
The skill of artifice or office mean;
Not that which justly gives heroic name
To person or to poem! Me, of these
No skilled nor studious, higher argument
Remains, sufficient of itself to raise
That name,

All the ancient epics are alike in at least one point: they all resemble Homer's *Iliad* and *Odyssey*, regarding the concept of the hero. J.A.K. Thomson very rightly says that all the European epics are faithful imitations of Homer's epics, and, consequently, the later epic poets' conception of the hero was formed in the dice of Homer. Milton was verily a traditionalist, in respect of ancient literature; but he did not sacrifice his individuality regarding the conception of the hero, nonetheless. T.J.B. Spenser is quite right when he says: "There is [then], in *Paradise Lost* not only a respect for the great cultural tradition of the past, but also a kind of witty devaluation of them, or inversion of them" (Patrides, 89). Milton ridiculed the struting, Viking-like hero, with a stentorian voice, perhaps, with an open and blood-dripping sword astride a courser, and peeling out a war-cry to his multitude of butchers. Contrarily, Milton's hero is meek; but he possesses enough fortitude; he strikes not anybody; he has immense power of bearing pain; and, above all, he has all these great attributes ready for the service of God. And, in forming a counter-concept of the hero, Milton has even pooh-poohed the traditional concept of the hero, as outlined in the just quoted passage from *Paradise Lost*. Therefore, T.J.B. Spenser truly says that "in some respects *Paradise Lost*, like *The Rape of the Lock*, is a kind of joke against the (traditional) epic" (Patrides, 93).

John Reesing has dealt at some length on the character-portrayal in *Paradise Lost*. His general commentary on the character-portrayal and other aspects of the epic is summarised in the following passage of his essay 'Miltonic sensibility in '*Paradise Lost*': "The narrator is in the poem, not story, and his voice comes to us from an angle different from that of the story's characters. His norm is fast and not very loud;

the characters tend to speak more slowly, and often considerably louder. So when on some occasions (not all) we hear the narrator's rather neutral tone and his brisk but unexcited pace commenting morally or theologically, we should understand simply that this is a part of the total proportioning Milton is working out in order to make a poem. The moral and theological comments are often pale because he intends them to be so; only by being unemphatic can they perform their proper action in the total structure of energy that is the poem" (Reesing, 108).

A few words about the verse of Milton. There may be differences of opinions about the justification of Milton's handling of the theme of the Fall, but most critics agree that his versification is superb. William Hazlitt, for one, in his *Lectures on English Poets and The Spirit of the Age* (J.M. Dent & Sons, 1955), has profusely praised the versification of Milton: "Milton's blank verse is the only blank verse in the language (except Shakespeare's) that deserves the name of verse." But T.S. Eliot has pointed out some serious faults in Milton's versification, and he thinks that the versification is not only bad, but this bad versification has left its unwholesome influence on the later generation of poets. Paul Merchant has written about Eliot's opinion about Milton's versifications: "One of his critics, T.S. Eliot, writing very much as a practical poet, saw his verse as a bad influence and a barrier to the development of eighteenth and nineteenth century poetry" (Merchant, 58). Merchant informs us that such criticism of Milton's versification has been repeated by F.R. Leavis and William Empson. But Merchant himself exonerates Milton of the charge by saying that "It should be remembered that for the blind Milton this [*Paradise Lost*] was truly an oral poem, and it is surely intended for the ear" (Merchant, 58). Merchant here means to say that Milton's epics should be heard as songs, and not as silent poems, and so the evaluation of his verse should be of a different kind. Frederick B. Arts, in his *From the Renaissance to Reformation*, has compared Milton's verse, particularly that of *Paradise Lost*, with the verse of Virgil: "In *Paradise Lost* Milton is closest to Virgil, especially in his use of verse paragraphs, where one line runs into the next, in the manipulation of the musical value of words, and in interjecting his own personality, as Homer does not. He could hardly reproduce Virgil's Latin because English lacks the multiplicity of case endings and verb forms and the variability of word order possessed by Latin, but he succeeded remarkably in producing something like the organ roll of *Aeneid*" (Artz, 197).

However, but for all its flaws *Paradise Lost* is certainly a supreme creation, its elements not being considered separately, but all these being taken as a whole. T.J.B. Spenser writes about this epic: "*Paradise Lost* is after all, a very entertaining poem. It is surely the most entertaining of the world's epics. The *Iliad* is full of excitement; the *Odyssey* is full of marvels. Still, *Paradise Lost* has probably a greater variety of amusement. When it comes to the question of amusement, the *Aeneid* is scarcely a competitor in this respect, for all its poetical merits" (Patrides, 96). But we may, perhaps, remind Spenser here that he has, perhaps, not enjoyed the two great Indian epics, *Ramayana* and *Mahabharata*, and had he read these two epics, he would certainly say that these two epics are far more entertaining than even Milton's *Paradise Lost*. Howbeit, the interest that we get from *Paradise Lost* arises, to William Hazlitt, out of only a few elements of it. Hazlitt writes in his *Lectures on English Poets and The Spirit of the Age:* "In a word, the interest of the poem arises from the daring ambition and fierce passion of Satan, and from the account of the paradisical happiness, and the loss of it by our first parents." On the other hand, Paul Merchant has found *Paradise Lost* to be of absorbing psychological interest pertaining to our "moral and spiritual equations". Merchant writes that the epic "is a great psychological narrative, probing into the deepest moral and spiritual questions" (Merchant, 55).

Paradise Lost has both its pungent critics and strong defenders. The pungent critics include T.S. Eliot, F.R. Leavis and Waldock, and the strong defenders include C.S. Lewis and Douglas Bush. The trenchant criticisms that have been labelled against the epic, besides those that have already been mentioned, may briefly be discussed here. First, epics may include mythological characters, but not allegorical personages; but in *Paradise Lost* we find that Sin and Death (the daughter and son of Satan, respectively) are also treated as living characters. Further, Johnson raises an objection as to the allegory of Sin and Death as used by Milton in the epic: "Milton's allegory of Sin and Death is undoubtedly faulty. Sin is indeed the mother of Death, and may be allowed to be the portress of hell; but when they stop the journey of Satan, a journey described as real, and when Death offers him battle, the allegory is broken" (Johnson, 129). Johnson adds: "This unskilful allegory appears to me one of the greatest faults of the poem..." (Johnson, 129).

Secondly, epic is verily an objective poem, and so there should be no scope left for ventilating the personal thoughts, feelings and emotions of the poet. But in *Paradise Lost* Milton's personal equations are at times very much obvious. For instance, how easy it has been to some critics to identify Satan with Milton, or Eve with Mary Powell! Thirdly, in *Paradise Lost* we find sort of conscious demonstration of scholarship: of latinism, of geographical and mythological knowledge, of philosophy and religion, of politics and history, of escatology, and even of scientific discoveries and astronomy. Such deliberate demonstration of scholarship has only made the epic into a caviare for the common readers. Fourthly, Milton's frequent and, perhaps, needless employment of puns and other sorts of word-play have further complicated the cumbrousness of the epic. Johnson writes in this regards "His [Milton's] play on words, in which he delights too often; his equivocations, which Bantly endeavours to defend by the example of the ancients; his unnecessary and ungraceful use of terms of art; it is not necessary to mention, because they are easily remarked, and frequently censured, and at last bear so little proportion to the whole, that they scarcely deserve the attention of a critic" (Johnson, 130).

Fifthly, Milton sometimes has used technical terms very ungracefully, as while describing the Pandemonium. Sixthly, he has sometimes, again, obstructed the course of events, or rather the course of the narration of the events, by introducing grotesque incidents and unnecessary digressions. Seventhly, John Dryden says that war is the hub of an epic — its main axle, which is conspicuously absent in *Paradise Lost.* And lastly, John Dryden, again, says that Milton's depiction of Nature is artificial, because he "saw Nature .... through the spectacle of books" (Johnson, 123).

However, Milton's defenders are also not rare. Here we are not going to relate what they all say in praise of Milton's *Paradise Lost*, but, perhaps, it will suffice if we only say what even Dr. Johnson, a pungent critic of Milton, says about *Paradise Lost.* Johnson has nothing to complain about the 'completeness or integrity' of the epic, because, he says, the poem follows the Aristotlean dictum that an epic must have a beginning, a middle and an end. Johnson writes: "There is, perhaps, no poem, of the same length, from which so little can be taken without apparent mutilation" (Johnson, 121). Johnson has also much more to praise the poem: "The *sentiments*, as expressive of manners, or appropriated to characters, are, for the greater part unexceptionably just. Splendid passages, containing lessons of morality, or precepts of prudence, occur seldom" (Johnson, 122). Again, Paul Merchant is struck by some of the beautiful and exact visual descriptions of the epic. In his slender book *The Epic*, Merchant cites two instances of Milton's supreme skill in painting visual images — one from Book IV (lines 771-773): "These lulled by nightingales imbracing slept,/And on that naked limbs the flowery roof/Showed roses, which the morn repaid"; and another, also from Book IV (line 500); "Squat like a toad, close at the ear of Eve". Again, though Milton's puritanical effusions in *Paradise Lost* have made the epic repellant to an extent, to some critics, and though there are some other faults in it, as other critics have called our attention to, Milton's grand conception and execution of the narrative, and his fine and sublime poetry in it, have made the epic able to surpass, and rise above, all its flaws. Glauco Cambon very justly writes: "Poetry survives in its own right; and so can afford to carry theology or time-bound philosophy on its shoulder" (Cambon, 105).

However, if we read *Paradise Lost* very closely we will find more and more curious things in it, and some critics have already found out some of them. John M. Steadman, for instance, in his book *Milton and the Renaissance Hero*, says that the epic deals with five aspects or elements of the Renaissance concept of heroism : *fortezza* or fortitude, sapience, leadership, magnanimity and amor. Both Satan and Adam display fortitude in their distress, and both of them show wisdom in their own ways. God is the 'good governor' or leader, and, likewise, Satan is also a leader, though in the pejorative sense of the term. God and Satan display magnanimity; of course Satan's magnanimity soon turns into vaingloriousness and pride. But Adam even transcended magnanimity, or what Aristotle calls *megalophycos*, through his obedience and charity. The fifth element of Renaissance heroism, *i.e.* amor, is of two kinds: illicit passion and 'holy wedlock', or lust and love. Satan shows illicit passion for Eve when he first discovers her in the garden of Eden. On the other hand, Adam and Eve had pure love for each other before they tasted the fruit of the Tree of knowledge; but after tasting the fruit, they became full of lust, instead. Steadman says that all these five virtues or heroic features or elements of heroism, that occupied the consciousness of the Renaissance man, are interrelated, and are governed by reason and by God. Steadman writes: "Wisdom, fortitude, leadership, love, magnanimity — none of the formulae.... exists in isolation. As philosophers pointed out, the virtues were inter-related; one presupposed the others. For classical ethics, all of them depended on right reason; for Christian ethics, on charity. No habit could be truly virtuous (the theologians insisted) unless it aimed at the glory of God" (Steadman, 161). Again, Frank L. Huntly found another curious thing in *Paradise Lost*. He discovered a sort of systasis in the pattern of the epic. He says that the epic shows four sorts of systasis or union of opposites: that between male and female, that between union with good and separation from good, that between good and evil, and that between the Creator and the created things (Patrides, 3).

Milton wrote his two epics and his only drama *Samson Agonistes* in his purblindness, and these three works are his best. One may, out of curiosity, here ask: Is there any relationship between blindness and poetic capability? The answer must be a simple guffaw. But C.M. Bowra finds some relationship, and a mysterious one at that, between blindness and poetic *elan*. Bowra's argument may here be quoted at some length; "In considering the social condition of bards, we have noticed incidentally that some, like Bernlef or Barba Slerios or the Yakut women, are blind, and indeed the bard's profession is often associated with blindness. The first examples come from the Greeks who had their legends of prehistoric poets like

> Bind *Thamyris* and blind *Maeonides*,
> And *Tiresias* and *Phineus* Prophets old.

Such legends seem to have been known to Homer, who tells the story of Thamyris, how he tried to surpass the Muses in song and was in consequence punished by them, being robbed both of his gift for song and of his sight. More significant is Homer's account of his own Demodocus:

> Him did the Muse love abundantly, and gave to
> him both good and evil;
> Him she robbed of his eyes, but gave him the
> gift of sweet singing.

Homer knew of blind bards, and it was, perhaps, inevitable that he was thought to be blind. .... "In modern times blind bards are quite common, though perhaps less common than is sometimes thought. They are sometimes found among the Turkomans and the Ainus. Among the Sudanese of western Java they are said to be more usual than sighted persons. Among the Sudanese an early example comes from 1547, when a blind soldier, conducted by his daughter, sang of Marko Kraljevic in Splijit to a large crowd. In the present century Murko says that they are rare, but a number of travellers have seen them. In Russia some bards of considerable renown have seen blind, notably Ivan Feponov, whom Gilferding met in 1870 and who was known a 'blind Ivan'; Kuzma Romanov, the rival of Trofim Ryabinin; Mina Efimov, who lived in the eighteenth century, travelled a great deal and was said to have learned his *byliny* in Moscow. Nor is it difficult to see why some bards are blind. If a child is born blind in a simple society, he can do nothing useful either as a worker or a soldier and is barred from helping his family and himself to live. He can, however, learn and practice the art of song, and, since blindness tends to strengthen the memory, it may even help a man to master the traditional formulae and theme. If he becomes blind in mature years, he can, if he becomes a bard, have a profession which will keep him from starvation and win him respect among his people" (Bowra, 420-422).

But, yet the question remains: how can a blind poet compose a long epical poem? And C.M. Bowra answers: "How does a [blind] bard compose a poem on such a scale? And how does he succeed, as some undoubtedly have, in giving a polish to the smallest details?... If we wish to understand how Homer composed, it is useful to remember that Milton composed *Paradise Lost* when he was blind and, though his daughters took down from his dictation, the actual composition was done in his head with no aid from writing. The illiterate composers of oral epics on a large scale must do something of this kind. But they differ from Milton in one important respect. When they have composed a part of a poem, they cannot have it written down and done with, and then pass on to the next section. They must carry the whole thing in their memories and work at it in their minds. They must not only plan the main shape and episodes and characters, but to large extent the actual words. Even if they are much helped in the last respect by formulae, it is clear from some of the poets that even these have received individual thought and attention. Such a process may well take years and implies an extraordinary gift not only of memory but of concentration and judgment" (Bowra, 440-441). By the by, an example of the fact that blindness cannot be an insurmountable hurdle to the expression of genius can be found in the Indian writer Ved Mehta (1934 —) who has been blind since his age of three. Mehta has produced a good number of books of some worth, and is "probably the most widely read Indian writer outside India, and a respected if occasionally controversial author within his own country" (Wordsworth Reference, 610).

Paradise Lost has achieved wide acclaim, and has produced great immediate and far-reaching influence. Milton's younger contemporary Andrew Marvell (1621-1678) liked the epic very much, and, in his poem 'On *Paradise Lost*', profusely praised it and its author :

> That majesty which through thy work doth reign
> Draws the devout, detering the profane;
> ....
> Rewards with prophecy thy loss of sight.

Even John Dryden, who was a puritan like Milton but was a scathing critic of him, was also a devout reader of the epic. In February 1674 (or earlier, may be), Dryden approached the ailing Milton for permission to write 'an heroic opera' on the theme of *Paradise Lost*. Milton at first asked him not to undertake such a venture, but next candidly agreed to his proposal. Dryden's operatic version of the epic is entitled *The State of Innocence, and Fall of Man* which was published in 1677, but was never acted. Afterwards, the great German poet Friedrich Gottlieb Klopstock (1724-1803) was much influenced by Milton, particularly, by his epic *Paradise Lost*. After this, John Keats (1795-1821) wrote his *Hyperion* following *Paradise Lost*.

Curious enough, we may find some parallels between *Paradise Lost* (particularly Book XI of it) and the *Gita*. Both of the two works are devotional poems, and both of them try to justify God's ways to men. We are not going here to dwell on all the parallels, but will only indicate some of them. Firstly, in *Paradise Lost*, Book XI, we find that Michael and Adam ascend "In the visions of God" and then Michael removes the 'film' from Adam's eyes, to show him future events: "Michael from Adam's eyes the film removed,/Which that false fruit that promised clearer sight/Had bred" (lines 412-414). Likewise, in the eleventh chapter of the *Gita* (*sloka* 8), God gives Arjuna the divine power of perception to see the Lord's immense body and power: "But as with human eye/Thou can never perceive/All these supreme objects,/ I do thee divine power give" (Sarker, 78). Secondly, in the same Book of the epic *Paradise Lost*, Michael teaches Adam the rule of "Not too much" (lines 530-534):

> 'There is,' said Michael, 'if thou well observe
> The rule of *Not too much*, by temperance taught
> In what thou eat'st and drink'st, seeking from thence
> Due nourishment, not gluttonous delight,
> Till many years over thy head returns...'

This is the rule of Aristotle, commonly known as the rule of the Golden Mean — the rule that dominated the ideals of the ancient Greek consciousness, in all spheres. And this rule or principle of moderation may also be found in the seventeenth chapter of the *Gita (slokas* 8-10 where God Krishna, the supreme Godhead, teaches Arjuna moderation in everything, including moderation in consumption of food (Sarker, 113):

> Sweet food, soft, nourishing,
> Does promote life and give
> Strength, health and joy;
> And on these the good live.
>
> Saltish, pungent, sour food,
> Or very hot, bitter,
> That pain and grief produce,
> The passionate prefer.
>
> Dear to the dull
> Are those tasteless, putrid,
> Unclean and stale,
> And those made without heed.

Thirdly, again, in Book XI, Michael Advises Adam to remain insoucient towards life (lines 553-554): " 'Nor love thy life, nor hate; but what thou liv'st/Live well' " Likewise, in the second chapter of the *Gita* (*slokas* 56-57), God advises Arjuna to remain indifferent toward both weal and woe, as the sages do. God tells Arjuna (Sarker, 18):

> Untroubled midst sorrows
> And free from desire, joy;
> Untouched by passion he;
> Such men true sage be.
>
> Good he relishes not
> Nor evil loathes.
> Without affection he, yet
> In wisdom firmly set.

And fourthly, *Paradise Lost* ends with Adam's gaining the knowledge that showing obedience to God is the only way to salvation, and with his avowal that since his gaining this knowledge he will heed God as his redeemer (Book XII, lines 561-573): " '... Henceforth, I learn that to obey is best,/And love with fear the only God,... /... whom I now/ Acknowledge my Redeemer ever blest.' " And the *Gita* ends with Arjuna's promise to God, the Lord (chapter 18, *sloka* 73): "By Thy grace to me, and/Doubt-free, now I shall act Thy will" (Sarker, 129). However, to conclude this chapter, Milton was very much attracted by the Latin and Italian languages, and, as if as a gesture of requiting gratitude, the Italians were attracted by Milton's *Paradise Lost* in Paolo Rolli's translation: "Between 1725 and 1742 Paolo Rolli, a resident teacher of Italian in London, translated *Paradise Lost*" (Goad, 217).

8

PARADISE REGAINED

1
(INTRODUCTION)

The seed of *Paradise Lost* was sown in the mind of Milton by himself, but that of *Paradise Regained* by his friend Thomas Ellwood. Regarding the origination of *Paradise Regained*, Hardin Craig writes: "When Milton was living at Chalfont St. Giles late in the year 1665, Ellwood had returned to him the manuscript of *Paradise Lost* and had said: 'Thou hast said much of *Paradise Lost*, but what hast thou to say to Paradise found?' When he visited Milton in London during the following year, Ellwood recounts, Milton showed him *Paradise Regained* and said, 'this is owing to you; for you put it in my head by the question you put me at Chalfont, which before I had not thought of' " (Craig, 256-57). For the story and theme of *Paradise Regained*, Milton owed much to Edmund Spenser's (1552-99) story of Sir Guyon or Temperance in the second Book of *The Faerie Queene*, and to Giles Fletcher's *Christ's Victory and Triumph*. The Satan of *Paradise Regained* resembles very much Spenser's Arch-imago.

As *Paradise Lost* follows the story of *Genesis* of the Old Testament so *Paradise Regained* follows the story of *The Book of Job* of the same Old Testament. Regarding length, *Paradise Regained* is about one-third of *Paradise Lost*. The two epics have some obvious similarities. Firstly, the theme of both the epics are the same temptation; in *Paradise Lost*, Satan tempts Adam through the agency of Eve, and in *Paradise Regained*, Satan attempts, in vain, to tempt Christ. Secondly, the themes of both the epics are taken from the Bible: the themes of the former from *Genesis*, and that of the latter from *The Book of Job* and the *Gospel of Luke*. Thirdly, both the epics are devotional. In fact, the theme of *Paradise Regained* was foreshadowed in Book X (lines 56-62) of *Paradise Lost*, where God tells Christ, his son :

'... To thee I have transferred
All judgment, whether in Heaven, or Earth or Hell.
Easy it may be seen that I intend
Mercy collage with justice, sending thee,
Man's friend, his Mediator, his designed
Both ransom and Redeemer voluntary,
And destined Man himself to judge Man fall'n.'

And, again, we find the foreshadowing in the same Book of *Paradise Lost* (lines 638-640) where God prophesys that at some future time Christ, his Son, will take charge of the whole creation, and " '...Then Heaven and Earth, renewed, shall be made pure/To sanctity that shall receive no stains...' "

But there are some differences between the two epics also. Firstly, in *Paradise Lost*, Satan has succeeded in tempting Adam, but in *Paradise Regained* he has failed to tempt Christ. Secondly, *Paradise Lost* is in the form of a narration, but *Paradise Regained* is written mostly in the dramatic form: dialogues between Satan and Christ dominate most of the second epic. Thirdly, while the earlier epic is a spiritual epic, the latter epic may be called an intellectual one. In *Paradise Lost*, Adam suffers from a spiritual conflict between yielding to Satan's temptation and keeping firm in the faith of God. In *Paradise Regained*, on the other hand, Christ is in an intellectual dialogue with Satan. Fourthly, *Paradise Lost* has all told four invocations: in Book I, to the Muse and the 'Spirit'; in Book III, to the Holy Light; in Book VII, to Urania and Bacchus; and in Book IX, to the 'celestial patroness'. But in *Paradise Regained*, the poet invokes the aid of only the 'Spirit', and that for only once. And lastly, unlike the Books of *Paradise Lost*, the Books of *Paradise Regained* are not capped with 'Arguments'.

Paradise Regained is divided into four Books. In Book I, Christ is proclaimed as the Son of God, and Satan vainly tries to tempt Christ. In Book II, Satan plans, once again, and this time with a different method, to tempt Christ, and again he fails. In Book III, Christ rejects Satan's third temptation; and in Book IV, Satan despairs of not being able to tempt Christ, and as the just consequence of his evil design, destroys himself. Whereas the total number of lines of *Paradise Lost* is 10,565, that of *Paradise Regained* is only 2,070. The break-up of the lines of *Paradise Regained* is as follows: Book I: 502 lines; Book II:496 lines; Book III: 443 lines; and Book IV: 639 lines. However, though there is some differences regarding theme and form between the two epics, they are certainly companion works; and not only that, *Paradise Regained* even begins with a skein of *Paradise Lost:*

> I, who erewhile the happy Garden sung,
> By one man's disobedience lost, now sing
> Recovered Paradise to all mankind,
> By one man's firm obedience fully tried
> Through all temptation, and the Tempter foiled
> In all his Wiles, defeated and Repulsed,
> And Eden raised, in the waste wilderness

2
(SUMMARY OF THE STORY OF *PARADISE REGAINED*)

Book I

Like Paradise Lost, Paradise Regained also begins with an invocation to the 'Spirit':

> Thou Spirit who led'st this glorious Eremite
> Into the desert, his victorious field
> Against the spiritual foe, and brought'st him thence
> By proof th' undoubted Son of God, inspire,
> As thou art wont, my prompted song,

God proclaims Christ as his Son. Satan, the Adversary, hears God's proclamation and is afraid, and calls forth a council of the fallen angels. He tells the congregation that they and he have escaped from hell and have conquered earth and air. But Christ has been born and has come of age with "All virtue, grace and wisdom to achieve/Things highest, greatest", and so he is afraid. Satan is afraid that "that fatal wound/ Shall be inflicted by the seed of Eve/Upon my head". He is afraid, moreover, because Christ has come down from heaven with peace to deliver to earth, and because he has heard God declare about Christ: "This is my Son beloved, in him am pleased." And, yet, Satan decides on his tempting, and thus destroying Adam :

> '... I, when no other durst, sole undertook
> The dismal expedition to find out
> And ruin Adam, and the exploit performed
> Successfully; a calmer voyage now
> Will waft me; and the way found prosperous
> Induces best to hope of like success.'

Satan, therefore, proceeds towards Jordan to seek out Christ, and to tempt him and thus to bring an end to his reign on earth. With the flash-back technique, Milton now describes the events of the birth of Christ. God, the Almighty, sends Gabriel to Galiles where virgin Mary will give birth to Christ. God tells Gabriel that He (God) will give Satan a free hand in his (Satan's) malicious designs, but, yet, he (Satan) will not be able to take Christ astray from his right path; rather, Satan, along with his host of fallen angels, will, at last, be forced to fall to hell: " 'at length/All his vast force, and drive him back to Hell —' ". All the celestial beings of heaven rejoice at this declaration of God. They rejoice because Christ will defeat Satan not by strength of arms but by that of wisdom.

Meanwhile, Christ is baptised by John in Bethabara. One day Christ walks through a desert expanse, and meditates, when he is only twelve years old, upon his duty of enhancing 'public good':

'... victorious deeds
Flamed in my heart, heroic acts, one while
To rescue Israel from the Roman yoke;
Thence to subdue and quell, o'er all the earth,
Brute violence and proud tyrannic power
Till truth were freed, and equality restored:
Yet held it more humane, more heavenly, first
By winning words to conquer willing hearts,
And make persuasion do the work of fear;
At last to try, and teach the erring soul,
Not wilfully misdoing, but unaware
Misled; the stubborn only to subdue.....'

Christ's mother Mary is pleased with such thoughts of his. She tells him that he is a 'messenger from God', and that he will sit "on David's throne,/And of thy kingdom there should be no end." She further tells him that after his birth angels became joyous and sang in praise of him. The angels told the shepherds who gathered to see him that he was the Messiah. Wise men from all over the world also came to Bethlehem, being guided by a star, to see Christ. Of course, righteous Simeon and prophetess Anna did not come to Bethlehem, but they saw the birth of Christ in their vision.

Hearing all these from his mother, Christ searches in the Laws of Prophets and finds that it is written there that his "'way must lie/ Through many a hard assay, even to death,/Ere I the promised kingdom can attain,/Or work redemption for mankind, whose sins'/Full weight must be transferred upon my head' ". Christ now goes out on a long and tedious journey through hills and wilderness infested with wild and ferocious beasts that do not harm him, and arrives at a dreary place. Satan, in the guise of an old man, accosts him and enquires of him for what purpose he does enter into that dreary place. Satan offers him to be his guide. Christ replies: " 'Who brought me hither/Will bring me hence; no other guide I seek.' " The old man tells Christ that he knows him as the Son of God, and that he knows that he (Christ) has been without food for many a day, and so Satan asks Christ to create bread (by magical means) and eat of it. Christ has full belief in God, and so, in reply, tells the old man that Moses and Elijah had been without food for forty days in a row. Christ tells the old man (Satan) that man does not live by bread alone. Christ further tells him that he can well recognise him (Satan). Being perplexed at this, Satan (in the guise of the old man) admits that he had a fall from heaven down to hell, but he frequently comes out of that 'bottomless Deep' and roams in the air and on the earth, and thus enjoys liberty. Satan further tells Christ that men know him to be their foe, but he wonders why they should call him their foe, because he thinks himself to be their well-wisher. Satan frankly admits that he is jealous of the fact that man, though fallen, will ultimately be redeemed, but he will never be redeemed: " 'This wounds me most (what can it less ?) that Man,/Man fall'n, shall be restored, I never more.' "

In reply, Christ heavily scolds Satan. He tells Satan that lying is his 'sustenance', and that God had rightly given up the people to his (Satan's) delusions, because they are idolatrous. But Satan will no more be able to mislead people by his oracles, such as he delivers at Delphos, because God himself has sent his oracles into the world. Satan is wounded at this, and yet keeps his aplomb. Christ, still angry with Satan, tells him that he knows his (Satan's) real purpose, and so warns him that he will not be able to achieve his objectives. Now night approaches and Satan melts into air. Thus, the first attempt of Satan at tempting Christ cannot fructify. Here ends Book I.

Book II

Christ, the 'new baptized', is soon found missing from among some other persons who are also baptized; " 'whither is he gone?' " Mary deeply bemoans the missing of Christ, and frequently recalls the adverse conditions through which she and her son, the Messiah, *i.e.* Christ, passed in the young days of her son — when Christ was only twelve years old. Meanwhile, Christ has been wandering through the wild dessert alone, thinking always about his high mission on earth. On the other hand, Satan sits in council with other fallen angels; and addressing them as 'Powers over Fire, Air, Water and Earth', tells them that they should now rule over the four elements — fire, air, water and earth "Without new troubles". And, innuendoing to the arrival of Christ on earth, cautions them of this new foe. He tells them that it is rather easier to allure Eve, and, through her, Adam, but Christ is more powerful than them, and so he is seeking their assistance, once more in his evil design of tempting Christ. Belial, the most sensualist of the fallen angels, advises Satan to try to allure Christ with the help of beautiful, amorous, persuasive and hideous virgins. But Satan tells him that all men are not like him (Satan) who "Cast wanton eyes on the daughters of men,/And coupled with them, and begot a race." Satan here refers to the race of dissolute persons. He tells Belial that there are also persons who, like 'that Pellean conqueror', took 'small account' of the allurements of the women-folk; and, on the other hand, there are persons who, like Solomon, like to wallow in ease and sensuality. Satan says that Christ is a different sort of person, and that in his case all allurements are ineffectual, particularly the allurement of beauty, because "Beauty stands/In the admiration only of weak minds/ Led captive; cease to admire, all her plumes/Fall flat, and shrink into a trivial toy,/At every sudden slighting quite abashed." So Satan tells them that they will rather tempt Christ with manly allurements:

> Therefore with manlier objects we must try
> His constancy, with such as have more show
> Of worth, of honour, glory, and popular praise
> (Rocks whereon greatest men have oftest wrecked);

Till now, Christ has been fasting for forty days for want of bread, and yet he is not despairing, because he thinks that he is " 'fed with better thoughts, that feed/Me hung'ring more to do my Father's will.' " Now night has fallen, and Christ sleeps under a grove of trees, and in a dream sees himself standing by the brook of Cherith. He sees ravens bringing food to Prophet Elijah in evenings and mornings, but Elijah is running away from the raven, and entering a desert to sleep under a juniper. After a sleep, Elijah wakes up and finds wholesome prepared food, and also angels who persuade him to eat the food. Elijah then eats the food which is sufficient for him to continue for forty days thereafter, without taking further food. Christ also sees, in his dream, that he too eats the food along with Elijah and Daniel. Now morning has come, and Christ wakes up, still fasting. He then goes up to the top of a hill and looks downwards, but sees no trace of human habitation. He only sees a grove of trees, and goes there to take rest, at noon. There in the grove, Christ sees a man who seems to him to be a man about town:

> When suddenly a man before him stood,
> Not rustic as before, but seemlier clad,
> As one in city or court or palace bred,

This man tells Christ that he (Christ) is in hunger, in that desolate place. The man, offering to bring food for him, further tells Christ that Nebaioth and his out-cast mother and the Prophet of Thebez came there and found food. Hearing this, Christ asks him: " 'What conclud'st thou hence?/They all had need; I, as thou seest, have none.' "

This old man is none else but Satan in disguise. Satan asks Christ why he refuses his offer to food. He tells him it is his duty, as it is anyone's to offer food to a hungry man, and then Satan again requests Christ "to sit and eat". No sooner has Satan ceased, Christ finds a richly spread table that contained meat, fish, wine and other items of sumptuous feast. About the table stand, 'stripling youths rich-clad'—youths who are more fair than Ganymede or Hylas. Near the table also stand a band of nymphs and ladies of incomparable beauty. The spot is enlivened with sweet songs and fragrance. Satan once again urges Christ to partake of the food:

> 'What doubts the Son of God to sit and eat ?
> These are not fruits forbidden; no interdict
> Defends the touching of these viands pure;
> Their taste no knowledge works, at least no evil,
> Cut life preserves, destroys life's enemy,
> Hunger, with sweet restorative delight.
> All these are Spirits of air, and woods, and springs,
> Thy gentle ministers, who come to pay
> Thee homage, and acknowledge thee their Lord.
> What doubt'st thou, Son of God? Sit down and eat.'

In answer, Christ indignantly tells Satan that, as he (Satan) has said, all things on earth are under his (Christ's) power, and if this is so, then he (Satan) should not offer those items of food to him (Christ) as gifts. Christ thus very bluntly rejects Satan's offer of delicious dishes, and tells him: " 'Thy pompous delicacies I contemn,/And count thy specious gifts no gifts, but giles.' " Satan grumbles at Christ's rejection of his offer, and then the spread-out feast vanishes.

But Satan is not yet to give in: he continues tempting Christ. He now tells Christ that he (Satan) knows that he (Christ) wants to do great things on earth, and that great things require great means to get done: " 'And all thy heart is set on high designs,/High actions: but wherewith to be achieved?/Great acts require great means of enterprise' ". But, Satan says, Christ has nothing of greatness, he being the son of a carpenter, and having no friend or acquaintance Satan tells him :

> 'Money brings honour, friends, conquest, and realms;
> What raised Antipater the Edomite,
> And his son Herod placed on Judah's throne,
> Thy throne, but gold, that got him puissant friends?
> Therefore, if at great things thou wouldst arrive,
> Get riches first, get wealth, and treasure heap —
> Not difficult, if thou hearken to me.
> Riches are mine, fortune is in my hand;
> They whom I favour thrive in wealth amain,
> While virtue, valour, wisdom, sit in want.'

Jesus Christ then replies that without virtue, valour and wisdom, wealth is but nothing, and that ancient empires possessed fabulous amounts of wealth, and yet those empires vanished. On the other hand, people who have these three supreme qualities — virtue, valour and wisdom — people like Gideon and Japhtha — become victorious, at the end. Christ further tells Satan:

> 'the shepherd lad
> Whose offspring on the throne of Judah sat
> So many ages, and shall yet regain
> That seat, and reign in Israel without end.'

Christ also tells Satan that he (Christ) wants to remain in poverty, as he is now, and yet he will accomplish great things, like those ancient great personages, or even more than what they could do. To Christ, riches are but 'the toil of fools' and 'wise man's cumbrance'. Christ also does not want the golden crown of a king, because

> 'a crown;
> Golden in show, is but a wreath of thorns,
> Brings dangers, troubles, cares, and sleepless nights,
> To him who wears the regal diadem,
> When on his shoulders each man's burden lies;'

Christ further tells Satan: "'Yet he who reigns within himself, and rules/Passions, desires, and fears, is more a king—/ ...../ To know, and, knowing, worship God aright,/Is yet more kingly,...' Therefore Christ rejects Satan's offer of wealth, etc. and so Satan fails in his attempt at tempting Christ, for the second time. However, the dialogue between Christ and Satan continues in Book III of the epic, where Satan advances still another temptation to Christ.

Book III

His offer of money and power being rejected by Christ. Satan stands there confounded. But soon he collects himself and began to flatter Christ by telling him that his (Christ's) heart " 'Contains of good, wise, just, the perfect shape' ". Satan asks Christ: " 'These god-like virtues wherefore dost thou hide?' " But Christ does not yield to Satan's persuasion. Satan then urges Christ to seek glory and fame, using all his god-like qualities, but Christ, again, despises his offer by saying that glory is but 'the blaze of fame', and that the public, on whom glory depends, is but a 'herd confused':

> 'For what is glory but the blaze of fame,
> The people's praise, if always praise unmixed?
> And what the people but a herd confused,
> A miscellaneous rabble, who extol
> Things vulgar, well weighed, scarce worth the praise?'

Christ further tells Satan that Job, the servant in heaven, as it is told in the Old Testament, did never seek glory and fame or public praise; and yet there are none who does not honour the same Job. Again, Socrates, the most memorable man, after Job, suffered even death-penalty for the cause of truth, and thus became " 'Equal in fame to proudest conquerors' ". Therefore, Christ tells Satan, he is rejecting his (Satan's) offer of glory and fame : " 'Shall I seek glory, then, as vain men seek,/Oft not deserved? I seek not mine, but his/Who sent me, and thereby wirness whence I am.' "

Yet, Satan does not demur, but continues to persuade Christ to understand that even God himself wants glory, and so he (Christ) should not reject his offer of glory. Christ retorts that God deserves glory because he has abounding grace, but man, having no grace at all, should not aspire after glory:

> 'Yet so much bounty is in God, such grace,
> That who advance his glory, not their own,
> Them he himself to glory will advance.
> But why should man seek glory, who of his own

> Hath nothing, and to whom nothing belongs
> But condemnation, ignominy and shame?'

Satan is awe-struck at the insoucience of Christ about glory, and yet, even then, does not abandon his attempt at tempting Christ. He proceeds with another ploy of temptation; he tells Christ that he (Christ) is the heir to his father David's possession of Judaea and 'all the Promised Land', all of which are now 'under Roman yoke' — under Tiberius. Satan therefore advises Christ to take possession of those lands by force of arms. If Christ is not interested in regaining and reigning his father's kingdom, yet he should, at least, show his zeal in reclaiming his father's kingdom from the hands of the heathens. Satan reminds Christ that it is rather his duty.

But Christ is not moved by the pleadings of Satan. He tells Satan that everything will be fulfilled only in their due time, and whatever God decrees must happen, and, therefore, he can take possession of his father David's kingdom only in due time, and according to God's decree. He also tells Satan that " 'Who best/Can suffer, best can do; best reign, who first/Well hath obeyed;....' " After this, Christ asks Satan:

> 'Why art thou Solicitous?
> What moves thy inquisition?
> Know'st thou not that my rising is thy fall,
> And my promotion will be thy destruction?'

In reply, Satan ironically tells Christ that he (Christ) is green in the experience of worldly affairs, and so he (Satan) "took/The Son of God up to a mountain high." From the top of that high mountain, Satan shows Christ many ancient kingdoms, and other places of renoun, such as Assyria, Nineveh, Babylon, Judah, Persepolis, Ecbatana, Susa, etc. Satan also shows him how in the ancient times kings and sovereigns were marching with huge armies forward to conquer lands, or to defend themselves, from or towards Arachosia, Candaor, Margiana, Caucasus, Atropatia, Susiana, Balsara, etc. Satan then tells Christ that unless he also engages himself in such raging wars that he was so long viewing, he will not be able to reclaim his father's kingdom. Satan tells Christ that without potent and appropriate means, he will not be able to win such wars, though there is prediction that he will win; rather, Satan tells him, the prediction itself will be revoked: " 'prediction still/In all things, and all men, supposes means;/Without means used, what it predicts revokes....' " Satan warns Christ that he (Christ) will not be able to secure his father's throne, which is a bone of contention between two strong opposing forces — the Romans and the Parthians — without befriending one of the opposing enemies. But Christ is not moved by this, apparently, wise advice of Satan. He rather tells Satan that he (Christ) will never resort to such means as arms to reclaim his father's kingdom, and to free his breathren in that kingdom. He tells Satan that the appropriate time for him has not yet arrived, and that when the appropriate time will come, he will not be 'slack', and will certainly deliver the 'Ten Tribes'. Thus, Christ, for the third time rejects the wileful offer of Satan.

Book IV

Satan could seduce Eve because 'Eve was Eve'— gullible and weak, but Christ is quite different — wise and strong. As regards Christ, Satan fails to "weigh/The strength he was to cope with". Nevertheless, Satan does not despair, even after successive failures, but, like bees that frequently swarm round wine-press, or as surging waves frequently break into bubles on shingles, "gives not o'er, though desperate of success,/And his vain importunity pursues." Satan now brings Christ to the western side of the high mountain, on the top of which they have so long been standing. From there Christ sees below another plain land by the sea, where "an imperial city stood,/With towers and temples proudly elevate/On seven hills". Satan tells him that that city is Rome, to which all nations show obeissance. He shows Christ some more things, and then tells him : " 'These having shown thee I have shown thee all/The kingdoms of the world, and all their glory...' " Satan further tells him that the old emperor of Rome had no son, and that he became lascivous, and that he converted the empire into a sty. Satan now instigates Christ to dethrone the emperor and occupy his throne :

'with what ease,
Endowed with regal virtues as thou art,
Appearing, and bringing noble deeds,
Might'st thou expel this monster from his throne,
Now made a sty, and in his place ascending,
A victor-people free from servile yoke !
And with my help thou may'st; to me the power
Is given, and by that right I give it thee.
Aim, therefore, at no less than all the world;
Aim at the highest; without the highest attained
Will be for thee no sitting, or not long,
On David's throne, be prophesied what will.'

But Christ is still unmoved by Satan's alluring pleas. He tells Satan that he does not want luxury and grandeur of the Roman empire — its gold, pearls, etc. He says that to him the enjoyment of such things is nothing, and that he is not interested in the throne of the barbarous emperor of Rome. He is, moreover, not interested in punishing the barbarous emperor, because he knows that the emperor's own conscience will punish him at some future time. Christ is confident that such empires, as that of Rome, will some day be torn into pieces, while his own kingdom will know no limiting boundary. Now, being once more bold in his attempt at tempting Christ, Satan offers him all the kingdoms of the world: " 'The kingdoms of the world to thee I give/(For, given to me, I give to whom I please),....' " At this swaggering of Satan, Christ becomes enraged, because he knows that the acceptance of Satan's offer only means showing subordination to, or rather worshipping of, Satan. Christ, therefore, tells Satan:

> 'It is written,
> The first of all commandments, "Thou shalt worship
> The Lord thy God, and only him shalt serve;"
> And dar'st thou to the Son of God propound
> To worship thee, accurs'd?'

Satan becomes afraid at this hot reply of Christ, and asks him not to feel offended. He tells Christ that he (Satan) now can understand that he (Christ) is inclined to something else — to meditation. Satan, therefore, asks Christ to earn fame by acquiring wisdom :

> 'slipping from thy mother's eye, thou went'st
> Alone into the Temple; there wast found
> Amongst the gravest Rabbis, disputant
> On points and questions fitting Moses' chair
> Teaching not taught. The childhood shows the man,
> As morning shows the day : be famous then
> By wisdom;

Saying so, Satan asks Christ to look at the city of Athens: " 'the eye of Greece, mother of arts/And eloquence, native to famous wits' ". There in Athens, Satan says, Chirst will find Plato's school, Lycium; the wits of Stoa; 'Aeolian charms' and 'Dorian lyric odes'; Alexander, the Great, and blind Melesigenes, later on called Homer, whose poem Phoebus claimed to be his own; and such other things and persons. Satan further tells Christ that there he (Christ) will also find the Greek tragedians, the famous orators, and there he will be able to learn from 'sage Philosophy'— from Socrates, the peripatetics, the epicurians, and the stoics.

And yet Christ will not give ear to Satan. He rather replies: " 'he who receives/Light from above, from the fountain of Light,/No other doctrine needs, though granted true;' ". To Christ, the things offered by Satan are nothing but dreams and fancies. Christ repudiates all the philosophies referred to by Satan, one by one, and then says about the philosophers: " 'Alas! what can they teach, and not mislead,/Ignorant of them-selves,....' ". Chirst tells Satan that the Greeks borrowed all their arts from Israel, and so they should not boast of all these. Satan now becomes confounded, and yet he naggingly asks Christ :

> 'Since neither wealth nor honour, arms nor arts,
> Kingdom nor empire, please thee, nor aught
> By me proposed in life contemplative
> Or active, tended on by glory or fame,
> What dost thou in this world?'

Satan, further, warns Christ that since he rejects all his offers, he (Christ) is doomed to suffer :

> 'Now contrary, if I read aught in Heaven,
> Or Heaven write aught of fate, by what the stars
> Voluminous, or single characters
> In their conjunction met, give me to spell,
> Sorrows and labours, opposition, hate,
> Attend thee; scorns, reproaches, injuries,
> Violence and stripes, and, lastly, cruel death.'

So saying, Satan takes Christ down from the top of the mountain, and leaves him in the former wilderness, he (Satan) feigning to have vanished.

Now, though night is approaching, Christ is not the least unnerved; he is only feeling hungry and cold. Presently, he takes rest under a bower, and soon falls asleep. But, Satan continues to disturb his sleep with agonising dreams. Then, to add to Christ's distress, storm, thunders, howlings, and shrieks — all at a time — begins to make the place hellish. Nevertheless, Christ "Sat'st unappalled in calm and sinless peace." Thus, passes the night, and then morning comes, and everything seems bright. After this, several more bids of allurements are done by Satan to distract Christ's mind, but all these are foiled by the Son of God. Satan then, desperately, plans his last bid of alluring Christ, and to this end, addresses Christ as the Son of God, and tells him that the previous night was in keeping with his (Satan's) prediction that he (Christ) will have to undergo extreme sufferings. Satan also renews his advice to Christ of reclaiming his father David's kingdom. But Christ curtly tells him that those horrible sights of the previous night were not sent by God, but by him (Satan). Saying so, Christ is about to go away. At this, Satan becomes 'swoll'n with rage' and tells him that he (Satan) is yet in doubt as to whether he (Christ) is really the 'Son of God'. Satan says that he had been watching Christ's birth and baptising — himself not being baptised — at the ford of Jordan, and since the baptisement of Christ, he has been studying very closely. " 'In what degree or meaning thou art called/The Son of God, which bears no single sense;' " Satan further tells Christ :

> 'The Son of God I also am, or was;
> And, if I was, I am; relation stands:
> All men are sons of God; yet thee I thought
> In some respect far higher so declared.
> Therefore I watched thy footsteps from that hour,
> And followed thee still on to this waste wild,
> Where, by all best conjectures, I collect
> Thou art to be my fatal enemy.

Satan confesses that through all his temptations he has been assaying if Christ is really the Son of God, and after much watching over him has found Christ to be really the Son of God. He admits that Christ is adamantine against all sorts of temptations.

Satan now catches hold of Christ and bears him through the sublime air and over plain, and at last lands him on top of the highest hill of Jerusalem. And then he tells Christ that it needs much skill to stand on that top. Satan then asks Christ to throw himself (Christ) down from there, to show the veracity of his claim that he is the Son of God: " 'I to thy father's house/Have brought thee, and highest placed: highest is best:/Now show thy progeny; if not to stand,/Cast thyself down; safely, if Son of God.' " Christ, Jesus, reminds Satan of the biblical warning: " 'Tempt not the Lord thy God.' " Satan is smiten with amazement at these words of Christ, and suddenly falls down from the highest top. Immediately afterwards, a band of resplendent angels takes hold of Christ, wafts him upwards, and places him in heaven. There in heaven, the angels entertain him with heavenly nourishment that they fetch from the Tree of Life and the Fount of Life, and they sing anthems in honour of Christ's victory: "Over temptation and the Tempter proud". In their anthem, the angels also sing about Christ's regaining the lost Paradise for Adam and his chosen sons. Then the angels take Christ, the Son of God, to a 'heavenly feast', and after he is refreshed, leaves him on his own way. And then Christ goes back to his mother's affectionate fold :

> Thus, they the Son of God, our saviour meek,
> Sung Victor, and, from heavenly feast refreshed,
> Brought on his way with joy; he, unobserved,
> Home to his mother's house private returned.

3
(A GENERAL DISCUSSION ON *PARADISE REGAINED)*

Paradise Regained, as has been told earlier, is based on Book of Job, and, yet, it is not a theological poem; it is poem of the practical advice that man must control his mind before going into any action. It teaches how to stick to one's own path of righteousness against all odds of distractions. In *Paradise Regained* Christ is determined to accomplish great actions, but Satan is continually trying to detract him. Christ is meek, but he is so only apparently: within his own mind, he is as strong as flint. On the other hand, Satan is strong only outwardly, and within himself he is a too weak being — an already defeated being. Christ is strong because he has faith in the righteousness of his great actions that he intends to accomplish; but Satan is weak because he knows that what he is going to do is wrong. Great actions demand great strength of mind, and to gather strength for the mind, the mind itself has to be regulated, controlled. The moral of the epic is that true conquest is the conquest of the inward realm, the subjugation of the passions that arise in the mind, from time to time, as allurements show themselves. In *Paradise Lost*, Milton protested against one man's rule over a multitude. There he advocated democracy — the rule of the many over the many, instead of that of the one, which he called tyranny. But in *Paradise Regained*, he has completely changed the concept of rule. Here he says that rule does not mean right over others, but only control over one's own self. In Book II of *Paradise Regained* (lines 466-472), Christ says:

> Yet he who reigns within himself, and rules
> Passions, Desires, and Fears, is more a king;
> Which every wise and virtuous man attains;
> And who attains not, ill aspires to rule
> Cities of men, or head-strong Multitudes,
> Subject himself to Anarchy within,
> Or lawless passions in him which he serves.

This is the moral of the epic *Paradise Regained.* But the poem may be interpreted in another way. It may mean the progress of the soul in this world. The soul has to move through diverse allurements and distractions, and so the soul has each moment the chances of falling down to its destructions. How than can the soul save itself? The only way out is to have the deepest faith in the goodness of God — the faith that one who surrenders himself to the disposal of God must be salvaged by God himself. One whose soul, unflinchingly, follows the loadstar of faith in god, never falls from God's grace; but one whose soul falters fails to get salvaged. In *Paradise Regained*, Christ teaches this supreme wisdom by showing his own life's examples.

In *Paradise Regained*, the strength of the Satan of *Paradise Lost* has been reduced to the minimum, while that of Adam of *Paradise Lost*, transmogrified into the person of Christ, has been increased to the maximum limit. In the earlier epic, Satan had his vertical rise, and could sustain the tenor of his rise at least up to the middle of the poem, and then, though the strength was reduced a little bit, it continued to remain with him, to the end. On the other hand, in the latter epic, the strength of Satan goes out of him, and he falls plump to his utter destruction. Again, in the earlier epic, we find the triumph of vice over virtue, but in the latter epic we find a just reversal. Further, in *Paradise Lost*, the bad characters outnumber the good characters, which may mean that the epic is over-weighed with evil; but in *Paradise Regained*, there is no preponderance of the evil. *Paradise Lost* is a narrative poem, while *Paradise Regained* is a dramatic poem. In *Paradise Lost*, the dialogues were introduced, as if to disperse possible tedium in the narrative; but in *Paradise Regained* the dialogue is the means of telling the story. Of course, both the poems contain stories; but the story of *Paradise Lost* is realistic, while that of the other epic is unrealistic, because unbelievable — it is almost oneiric. Nevertheless, the two epics converge on at one point; the point of humanity. In *Paradise Lost.* Satan, though a diabolical character, possesses all the human attributes; and in *Paradise Regained*, though almost up to the end of the poem Christ seems to be an abstraction, at the fag end of the poem he discloses his human attributes, when the poet says of him : "Home to his mother's house private returned."

Regarding the structure of *Paradise Regained*, Milton possibly imitated mostly Virgil's *Georgics*. This conjecture has been made by E.M.W. Tillyard, for two reasons. Firstly, both *Georgics* and *Paradise Regained* contain almost equal number of lines — the former 2188 lines and the latter 2070 lines. Secondly, *Paradise Regained* like *Georgics*, is divided into four Books, though the narration might have been divided into just two Books, because there is only one shift in the course of the narration after Book I. However, Tillyard has broken down the totality of 2070 lines of *Paradise Regained* into the following six headings (Tillyard, 1956, 323) :

i.	Preludes	182 lines
ii.	First temptation	320 lines
iii.	Prelude to second temptation	241 lines
iv.	Second (or main) temptation	1081 lines
v.	Thris temptation	187 lines
vi.	Epilogue	59 lines

Paradise Lost showed us the dire consequences that we are to face when we are guided solely by our passions, *i.e.* when our rationality is clouded by our passions. *Paradise Regained* shows us how we may enjoy the bliss of paradise within us should we choose to be guided by our rationality. In *Paradise Regained*, Satan thrice attempts to corrupt Christ by tempting him with objects that, generally, attract our passions, and rather naturally. Christ is Milton's ideal man, or model of humanity, — Christ who shows absolute control over his passions. Here Milton was, perhaps, influenced by the Moralities of the pre-Elizabethan period, where temptations fail against uprightness and self-control, where, that is, rationality prevails over passions. As we have said before, there are three temptations in *Paradise Regained*. E.M.W. Tillyard writes about these three temptations: "Milton treats the first temptation, to turn stones into bread, as a prelude; the second temptation, the vision of the kingdoms of the world, is the body of the poem; the third temptation, when Christ is set on the pennacle of the temple, is less a temptation than the brief and sudden rout of Satan" (Tillyard, 1956, 323).

Paradise Regained is, generally, treated as a sequel to *Paradise Lost*. The apparent association between the two poems rests on several factors. Firstly, there is a similarity between the titles of the two poems. Secondly, both deal with something relating to paradise. Thirdly, some of the principal characters of the two epics are common, such as Satan, Christ, God, etc. And lastly, Milton himself innuendoes to some connections between the two poems just at the very beginning of *Paradise Regained*: "I who erewhile the happy Garden sung". Besides, there was a foreshadowing of *Paradise Regained* in the earlier epic.

But, as has been hinted at earlier, there may not be any relation between the two epics. Tillyard, particularly, believes that *Paradise Regained* is, in no wise, a sequel to *Paradise Lost*. Tillyard writes: "The mistaken idea that *Paradise Regained* is a sequel to *Paradise Lost* rests partly on the title of the two poems and the opening lines of *Paradise Regained*, partly on the statement of Thomas Ellwood [that he suggested a sequel to Milton]. When Milton writes

> I who erewhile the happy Garden sung,
> By one man's disobedience lost, now sing
> Recover'd Paradise to all mankind,

he might appear to mean that he will now complete *Paradise Lost* by a supplementary poem. But he cannot really mean this, because the recovery of Paradise is an essential part of *Paradise Lost*, treated at considerable length in the poem. All he can mean is that he is now going to write a poem in which the recovery of Paradise is to be the principal not the second subject" (Tillyard, 1956, 297). But Tillyard actually does not say something very different from saying that *Paradise Regained* is a sequel to *Paradise Lost*. Because, if the recovery of Paradise is "an essential part" of *Paradise Lost* and if this, again, is the theme of *Paradise Regained*, Tillyard should like to say that the second epic is just an elaboration of a part of the first epic. And, in that case, if we say that the second epic is a sequel to the first, it does not mean something very different from saying that the second epic is the elaboration of a part of the first. Besides, *The Wordsworth Companion to Literature in English* also says that *Paradise Regained* is a sequel to *Paradise Lost* (Wordsworth Reference, 706).

It is true that *Paradise Regained*, as a whole, has failed to achieve the poetic height of *Paradise Lost*. The cause of this may be four-fold. Firstly, any noble poetic work, of the length of an epic, needs much time to get incubated or gestated in the mind of the poet. The poet has to gather experiences — both subjective and objective — which are to be utilised as raw-material of the poem. Milton conceived of the theme of, and thought much about the style of, *Paradise Lost*, for a long time. His anti-establishment and anti-catholic attitude did not develop overnight. His ideals of manhood, womanhood, marriage, nuptial love, etc. were not the products of a single day, or of a single sitting on meditation. All these grew out of his long study and experiences, and long participation in the social and political affairs of his country. And so all these concepts and ideals belonged not only to his head but also to his heart — they were emotionally surcharged concepts and ideals. So the thoughts and emotion of *Paradise Lost* had enough time to get formed and expressed. But this did not happen in the case of *Paradise Regained*: Milton almost as soon as sat down for dictating the epic as Ellwood requested him to write the same. Secondly, good poetry cannot be supplied when ordered for, but it comes out of the poet's inspiration — out of some sort of insuperable urge to unburden the poet's heart of some heavy pressure of creative energy. The poet can rise high up in poetic flight only when he feels a great urge to sing full-throated, only when there is a pent-up emotion that strives to come out with a gusto. Poetry is no artifice; it is a creation. An artifice can be tailored to suit an order; but good poetry is rather a shading off of the poet's emotional burden, and so to write a good poetry, the poet must be able to feel the emotion that he is going to express in his poetry. And so good poetry cannot be expected when the poet creates or imagines an artificial emotion within his heart. It was for this reason that the ancient Greeks believed that poetry comes out of divine afflatus. The spirit of *Paradise Lost* was the spirit of Milton that grew within him out of his own nature and out of his learning and experiences. So the emotion he is natural, immaculately natural, and so the epic is superb. But, in the case of *Paradise Regained*, the poet's emotion is deliberate and artificial, and so the poem has failed to achieve the appropriate poetic height. Thirdly, great poetry does not emerge out of rationality, but out of intense emotion. The fount of *Paradise Lost* was Milton's genuine and intense emotion, but *Paradise Regained* grew out of a debate, and so as a discursive poem it has failed to rise to the pinnacle of poetic height. And lastly, good poetry depends largely on fancy and not on faith, and *Paradise Regained*, unlike *Paradise Lost*, is more full of faith than of fancy.

We find a major change in Milton's style and content when he moves from *Paradise Lost* to *Paradise Regained*. Whereas in the former narration predominates, in the latter dialogue is predominant. The theme of the two epics are different: in *Paradise Lost*, the theme is the loss of Paradise to Adam, due to himself, but the theme of *Paradise Regained* is the salvaging of Adam through showing the example of Christ. In the earlier epic, Christ is almost absent, but in the later epic, he has the principal part. In the earlier epic, Satan is the seeming hero, but in the later epic, he has to eat the humble pie. Adam may be said to be the hero of the earlier epic, but Christ is certainly the hero of the later epic. In *Paradise Lost*, we may find, if we like, some autobiographical elements, but *Paradise Regained* is devoid of any. In the former epic, Milton sometimes refers to his contemporary political situations, but in the latter epic no such references are available. Lastly, in *Paradise Lost* both Satan and Adam show disobedience to God — the former rather parades his disobedience; but in *Paradise Regained* the general tune is not that of defiance, but of obediences, of submission. In the former, Satan is as adamentinely disobedient to God as in the latter Christ is obedient to him. Regarding the amount of classical allusions and obsolete geographical and person names, both the epics stand at par. As we have said earlier, in poetic quality, the former epic is far superior to the latter epic. Nevertheless, in may places, *Paradise Regained* is excellent in poetic quality and noble in thought. Dr. Johnson writes about *Paradise Regained*: "Of *Paradise Regained*, the general judgment seems now to be right, that it is in many parts elegant, and everywhere instructive" (Johnson, 130). But Johnson has also found some faults in it: "The basis of *Paradise Regained* is narrow; a dialogue without action can never please like an union of the narrative and dramatick powers" (Johnson, 131). We may find another great fault in *Paradise Regained.* In it, why should Satan be able to bear Christ up a hill, rising over Jerusalem, without Christ's consent, to throw him down? Here Milton has certainly degraded the divine stature of Christ.

However, in spite of some of its faults, *Paradise Regained* was Milton's favourite. We have mentioned some of the reasons of the failure of this epic, but, perhaps, the most potent cause of its failure lies in the fact that it could not give vent to the sentiment of the poet's contemporary age. Herbert Read, in his scholarly book *Phases of English Poetry*, is quite perceptive when he writes: "An epic is, intimately, related to the aspirations of its age, and almost every age has its epic, though we do not always recognise them as such" (Read, 132). *Paradise Lost* could express the sentiment of the age — an age that mingled the Renaissance spirit with the humanism of the Reformation; but, in its abstraction, *Paradise Regained* remains unconcerned about the sentiment of the people, and so the people found it not so interesting. Milton says that both the poems are prompted to him by divine powers. In *Paradise Lost* he invoked the divine Muse and the Holy Spirit, and in *Paradise Regained* he urges the Spirit (the Holy Spirit) to inspire him: "inspire/ As thou art wont, my prompted song" (Book I, lines 11-12). But, while in *Paradise Lost* the divine Spirit and the Holy Spirit inspired the poet to sing divine song against the earthly aspirations of his contemporary people, in *Paradise Regained* the Spirit inspired him to sing divine song, being abstracted from the aspirations of his contemporary society. Only that, that shows interest in people, can make people interested in it. Certainly, *Paradise Regained* failed here. However, to conclude this section, *Paradise Regained* will always be remembered for, among other things, its many quoteable quotes, such as "Man lives not by bread only" (Book I, line 349) and "The childhood shows the man,/As morning shows the day" (Book IV, lines 220-221).

9

SAMSON AGONISTES

1
(INTRODUCTION)

We know that in his early life, Milton thought of writing plays, but urgent circumstances prevented him from producing any. Such urgent conditions were many. Firstly, he was drawn to active politics, and with political objectives in view turned out, or rather had to turn out, a spat of pamphlets. Secondly, as the Commonwealth of Cromwell began to dwindle, he sat down to write two epics in quick succession — *Paradise Lost* and *Paradise Regained*. Consequently, he could not so long find time to write any play, though he had by then shown his metier as a dramatist in his *Arcades* and *Comus*. And only at the fag end of his life, he found time to produce his only drama — *Samson Agonistes*. This play and the epic *Paradise Regained* were published in the same year, *i.e.* in 1671; but we do not know the exact date of writing the play. Though Milton never intended *Samson Agonistes* to be acted, it was licensed in July, 1670, though it was never produced either during Milton's life time or some time after that. However, much later on it had been successfully staged. Milton intended *Samson Agonistes* to be a closet drama because, maybe, the Puritans, at the time of writing it, did not favour plays being staged. *Samson Agonistes* had inspired the great German music composer Geroge Frederick Handel (1685-1759) to compose an oratorio — *Samson*. However, as we have said, we do not know the exact date of the composition of *Samson Agonistes*. But some commentators believe that the play was written in 1667, though others say that it was written some time between 1666 and 1670. In any case, the writing of the play was not undertaken before the Restoration. There is yet another debate regarding whether *Paradise Regained* was written before *Samson Agonistes*, or the other way round. Without going into the details of the debate, we may, from the internal and circumstantial evidences of the epic and the play, perhaps, say that the epic preceded the play. After the Restoration, as time went by, Milton's confidence in the ultimate victory of the Puritan movement gradually waned, and this is better perceptible in the play than in the epic.

An inkling of the coming into being of *Samson Agonistes* may be found in *Paradise Lost* (Book IX, lines 1059-1063) :

So rose the Danite strong,
Herculean Samson, from the harlot-lap
Of Philistean Dalilah, and waked
Shorn of his strength; they destitute and bare
Of all their virtue.

According to E.M.W. Tillyard, in *Paradise Regained*, Milton argues for inactivity, following simple faith in God; but after this spell of inaction, he reverts once again to activity in *Samson Agonistes* — the activity that we saw in *Paradise Lost*. Tillyard writes: "*Paradise Regained* has the narrowest scope of Milton's three long poems; it concerns itself with a single idea, namely that action is to be distrusted and that what matters almost exclusively is that inner paradise which it is in the power of every individual to attain. But Milton seems to have changed and by the time of *Samson* to have regained his faith in action. He makes a deed, not a thought, the centre of the drama" (Tillyard, 1956, 328). However, in a sense, Milton's two epics and *Samson Agonistes* are very much inter-related, because the play may be said to be an example of the ways in which God behaves with human beings, and so it is rather merely a dramatic presentation of what was said in the two epics.

As *Paradise Lost* was moulded on the story of *Genesis*, or as *Paradise Regained* was conceived on the story of *Book of Job*, so *Samson Agonistes* was structured following the Samson myth contained in *Book of Judges* (of the Old Testament). "The book of *Judges* is composed of stories from the lawless period of Israel's history between the invasion of Canaan and the establishment of the monarchy. These stories are about the exploits of national heroes called 'judges', most of whom were military leaders, rather than judges in the legal sense of the word. One of the better known of them was Samson whose deeds are recorded in chapters 13-16 [of *Book of Judges*]" (The Bible Society of India, 233). The origin of the story of Samson goes back to about 1,200 B.C. when the Israelites had been being ruled by the Philistines for about 40 years. Samson's father was Manoah, a man of the town of Zorah and a man of the tribe of Dan. Manoah's wife did not conceive, but one day Lord's angel came to her and told her: "'You have never been able to have children, but you will soon be pregnant and have a son. Take care not to drink any wine or beer, or eat any forbidden food; and after your son is born, you must never cut his hair, because from the day of his birth he will be dedicated to God as a Nazarite. He will begin the work of rescuing Israel from the Philistines' " (The Bible Society of India, 249). Manoah's wife gave birth to a son who was named Samson. Samson came of age, and one day was attracted by a Philistine girl, Timnah, but his father and mother tried to dissuade him from going to marry her. But Samson was determined to marry her, because God wanted to find a chance of punishing the Philistines. A few days later, Samson was going to marry the girl, and on the way he killed a lion. Since then he did some other deeds of prowess. The Philistines thought Samson to be dangerous for them, and one day, with the intention of killing him, surrounded Samson at Lehi, and began shouting at him in order to bring him into a brawl, and then to kill him, but when the skirmish began, Samson routed the whole host of them. On another day, Samson went to Gaza and lay with a prostitute. At this, the people of Gaza became angry, and in order to kill him laid a siege where he laid, and thought of killing him at day-break. But Samson woke up at midnight, cognized what was going on around the house in which he slept, and so pulled down the city-gate and bore it to the top of a hill, and thus he saved himself. These are only some of the instances of his incomparable physical prowess.

After this, Samson fell in love with another Philistine maid, named Delilah, who lived in the valley of Sorek. Five Philistine kings, intent upon killing Samson, went to Delilah, and with allurements of rewards and on pain of punishment asked her to know from Samson what made him so strong, and to know from him how he could be tied up immoveably. On Delilah's enquiry, Samson told her that if he were tied with "seven new bowstrings that are not dried out", then he could be immoveably tied up and made weak. The five kings grafted Delilah to tie him up in like manner by her, but Samson easily snapped the tie. Dalilah then asked Samson how he could be tied, and he said that she could do so with unused ropes meant for sails. But this ploy also failed. Then Samson told her that he could be inextricably tied up with his own hair made into a loom. The third attempt at nabbing Samson with this device also came a cropper. Dalilah then naggingly, repeatedly, and with womanly wiles asked him to tell her the way in which he could be tied up. She told him that should he not tell her this, she would think that he did not love her at all. Henpecked, Samson then, ultimately, told her the truth: he told her that if his hair, that was dedicated to God and which was never cut, was cut, he would become as weak as any other man. Dalilah then lulled him into deep sleep, and cut off "Samson's seven locks of hair", and, consequently, Samson lost his divine strength. The Philistines then captured him, pulled out his eyes, took him to Gaza, and there bound him with bronze chains. In addition to all these, Samson was ordered to grind at a mill while in a prison. Curiously, the hair of Samson began to grow in the prison, which meant that he began to grow in strength, too. And this happened according to the will of God.

On the other hand, to celebrate their victory over Samson, the Philistine kings gathered at a place to offer a great sacrifice to their highest god Dagon (the Hebrew word 'dagon' means 'corn'). To add to their joy and hilarity, they brought Samson, from out of the dark prison, to the sacrificial place, and made him stand between two pillars that held up the vast roof under which almost all the Philistines gathered to witness and enjoy the great sacrifice. Then songs were being sung in praise of the heathen god Dagon. Samson could not bear with all this heathen affairs, and so invoked God for strength, and God granted his prayer. He then asked the boy who conducted him there from the prison to bring him near a pillar, to let him take some rest, and the boy did accordingly. Then Samson plucked his courage, gathered his strength, and pulled at the pillar against which he was reclining. On the impact of the pull, the roof caved in, and all the men and women who stood under it were killed, and with them Samson himself, too. Before pulling the pillar, Samson shouted: " 'Let me die with the Philistines!' " Such is the myth of Samson.

Milton added a sort of preface to his play *Samson Agonistes*, and entitled it 'Of that sort of dramatic poem which is called tragedy'. In it he has discussed the objective of a tragedy, agreeing with Aristotle's view of tragedy: "by raising pity and fear, or terror, to purge the mind of those and such-like passions; that is to temper and reduce them to just measure with a kind of delight, stirred up by reading or seeing those passions well imitated." He also agreed with Aristotle regarding the unity of time (as he agreed with Aristotle regarding the unity of two other things: place and action): "The circumscription of time, wherein the whole drama begins and ends, is, according to ancient rule and best example, within the space of twentyfour hours." Though his own puritan political party supported banning of staging of plays, Milton wrote in the Preface that tragedy was not unwholesome, and that even Apostle Paul "thought of it not unworthy to insert a verse of Euripides into the text of Holy Scripture, 1 Cor. xv. 33". Milton also said in the Preface that a drama should be confined within the space of five acts.

Milton also wrote a two-sentence Argument or summary of the story of the play. We may profitably quote it in full. It runs thus: "Samson, made captive, blind, and now in the prison at Gaza, there to labour as in a common workhouse, on a festival day, in the general cessation from labour, comes forth into the open air to a place nigh, somewhat retired, there to sit a while and bemoan his condition: where he happens at length to be visited by certain friends and equals of his tribe, which make the Chorus, who seek to comfort him what they can; then by his old father, Manoa, who endeavours the like, and withal tells him his purpose to procure his liberty by ransom; lastly that this feast was proclaimed by the Philistines as a day of thanks giving for their deliverance from the hands of Samson — which yet more troubles him. Manoa then departs to prosecute his endeavour with the Philistian lords for Samson's redemption: who, in the meanwhile, is visited by other persons, and, lastly, by a public officer to require his coming to the feast before the lords and people, to play or show his strength in their presence; he at first refuses, dismissing the public officer with absolute denial to come; at length, persuaded inwardly that this was from God, he yields to go along with him, who came now the second time with great threatenings to fetch him; the Chorus yet remaining on the place, Manoa returns full of joyful hope to procure ere long his son's deliverance; in the midst of which discourse an Hebrew comes in haste, confusedly at first, and afterwards more distinctly, relating the catastrophe, what Samson had done to the Philistines, and by accident to himself; wherewith the Tragedy ends."

The *dramatis personae* of *Samson Agonistes* are:

i. *Samson* : the hero of the play, a member of the Israelite tribe called Dan. (The Hebrew word 'Samson' means 'sun'. About 1600, a verb was derived from the term 'Samson' — 'sampsoun' which means 'to cast down in dejection and anguished thought'. In *The Book of Judges*, in the *Old Testament*, Samson is a 'Judge' or military leader.)

ii. *Manoa* : Father of Samson. (In *The Book of Judges* of

	the *Old Testament*, he is called Manoah. The Hebrew word 'Manoa' or 'Manoah' means 'rest').
iii. *Dalila* :	second wife to Samson. (In *The Book of Judges*, her name is Dalilah. The Hebrew word 'Dalila' or 'Dalilah' means, roughly, 'hang like a leaf'. (See lines 727-728 of the play.) She is a woman of Palestine stock.
iv. *Harapha* : *of Gath*	A Palestinian giant. (The Hebrew word 'Harapha' means 'giant'.)
v. *Public* : *Officer*	of the Philistines.
vi. *Messenger*	
vii. *Chorus of* : *Danites*	consisting of people of the Dan tribe to which Manoa and Samson belong.

The drama occurs before the prison in Gaza (or Azza)

2
(SUMMARY OF THE STORY OF *SAMSON AGONISTES*)

The play begins with a speech of Samson, which may be called the prologue of the play, in which Samson, the hero, bewails his fallen state. He is incomparably strong, both in body and in mind. An angel promised or foretold that he (Samson) would deliver Israel from the overlordship of the Philistines but, contrarily, he is now blinded and imprisoned in Gaza. He complains:

> Blind among enemies, O worse than chains,
> Dungeon, or beggary, or decrepit age
> Light, the prime work of God, to me is extinct,
> And all her various objects of delight
> Annulled,......................................

Samson now sees only darkness covered by darkness: "O dark, dark, dark, amid the blaze of noon". He is now 'Eyeless in Gaza', and 'a living death'. He thinks that he himself is responsible for this his fallen state, a pitiful plight. Because at some moment of weakness, he revealed his secret to a woman: "But weakly to a woman must reveal it,/Overcome with importunity and tears." This day, the victorious Philistine kings and people are holding a solemn feast in honour of their heathen deity Dagon — the sea-idol. Under the order of the kings, Samson is being taken to the place of the feast, by a boy. As he is being led out of the dark and unwholesome prison, Samson feels better in the open air. He asks the boy; "here leave me respire."

The chorus now discovers Samson, and delivers a speech which may be taken to be the parode. The chorus wonders at the crest-fallen state of Samson: "Thou art become (O worst imprisonment!)/The dungeon of thyself". After this, begins the 1st episode of the play. Samson faintly hears human voices — the voices of the Chorus. The Chorus approaches him, and introduce themselves to Samson as his friends, and offer counsel and consolation. Samson tells them that he has been cheated by a woman, and now is being published as a fool. The Chorus asks him not to grive, because even "Wise men/Have erred, and by a bad woman been deceived". They ask him why he married a Philistine wife and not a woman of his own tribe. Samson tells them that at first he had impulsively wedded Timna, the daughter of an infidel, and that she proved herself false; and then he wedded Dalila of the valley of Sorec, and that she has proved herself to be his 'accomplished snare'; and also that at some weak moment of his, he disclosed the secret of his strength with which, as divinely predicted, he wanted to vanquish the Philistines. The Chorus assures him that he was never amiss in provoking the Philistines. Samson tells the Chorus that he was imprisoned, not due to him, but due to the fault of the governors of Israel, because they did not support what he wanted to do. The Chorus then sings a 'stationary song' or *stasimon* in which it says that "Just are the ways of God,/And justifiable to men,/Unless there be who think not God at all." The Chorus says that Samson could certainly free the Israelites had he not married Dalila — his "fallacious bride,/Unclean, unchaste." Meanwhile Manoa, Samson's father, appears, and the Chorus wonders how Samson will receive his father who is wearing "locks white as down". The play is not divided into Acts, but, if we like, we may say that the first Act (or the first episode) of the play ends here.

At the beginning of the second Act (or episode), we find Samson more aggrieved at the sight of his father, Manoa. Manoa also bewails the crest-fallen plight of Samson who had once been "Himself an army — now unequal match/To save himself against a coward armed/At one spear's length." Samson asks his father not to hold heaven responsible for his fallen state, because it was he himself who was so, as it was he himself who disclosed the secret of his strength to Dalila. Manoa knows well that Samson married Dalila being goaded by "Divine impulsion". Manoa now reveals before Samson the occasion of the feast. He says that the Philistines are holding the feast with much pomp in honour of their chief god, Dagon, after their victory over the Israelites. But Samson is confident that God must subdue the votaries of Dagon, before long. Manoa tells Samson that he (Manoa) has arranged ransom for his (Samson's) release, but Samson will not get freed on his father's payment of ransom, because he wants to suffer punishment at the hands of the Philistines for his own foolery in divulging the secret of his divine strength to Dalila. Manoa advises him not to be so contrite, and decide on his death at the hands of the Philistines, but to repent for his sin and pray for God's mercy. Samson replies that he certainly seeks God's pardon; but he asks his father what he (Samson) will do with his life? In a heavy mood, then, Samson muses on his former and present state:

> Fearless of danger, like a petty god
> I walked about, admired of all, and dreaded
> On hostile ground, none daring my affront.
> Then, swoll'n with pride, into the snare I fell
> Of fair fallacious looks, venereal trains,
> Softened with pleasure and voluptuous life,
> At length to lay my head and hallowed pledge
> Of all my strength in the lascivious lap
> Of a deceitful concubine, who shore me,
> Like a tame wether, all my precious fleece,
> Then turned me out ridiculous, despoiled,
> Shaven, and disarmed among my enemies.

The Chorus says that Samson has always been a teetotoller. But Samson ironically tells the Chorus that he has certainly avoided one kind of intoxication, but he has been a slave to another kind of intoxication — that of feminine charms. His purpose of life having been defeated, Samson feels dejected :

> To what can I be useful? wherein serve
> My nation, and the work from Heaven imposed
> But to sit idle on the household hearth,
> A burdenous drone; to visitants a gaza,
> Or pitied object;....................
>
> ....
>
> Here rather let me drudge, and earn my bread
> Till vermin, or the draft of servile food,
> Consume me, and oft-invocated death
> Hasten the welcome end of all my pains.

Samson now thinks that all his hopes are gone, but Manoa asks him not to despair, because he will fetch his (Samson's) deliverance by ransom. Nevertheless, Samson continues to despair : "Sleep hath forsook and given me o'er/To death's benumbing opium as my only cure". After this, the Chorus sings the second *stasimon*. It sings about the benefit of fortitude, and about the destiny of human beings that "Grow up and perish as the summer fly", and also about great men who serve God. Lastly, the Chorus sings about the infirmities and sufferings of old age, and then announces the appearance of Dalila. Here the second Act (or episode) ends, and the third Act (or episode) begins.

As Dalila approaches near him, Samson begins to burn in rage, and cries aloud: "My wife, my traitress, let her not come near me." Yet Dalila inchingly and ditheringly comes close to him. The Chorus describes Delila's hasitation in coming close to Samson :

> Yet on she moves, now stands and eyes thee fixed,
> About to have spoke, but now, with head declined
> Like a fair flower surcharged with dew, she weeps
> And words addressed seem into tears dissolved,
> Wetting the borders of her silken veil:
> But now again she makes address to speak.

Dalila tells Samson that she is repentant of her evil behaviour with him, and that she will willingly do anything in her power to alleviate his sorrows. But Samson reproaches her, calling her a hyaena, and asks her to go away. He tells her that she must have come, this time, to make another assail upon him and to try his residual strength. Dalila admits her faults once again — a fault, she says, that is ubiquitous among women folk. She mildly accuses Samson of trusting a woman like her, because frailty is elemental to women; "Nor shouldst thou have trusted that to woman's frailty:/Ere I to thee, thou to thyself was cruel." (We may here recall Eve's accusation of Adam, in *Paradise Lost*, after their fall.) Dalila submits that she found him changeable as his fancy changes: he once took fancy with a girl at Timna, and then left her, and then fell in love with herself. It was for this reason that she wanted to know the secret of his strength, so that she could control his fancy. She further told him that she revealed the secret of his strength to the Philistines only because they assured her that no harm would be done him by them :

> I saw thee mutable
> Of fancy; feared lest one day thou would leave me
> As her at Timna; sought by all means, therefore,
> How to endear, and hold thee to me firmest :

No better way I saw than by importuning
To learn thy secret, get into my power
The key of strength and safety: thou wilt say,
'Why, then, revealed?' I was assured by those
Who tempted me that nothing was designed
Against thee but safe custody and hold.

At this pleading of Dalila, Samson becomes somewhat softened, and pardons her, thinking, as she reminded him, that the actual fault lies with himself: "I to myself am false ere thou to me./Such pardon, therefore, as I give my folly/Take to thy wicked deed". He excuses her also because, as she pleaded, she was a weakling; "weakness is thy excuse". Samson also excused her of her guilt of revealing the secret of his strength, on receipt of, or on assurance of receiving, gold from the Philistines. But Dalila denies the charge that she received gold, or the charge that she was assured of the receipt of gold, from the Philistines. She says that she was never allured by gold. She says that she was repeatedly and importuningly asked by the magistrates, princes and other notables to divulge the secret. All these people also threatened her of dire consequences if she did not reveal the secret. They further, argued that not to reveal the secret was sacrilegious and anti-national. She tells Samson that with such mighty persons of the state the priest joined hands in persuading her to reveal the secret, and so it was beyond her power not to yield to their persuasions :

thou know'st the magistrates
And princes of my country came in person,
Solicited, commanded, threatened, urged,
Adjured by all the bonds of civil duty
And of religion — presses how just it was,
How honourable, how glorious to entrap
A common enemy, who had destroyed
Such numbers of our nation: and the priest
Was not behind, but ever at my ear,
Preaching how meritorious with the gods
It would be to ensnare an irreligious
Dishonour of Dagon: what had I
To oppose against such powerful arguments?

Samson wonders that Dalila took him to be an enemy of hers and her country, and not as her husband. He asks her why then she once did accept him as her husband, and reminds her that after their marriage, she belongs to him, and not to her people. He further tells Dalila that he knows well that what she has done she has done to please her heathen gods, particularly to please Dagon.

Now Dalila asks Samson for forgiveness, and assures him of her redoubled care, in future, in his blindness. She promises that she will fetch for him maximal delight, possible for her. But Samson is yet not fully reconciled to her: "No, no! of my condition take no care". Nevertheless, Dalila fondly asks him to let her touch his hand: "Let me approach at least, and touch thy hand." But, though he has pardoned her, yet Samson is still burning in rage at her, and so will not allow her to touch his hand. Frustrated, Dalila now leaves Samson to himself: "I leave him to his lot, and like my own." Dalila is confident that one day she will become famous as a saviour of her own country and countrymen;

> I shall be named among the famousest
> Of women, sung at solemn festivals,
> Living and dead recorded, who, to save
> Her country from a fierce destroyer, chose
> Above the faith of wedlock-bonds; my tomb
> With odours visited and annual flowers.

Saying so, Dalila goes away, leaving Samson behind to his fate. But Samson still nurses within his heart an attraction for the beauty and charm of Dalila. The Chorus now sings the third *stasimon*. It says that God gave man despotic power so that he may not have to suffer female usurpation. After this, the fourth Act (or episode) begins, with the Chorus announcing the approach of a storm.

Samson perceives good days coming through the storm. The Chorus tells him about the coming of the giant Harapha of Gath. Harapha tells Samson that he has come to see his strength, whereupon Samson asks Harapha to test his (Samson's) strength. Harapha jeers at Samson's 'ass's jaw' and at his being 'unforeskinned'. Samson then invites Harapha to a duel, but Harapha says that he is not willing to fight with a blind and ugly man. Yet Samson asks him to come fully armed to fight with him, and tells him that he will fight with him (Harapha) with nothing else than only "an oaken staff". Harapha presumes that Samson's strength lies in his spell or charm, but Samson tells him that his strength resides not in any spell, but in his belief in the 'Living God'. He further tells Harapha that with his strength, he (Samson) challenges his (Harapha's) god, Dagon. In reply, Harapha ridicules Samson by saying that Samson's God has reduced him to an abject being. To Harapha's ridiculing, Samson retorts that in bringing him down to an abject condition, God acted but very justly, and that God, ultimately, will certainly pardom him. Saying this, Samson once again invites Harapha to a duel, to prove "whose god is God". This is followed by mutual accusations and counter-accusations between Samson and Harapha. Harapha calls him a murderer, because he killed "thirty men", *i.e.* thirty Palestinians. In reply, Samson tells him that whatever he did he did according to the "Command from Heaven". But, in indignation, Harapha calls Samson 'Baal-zebub', and, at this, Samson, much infuriated, warns him thus:

> Go, baffled coward, lest I run upon thee,
> Though in these chains, bulk without spirit vast,
> And with one buffet lay thy structure low,
> Or swing thee in the air, then dash thee down
> To the hazard of thy brains and shattered sides.

Exasperated, Samson gets ready to fight against Harapha, because he believes that whatever may be the consequence of the duel, the duel will be his best : "The worst that he can give, to me the best." Samson foresees the fall-out of the fight: "Yet so it may fall out, because their end/Is hate, not help to me, it may with mine/Draw their own ruin who attempt the deed." Now the Chorus sings the fourth *stasimon*. It sings in praise of patience :

> But patience is more oft the exercise
> Of saints, the trial of their fortitude,
> Making them each his own deliverer,
> And victor over all
> That tyranny or fortune can inflict.

Now the fifth Act (or episode) begins. The Chorus announces the coming near of a public officer of the Philistines:

> For I descry this way
> Some other tending; in his hand
> A sceptre or quaint staff he bears,
> Comes on amain, speed in his look.
> By his habit I discern him now
> A public officer, and now at hand.
> His message will be short and voluble.

The public officer tells Samson that a great feast is going to be held in honour and worship of Dagon, the highest god of the Philistines, with boundless pomp and gaity. The public officer asks Samson to go to the place of the feast, with him, and there show his incomparable physical strength. Samson replies that he is a Hebrew, and so he cannot attend the feast given in honour of a heathen god. Offended at this, the officer departs, warning Samson about the consequences of his refusal. Then the Chorus tells Samson that even if he joins the feast, he will thereby commit no sin, because, he says: "Where the heart joins not, outward acts defile not." But Samson tells the Chorus that he cannot obey the Philistines because that will be tantamount to displeasing his God, and that will be a sinful act on his part:

> If I obey them,
> I do it freely, venturing to displease
> God for the fear of man, and man prefer,
> Set God behind; which, in his jealousy,
> Shall never, unrepented, find forgiveness.

Nevertheless, Samson elects to follow the public officer, and tells the Chorus :

> If there be aught of presage in the mind,
> This day will be remarkable in my life
> By some great act, or of my days the last.

Earlier, the public officer went away, but he soon returns, and tells Samson that he has been commanded for the second time to take him (Samson) to the place of the grand feast. Samson now agrees to go with him. He says very wisely; "for a life who will not change his purpose?/ (So mutable are all the ways of men)". The officer is contented, and releases Samson from the chains. The officer assures Samson of his possible manumission, on the pleasure of the Philistine lords. Immediately after Samson's departure, the Chorus finds Manoa who says that he has settled an arrangement with Samson's captivators for his release, on condition of paying a ransom. But, on a sudden, Manoa hears a great noise and shouts that rend the sky. The Chorus presumes that the din and bustle may be coming from the rejoicing of the people at the sight of the great hero Samson. Withdrawing his attention from the hue and cry, Manoa says that he is ready to live the poorest man, but he must delightfully get his son released with a ransom. Manoa again hears a shout which is unlike the former noise and screech. The Chorus tells him that it seems to be a heavy groaning due to blood and death and destruction:

> Noise call you it, or universal groan,
> As if the whole inhabitation perished?

> Blood, death, and deathful deeds, are in that noise,
> Ruin, destruction at the utmost point.

The Chorus further tells Manoa that his son, Samson, is perhaps killing the Philistines. Manoa is utterly apprehensive, but if what the Chorus says is true, he will be the most happy.

Meanwhile, a messenger arrives, who seems perplexed. He reports that an accident has occurred. Manoa asks him to briefly narrate the accident: "Tell us the sum; the circumstance defer." The messenger tells him that all the Philistines are killed: "Gaza yet stands; but all her sons are fall'n". He further tells them that Samson has killed the Philistines, but Samson himself is dead. Manoa heavily grieves for the death of his son, and asks the messenger to tell him how he died. The messenger reports :

> Inevitable cause
> At once both to destroy and to be destroyed;
> The edifice, where all were met to see him,
> Upon their heads and on his own he pulled.

At this, Manoa is taken aback: "O lastly over-strong against thyself !" He asks the messenger to narrate the particulars of the incident. The messenger tells him that, on this day, early in the morning, trumpets were blown and people (the Philistines) gathered at the place where revelry was being held, to see the physical strength of Samson, in a specious building whose roof was held up by two high pillars. At high noon, feast was served, sacrifice was done, and the people were rejoicing. In no time, Samson, clad in stately costume, was brought there, being watched by guards and militia. Samson was "patient, but undaunted". During the intermission of the feast, Samson was stationed between the two pillars. Samson requested the guard: "As over-tired, to let him lean a while". The guard granted his request. Samson kept his blind eyes up-lifted for a while "as one who prayed", and then cried aloud:

> 'Hitherto, Lords, what your commands imposed
> I have performed, as reason was, obeying,
> Not without wonder or delight beheld
> Now, of my own accord, such other trial
> I mean to show you of my strength, yet greater;
> As with amaze shall strike all who behold.'

Uttering these words, with all his gathered strength, Samson shook the pillars, and the whole roof caved in upon all assembled, and killed them, along with Samson himself; only a few vulgar Philistines could escape the tragedy, as they stood away from the roof:

> This uttered, straining all his nerves, he bowed;
> As with the force of winds and waters pent,
> When mountains tremble, those two massy pillars
> With horrible convulsion to and fro
> He tugged, he shook, till down they came, and drew
> The whole roof after them with burst of thunder
> Upon the heads of all who sat beneath,
> Lords, ladies, captains, counsellors, or priests,
> Their choice nobility and flower, not only
> Of this, but each Philistian city round,
> Met from all parts to solemnize this feast.
> Samson, with these inmixed, inevitably
> Pulled down the same destruction on himself;
> The vulgar only escaped, who stood without.

The Chorus praises Samson for taking a just revenge. Then the first Semichorus says that when the Philistines were beside themselves in merry-making, the 'living Dread', *i.e.* God, who dwells in his brightest sanctuary in Silo, sent a spirit of frenzy, and by it killed them. Thus, when men fall victims to the wrath of God, they kill themselves. After the first Semichorus finishes, the second Semichorus says that though Samson was physically blind, his 'inward eyes' were very perceptive, and the strength of his virtue, like the mythological bird Phoenix that comes back to life from out of its own ashes, came to him from out of his state of depression, and made a rightful holocaust. Manoa now asks all around not to mourn, because "Samson hath quit himself/Like Samson". Whatever has occurred seems to him to be "well and fair". He asks his friends — those that gathered there — to arrange for Samson's funeral, and thus bid farewell to him (Samson) who is going to the presence of God: "Home to his father's house".

Meanwhile, Manoa becomes swayed by emotion, in spite of himself, and says that he will build a monument for Samson and decorate it with palms and laurels :

> there will I build him
> A monument, and plant it round with shade
> Of laurel ever green and branching palm,
> With all his trophies hung, and acts enrolled
> In copious legend, or sweet lyric song.

Thither shall all the valiant youth resort,
And from his memory inflame their breasts
To matchless valour and adventures high;
The virgins also shall, on feastful days,
Visit his tomb with flowers, only bewailing
His lot unfortunate in nuptial choice,
From whence captivity and loss of eyes.

And lastly, the Chorus says that we sometimes doubt that God is perceptive and just, and that God's ways are just and best; but this is wrong, because God is certainly and always just: "All is best, though oft we doubt". The Chorus says that sometimes, again, God may seem to be insoucient about, and imperceptive of, evils, but, in fact, he is always perceptive: "Oft he seems to hide his face,/But unexpectedly returns". The Chorus closes the play saying that while the whole of Gaza mourns, Samson is glorified, because his "uncontrollable intent" has wrought the most glorious deed. Samson's turbulent life having ended, he enjoys unperturbed and unperturbable perpetual peace: "And calm of mind, all passion spent."

3
(THE SOURCES OF *SAMSON AGONISTES*)

As told earlier, the myth or legend of Samson can be found in *The Book of Judges*, of the Bible, chapters xiii-xvi. As we know, Milton grew up in the puritan atmosphere of his family. In his young age, he avidly read and re-read the Bible, and thus was immensely influenced by the myths and legends of the Bible. Naturally, we may presume, Milton took the theme of *Samson Agonistes* principally from the Bible. The origin of the biblical myth of Samson, as we have said, goes back to about 1,200 B.C. The Israelites, after being driven by the people of Egypt (who once invited the Israelites to succour their country from agricultural depression), were wandering hither and thither, and then settled in Sinai. Next, they defeated the Canaanites, and settled in Canaan. They had to fight frequent battles against the Canaanites who used to surprise them from the north-west, and against the Philistines who made frequent inroads on them from the south-west of the country of Canaan. Though, ultimately, the Israelites won the land, they were yet dominated by the Philistines who were in majority. The Israelites were not a monolithic nation, but were divided into a number of tribes, among which Dan, to which Samson belonged, was one. The individual tribes of the Israelites had no king, but it was ruled by a chieftain, or a guerrilla leader, who used to be called 'judge'. Some such 'judges' were Jephtha, Jael and Gideon. Samson actually was not a 'judge', but simply a hero of the Israelites. In his youth, he committed some irreligious and immoral acts, but, in course of time, he rectified himself, and then did some deeds of valour for his country, for which reason he was lionized by the people, and was made a national hero, particularly, in the latter part of the Middle Ages and during the Renaissance.

Who the Philistines actually were, we do not know for certain, but they probably came from Crete and settled in the furtile parts of Gaza, in the south-west part of Palestine. There they traded in olive, wheat, iron and gold ornament. The Philistines were a highly cultured people, though the term 'philistine', later on, came to mean 'an uncultured people'. The Philistines were dead enemies of the Israelites. Like the Israelites, the Philistines also had no kings, but they had their 'lords' who ruled particular clans, in absolute terms. These 'lords' were both civil heads and military heads. The common people would regard the 'lords' as gods. The chief god of the Philistines was known as Dagon, or fish-god, though the word 'dagon', in Hebrew, means 'corn'. This god travelled to Palestine probably from Babylon. However, it was with these Palestinians that Samson, probably, once fought.

For the story of Samson, besides the biblical source, Milton might have resorted to other sources. One of such probable sources is an Italian play by Roselli, on the theme of Samson. Another probable source is Vondel's play on the same theme, published in 1660 — a play which was, like Milton's, modelled on the classical plays. A third probable candidate for Milton's source may be Francis Quarles' (1592-1644) *History of Samson*. Hardin Craig suggests some more sources of *Samson Agonistes*. He writes. "It is thought that Milton drew some small details from Josephus' *Antiquities of the Jews* and that his [Milton's] description of the architecture of the theatre of the Philistines may have come from George Sandy's *Relation of a Journey* (1615)" (Craig, 260). However, we may say that the principal source of *Samson Agonistes* was the biblical story of Samson, contained in *The Book of Judges*. This is evident in the heavy religious overtone of the play. Notice, for instance, how ungrudgingly Samson is bearing with his pain that, he believes, "God inflicted on me/Justly"; or how much confident he is that whatever he is doing he is doing according to the "Command from Heaven"; or notice what he says, at the end of the play, about the justness of God's deeds :

> All is best, though oft we doubt
> What th' unsearchable dispose

Of highest Wisdom brings about,
And ever best found in the close.

But, we should not forget that many things of the play Milton took from his own experiences of life. We find many parallels between elements of the play and Milton's own experiences. Milton was blind like Samson; after the fall of the Commonwealth, he was made, as if, a prisoner of the royalists; his first wife Mary Powell was not very different from Dalila; etc. Milton lived in a very hostile environment. His own brother was a royalist, like his [Milton's] nephew Edward Phillips, and his grandfather was a Roman Catholic. But among all these and other hostile kins of his, Milton was a dedicated puritan. He was, as if, an upright Israelite, and so he thought all these kins to be Philistines. It may be that Milton had for long been thinking about creating an art product out of the pent-up and torturing emotion that he had been gestating in his mind for long, and ultimately he found an appropriate story, in the myth of Samson, and wrote this play to give himself relief from that pent-up emotion. We may therefore legitimately say that the source of *Samson Agonistes* at least partially lay in the life experiences of Milton himself.

4
(AUTOBIOGRAPHICAL ELEMENTS IN *SAMSON AGONISTES*)

Drama is said to be the most objective among all literary types, and yet it is true that there are very few dramas that are as autobiographical in tone and spirit as *Samson Agonistes*, and this is so because Milton had a strong autobiographical inclination, while writing. from the beginning to the end, *Samson Agonistes* contains many obvious suggestions to Milton's personal life and personal equations. To begin with, why did Milton take up the theme of revolt for his play, and that at the fag end of his life? The reason, perhaps, is this. In 1660, Milton's wished-for Cromwellian Commonwealth was subplanted by his hated old monarchical form of government. At that time, though he had to reconcile himself with the inevitable, Milton nursed within the core of his heart an impulse to throw away the hated monarchy of Charles II — the instrument of tyranny and oppression, manouvred by the royalists and the corrupted clergy, who, perhaps, are represented by the Philistines of the play *Samson Agonistes*. E.M.W. Tillyard justly writes: "As a political manifesto Milton must have enjoyed writing *Samson Agonistes*. It is nothing less than stark defiance of the restoration government and a prophecy that it will be overthrown" (Tillyard, 1956, 329). The poet also nursed a great hatred for the clergy as such and its concomitant corrupted theocracy that preceded and followed the Commonwealth. He also wished to overthrow the irreligious religion of the clergy. In the play *Samson Agonistes*, Dagon may reflect the contemporary corrupted theocracy that seemed to the poet to be the other name of heathenism. He wanted to free his country of this corrupted and tyrannical theocracy. Milton opens his mind when Samson, at the beginning of the play, says: "Promise was that I/Should Israel from Philistine yoke deliver".

At line 882 of the play, Samson says that he is now deemed an enemy, and is encircled, by the Philistines: "now am judged an enemy". This may refer to Milton's alleged brief imprisonment immediately after the collapse of the Commonwealth, or to the ill treatment meted out to him by the royalists, after the restoration of the monarchy. After the Restoration, Milton never again raised his voice against the new monarchy, but recoiled himself within the cocoon of his self. Since then he bore with everything of the new regime, thinking that resistance was but impossible, and that meek obedience was rather the best policy. This dispair of Milton we may discern in what Samson tells the Public Officer, in the last quarter of the play. The Public Officer has come to conduct Samson to the site of the feast given in honour of Dagon. Composed even in his defeat, Samson tells the Public Officer (lines 1403-1407) :

I am content to go.
Master's commands come with a power resistless
To such as owe them absolute subjection;
And for a life who will not change his purpose?
(So mutable are all the ways of men)

But, *Samson Agonistes* does not reveal so much of Milton's political motive and suffering as it does his painful relation with his first wife, the wretchedness he suffered due to his blindness, and his unflagging faith in the rightfulness of the ways of God. We should not forget the fact that Milton wrote the drama in the evening of his life, when it was natural for him, particularly in his blindness, to see kaleidoscopically the whole of his long past life, and make comments on the outstanding events of it. After his long life of sufferance, he thought himself principally responsible for all his sufferances. Milton married his third wife Elizabeth Minshull in 1662, and though handicapped for his blindness, lived a happy life with this sympathetic and accommodating lady. His second wife Catherine Woodcock, whom he married in 1656 and who died in 1658, was also a comfortable wife. But his rash marriage with Mary Powell, who was about 18 years younger than himself, brought for him only a world of woes; and though at the height of the bitterness of their relation, Milton could procure a divorce, he could never forget that bitterness — the bitterness that can be traced in the bitter and mutual accusations between Adam and Eve in *Paradise Lost*, Book IX. What was the cause of the quarrel we are quite in the dark about, but we know that this bitterness inspired Milton to write his famous tract on divorce justifying the institution.

As we know, Milton married the daughter of a Catholic — Mary Powell — in the spring of 1642, when he was about 34 and Powell was only about 16. In 1645, Powell precipitately left her husband's house for her father's house, intending not to return. But before long, she came back to her senses and came back to Milton's fold, with penitential tears, and since then was living in uneasy reconcilation with him till 1652 when she died of childbirth. The somewhat abnormal difference between the ages of the spouses might have been the cause of their maladjustment. Or, the cause may be their divergent mental make-ups, and the consequential differences in their perceptions, Milton being a strong disciplinarian, a high intellectual, a keen moralists and an eager puritan, and Mary Powell being a popinjay and a flighty wife. It may be noted here that Milton began growing blind after his marriage with Powell, and became purblind in 1652, the year in which Powell died. All these facts are so vividly described in *Samson Agonistes* that one may think that Milton simply put in record in the play the circumstances of his blindness and the bitter relationship between himself and his first wife. And it may not be far from truth if we think that Milton verily identified himself with Samson, and found a replica of Mary Powell in the character of Dalila. Let us now look at some places of the play to see how far our conjectures are warranted.

At the very beginning of the paly, Samson, in a long speech, bitterly laments for, among other things, his blindness (lines 70-82):

> Light, the prime work of God, to me is extinct,
> And all her various objects of delight
> Annulled, which might in part my grief have eased,
> Inferior to the vilest now become
> Of man or worm, the vilest here excell me,
> They creep, yet see; I, dark in light, exposed
> To daily fraud, contempt, abuse, and wrong,

Within doors, or without, still as a fool,
In power of others, never in my own;
Scarce half I seem to live, dead more than half.
O dark, dark, dark, amid the blaze of noon,
Irrecoverably dark, total eclipse,
Without all hope of day!

The lamentation continues till line 109, and after a break, again resumes at line 159, and continues till line 161:

In real darkness of the body dwells,
Shut up from outward light
To incorporate with gloomy night;

But, only a few lines afterwards Samson ceases to lament for his blindness (lines 194-196):

How many evils have enclosed me round;
Yet that which was the worst now least afflicts me,
Blindness;

After this, Milton takes up his scourging cudgel to chastise the wanton woman, Mary Powell. In the play, Samson bitterly vituperates Dalila, and in course of his vituperation, at times censures his own rash action of marrying Dalila. He calls Dalila abject names: 'accomplished snare', 'fallacious bride', 'hyaena', and 'a thorn/Intestine'. The Samson-Dalila episode in *Samson Agonistes* is extended from line 710 to 1060. When the Chorus announces the approach of Dalila, Samson flies into a rage: "My wife, my traitress, let her not come near me." Then Samson is heaping up accusations upon Dalila, non-stop (lines 748-765):

These are thy wonted arts,
And arts of every woman false like thee,
To break all faith, all vows, deceive, betray;
Then, as repentant, to submit, beseech,
And reconcilement move with feigned remorse,
Confess, and promise wonders in her change;
Not truly penitent, but chief to try
Her husband, how far urged his patience bears,
His virtue or weakness which way to assail:
Then, with more cautious and instructed skill,
Again transgresses, and again submits;
That wisest and best men, full oft beguiled,
With goodness principled not to reject

The penitent, but ever to forgive,
Are drawn to wear out miserable days,
Entangled with a pois'nous bosom snake,
If not by quick destruction soon cut off,
As I by thee, to ages an example.

We will not be able to fully comprehend the meaning of the above passage, unless we recount the bitter dealings between Milton and Mary Powell. The difference between the two personalities was serious: Milton was grave, she was light; Milton was puritan, she was romantic; Milton took marriage as something of vow and trust, she took it as a convenience; Milton thought love as of secondary importance beside honesty and duty, Powell thought love to be equivalent to life. Powell left her husband in the lurch and went away to her father's house, and thus broke her marriage vow, proved herself unfaithful, and deceived and betrayed her husband ("break all faith, all vows, deceive, betray"). But Powell, before long, as told earlier, returned to Milton with a repentant mien. She submitted herself to Milton and begged his pardon ("as repentant, to submit, beseech"). And then there was an uneasy reconcilement between the husband and the wife ("reconcilement move with feigned remorse"). After Powell left him, Milton was patiently waiting for her mind to be changed, and as she returned, though she actually did not change in behaviour nor was she really penitent, Milton bore with her defiant attitude with all patience, though his heart was sore with her misbehaviour ("how far urged his patience bears"). Whenever the puritan Milton became imposing, Powell submitted, but only soon to spring back to her original nature ("Again transgresses, and again submits"). Milton was well aware of his intellectual superiority, and thought that, like all wise men, he was fated to be duped by women ("wisest and best men, full oft beguiled").

Powell came back into the fold of Milton with tears in her eyes, begging her husband's forgiveness. She approached Milton perhaps with such words as Dalila speaks to Samson: "I was a fool. Too rash, and quite mistaken/In what I thought would have succeeded best./Let me obtain forgiveness of thee Samson". Powell, maybe, begged Milton's forgiveness very affectionately and naggingly, and Milton ultimately pardoned her and lived with her for the rest and brief period of her life. In *Samson Agonistes* also Dalila begs Samson's pardon very touchingly, and at first giving vent to his ire, Samson also pardons her:

Dalila. Let me approach at least, and touch thy hand.

Samson. Not for thy life, lest fierce remembrance wake
My sudden rage to tear thee joint by joint.
At distance I forgive thee; go with that;

Milton never had a very sympathetic opinion about womenfolk. Not that even in his youth he for once was never attracted by the 'softness' and the 'attractive grace' of the fair sex, but very early in his adulthood he became insoucient and psychologically abstemious about them. He thought that women were inferior to men in both physical and psychological properties. He thought that women had no other alternative but to be governed absolutely by men, should men wished to make the conjugal life blissful. Milton believed that men should be weary about the female wiles. In this case of his belief system, he was perhaps taught by his experiences with Mary Powell. All such notions of Milton, regarding the psychology of the fair sex and about the psychology of the superiority of the menfolk may be discerned in the last part of a speech of the Chorus in *Samson Agonistes* (lines 1053-1060) :

Therefore God's universal law
Gave to the man despotic power
Over his female in due awe,
Nor from that right to part an hour,
Smile she or lour:
So shall he least confusion draw
On his whole life, not swayed
By female usurpation, nor dismayed.

Milton's puritan conviction is also evident in *Samson Agonistes.* Milton was a deeply religious person, and he got all his inspiration from the Bible, but he rejected extra-religious rites of the church, to remove all of which he fought, determinedly, and wrote a number of philippic pamphlets charging the clergy. He believed that God is always just, though we sometimes doubt his righteousness. In both of his two epics, he strove to prove this very fundamental truth of his belief system. And, as God is always just, in *Paradise Lost*, he advised us to meekly obey the commands of God: "to obey is best". He believed that one who obeyed God needed not any religious rites to perform. This he expressed in *Paradise Regained* through the mouth of Christ: "he who receives/Light from above, from the Fountain of Light,/No other doctrine needs, though granted true". In *Samson Agonistes*, besides in the two epics, Milton has expressed his third religious conviction: everything is fore-ordained by God. Samson's marriage with Dalila was due to "Divine impulsion"; he has received some "command from Heaven,/To free my country"; and before pulling down the pillars, he stood in prayer to God for aid: "he stood, as one who prayed". Samson, like Milton, believes that nothing can be done if it is not commanded from above to be done. And lastly, like Milton again, and as the Chorus says, Samson believes that God is always just: "Just are the ways of God,/And justifiable to men".

Another autobiographical element in *Samson Agonistes* is Milton's heart-harrowing pain of blindness. References to his blindness are there in both *Paradise Lost* and *Paradise Regained*, but in *Samson Agonistes* such references are the most urgent. Notice, for instance, that the words 'light' and 'darkness ' occur in the play very frequently . And at line 80, Milton cries out for his lack of light so loudly that, as if, the whole heaven is rent into pieces: "O dark, dark, dark, amid the blaze of noon". Now, all these may, perhaps, prove that *Samson Agonistes* is the most autobiographical among all his works . Regarding how far the play is autobiographical, H.A. Mason truly writes that it is Milton's "condensed autobiography" (Craig, 260). Like Mason, Frederick B. Artz is also very clear about the autobiographical nature of the drama. Artz writes: "*Samson Agonistes*, a classical play with choruses, recounts the blind poet's despair, and the victory of his will and mind over fate and matter. The play is the tragedy of a hero like himself, a blind and surrounded by Philistines" (Artz, 197). And, lastly, Professor Grierson dittoes both Mason and Artz. Grierson writes about *Samson Agonistes*: " 'Into no poem has Milton put more of his deepest feeling, his own sufferings physical and mental (but dramatized and so held at a distance) and those haunting doubts about God's ways which had looked out even in his early exultant prose' " (Tillyard, 1957, 65).

5
(THE THEME, AND THE INTERPRETATION OF MEANING OF *SAMSON AGONISTES)*

The three principal works of Milton — *Paradise Lost*, *Paradise Regained*, and *Samson Agonistes* — were written in particular period of time, approximately from 1667 to 1671. It is not unnatural, therefore, that there are some similarities among the themes of the three works. The theme of *Paradise Lost* is man's Fall, with an assurance of redemption; that of *Paradise Regained* man's redemption, through the agency of Christ; and that of *Samson Agonistes*, again, man's Fall, and redemption — but, this time the redemption is achieved through revenge. In the first epic, the Fall is from heaven, and in the second, redemption is procured through divine agency; but in the drama, the fall is from earthly grace and happiness, and the redemption is achieved through personal striving, though, here, behind both the fall and the redemption, there is the divine plan working invisibly. Perhaps, after the establishment of his wished-for Cromwellian Commonwealth, Milton thought that Almighty God himself would sustain it, but when the Commonwealth fell through in 1660, he realised that 'God helps those that help themselves'. Therefore, after writing his two epics, where he kept man behind God, he brought man before God, in his *Samson Agonistes*, where Samson is more active than Adam and Christ, in the two epics. In the two epics, Milton had shown that God acts through his chosen representatives (Christ, Michael and such others), but in the last stage of his life, he has shown, in *Samson Agonistes* that God sometimes also communicates directly with man. In the drama, therefore, the God-man relation is much closer than in the two epics. Again, in the two epics, man is a passive being, sometimes like a marionette at the hands of God, but in the drama man is ceaselessly active. But this activity should not be stretched too far, because Samson himself, to an extent and by nature inactive and impotent, only when his divine hair grows on his head, does become active and puissant.

That the three literary pieces of Milton are, in some respect, of the same ilk is evident from the motto or moral of the three: God is always good, and whatever He does is good. This motto was first announced by Milton at the beginning of *Paradise Lost*: "I may assert Eternal Providence,/And justify the ways of God to men." *Paradise Regained* has a direct link with its predecessor — in it the poet begins with these words: "I, who erstwhile the happy Garden sung,/By one man's disobedience lost, now sing/Recovered Paradise". And in *Paradise Regained* also the poet says that God is always good. God is so good that he must redeem everyone of us, — everyone that will obey him. It is for this reason that the poet says: "To know, and, knowing, worship God right,/Is yet more kingly". Like *Paradise Regained, Samson Agonistes* was also foreshadowed in *Paradise Lost* (Book IX, lines 1059-1063) where Milton narrates the physical love between Adam and Eve, and tells of the consequent birth of shame and loss of virtues :

> So rose the Danite strong,
> Herculean Samson, from the harlot-lap
> Of Philistine Dalilah, and walked

> Shorn of his strength; they destitute and bare
> Of all their virtue.

And, in *Samson Agonistes* also Milton says that God is good . In the drama, the Chorus says that God's works are certainly good, though we may have doubts about them: "Just are the ways of God" and "All is best, though we oft doubt/.../Oft he seems to hide his face,/But unexpectedly returns". The two epics and the drama have another point in common: in all of them the heroes submit to the divine providence. In *Paradise Lost* (Book XII, line 561), Adam says: "Henceforth, I learn that to obey is best". In *Paradise Regained* (Book IV, lines 288-290), Christ tells Satan: " 'he who receives/Light from above, from the Fountain of Light,/No other doctrine needs, though granted true". These are, clearly, words of surrender, of obedience. And in *Samson Agonistes*, Samson surrenders to the "Divine impulsion".

Thus, we find that in all his three masterpieces, Milton wanted to "justify the ways of God to men." But whereas in the two epics he, as if theoretically, proved the justifiability of "the ways of God to men", in *Samson Agonistes* he has given a concrete example of how actually God behaves with men. God will teach the polytheistic and idolatrous Philistines that only he is the 'Living God', and he will teach mankind that 'not a sparrow falls without the command of God'. God will teach mankind that everything works according to his plan. Even sins that are committed by men are planned by him (Samson married Dalila according to the will of God; this seemed an evil at the beginning, but at the end it proved an usherer of good). It was for this reason that Samson felt the 'Divine impulsion' to marry Dalila. Apparently, such acts seem incongruous with the nature of God. But Milton says that it serves a two-fold purpose. Firstly, Samson suffers through his marriage, and thus acquires knowledge, proving that knowledge is possible only through sufferance — '*pathei mathos*'. Again, Samson gets deliverance also through sufferance, because only through sufferance man may achieve strength, or, only after due sufferance does God bestow upon man enough strength for his deliverance. Secondly, God creates conditions for men for committing sins, so that he (God) can punish the sinners and thus teach mankind with concrete examples. Even the physical strength necessary for punishing sins of man, by man, is supplied by God himself. In *Samson Agonistes*, God bestows strength upon Samson by growing hair, once again, on his tonsured head, while he was in prison, in order to punish the Philistine sinners.

Samson Agonistes further shows that our assumption that sometimes God is indifferent to our sufferings is wrong. God always seeks the right moment for doing the right deed. He waits for the right moment so that the appropriate situation or opportunity is available for punishing the wrongers. We cannot bear with the delay, and hence we sometimes say that God is insoucient about the wrongs: this is our mistakes, not God's. Further, sometimes even God himself arranges for the appropriate opportunity for punishing the sinners. We know that Samson, ignoring his father's objection to his proposed marriage with Dalila, wedded her. He did this being driven by 'Divine impulsion'. It was only to arrange for the appropriate opportunity of punishing the Philistines that God had willed that Samson would will to marry the coquettish Dalila. Dalila divulges to the Philistines the secret of the strength of Samson, and soon after the Philistines nab Samson, blind him, and throw him into the dark prison. This act of God seems confusing to us: why should God let innocent Samson be caught in the net of the Philistines, after his marriage with Dalila — marriage that was due to "Divine impulsion"? But we people are myopic, while God has farsightedness. God knows that Samson's sufferings in the prison is only prodromal to the high drama of divine justice, in which drama Samson, a host in himself, will kill the whole host of the Philistines, and thus will deliver the Israelites, and in course of killing the Philistines, will kill himself and thereby deliver himself, withal. Therefore, when, just before pulling down the pillars, Samson prayed to God for strength and God granted his prayer. And with God's strength and according to God's plan, Samson did what he did. So we see that, unlike in *Paradise Lost* and *Paradise Regained*, in *Samson Agonistes* God is in direct communication with a human being, with Samson. But, all the same, like the two epics, *Samson Agonistes* also proves that God is always just, though we often doubt.

6
(THE CHORUS IN *SAMSON AGONISTES*)

The Elizabethan stage was almost absolutely devoid of the institution of chorus in plays (the Greek word 'chorus' means 'dance'). Even Shakespeare, who handled all the devices of drama, employed chorus very sparingly, and only with minor purposes. Milton, therefore, deserves the credit of introducing the chorus, in his play, with all the importance that it once enjoyed in the classical dramas. In this regard, he is the forerunner of such classicists as Matthew Arnold, who used the chorus in his poetic play *Merope*, and T.S. Eliot, who profitably employed the chorus in his poetic play *Murder in the Cathedral*. In his Preface to

Samson Agonistes, entitled 'Of that sort of Dramatic Poem called Tragedy', Milton says that he has introduced chorus in his tragic drama following the Greek dramatic tradition: "... Chorus is here introduced after the Greek manner, not ancient only, but modern, and still in use among the Italians." In *Samson Agonistes*, the chorus performs the same important functions as it did in ancient Greek and Roman tragedies — the chorus interpretes situations, flashes forward and backward, and weaves together the different episodes of the play. And, like in the ancient tragedies, the chorus of *Samson Agonistes* also remains present throughout the play. He appears just after the opening speech of the drama to be delivered by Samson, and closes the drama with a brief comment of his on the whole of the play and with a short moral.

In the ancient tragedies, the choruses played different roles at the hands of different tragedians. For instance, Aeschylus used the chorus as the ideal spectator, and, generally, his chorus would not take part in the actions of the play. Of course, this did not dovetail with the Aristotlean principle of the chorus, according to which the chorus has to be 'a sharer of the action' of the play. Sophocles followed the Aristotlean dictum regarding the chorus, and so his chorus takes active parts in the play, in addition to its other functions, such as working as an ideal spectator, interpreting situations, and expressing the sentiments of the ideal sepctator. Euripides took an altogether different path: his chorus expresses and intensifies the emotion of the audience (or of the ideal spectator, that he is), but does not participate in the action. Milton has, perhaps, followed in the footsteps of Sophocles in the use of the chorus in *Samson Agonistes*. It is for this reason that Milton's chorus differs from Shakespeare's, as Shakespeare's chorus participates in the actions of a play. In Shakespears's *King Henry the Fifth*, for instance, the chorus appears before the beginning of each Act and at the close of the play, but never does he participate in the action, like the chorus in T.S. Eliot's *Murder in the Cathedral*. T.S. Eliot has also followed Aeschylus, regarding the chorus, because only in his *The Family Reunion* does the chorus participates, but that too very rarely. But Milton has followed Sophocles, as we have said, and thereby Aristotle, because his chorus takes part in the action. For instance, in *Samson Agonistes* (lines 237-239), the chorus tells Samson: "In seeking just occasion to provoke/ The philistine, thy country's enemy,/Thou never wast remiss, I bear thee witness".

Both Voltaire and Dr. Johnson have severely criticised the presence of chorus in a play. Johnson "calls the chorus an encumbrance" (The

Wordsworth Poetry Library, 1995,305). And Voltaire says about the chorus that if it repeats what has already happened, its speech will be 'tiresome'; and if it foretells, or alludes to what is going to happen, then it will diminish the dramatic surprise. But Matthew Arnold pleads very strongly for the presence of the chorus in the play, following the arguments of the ancient masters. He says that for the Greeks "the aim of tragedy was *profound moral impression:* and the ideal spectator, as Schlegel and Müller have called the chorus, was designed to enable the actual spectator to feel his own impressions more distinctly and more deeply. The chorus was, at each stage of the action, to collect and weigh the impressions which the action would at that stage naturally make on a pious and thoughtful mind; and was, at last, at the end of the tragedy, when the issue of the action appeared, to strike the final balance. If the feeling, with which the actual spectator regarded the course of the tragedy, could be deepened by reminding him of what was past, or by indicating to him what was to come, it was the province of the ideal spectator so to deepen it. To combine, to harmonize, to deepen, for the spectator, the feelings naturally excited in him by the sight of what was passing upon the stage — this is one grand effect produced by the chorus in Greek tragedy" (The Wordsworth Poetry Library, 1995, 306). After so much, Matthew Arnold opines that the chorus performs a great role in *Samson Agonistes*: "Few can have read the *Samson Agonistes* of Milton without feeling that the chorus imparts a peculiar and noble effect to that poem" (The Wordsworth Poetry Library, 1995, 307).

The chorus in *Samson Agonistes* occupies more than one quarter of the total of 1,758 lines of the drama. In addition to this, Semichorus I has 18 lines and Semichorus II has 21 lines to deliver. The first, tenth and the fourteenth speeches of the chorus are the longest: the first speech consists of 61 lines, the tenth 73, and the fourteenth 52. The chorus in *Samson Agonistes* performs a number of important functions. To begin with, the chorus intensifies our feeling, otherwise, aroused within us. For instance, the very first speech of the chorus makes us sympathetic to the chop-fallen Samson almost immediately : at the very beginning of the play we become at once one with him :

> This, this is he; softly a while;
> Let us not break in upon him.
> O change beyond report, thought, or belief!
> See how he lies at random, carelessly diffused,
> With languished head unpropped,

As one past hope, abandoned,
And by himself given over,
In slavish habit, ill-fitted weeds
O'er-worn and soiled.

Secondly, sometimes the chorus becomes deductive, moralising. For instance, the chorus teaches the Public Officer of the Philistines, who has come to fetch Samson to the site of the grand feast, about the great benefits of patience and fortitude:

But patience is more oft the exercise
Of saints, the trial of their fortitude,
Making them each his own deliverer,
And victor over all
That tyranny or fortune can inflict.

Thirdly, sometimes, again, the chorus gives us practical advices about worldly affairs. Samson has been betrayed by his wife Dalila, because he was over-indulgent. The chorus therefore tells Samson that it is the 'universal law' that the husband must be despotic and over-bearing about the wife, innuendoing thereby that had Samson been so, he would not be betrayed (lines 1053-1060):

Therefore God's universal law
Gave to the man despotic power
Over his female in due awe,
Nor from that right to part an hour,
Smile she or lour:
So shall he least confusion draw
On his whole life, not swayed
By Female usurpation, nor dismayed.

Fourthly, the chorus sometimes introduces characters and announces their approaches on the stage. For example, the chorus announces the coming of Manoa to blind Samson: "But see! here comes thy revered sire". And he introduces to the audience the relation between Samson and Dalila: "And now, at nearer view, no other certain/Than Dalila, thy wife."

That the chorus occupies a place of great importance in *Samson Agonistes* may, at least to some extent, be ascertained from the fact that the chorus has, as we have said, as many as 430 lines, or about one quarter of the total 1758 lines of the drama, to be delivered, besides the 18 lines of the first Semichorus and the 21 lines of the second Semichorus. The chorus speaks 38 times, and his longest speech, when he speaks for the 10th time, consists of as many as 73 lines (his first speech is also very long, of 61 lines). Of course, the play does not open with a prologue, but the very second speech of the play is that of the chorus, and the play closes with a speech, again, of the chorus. Besides, Milton has, again as we have said, introduced two Semichoruses in the drama. Semichorus I narrates the circumstance in which the Philistines were killed, when Samson pulled down the pillars, and ends with a moralising: "So fond are mortal men,/Fallen into wrath divine". Semichorus II, on the other hand, tells us that Samson, though dead, will live eternally like "that self-begotten bird", Phoenix, upholding virtue. The speech of the second Semichorus, therefore, reminds us of the conventional concluding part of an elegy — of a happy ending.

A question may here be raised: who are the chorus? In the *dramatis personae* of the play, Milton is not explicit: he only says that the chorus consists of (some) Danites. But from this we do not understand the relation between the chorus and Samson, or, that between the chorus and any other character. However, though the composition of the chorus is not clear from the drama itself, in the 'Argument' prefaced to the play, Milton has explicitly said that the chorus consists of a few of Samson's friends and equals of his tribe. Samson, made blind, is taken out of the prison, where he sits and "bemoans his condition", and there "he happens at length to be visited by certain friends and equals of his tribe, which make the Chorus". Christopher Hill writes that in the drama, not only Samson but also the chorus are re-educated through sufferance, and through them, the audience: "They [the chorus] as well as Samson were to be re-educated; and through them the audience" (Hill, 312).

Lastly, the verse-form of the chorus has an obvious peculiarity. Whereas the whole of the drama, excepting the chorus, is in the heroic blank verse form, the chorus is composed in sprung rhythm. The sprung rhythm is a pattern of rhythm that is based only on the number of accented syllables in a line, ignoring the number of unaccented syllables. For instance, the following two lines are in sprung rhythm: "Óne, twó/ Búckle my shóe." Though Gerard Manléy Hopkins (1844-1899) coined the term 'sprung rhythm' and though Hopkins is said to have invented the sprung rhythm, in fact the sprung rhythm is as old as, if not older than, *Piers Plowman* which is also in sprung rhythm. Therefore, the credit of re-introducing the sprung rhythm, for the first time after the Middle Age, should go to Milton, and not to Hopkins.

7
(A GENERAL DISCUSSION ON *SAMSON AGONISTES*)

According to Christopher Hall, *Samson Agonistes* is an allegorical drama, because there are in it two levels of meaning: on the surface level, the drama presents a myth — a biblical myth; but on its deeper level of meaning, it represents Milton's political view about his contemporary England. Hall claims that like Dryden's *Absalom and Achitophel*, which has also adopted another biblical myth, Milton's *Samson Agonistes* is a political tract presented in a dramatic garb. Hall writes: "He [Dryden] was advising the Duke of Monmouth on action to be taken in England at the time of writing, just as — I suggest — Milton in *Samson Agonistes* was offering advice to God's servants in England" (Hall, 312). In the drama *Samson Agonistes*, we may notice two very important things: one, a *priest* urges Dalila to betray Samson; and two, when the roof is pulled down by Samson, all the Philistine people who gathered in the feast, except the *common ones*, perished ("the *vulgar* only 'scaped who stood without' "). The priest represents the clergy of the contemporary England, and the 'vulgar' people represent the then common people who were not politically conscious, *i.e.* who stood outside politics. The Philistines of the drama are the representatives of the royalists and the aristocracy. Hall says that all these representatives are Milton's inventions. He writes; "I see no reason for these innovations of Milton's except to condemn the clergy and aristocracy whom he [Milton] regarded as the principal enemies of God in the Restoration England; and perhaps to show that he now had more hope of 'the vulgar' responding to a purged and purified leadership than when he wrote *Paradise Regained*" (Hall, 314-315).

There is close resemblance between the pamphlet *De Doctrina Christiana* (1655) and *Samson Agonistes* (1671), at least in certain respects. In the pamphlet, Milton justifies his hatred for the enemies of God. Christopher Hill writes in this regard: "And if Milton did believe it a Christian duty to hate God's enemies, who could be more clearly God's enemies than the Philistine aristocracy and priests, or their counterparts in restoration England?" (Hill, 317) In *Samson Agonistes*, Milton wants to prove that God is right and his ways are justifiable — a theme that we saw in *Paradise Lost*: "And justify the ways of God to men." In *Samson Agonistes* (lines 293-295), the chorus says: "Just are the ways of God,/And justifiable to men,/Unless there be who think not God at all." However, we may, perhaps, say that *De Doctrina Christiana* is the negative, and *Samson Agonistes*, along with *Paradise*

Lost and *Paradise Regained*, is the attestation of Milton's deep faith in Christianity. In fact the two epics and the drama hold up related ideas and sentiments. Christopher Hall writes : "There are analogies in the 'subjects' of Milton's last three poems. *Paradise Lost* deals with a man and a woman who were tempted and fell; *Paradise Regained* with a perfect man who withstood temptation; *Samson Agonistes* with a fallen man who recovered by overcoming temptation" (Hill, 310). But there is a difference between the two epics, on the one hand, and the drama, on the other. While the epics are concerned with human condition and salvation, *i.e.* while the epics are soteriological, the drama concerns itself with a lesser theme — the deliverance of the Israelites from the tyranny of the Philistines. As Christopher Hill suggests, *Samson Agonistes* is not a pietistic drama, as some suppose it to be, but is a play of deliverance by force — by 'war'. In *Paradise Lost*, Milton rejected war, and hence in it war brings no good. In *Paradise Regained*, again, Milton avoided war. But in *Samson Agonistes*, he suggests that sometimes war brings good. Hardin Craig beautifully sums up the relations among the three: "*Samson Agonistes* is of one piece with *Paradise Lost* and *Paradise Regained*: barer and sterner than either of them, but transmitting with at least equal force and clarity the message of the poet-statesman to the world" (Craig, 261). Again, W.P. Ker has found in Milton's poem 'Hymn for the Morning of Christ's Nativity' another parallel to *Samson Agonistes*. Ker writes: "I will add this that Milton's last poem throws a reflection back to his earliest, the *Hymn for the Morning of Christ's Nativity*. The song of triumph over the rout of the old gods of the nations :

"Peor and Baalim
Forsake their temples dim
With that twice-batter'd god of Palestine"—

that triumph is repeated in another mood forty years later, and the earlier poem, if you look back to it, takes fresh light from the victory of Samson" (Caircross, 67).

There are four characters in *Samson Agonistes* — Samson, Dalila, Manoa and Harapha. But Frederick S. Artz justly says that only one character, among the four, is rounded — that of Samson. The character of Samson grows, changes, undergoes mutation, and Samson himself admits this: "And for life who will not change his purpose?/ (So mutable are all the ways of men)". He was the unquestioned and indomitable hero; but for his own *hamartia*, he has been captured, blinded, imprisoned. He, who once would never yield to his enemies, now while humbled by the Philistines through trickery, changes: he obeys the order of the Philistine lords to present himself at the place of the Philistines' feast. But, soon his former pride and sentiment return to him; and he determines that as a servant of God he must destroy the Philistines, if necessary, even by sacrificing himself, along with them. He prays to God, and then does the work of God, *i.e.* he destroys the Philistines, and thus proves that he is now his former self. Manoa truly says: "Samson hath quit himself/Like Samson". Again, Samson had been sceptic about Dalila, but Dalila's womanly wiles conquered his reservation, and he disclosed to her the secret of his strength. So Samson is a character with all the human qualities. But all the three other characters are flat — the characters of Manoa, Dalila and Harapha. They do not develop; they remain what they are throughout the drama. Of course, this does not devalue the drama in any way, because as the drama is as it is, our total attention is concentrated exclusively on the character of, or rather on the destiny of, Samson.

Dr. Johnson has complained that *Samson Agonistes* has a beginning and an end, but no middle, and so he insinuates that the drama is not true to the Aristotlean principle of drama. Dr. Johnson, perhaps, thinks that there are only two parts or points in the drama: Samson is suffering in captivity, which is the 'beginning' and he takes revenge on the Philistines, which is the 'end'. But, perhaps, we should not forget that there is also a 'middle', though it is really thin. While in prison, Samson's hair again grows, due to some divine plan, and out of the extremity of his dejection he grows absolute conviction of the justness of God, and courage, within him. He was, so long, as if, hybernating and thus generating enough strength in him, and when he has got that strength he warns the Philistine lords:

'Hitherto, Lords, what your commands imposed
I have performed, as reason was, obeying,
Not without wonder or delight beheld.
Now of my own accord, such other trial
I mean to show you of my strength, yet greater;
As with amaze shall strike all who behold.'

Is this not generation of strength, in the middle of the drama? Dr. Johnson also objects to Milton's mingling of Christian ideas with pagan mythology in *Samson Agonistes*. But David Daiches sets aside this objection of his. Daiches writes; "Such a mingling is, however, a commonplace in English poetry. In Spenser's *Faerie Queene* the very texture of the work is woven out of a combination of pagan and Christian images,..." (Daiches, 1993, 258). By the by, Daiches finds a difference between Spenser's and Milton's use of both pagan and Christian elements, in a single work. Daiches writes: "There is an important difference, however, between Milton's use of pagan references and Spenser's; Milton uses his as analogies rather than as symbols, while Spenser can see a figure from a pagan myth as a symbol as rich in moral and even religious meaning as his more specifically Christian material" (Daiches, 1993, 258).

Matthew Arnold's objection to the play is regarding another aspect of it. The story of *Samson Agonistes* is a Hebrew story; but Milton has, says Arnold, used this story very incongruently to the Greek form of drama. Arnold writes: "The story of Samson, although it has no mystery or complication, to inspire, like tragic stories of the most perfect kind, a foreboding and anxious gloom in the mind of him who hears it, is yet a truly dramatic and noble one; but the forms of Greek tragedy, which are founded on Greek manners, on the practice of chorus-dancing, and on the ancient habitual transaction of affairs in the open air in front of the dwelling of kings, are better adapted to Greek stories than to Hebrew or any other" (The Wordsworth Poetry Library, 1995, 307). But W.P. Ker does not agree with Arnold. Ker says that Milton thought it proper to adapt the Greek form of drama, even though the story was Hebrew, in inspiration, and Ker means to say that Milton was right in this regard. Ker writes: "*Samson Agonistes* was not written merely as an experiment in Greek poetic form. It was written because the Greek form was the right form for something that Milton wanted to say... In *Samson Agonistes* Milton is able to express himself fully, his poetic strength and fire at their utmost pitch, his genius undistracted. He finds in the form of Greek tragedy exactly the right measure and mode for something not yet accomplished in his poems" (Cairncross, 57-58).

W.P. Ker has an encomium for *Samson Agonistes*. He says that the play is certainly narrow in scope, but it is very intense in emotion. Ker writes: "in *Paradise Regained*, undoubtedly, there is more appearance of an even contest than in *Paradise Lost*, and within the narrower limits the tide runs stronger. In *Samson* the channel is narrowed still more, and the mass of the flood goes through, full and strong — no large spaces like *Paradise Lost*, no bays and inlets as in *Paradise Regained*, but all one unhindered, unbroken force" (Cairncross, 63). Like in the ancient Greek tragedies, the action of the play begins abruptly in the middle of the story, and reaches the climax, and then comes the catastrophe, unhindered by accessories. The feeling aroused is very intense and pointed; and there is no space for normal breathing. The drama is true to the three Aristotlean principles of unity — unity of place, time and action. The action takes place within the precinct of the Philistine king; the action occurs within the space of just 24 hours or so; and there is only one action — Samson's taking revenge on the Philistines. *Samson Agonistes* is therefore a classical drama in the exact sense of the term.

In *Samson Agonistes*, Milton has employed a variety of metres, sometimes rhymed and sometimes not, as occasions have suited. But, F.R. Leavis has scathingly attacked the versification of the drama. His trenchant comment on the versification of *Samson Agonistes* runs thus: "How many cultivated adults could honestly swear that they had read it through with enjoyment?" (Leavis, 1959, 67). Leavis says that the versification is "externally managed, not internally." According to Leavis, the versification of *Samson Agonistes* is mechanical, stiff, arid, exhausted and uneloquent. T.S. Eliot and Middleton Murry also think that the versification of the drama is inferior.

However, despite some minor objections raised against it, *Samson Agonistes* has been highly praised. Matthew Arnold writes: "These reserves being made, it is impossible to praise the (sic) *Samson Agonistes* too highly: it is great with all the greatness of Milton. Goethe might well say to Eckermann, after re-reading it, that hardly any work had been composed so entirely in the spirit of the ancients" (The Wordsworth Poetry Library, 1995, 307-308). Regarding the verse of the drama, Arnold further writes: "Milton's drama has the true oratorial flow of ancient tragedy, produced mainly, I think, by his making it, as the Greeks made it, the rule, not the exception, to put the pause at the end of the line, not in the middle" (The Wordsworth Poetry Library, 1995, 308). Frederick B. Artz also admires the verse and the poetry of *Samson Agonistes*, but he says that the drama fails to create appropriate tension that is essential for a good play. Artz writes about the drama: "the work though it contains some sublime poetry, lacks the tension of true drama" (Artz, 197). To conclude this chapter, if we raise the question whether there are dramatists who have written only one play each and, nevertheless, have proved themselves to be great dramatists, Milton's name must be pronounced first.

10

A CRITICAL APPRECIATION OF MILTON

In Tennyson's folio edition of *Paradise Lost* (1698), John Dryden, the father of English criticism, wrote about Milton :

> Three Poets, in three distant Ages born,
> *Greece, Italy*, and *England* did adorn.
> The first in Loftiness of Thought surpass'd,
> The next in Majesty, in both the last:
> The Force of Nature could no further go;
> To make a third she join'd the former two.

Milton has not written much poetry : his three principal works — *Paradise Lost*, *Paradise Regained*, and *Samson Agonistes*, besides a number of sonnets and other poems are his all. The three principal works, upon which his fame largely depends, consist in only some 375 pages, and yet, after Chaucer and Shakespeare, he stands like a tower in the history of English literature. And this is due to at least two qualities of his poetry: 'form and coherence' and 'stateliness' of manner. Milton had a life-long devotion for 'form and coherence' and, in this regard, his poetry is quite different from the poetry of the Romantics. The quality of having 'form and coherence' in Milton's poetry is evident even in his early works, such as 'L'Allegro', 'Il Penseroso', 'Comus' and 'Lycidas'. His form or style has the stamp of individuality: any one reading any piece of his works, will immediately be able to identify it as Miltonic. Again, he has always an eye on the relation between the parts and the whole of any of his works. The other rare quality of Milton's poetry is its 'stateliness' of manner. Milton can never come down to the paltry. It is not only at the beginning of *Paradise Lost*, for instance, that the poet "no middle flight intends to soar", but always and everywhere. Yet again, his verse has an organic voice, and yet, nowhere does it show any lack of lyricism. However, it is largely his 'stateliness of manner' for which Milton stands unique in English Literature.

Besides these two great qualities, Milton's poetry has some other qualities as well. Milton had a penchant for musicality — musicality that, according to T.S. Eliot, is an essential quality of great poetry. He had also immense imaginative sweeps that touched the high heaven and the deep abyss. C.V. Wedgwood, speaking about the qualities of Milton as a poet, enumerates these and some other qualities of Milton: "Milton's natural gifts were an exquisitely sensitive ear; an unusually powerful sensual imagination; a tenacious memory whether for facts, words, physical sensation, or, it must be admitted, other people's poetry; singleness of purpose; and immense power of concentration" (Wedgwood, 110). As we all know, T.S. Eliot is a bitter critic of Milton's so many things, but all the same, Eliot could not but praise Milton's musicality. Eliot writes that Milton's verses are principally phonological: "the sensuous effect of these verses is entirely on the ear." (Eliot, 140). True Eliot has many reservations about Milton's poetry, but, nevertheless, he agrees with Johnson on the total effect, or rather on the excellence of Milton's poetry. Johnson writes, in his *Lives of the English Poets*, about Milton: "such is the power of his poetry, that his call is obeyed without resistance." And T.S. Eliot writes about Milton's poetry: "I do not think that any modern poet, unless in a fit of irresponsible peevishness, has ever denied Milton's consummate powers" (Eliot, 159-160).

On the other hand, L.A. Cormican has encomium for Milton for the latter's linguistic uniqueness and power, and for his skill in welcome mingling of diverse attitudes and cultures in his poetry. Cormican writes: "The last three poems [of Milton] represent a kind of triumph of language which has no parallel elsewhere in English. Milton lived and worked in three worlds which were in conflict along various fronts: the medieval, the Renaissance, and the Puritan. It was Milton's great achievement to draw on all three, to harmonize the wide range of medieval beliefs with the intense seriousness and sense of responsibility of the Puritan mind and with the Renaissance discussions of the good life and the ideal state. If his psychological insight was weak, he at least shows some of the forces which were at work when modern England was coming into being. His verse is one of the great vehicle by which we come to know the cultural and political vitality of his times. If it has serious and disconcerting limitations, if it presents no vivid portrait of human beings, it does give a special insight into a religious doctrine and mentality without which we cannot understand what England then was or later became" (Ford, 191-192). All the foregoing critics have shown their regard for Milton while keeping their reservations with them, but Professor Grierson, as E.M.W. Tillyard says, is all praise for Milton's poetic art: "'Milton as an artist is altogether a larger and more splendid luminary in the poetic heaven than Wordsworth. He is the supreme master of poetic evolution and poetic diction — a style sensuous, impassioned, elaborate, musical, a very cloth of gold' " (Tillyard, 1957, 64).

Milton had his own conception of heroism, as we have said, and here he had shown enough courage to deviate from the ancient masters. His concept of heroism grew out of his strong religious conviction. Walt Whitman rightly says that Milton was "the true son of God." Milton believed that a hero is not necessarily a war-monger, and that enormous physical strength is not an essential attribute of the hero. He believed that true strength of the hero lies in the core of his heart, and that this strength is not sadistic, but masochaistic — that is, the strength is not meant for inflicting pain on others, rightfully or wrongfully, but is meant for undergoing sufferance for the cause of establishing right and dispelling wrong; in short, for the cause of God. *Comus*, *Paradise Lost*, *Paradise Regained* and *Samson Agonistes* present us with instances of the Miltonic hero: militant chastity as against an evil design is presented in *Comus*; in *Paradise Lost* the heroic quality of patience and forbearances is presented; *Paradise Regained* shows us Christ, the supreme hero, who teaches us that the power of God is invincible; and *Samson Agonistes* shows us the supreme example of martyrdom. Milton's concept of heroism is certainly an addition to the English theory of heroism.

Milton is not only a great poet, but also a great dramatist. Hardin Craig writes about Milton the dramatist: "Milton was a poet of real dramatic talent. He shows it in all his poems, in his sonnets, and particularly in *Comus*, which dramatizes the very problem of good and evil he was later to treat in *Paradise Lost*. At the end of his career appeared the drama, *Samson Agonistes*.... He chooses dramatic moments with great certainty, and his emphases are dramatic" (Craig, 249). In his dramatic works, Milton is not so much interested in human actions as he is in divine interferences into human affairs. John Reesing, in his *Milton's Poetic Art*, writes about Milton's dramatic arts "In *Lycidas*, *Paradise Lost* and *Samson Agonistes*, Milton dramatizes actions involving characters who at some juncture in their experience are strongly tempted to believe that God is unjust. The discovery may come late, but it always does come, that He is not only just but merciful; that, in fact, divine Justice toward man is Mercy. From *Lycidas* to *Samson Agonistes*, each of Milton's plots eventuates in a resolution wherein more good has been received by the main character (s) than has been expected or even desired by them. Hence, the feeling of surprise and wonder so prominent in all these works... It is from the feeling of amazement which Milton always experiences in contemplating that action of God as his works arises" (Reesing, 124). John Reesing further writes: "From *Lycidas* onward, all of Milton's protagonists move to a profound sense of joy and gratitude by discovering how God deals with men" (Reesing, 126). In *Comus* and *Samson Agonistes*, principally, and in the two epics of Milton, there is, to an extant, a strain of the Miracle plays where supernatural powers interfere to solve apparently insoluble human problems. Milton's supernatural powers are humane and are always in communication with human beings. M.V. Rama Sarma writes in this regard: "Milton humanises the devil, makes God a justiciar and Adam and Eve, especially after their fall, look like Everyman and Every woman. This human touch is given so as to create an interest in the figures participating in the narrative" (Sarma, 15). But, Sarma says, this "humanising aspect has its own limitations in the sense that Milton's God is often dubbed as a school divine noted for his bungling inefficiency" (Sarma, 15).

Frederick B. Artz calls Milton "the greatest genius of the Baroque in England" (Artz, 196), but certainly not in any pejorative sense. But what does Artz mean by baroque, here? Artz writes: "Originally used as term in Scholastic logic, it came, in Italy, in the sixteenth century, when Scholasticism was going out of fashion, to stand for the whole of Scholasticism. Then by the eighteenth century it was used for anything queer, overelaborate, contorted, or involved. This seems to have been the history of the word in Italy. In Portugal, Spain, France, and England, the use of the word came partly from Italy and partly from a Portuguese word meaning a rough or imperfect pearl. In the eighteenth century Milizia, a Neo-Classical art historian and critic, used the term 'baroque' for 'the ultimate of the bizarre, the ridiculous carried to extremes.' Another Neo-Classical critic refers to the Baroque as 'a Jumble of oddities and witticisms'. This idea that the Baroque represented a corrupt taste, and a senseless love of novelty, was continued in the nineteenth century" (Artz, 158). The baroque may here be contrasted with mannerism that urged art to follow the manners or styles of earlier masters. The baroque style is "at once, robust, positive, forceful, demonstrative, exuberant, and superlative. It is addressed even more to the imagination and the emotion than to the reason, but to an imagination and emotion that recognise the order that reason can work" (Artz, 162-163). Milton was not only a baroque artist but also a mannerist, or, rather, let us say, he made a happy combination of the two : the baroque and the mannerism. His 'Lycidas' was written in a manneristic style, but his *Paradise Lost*, for instance, was composed in the baroque style.

According to Murry, "unlike Shakespeare's, Milton's mind was simplistic without having any knowledge of the intricacies of human behaviour. Murry says that Milton was content with the large outline" (Tillyard, 1957, 43). But Milton should not be devalued for that because he was a different sort of poet, to wit, he was what Grierson calls a 'prophetic poet'. The prophetic poets are those who strive for reaching out to notions beyond " 'the thought and feeling of the society in which they live, the civilization which has shaped their minds and hearts' " (Tillyard, 1957, 62). E.M.W. Tillyard writes that "they do not merely utter their private and unique feelings. They have a new message for that society whose thought and feeling they are *not* expressing. They are, then, if I understand Professor Grierson aright, men who are in advance of their age (as we say), groping for something they know not consciously what, and saying it brokenly though impressively and as if burdened with the weight of their message" (Tillyard, 1957, 62-63). Now, if we agree with Grierson that there are prophetic poets, we should say that Milton is certainly a prophetic poet. Milton, the man, always looked forward and visualised a new, better, and ideal condition of human existence that was not available in his contemporary society. He saw the degradation in the political, religious and private spheres of human existence; but he did not take the prevailing state of affairs as granted; he rather visualised that man would be saved from his degraded state by some agency of God. In this sense, Milton, the man, was a prophet; and so what he sang was also prophetic.

Regarding the story of the Fall, as in *Paradise Lost*, one legitimate question may be raised: why did God, who is all good, create Satan who harbours heinous evils, or why should Adam, who was created in the image of God himself, disobey the sovereign dictator? If evil originates in God, — and otherwise where did Adam and Satan get their evils from? — how can we think that God is good? This is a very intriguing question about which the clergy and philosophers have laboured so much but have failed to answer it. And this flaw in the conception of the story of the Fall still remains, and it remains also in *Paradise Lost*. Perhaps, Milton did not notice this flaw, or, may be, he was quite aware of the flaw but ignored it. And, perhaps, the only probable solution of such a tricky question lies in the Indian Advaita philosophy of Vallabha, according to which whatever God does he does playfully for his own enjoyment, and according to which, therefore, evil has no ontological status, *i.e.* evil is not actually real. But the Christian conception of evil does not admit of such an explanation, as according to it evil is real. According to Christianity, God created evil for "soul making", *i.e.* through sufferance due to evil, the imperfectly created man will become perfect. But, yet the question remains: why did not God create man as a perfect being ? However, in any case, if there be any wrong or evil in the creation, it must have come from heaven. And the wrong is bent upon ruining the creation — the creation that was done by the heaven itself. Milton himself admits of such a syllogism in *Paradise Lost* (Book VI, line 868): "Heav'n ruining from Heav'n". Following this logic, C.S. Lewis writes that Satan "also is 'Heaven' — diseased, perverted, twisted, but still a native of Heaven" (Lewis, 97). So we see that there is a self-contradiction in the conception of the story of the Fall. C.S. Lewis is perceptive of such a contradiction in *Paradise Lost*: he says that Satan's revolt against the Almighty also involves a contradiction. Lewis writes: "Hence, his [Satan's] revolt is entangled in contradictions from the very onset, and he cannot even raise the banner of liberty and equality without admitting in a tell-tale parenthesis that 'Orders and Degrees Jarr not with liberty' (V, 789). He [Satan] wants hierarchy and does not want hierarchy" (Lewis, 96).

In his epics, Milton used bare, unembellished blank verse, and not heroic couplet. In Milton's time the blank verse did not reach perfection, and yet he persuaded himself to use blank verse. C.V. Wedgwood writes: "The fashion of poetry in the middle years of the [seventeenth] century, while Milton's genius was growing in its long incubation, was away from blank verse. With Waller, Denham, and Davenant the heroic couplet was being born. The long narrative poem had never died. There had been Davenant's unreadable *Gondibert*; there had been Shackerly Marmion's enchanting *Cupid and Psyche*, Chamberlayne's *Pharonnida*, Chalkhill's *Thealma and Clearchus*. Cowley, by many still thought to be the outstanding poet of the time, was at work on *Davideis*, an ambitious epic on a sacred theme, ingenuously handled in heroic couplets, with an occasional alexandrine to break the surface. But Milton determined on blank verse" (Wedgwood, 113-114). Milton has shown extreme courage and skill in using blank verse in his epics, and that with commandable perfection, without having any good model before him.

He has gone even further: he has shunned all possible and expected embellishments of the blank verse, and yet his blank verse stands out unique. C.V. Wedgwood writes in this regard: "At the close of *Comus* and in those intervening sonnets, he [Milton] had stripped his poetry of all superfluous ornament, leaving it no other beauty but that of economy and aptitude of words wedded to a perfectly modulated metre. Now he casts away the last facile adornment left to his muse. He abandoned rhyme. By doing so he lost the chance of popular success, but he was far beyond caring about that" (Wedgwood, 114). And, it may be added, even Marvell and Dryden acclaimed the unadorned blank verse of *Paradise Lost*.

But Milton's verse has not been able to satisfy all. Addison, for instance, said, in 1712, about Milton that English language "sunk under him". T.S. Eliot agreeing with Johnson labelled at least three criticisms against Milton's language : firstly, Miltons uses a language which is "far removed from use", and so it causes difficulty to the common readers; secondly, Milton is objectionably but highly "desirous to use English words with foreign idiom"; and thirdly, Milton's style is "not modified by his subject; what is shown with greater extent in *Paradise Lost* may be found in *Comus*." Eliot further writes about Milton's poetic language: "And it must be said that Milton's diction is not a poetic diction in the sense of being a debased currency. when he violates the English language he is imitating nobody, and he is inimitable. But Milton does, as I have said, represent poetry at the extreme limit from prose; and it was one of our tenets that verse should have the virtues of prose, that diction should become assimilated to cultivated contemporary speech, before aspiring to the elevation of poetry. Another tenet was that the subject-matter and the imagery of poetry should be extended to topics and objects related to the life of a modern man or woman; that we were to seek the non-poetic, to seek even material refractory to transmutation into poetry, and words and phrases which had not been used in poetry before. And the study of Milton could be of no help here: it was only a hindrance" (Eliot, 160). We may here agree with Eliot on the point that Milton unnecessarily widened the chasm between the poetic language and the language of prose, but we should not forget that Eliot is criticising Milton's diction from the modern perspective of poetry, which is unjust. A poet should be evaluated from the perspective of his own age, and during Milton's time we could not go so far as to say what Eliot has said — that "verse should have the virtues of prose". Further, Milton's ideas and images, in his poetry, are so noble and elevated that, perhaps, the language of prose, or prose-like diction, would not be able to measure upto those.

T.S. Eliot is the most pungent critic of Milton. He was not satisfied with only one essay on Milton, to express his bitterness, and so he wrote two — one in 1936, and another in 1947. In the first essay, Eliot writes about Milton: "While it must be admitted that Milton is a very great poet indeed, it is something of a puzzle to decide in what his greatness consists. On analysis, the marks against him appear both more numerous and more significant than the marks to his credit.... His greatness as a poet has been sufficiently celebrated, though I think largely for the wrong reasons, and without proper reservations. His misdeeds as a poet have been called attention to as by Mr. Ezra Pound, but usually in passing. What seems to me necessary is to assert at the same time his greatness — in that what he could do well he did better than any one else has ever done — and the serious charges to be made against him, in respect of the deterioration — the peculiar kind of deterioration — to which he subjected the language" (Eliot, 138). From the above quotation from Eliot, it is clear that Eliot's main objection to Milton is regarding the latter's language. However, Eliot further writes: "even in his mature work, Milton does not infuse new life into the word, as Shakespeare does" (Eliot, 140). And so Eliot concludes: "... Milton writes English like a dead language" (Eliot, 140). Francis Birrell, says E.M.W. Tillyard, also speaks about Milton's language in the same vein. Birrell writes: " 'For 200 years Milton has been the schoolmaster of English poetry, and a worse schoolmaster could in some ways hardly be imagined; for, in obedience to his temperament, he twisted diction and prosody into shapes for which they were never intended' " (Tillyard, 1957, 105).

T.S. Eliot has also criticised Milton's style, commonly known as 'Miltonics'. Eliot accuses Milton for the latter's 'hypertrophy of the auditory imagination'. Eliot writes: "A disadvantage of the rhetorical style [of Milton] appears to bet that a dislocation takes place, through the hypertrophy of the auditory imagination at the expense of the visual and tactile, so that the inner meaning is separated from the surface, and tends to become something occult, or at least without effect upon the reader until fully understood. To extract everything possible from *Paradise Lost*, it would seem necessary to read it in two different ways, first solely for the sound, and second for the sense. The full beauty of his long periods can hardly be enjoyed while we are wrestling with the meaning as well; and for the pleasure of the ear the meaning is hardly necessary, except in so far as certain key-words indicate the emotional tone of the passage" (Eliot, 143). Eliot has found Shakespeare's works profusely coloured with 'visual imagination', but says he, "At no period is the visual imagination conspicuous in Milton's poetry" (Eliot, 139). This lack of 'visual imagination' in Milton's poetry may be due to the poet's unfortunate lack of vision, and this lack of 'visual imagination' has unfortunately, but certainly, marred his poetry, to a great extent. Milton's high-falutin rhetorics has obfuscated all other qualities of his poetry. His verse is artificial and extremely controlled, and yet such an artificial verse once attracted Keats who wrote his *Hyperion* in the Miltonic style; but soon he became averse to the Miltonic style and left it altogether and for ever. A few beginning lines from Keats' *Hyperion* (Book I) may be quoted below to show how far Keats used 'Miltonics':

> Deep in the shady sadness of a vale
> Far sunken from the healthy breath of morn,
> Far from the fiery noon, and eve's one star,
> Sat grey-hair'd Saturn, quiet as a stone,
> Still as the silence round about his lair;
> Forest on forest hung about his head
> Like cloud on cloud.

L.A. Cormican, in his essay 'Milton's Religious Verse', has found several flaws in Milton. Firstly, says he, "We do not find in Milton either the constant sensuous contact with physical reality, or the frequent alternation of swift intensity with calm slowness, or the profound insight into character and motive which keep most people's interest in Shakespeare alive; and only rarely do we find the short, pregnant phrase which strikes us immediately because of its concrete, aphoristic, or poignant quality" (Ford, 188). Secondly, writes Cormican, "Milton's verse moves with relatively little variety of speed or emphasis. The main point of interest, instead of being precisely localised or standing in sharp relief from the rest, is often lost in the successive surge of clauses. In spite of his close attention to the Psalms and to the Latin periodic sentence, Milton learnt neither pointedness from the one nor strong emphasis from the other. The shifting of focus which enables him to achieve a wide survey in the better sentences leads him into diffusiveness and pointless piling up of effects in the worse. Occasionally, he smothers the main idea by prolonging the sentence too far; by the time we come to line 208 or 355 in *Paradise Lost*, Book I, the point of the comparison has been lost in rather wanton luxuriance. What is true of individual sentences is true of whole passages" (Ford, 188-189).

Thirdly, writes Cormican, "While Milton had the well-constructed Christian in mind as his reader, the three great poems are not addressed to any particular public in the same sense as, say, Shakespeare's plays. He thought of himself as writing 'general' or 'Catholic' works in the manner of the epistles of James and Peter in the New Testament (as contrasted with the 'local' epistles of Paul). It is from this, as well as from the special qualities of his character and genius, that the characteristics of his style derive... He thus achieves full scope for the use of Biblical references (and for a more technical use of them than Shakespeare employed) and for the long-sustained sentence in which he is often at his best. But the fact that he is engaging in so solitary a poetic effort and has no definite group of human beings in mind, encourages him also to indulge his own foibles (as when his love of argument reduces God to a seventeenth-century controversialist — III. 106-28; his views on women make Eve ridiculous and the verse naive and tumid — VIII. 39-58; or his desire to remain dignified urges him into a pompous parody of his own style — VIII. 4-38)" (Ford, 189). Fourthly, Milton's "Puritan solemnity eschewed the homely, familiar manner of speaking about divine things which is found in the Psalms and in the medieval plays" (Ford, 190). Fifthly, "... Milton's implied theory of epic is not related to the experience of men in the way in which theory of epic in Homer or of tragedy in Shakespeare grows out of the way in which men actually feel and speak" (Ford, 190).

Ezra Pound, T.S. Eliot and Sir Herbert Read found more faults than one in Milton, but they were particularly unhappy with his verse. Pound and Read found Milton's verse "uninspiring and mechanical", and T.S. Eliot found dissociation of sensibilities in Milton. M.V. Rama Sarma writes: "Ezra Pound and Sir Herbert Read found Milton's verses uninspiring and mechanical. Pound censured Milton's diction and syntax. T.S. Eliot's essay on Milton in 1935 helped practitioners of poetry to try to put down Milton from his pedestal. Eliot referred to the dissociation of sensibility in the seventeenth century with the influence of the most powerful poets of the century, Milton and Dryden. To him Milton was thoroughly unsatisfactory 'either from the moralist's point of view, or from the theologian's point of view, or from the psychologist's point of view, or from that of the political philosopher, or judging by the ordinary standard of likableness in human beings' " (Sarma, 7). T.S. Eliot says, in his essay 'The Metaphysical Poets' (1921), that in the 16th and 17th centuries, there was, particularly in John Donne, unity of thought and feeling, but after Donne, in Milton and Dryden, there was 'dissociation of sensibility' — 'a mechanism of sensibility which could not devour any kind of experience' and which could not make for 'a direct sensuous apprehension of thought'. But here E.M.W. Tillyard differs from Eliot. Tillyard says that Milton sometimes works wonders even without sensual appeal. Tillyard also does not agree with Eliot when the latter says that Milton failed to "infuse now life into the word." To explain his point, Tillyard takes the following four lines from *Samson Agonistes*, as an example :

> The sun to me is dark
> And silent as the Moon,
> When she deserts the night
> Hid in her vacant sublunar cave.

Tillyard goes on to write: "Mr. Eliot gives this as an example of Milton's failure to 'infuse new life into the word'. He thinks 'interlunar' a stroke of genius but that it is 'merely combined with 'vacant' and 'cave', rather than 'giving and receiving life from them'. On the contrary, it is by the new life Milton infuses into words mostly familiar, yet without the use of any vivid picture or metaphor, that he gets a most powerful effect" (Tillyard, 1957, 101).

Milton is, till today, celebrated for his grand style, but some critics, including F.R. Leavis, consider the grand style of Milton uninspiring. Sarma writes about F.R. Leavis' opinion about Milton's grand style: "F.R. Leavis considered the Grand Style to be monotonous and mechanical 'as mechanical as bricklaying' " (Sarma, 7). Many critics, again, object to the artificial language of Milton. They say that his language is inordinately influenced by the Latin syntax as a result of which his English is not the English that we know it to be, and that his artificial language is uninspiring, dead. Sarma again writes: "The consensus on the whole was that Milton wrote a language quite foreign and remote from the native diction and that his influence on the later poets was positively bad. Milton's poetry was a dead end. His language was 'artificial and conventional' and it had very little to do with the ordinary spoken language" (Sarma, 7).

T.S. Eliot further accuses Milton for the latter's using words not so much for arousing our sight as for arousing our hearing. Eliot writes: " '... in reading *Paradise Lost* ... our sense of sight must be blurred, so that our *hearing* may become more acute' " (Leavis, 14). But F.R. Leavis does not agree with Eliot. Leavis says that Milton's music is not as much acute as it can make us ignorant or unmindful of the images —

that would be too much to say about Milton's musicality. Leavis writes; "The Miltonic 'music' is not the music of the musician; what our 'hearing' hears is words; and the sense in which Milton's use of words is characterised by a 'musical' bias can be explained only in terms of a generally relaxed state of mind he induces in us" (Leavis, 14). Another objection of T.S. Eliot is to Milton's use of 'organic sound' that, Eliot thinks, obfuscates the meaning he [Milton] wants to convey, and we think that here Eliot is quite right. Eliot writes: " 'We have to read Milton twice, once for the sound and once for the meaning' " (Leavis, 14-15). E.M.W. Tillyard has two other different but relevant charges against Milton, regarding the latter's style. Tillyard writes: "The first is that Milton's style hardened into a remote grandeur, forsaking the common English speech and the common feelings of men, becoming in Mr. Welby's words the 'arteriosclerosis of English poetry'. The second is that Milton's poetic method was inorganic, that he clothed prose notions in a magnificent poetic dress rather than conceived notion and clothing in a single act of the imagination. Mr. Welby called his art the 'stationing the deliberately selected fact' " (Tillyard, 1957, 115). Tillyard has also criticised Milton's latinised English, saying that it is neither purely latinised nor does it follow either English grammar or Latin grammar: "The main peculiarities or heightening of Milton's style in *Paradise Lost* are quite unlatin, indeed quite alien to the genius of Latin tongue. Mr. Empson has put his finger on the right spot when he talks of Milton's 'vague or apparently disordered grammar'." (Tillyard, 1957, 124), And, about Milton's faults, C.V. Wedgwood writes: "His natural defects were lack of humour and fundamental lack of interest in ordinary human beings. (That he is far more interested in God, Satan, and the angels than he is in Adam and Eve is a truism; but even in *Comus*, written before he was thirty, he puts his richest treasure of poetic imagery at the disposal of Comus than of the Lady and her brothers)" (Wedgwood, 100).

In the modern age few people are interested in Milton, and this is due to more than one reasons. Firstly, Milton's religious convictions are now discarded, and so reading of Milton suffers from lack of mental set. Secondly, Milton's religious convictions are not universal but committedly Christian, and in course of narrating a Christian story, Milton, at places, has shown disregard to some non-Christian religious convictions. This has given rise to emotional apathy in some persons towards Milton, and this, in turn, has made some persons disinterested in his works. Thirdly, Milton has always been didactic, but in our modern age we do not go to literature for any moral edification. There may be many more reasons for Milton's unpopularity now-a-days, but, perhaps, these three are the foremost. In any case, Milton is one of the most controversial poets: to some, as a poet he is next only to Shakespeare; but to others, he has unjustly been lionised. Again, to some, Milton has highly enriched the English language and English verse, but to others (like Ezra Pound, T.S. Eliot, *et. al*), Milton has left behind him a hideously bad effect on English language and verse. However, we may have an idea about the worth of Milton's works from a relatively reliable objective survey of public opinion about the value of Milton's works, against the backdrop of the values of the works of some other poets, done in the eighteenth century. In 1758, the *Literary Magazine* evaluated several poets, including Milton, using some 'poetical scale'. "The scale gave a possible eighty points to poets for 'Genius, Judgment, Learning, Versification'. Pope came top with 80 points, then came Milton and Dryden with 69, Addison with 68, Shakespeare and Cowley with 66 and Spenser with 62" (Hammond, 13). But, we should remember that this evaluation was done in the eighteenth century, and that, like fashion and all that, literary tastes also change. So even if one may guess about Milton's standing as a poet, from the survey just mentioned, we cannot be sure about Milton's evaluation in our modern age, until we do another such survey. And before we can make such a survey, it would, perhaps, not be unwise if we hold fast to what William Wordsworth says of Milton, in his 'Sonnet on Milton':

> Thy soul was like a star and dwelt apart;
> Thou hadst a voice whose sound was like the sea —
> Pure as the naked heavens, majestic, free;....

And let these lines be the *finis coronat opus*.

BIBLIOGRAPHY

(ONLY THE TITLES REFERRED TO IN THIS BOOK)

Artz, Frederick B., *From the Renaissance to Romanticism,* 1975, University of Chicago, Chicago and London.

Bowra, C.M., *Heroic Poetry,* 1966, Macmillan, London, etc.

——, *From Virgil to Milton,* 1967, Macmillan, London, etc.

Bible Society of India (The), Bangalore, *Good News Bible,* 1983.

Bridges, Robert, *Milton's Prosody,* 1967, Clarendon Press, Oxford.

Brown, Calvin S. (ed.), *The Reader's Companion to World Literature,* 1964, A. Mentor Book.

Cuddon, J.A., *A Dictionary of Literary Terms,* 1979, Penguin Books.

Compton-Rickett, Arthur, *A History of English Literature,* 1992, Universal Book Stall, New Delhi.

Cambon, Glauco, *Dante's Craft,* 1969, John Hopkins Press, University of Minnesota, Minneapolis.

Caircorn, A.S. (ed.), *Modern Essays in Criticism,* 1947, Macmillan, London.

Craig, Hardin (ed.), *The Literature of the Renaissance,* (Vol. 2 of *A History of English Literature,* Gen. Editor : Harding Craig), 1966, Collier Books, New York.

Daiches, David, *Critical Approaches to Literature*, 1993 (Oriental Longman, London), Printed in India by Ananda Press & Publishers, Calcutta.

——, (ed.), *The Penguin Companion to English Literature,* Vol. I, 1971, Penguin Books.

——, *Milton,* 1968, Hutchinson University Library, London.

Evans, J.M., *Paradise Lost and the Genesis Tradition,* 1968, Oxford University Press.

Eliot, T.S., *On Poetry and Poets,* 1957, Faber and Faber, London.

Ford, Boris (ed.), *From Donne to Marvell* (Vol. 3 of *A Guide to English Literature*), 1956, Penguin Books.

Goad, Harold, *Language in History,* 1958, A Pelican Book.

Gardner, Helen, *A Reading of Paradise Lost,* 1965, Oxford University Press, London.

Hammond, Gerald (ed.), *The Metaphysical Poets : A Casebook,* 1988, Macmillan, London.

Heighet, Gilbert, *The Classical Tradition : Greek and Roman Influences on Western Literature,* 1959, Oxford University Press, London.

Hill, Christopher, *The Experience of Defeat : Milton and Some Contemporaries,* 1984, Faber and Faber, London.

Hazlitt, William, *Lectures on English Poets and The Spirit of the Age,* 1955, J.M. Dent & Sons, New York.

Hughes, A.D.M. (introduced by), *Milton : Poetry and Prose,* 1962, Clarendon Press, Oxford.

Johnson, Samuel, *Lives of the English Poets,* Vol. I, 1961, Oxford University Press, London.

Leawis, F.R., *The Common Pursuit,* 1953, Chatto & Windus, London.

——, *Revaluation : Tradition & Development in English Poetry,* 1959, Chatto & Windus, London.

Lewis, C.S., *A Preface to Paradise Lost,* 1967, Oxford University Press, London.

Long, William J., *English Literature : Its History and Its Significance,* 1989, Kalyani Publishers, New Delhi and Ludhiana.

Merchant, Paul, *The Epic*, 1984, Methuen, London and New York.

McArthur, Tom (ed.), *The Oxford Companion to the English Language,* 1992, Oxford University Press.

MacCaffrey, Isabel Gamble, *Paradise Lost as 'Myth',* 1967, Harvard University Press, Cambridge, Massachusetts.

Patrides, C.A. (ed.), *Approaches to Paradise Lost*, 1968, University of Toronto Press, Toronto.

Progress Publishers, Moscow, *A Dictionary for Believers and Non-believers,* 1989.

Preminger, Alex, *Princeton Encyclopedia of Poetry and Poetics,* 1975, Macmillan.

Read, Herbert, *Phases of English Poetry,* 1950, Faber and Faber, London.

Reese, William, *Dictionary of Philosophy and Religion,* 1980, Humanities Press, New Jersy, etc.

Reesing, John, *Milton's Poetic Art,* 1968, Harvard University Press, Harvard.

Ricks, Christopher, *The Force of Poetry,* 1984, Clarendon Press, Oxford.

Russell, Bertrand, *History of Western Philosophy,* 1961, George Allen & Unwin, London.

Russell, Stella Pandell, *Art in the World,* 1975, Rinehart Press, San Francisco.

Scruton, Roger, *A Dictionary of Political Thought,* 1982, Pan Books, Macmillan.

Sutherland, James (ed.), *The Oxford Book of Literary Anecdotes*, 1976, A Kangaroo Book.

Sarma, M.V. Rama, *The Heroic Argument : A Study of Milton's Heroic Poetry,* 1971, Macmillan & Co. Madras, etc.

Sarker, Sunil Kumar, *The Gita : in English Verse,* 1996, Atlantic Publishers & Distributors, New Delhi.

Steadman, John M., *Milton and the Renaissance Hero,* 1967, Clarendon Press, Oxford.

Thomson, J.A.K., *Classical Influences on English Poetry,* 1951, George Allen & Unwin, London.

Trevelyan, G.M., *English Social History,* 1982, Penguin Books.

Thorlby, Anthony (ed.), *The Penguin Companion to Literature,* Vol. 2 (European), 1969, Penguin Books.

Tillyard, E.M.W., *Milton,* 1956, Chatto & Windus, London.

——, *The Miltonic Setting : Past and Present,* 1957, Chatto & Windus, London.

Wells, H.G., *A Short History of the World,* 1965, A Pelican Book.

Wedgwood, C.V., *Seventeenth-Century English Literature,* 1956, Oxford University Press.

Wordsworth Poetry Library (The), *The Works of John Milton,* 1994.

——, *The Works of Matthew Arnold,* 1995.

Wordsworth Reference, *Companion to Literature in English*, 1992.

INDEX

D

E

9788171567942